English Vocabulary in Use

Advanced

Michael McCarthy
Felicity O'Dell

CAMBRIDGE
UNIVERSITY PRESS

CAMBRIDGE UNIVERSITY PRESS
Cambridge, New York, Melbourne, Madrid, Cape Town,
Singapore, São Paulo, Delhi, Mexico City

Cambridge University Press
The Edinburgh Building, Cambridge CB2 8RU, UK

www.cambridge.org
Information on this title: www.cambridge.org/9780521653978

First published 2002
17th printing 2012

Printed in Italy by L.E.G.O. S.p.A.

A catalogue record for this publication is available from the British Library

ISBN 978-0-521-65397-8 Paperback
ISBN 978-0-521-67746-2 Paperback with CD-ROM

Contents

Travel

The environment

Society and institutions

The media

Health

Technology

Basic concepts

Functional vocabulary

Idioms and phrasal verbs

Aspects of variation

To the student

Why was this book written?

It was written to help you to improve your English vocabulary and to take you to an advanced level of knowledge of English words and phrases. It will help you to learn not only the meanings of words but also how they are used, how they combine with one another (*collocate*), and how they form longer expressions. It will help you to distinguish better among the large number of words you already know and the new ones we introduce you to.

What is special about this book?

You can use this book either with a teacher or for self-study. The book aims to build your vocabulary by helping you to learn about 2000 new words and expressions, but it also helps you to learn many collocations (combinations that are typical of English but which are difficult to predict) and longer expressions. It helps you understand the more subtle features of meaning, such as how formal or informal the words are, whether they have negative or positive connotations, how they function as metaphors, and so on. To help us make the language in the book as natural as possible, we consulted a 250 million-word database (called a *corpus*) of spoken and written English, taken from newspapers, novels, magazines, everyday conversations in people's homes, in shops, offices, etc. We used computers to analyse the database and tell us which words are most useful at the advanced level, what their most typical collocations are, and in what contexts they are normally used. So the language you are studying here is based on what actual native-speakers of British English have said and written. To make the language more natural, we have often included longer texts, not just sentences, so that you get a more detailed context for the key words, and can see how they form collocations. Reading and observing how words go together is a very important learning strategy at advanced level. Also at this level, you will want more and more to relate the words you learn to your own personal world and your own goals in learning English, so we have included exercises that encourage you to personalise the vocabulary you learn. We chose topics which we consider useful for students who want to use their English in the world, to be able to socialise and talk about a wide range of adult subjects related to ourselves, society, cultures and the world around us.

How is the book organised?

The book has 100 two-page units. In most units, the left-hand page explains the words and expressions to be studied in that unit. Where appropriate, it gives information about the typical contexts in which the words are used, and what the most useful collocations are, as well as their meaning. The right-hand page checks that you have understood the information on the left-hand page by giving you a series of exercises practising what you have just learnt. Occasionally the right-hand page will also teach you some more new words to challenge you and extend your vocabulary even further.

We also include, from time to time, learning tips. These consist of suggestions which will help you to organise your learning better and encourage you to think about your own strategies for learning vocabulary. Additionally, many units have a follow-up activity which will take you beyond the book, for example to a website or to other sources where you can expand your vocabulary on the topic of the unit.

There is a key at the back of the book. The key does not always give you simply one right answer. It sometimes also comments on the answers and will help you learn more about the words studied in the unit.

There is an index at the back of the book. This lists all the words and phrases covered in the book and refers you to the units where these words or phrases are discussed. It also gives pronunciation, using the International Phonetic Alphabet. The symbols you need to know are listed at the beginning of the index.

How should I use this book?

The book is divided into a number of sections. Complete the eight introductory units first (the section called *Aspects of vocabulary learning*). These units not only teach you some new vocabulary, but they also help you with useful techniques for vocabulary learning in general, and introduce you to some concepts about the way vocabulary is used in English. After completing those units, you might want to work straight through the book or you might prefer to do the units in any order that suits you.

What else do I need in order to work with this book?

You need some kind of vocabulary notebook or file where you can write down the new words, collocations and expressions you are learning. You also need to have access to a couple of good dictionaries. This book selects words that are useful for you to learn at advanced level and it gives you the most important information about those words, but you will sometimes need to refer to a dictionary as well for extra information about meaning and usage. Some exercises tell you to use a dictionary; these help to train you in getting the best out of your dictionary. Firstly, you need an English–English dictionary for foreign learners. Good ones are the *Cambridge Advanced Learner's Dictionary*, the *Longman Dictionary of Contemporary English*, the *Oxford Advanced Learner's Dictionary* and the *Collins Cobuild English Language Dictionary*, for example. Secondly, you will also find a good bilingual dictionary useful. Ask a teacher to recommend a good one for you. (See Unit iii for advice on using your dictionaries.) Don't forget that many dictionaries are available on CD-ROM. If you want more information about different types of dictionaries, visit Cambridge University Press's website at dictionary.cambridge.org.

i Strategies for learning

Aims of this book

The aim of this book is to help you, as an advanced learner of English, to extend and improve your vocabulary by:
- increasing the number of words that you know.
- helping you to use words in a more natural, more accurate way.
- improving your knowledge and active use of collocation.
- presenting additional meanings or metaphorical uses of words you may already know.

Using the book

Do the first eight units, i–viii, before you start on any other units.

Then do not just work through the book from the first to the last page – choose the units you need most or that appeal to you most and do them first.

When you are working on any of Units 1 to 100:
- read the left-hand page.
- attempt the exercises on the right-hand page.
- check your answers in the key.

When checking your answers in the key, you will find that it sometimes contains extra useful information about the area of language you are working on. So, read it carefully and make notes of any interesting language that you learn from it.

Revising

You will learn most effectively if you revise the units you study:
- a week after you first worked on the unit.
- again after a month.

Dictionaries

You will also be able to gain much more from the language presented in this book if you follow up words that especially interest you in a good learner's dictionary (see Unit iii). By doing this, you can extend your vocabulary still further.

You may find, for example:
- other useful collocations.
- other meanings for the words you look up.
- other words based on the same root.

Personalising words

Research studies show that we remember new words much more easily if we think about them in relation to our own experience and use them in a context that is meaningful to us as individuals. So, as well as doing the exercises here, write any new words or phrases that you particularly wish to learn in a context that has some personal meaning for you. You could, for example, use the language you wish to learn in a sentence about an experience you have had personally, or about a story you have read in a newspaper or magazine, or about a film or TV programme you have watched.

This helps in two ways by:
- revising language you have already worked on.
- making language personally more meaningful and, thus, more memorable.

Grouping words

Research shows that it is very useful to organise a set of vocabulary items being studied into groups. It does not matter how you group those words or whether your groupings would make sense to anyone else or not. It is thinking about the words enough to create groups that improves how we learn those words.
- As another revision technique, try organising the words you have worked on in a unit into three or four (or more) groups in any way that you find appropriate.

Going beyond this book

Although this book deals with many useful words and expressions for advanced learners, it is clearly impossible to cover all the words that you may come across in English. The best way to increase your vocabulary further is to read and listen to as much English as you can and there are a lot of tips in the book suggesting ways in which you can do this.

Remember you can also usefully expand your vocabulary by:
- reading – novels, newspapers or magazines
- exploring websites
- reading things in English that relate to your job or academic interests
- watching films or videos
- watching cable TV
- listening to the radio
- listening to songs
- listening to audio books.

So, good luck with your advanced study of English vocabulary. We hope that you will learn a lot from using this book and that you will enjoy working with it.

ii Types of meaning

A Basic meaning

When you look up a word, the main thing that you want to know is its basic meaning. For example: in *She has fair hair* the word *fair = light, opposite of dark* or in *It's time to wind up the discussion now* the words *wind up = end.*

However, there are a lot of other aspects of meaning that it is important to be aware of, particularly when you are studying at a more advanced level of English.

B Polysemy or multiple meanings (see Unit v)

A great many words in English have more than one meaning.
Look at *fair* and *wind up* /waɪnd ʌp/ and their different meanings in these examples:

That wasn't a very **fair** thing to say! [adjective: just]
The handsome knight fell in love with a **fair** maiden. [adjective: beautiful]
His knowledge of French is **fair**. [adjective: neither very bad nor very good]
She has a **fair** chance of winning the prize. [adjective: reasonable]
Fair weather is forecast for tomorrow. [adjective: dry and pleasant]
There's a **fair** on at the park this week. [noun: public event with games and rides]

Don't forget to **wind up** your watch. [turn a knob on a clockwork watch so it keeps going]
She seems to enjoy **winding** him **up**. [tell someone something in order deliberately to annoy]
If he carries on like this, he's going to **wind up** in prison. [end up in an unpleasant situation]

C Synonymy

English has a lot of different words with similar but slightly differing meanings. Look at these words that are synonymous with *fair* and *wind up* (with the meanings illustrated in A):
fair – light, blonde, pale, colourless, bleached
wind up – end, finish, complete, close, stop, conclude, terminate, discontinue, abort

D Collocation (see Unit iv)

Words are used with each other (or collocate) in fairly fixed ways in English. You cannot, for example, use all of the synonyms in C as replacements in the example sentences in A. *Hair* can be *fair, light, blonde* or *bleached* (though each of these has a slightly different meaning), but it is not usually described as *pale* or *colourless.*
Skin can be *fair, light* and *pale* but it is not usually described as *blonde, colourless* or *bleached. Colourless* collocates with, for example, *gas* or *liquid.*

E Connotation (see Unit viii)

Words do not only have meanings, they also have associations. At an advanced level of English, it is important to develop an impression of what connotations certain words have. The sentence *Who is the fairest of them all*, for example, immediately makes English speakers think of the wicked stepmother in the children's fairy tale *Snow White* and *the fairer sex* refers to women. *Fair* meaning beautiful or attractive is an old-fashioned word and it has associations with fairy tales and stories about the past.

F Register (see Unit vii)

It is important also to note whether any words you are learning have a particular register. For example *apparel* is a formal or literary word for clothing and *to wind someone up* is both British and informal.

Exercises

ii.1 The underlined words in the sentences below have a number of different meanings. What is their meaning in the contexts of these sentences?

1 What does polysemy <u>mean</u>?
2 Make a <u>note</u> of any special register characteristics that a word has.
3 The judge increased the <u>sentence</u> to life imprisonment.
4 We had a <u>light</u> lunch.
5 Carl is very good at <u>putting on</u> different accents.
6 Does Spanish writing use any different <u>accents</u>?
7 Where does the <u>stress</u> go on the noun 'photographer'?
8 There are a lot of <u>points</u> to think about when considering the meaning of words.

ii.2 Choose a synonym from the box in order to complete the response to these statements.

worn out	famished	annoying	excruciating	pouring
appropriate	brilliant	gorgeous		

1 Are you hungry? Yes, I'm ....
2 Is she an intelligent girl? Yes, she's absolutely ....
3 Your little boy looks tired. Yes, he's ....
4 I like her dress. Yes, isn't it .... ?
5 Is it raining? Yes, it's ....
6 The film was pretty bad, wasn't it? Yes, I thought it was ....
7 Did you think the sentence was fair? Yes, I thought it was ....
8 Does she deliberately wind him up? Yes, she loves .... him.

ii.3 Match the words on the left with the words they collocate with on the right.

1 to contemplate	a worker
2 to dismiss	a mistake
3 to do	a good time
4 to dribble	your future
5 to have	a rope
6 to make	a compliment
7 to pay	innocence
8 to plead	cards
9 to set	some gardening
10 to shuffle	an opportunity
11 to waste	a ball
12 to wind	an example

ii.4 Answer these questions about connotation and register.

1 Which of these things have lucky connotations in British English – horseshoe, mascot, black cat, the number 13?
2 Mistletoe is a kind of parasitic plant, but what are its special connotations?
3 Give the standard meaning and the informal meaning of the following words – loaf, bread, nick, kid, wicked.
4 What does the word *register* mean for a) a linguist, b) a school teacher, c) a musician?

TIP When you are looking up a new word, make sure that you check what other meanings and forms it may have. Also note down any points relating to collocation, connotation or register.

iii Making the most of your dictionary

A Types of dictionary

type	*comments*
alphabetical	the most common type; words are arranged in alphabetical order
thesaurus /θɪˈsɔːrəs/	the words are arranged according to meaning, usually under a broad heading, e.g. under *walk* we would find *stroll, plod, stride*, etc., with explanations
monolingual	in one language only; popular learners' dictionaries of English are often monolingual, and have detailed explanations in English, with examples of use
bilingual	in two languages, usually yours and the language you are learning; useful because they give translations, but may not be so good for distinguishing between possible translations
dictionaries of synonyms /ˈsɪnənɪmz/	words are grouped according to their closeness in meaning, e.g. *start* and *begin*; sometimes antonyms (opposites) are also given and explanations of differences in meaning
dictionaries of false friends (or **cognate words**)	these give advice on words which are easily confused with similar-looking words in other languages, e.g. see Unit 6 of this book
CD-ROM and **online dictionaries**	some publishers include a CD-ROM with their learners' dictionaries and/or have put their dictionaries on the Internet; with these dictionaries, searching is very quick and easy – you can search for words, meanings, examples, words you only half-know, all much faster than using a book

The publisher of this book, Cambridge University Press, includes a CD-ROM with the *Cambridge Advanced Learner's Dictionary*, the *Cambridge Dictionary of American English* and the *Cambridge Learner's Dictionary.* You can also look up words online in these three dictionaries, as well as in the *Cambridge International Dictionary of Phrasal Verbs* and the *Cambridge International Dictionary of Idioms*.
The web address is: dictionary.cambridge.org

B Information in dictionaries

A good dictionary will tell you some or all of the following:

information	*comments*
word	regional alternatives may be given, e.g. *nappy* (UK) versus *diaper* (US)
spelling	perhaps more than one correct spelling exists, e.g. *encyclopedia* and *encyclopaedia*, or regional spellings, e.g. *centre* (UK) versus *center* (US)
pronunciation	this may involve phonetic symbols; the dictionary usually gives a list of the symbols used; alternative and/or regional pronunciations may be given, e.g. /təˈmɑːtəʊ/ (UK) versus /təˈmeɪtəʊ/ (US)
meaning	a definition, or a picture, or a diagram; regional differences in meaning may also be given, e.g. *Slim* in East African English means the disease AIDS
senses	the word *face* has several different senses, including (1) the eyes, nose, mouth, etc., (2) one's expression (*a sad face*), (3) the front, vertical part of something, e.g. *a cliff face*. (See Unit v.)

information	*comments*
grammar and word class	Is the word a noun? Can it also be a verb? Which prepositions follow it? (e.g. is *compared with* the same as *compared to*?)
collocations	What words normally combine with this word, e.g. *alibi* and *cast-iron*, see Unit 77? (See also Unit iv.)
register	Is the word formal or informal? Is it old-fashioned, poetic, academic? (See Unit vii.)
connotations and cultural information	Does the word have a positive or negative association, e.g. see the verb *cause* in Unit 70? Is it often used ironically? Does the word have an interesting history? Was it borrowed from another language? (See Unit viii.)
related words	Is it a synonym or antonym of another word? (See Unit ii.)
examples	Good learners' dictionaries give example sentences or phrases. Examples are often taken from computer databases of real texts or else written specially to illustrate key features of meaning and use.

TIP When buying a dictionary, take a checklist based on B above, and see how many of the types of information each dictionary offers, then choose the one that is best for your needs.

Exercises

iii.1 **In a good dictionary, such as the *Cambridge Advanced Learner's Dictionary*, look up the word *dissimilar*. Are there any special aspects of usage that you should make a note of?**

If your dictionary does not tell you anything special about its usage, look at the notes about usage of *dissimilar* in Unit 71.

iii.2 **Look in your dictionary and find out which two prepositions normally follow the adjective *liable*.**

iii.3 **Find a dictionary which has the word *aught* in it. What special information does the dictionary give about its usage?**

iii.4 **If you can access the Internet, go to the website for Cambridge University Press dictionaries at dictionary.cambridge.org and find out if the two phrasal verbs *catch up with* and *catch up on* are the same, or whether there are differences in meaning.**

iv Collocation

A

Collocation is concerned with the way words occur together, often in unpredictable ways. It is a very good idea when learning new words to learn any typical collocations that go with them.

Adjective + noun collocations

Nouns often have typical adjectives which go with them. Here are some examples.

Compare **article** and **thing**:

We say	*but not usually ...*
the **real thing**	the genuine thing
the **genuine article**	the real article

Examples:

I don't like recorded music, I prefer the **real thing.** [i.e. real, live music]

These trainers are the **genuine article.** Those others are just cheap imported copies.

Other examples:

You can give a **broad summary** of something. (*Not:* ~~a wide summary~~)
You can describe something in **great detail.** (*Not:* ~~in big detail~~)

Some adjectives go with a restricted range of nouns.
For example: a **formidable task/opponent/amount/person**

B

Verb + adverb collocations

Often, verbs have typical adverbs that collocate with them. The lines in the chart show which collocations are normal:

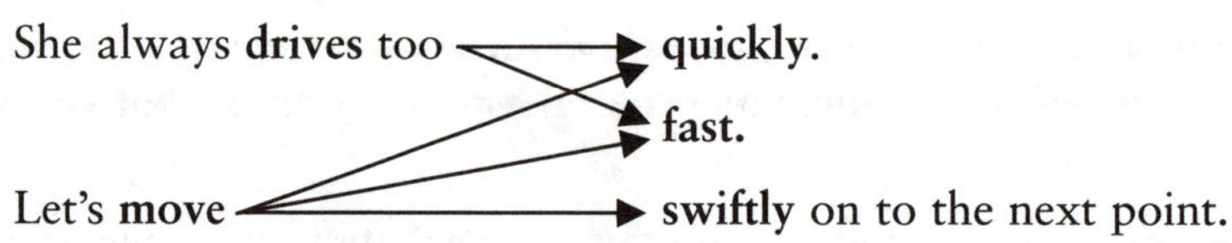

Other examples:

It's something I **feel strongly** about. (*Not:* I ~~feel powerfully about~~)
If I **remember rightly**, it happened at about six-thirty. (*Not:* ~~If I remember perfectly~~)

C

Adverb + adjective collocations

It is useful to learn which adverbs most typically modify particular types of adjectives. For example, the adverb **utterly**, which means totally or completely, generally occurs before an adjective. The majority of these adjectives have a negative connotation. Typical examples are: **alien, appalling, blank, dismal, depressed, disgusting, distasteful, false, fatuous, impossible, lost, ludicrous, naïve, ridiculous.** Try to notice this kind of regularity when learning words.

D

Verb + object collocations

Verbs and their objects often form collocations.

You **raise your hand** to ask a question. (*Not:* ~~lift your hand~~)
You can **raise a family.** (i.e. bring up children; *not:* ~~lift a family~~)
You can **visit / go to / check out a website** on the Internet.

Exercises

iv.1 **Choose between *real* and *genuine* in these sentences. Circle the more normal collocation. If both are acceptable, circle them both.**

1 The Egyptian Pyramid hotel in Las Vegas is great, but I'd prefer to see the real/genuine thing.
2 He just doesn't live in the real/genuine world. He lives in a fantasy world all the time.
3 This briefcase is made of real/genuine leather.
4 She is a very real/genuine person. If she promises something, she'll do it.
5 This home-made champagne is nice, but it's not as good as the real/genuine article.

iv.2 **Choose one of the words below each sentence to fill the gaps. In each case only one of them is the normal collocation for the underlined word.**

1 After his death, she went to the hospital to collect his personal ....
a) affairs b) objects c) effects d) extras
2 He made a rather .... attempt at an apology, but it didn't convince anyone.
a) faint b) frail c) fragile d) feeble
3 George was a .... opponent, and I respected him for that.
a) formidable b) dreadful c) forbidding d) threatening
4 I was feeling .... anxious when she didn't arrive.
a) totally b) pretty c) utterly d) blatantly
5 She seemed to be .... bewildered by the answer they gave her.
a) vividly b) strongly c) utterly d) heavily

iv.3 **Circle the most suitable collocation in these sentences. The word you choose should have the approximate meaning given in brackets.**

1 A brisk/brusque/brash (quick and energetic) walk before breakfast helps to enforce/sharpen/grow (increase, make stronger) the appetite.
2 The death tally/tale/toll in the earthquake has now risen to 20,000. (number or total)
3 Let's take a sluggish/plodding/leisurely stroll along the beach, shall we? (slow and not energetic)
4 If you want to stay at home tonight, that's utterly/perfectly/blatantly OK with me. (completely, 100%)
5 My aunt bequeathed/bequested/bereaved £20,000 in her will to cancer research. (gave after her death)
6 If I remember rightly/keenly/fairly she had two brothers, both older than her. (correctly)
7 If you want information about the publisher of this book, you can accede/call/visit their website at www.cambridge.org (consult, look at).
8 Eating all those peanuts has spoilt/attacked/lowered my appetite. I don't feel like dinner now. (destroyed, decreased)

iv.4 **Which collocation is more likely? Circle the correct answer.**

1 a strong car / a powerful car
2 strong tea / powerful tea
3 auburn hair / auburn carpet
4 a doleful party / a doleful expression
5 a lengthy car / a lengthy meeting

FOLLOW UP
During the next seven days, try to find one new collocation that you were not aware of before for each of these categories:
ADJECTIVE + NOUN VERB + OBJECT VERB + ADVERB

V Polysemy

Polysemy is concerned with the way words often have a number of different meanings.

A

Look at these sentences and think about how you would translate the words in italics into your own language.

It's only *fair* that we should share the housework.
The Frankfurt Book *Fair* is a very important event for most publishers.
Our caravan gives us shelter through *fair* weather or foul.
I've got *fair* eyelashes and my eyes look awful without mascara.
His marks in his final exams were *fair* to disappointing.

The firefighters managed to save the children from the burning third-floor *flat.*
The countryside round here is terribly *flat* and boring.
To join the Fitness Club you pay a *flat* fee of £500.
The tune is in B *flat* minor.
He erected the shed in five minutes *flat.*

You probably need a different word to translate *fair* and *flat* in each sentence.

These sentences illustrate what linguists call **polysemy**, i.e. the fact that many words in English have more than one meaning. Sometimes the meanings are clearly related – *flat* as in *countryside* has a connection with *flat* as in *apartment* in that they both include an idea of being on one level. Sometimes, however, there is no connection at all.

For example, the meaning of *fair* as in Book *Fair* does not seem to be connected in any way with any of the other meanings of *fair*. Words like this can also be called **homographs** (same spellings but different meanings).

Here is another example. Which polysemous word can fill the gaps in all these sentences?
He struck a .... and we slowly began to look around the dark cave.
The teenage cooks in the competition were a .... for any of the adults.
Their marriage has been called a .... made in heaven.

B

One element of polysemy in English is that the language is very flexible and words can sometimes be used as different parts of speech. *Flat* with its *apartment* meaning, for instance, can become an adjective, e.g. a set of *flat keys*.

C

It is useful to be aware of polysemy in English for two main reasons.

- You need to be aware that the meaning you first learnt for a word may not be the one that it has in a new context.
- Learning about the range of meanings that a word can have can help you, as it were, to learn several meanings for the price of one.

D

The context of a word with multiple meanings will usually make it absolutely clear which of the word's possible meanings is intended. What, for example, would the noun *drill* probably mean in (a) a dental context, (b) an army context, (c) a road-building context?

We shall deal with some examples of polysemy at different places in this book. However, you should also be aware of it when you are using your dictionary and should note down any useful additional meanings for words that you have looked up.

vi Metaphor

Metaphor is concerned with using words in abstract rather than literal ways.

A

Metaphor is a way of expressing something by comparing it with something else that has similar characteristics.

If we call a city a jungle, for example, we are using a metaphor. We are suggesting that a city is like a jungle in that it is wild and full of dangers.

If we say that someone lights up our life, we are using a metaphor. We are suggesting that person is like a light in our life in that they bring us great happiness.

B

Many idioms are metaphorical expressions which are in common use. For example: *to be on the ball* [to be very aware of things and ready to act – like a good footballer], or *to keep someone or something on a tight rein* [to have a lot of control over someone or something – like a rider having control over a horse] are also metaphors.

vi.1 Here are some more idioms which are based on metaphors. What is the idiom in each sentence and what does it mean? What aspect of life does it draw its image from?

a) Jane's going to be in the saddle while the boss is on holiday.
b) It's hard to know what to do when management keeps moving the goalposts.
c) Starting his own decorating business was just another of his half-baked ideas.
d) We've had to tighten our belts since Sam lost his job.

vi.2 More unusual and original metaphors are used a great deal in literature. Here are some famous metaphors from Shakespeare. Underline the metaphors in each case and explain what they suggest.

a) All the world's a stage and all the men and women merely players.
b) Night's candles are burnt out; and jocund day stands tiptoe on the misty mountain tops.
c) There is a tide in the affairs of men, which, taken at the flood, leads on to fortune.

C

Many words in English are so frequently used in a metaphorical way that English speakers may no longer notice that they are metaphors. Here are some examples.

- Intelligence is equated with light; for example, a clever person is called *bright* and a less intelligent person *dim*.
- Intensity of feeling or passion is equated with temperature; someone who is enthusiastic at one time and not at another is said to *blow hot and cold*.
- The movement of people is equated with the movement of water; we can, for example, talk of people *flooding* or *trickling* out of a hall.
- Time is equated with money; both can be *spent* or *wasted* or *used profitably*.
- Business is likened to a military operation; *strategies, tactics* and *campaigns* are used in both.

vi.3 Here are some more examples of the five metaphorical concepts above. Underline the metaphor and say which concept it exemplifies and what it suggests.

a) This book throws a great deal of fresh light on the history of the period.
b) We could save half an hour at least if we went through the wood.
c) Try to keep cool even if he argues with you.
d) She spent all her life fighting to get her company recognised.
e) Police tried to control the flow of the fans as they left the concert.

vii Register

Register is concerned with the overall tone of a text or conversation, and the relationship that is built between the speaker and listener, or reader and writer. It is important to speak and write in the appropriate register for the situation.

A Formal and informal words

Some words may be more formal or informal, while other words may be quite neutral. It is a good idea to mark words as formal or informal if they have such associations.

Is your **other half** not with you today? [informal: husband/wife]
She brought her new **bloke** to the party. [informal: boyfriend]
I saw him **conversing** with a woman in a red car. [formal: having a conversation]

Sometimes it is possible to arrange words into sets of neutral, formal and informal words:

neutral	*formal*	*informal*
TV/television		the box/telly
glasses	spectacles	specs
clothes	clothing/garments	clobber/kit

B Speech and writing

Some words are more associated with *either* spoken *or* written language. Again, in such cases, it is worth noting if a word has a particularly strong association with speech (S) or writing (W).

word/phrase	*S/W*	*comment and example*
subsequently	W	conjunction: in speech more likely to be 'later' or 'afterwards', e.g. The police found some important clues. **Subsequently**, three people were arrested.
in sum	W	conjunction: means 'to sum up', e.g. **In sum**, we may say that most, but not all, English adverbs end in -ly.
whatsisname/ whatsername	S	vague word: used when we cannot remember the name of a person, e.g. I met **whatsisname** at the party, you know, the guy who works at the university.
thingy	S	vague word: used as a noun, of people and things whose name one cannot remember, e.g. Give me that **thingy** there, yes, that bottle opener.
mind you	S	discourse marker: used to bring attention to an important point, e.g. He's a good actor. **Mind you**, he should be; he went to the best drama college.
now then!	S	discourse marker: used to get people's attention when something is about to happen, e.g. **Now then!** I want everyone to put their luggage together in one pile.

C Outdated words

Some words and expressions may be correct, but may sound archaic (outdated) or old-fashioned, e.g. **asylum** [hospital for the mentally ill], **frock** [dress], **wireless** [radio], **consumption** [tuberculosis/TB], **eyeglasses** [glasses].

Exercises

vii.1 Make the underlined words in these sentences formal or informal, as instructed.

1 She works in a shop that sells <u>women's clothes</u>. (formal)
2 I've got some new <u>spectacles</u>. Do you like them? (informal)
3 Did you see that documentary about Wales on <u>TV</u> last night? (informal)
4 Have you met Lily's new <u>boyfriend</u>? (informal)
5 I spent the morning <u>talking</u> with the Director. (formal)
6 Molly was there with her <u>other half</u>. He's a nice <u>chap</u>. (formal)

vii.2 Complete the table using the words from the box. Do not fill the shaded boxes.

shades meal kids cop ensure umbrella children

neutral	*formal*	*informal*
	offspring	
sunglasses		
policeman/woman	police officer	
		brolly
	repast	
make sure		

vii.3 Decide whether these words are more likely to be associated with everyday spoken or everyday written English. Write S or W next to the word.

1 frequently   2 start   3 begin   4 maybe   5 moreover

vii.4 What do you think are the present-day equivalents of these now outdated English words? Use a dictionary if necessary.

1 apothecary   2 damsel   3 poesy   4 whither

vii.5 Look at these text extracts and decide which register types you would classify them in. Underline key words which help you decide the register. For example, if you think the text is 'formal, poetic, archaic and written', which word(s) make you think that?

Some register types:

literary/poetic/non-literary
archaic/modern
spoken/written
academic/non-academic
technical/non-technical
formal/informal

1 When using a .pst file that is stored in a shared directory, or else one that is located on a file server, use the Macron file system to restrict access to the .pst file.

2 Views are certainly divided on the answers to the questions listed above; even whether it matters that pluralism and different paradigms reign in SLA is a matter of ornery and splenetic debate. (Block 1996; Gregg et al 1997)

3 Sweetest love, I do not go,
For weariness of thee,
Nor in hope the world can show
A fitter love for me;
But since that I
Must die at last, 'tis best,
To use my self in jest
Thus by feigned deaths to die.

4 And so, my fellow Americans: ask not what your country can do for you – ask what you can do for your country. My fellow citizens of the world: ask not what America will do for you, but what together we can do for the freedom of man.

5 Mind you there was a lot of rain in Germany over Christmas wasn't there, cos I saw the river in Bonn on the news on telly. The Rhine. Yeah. The river in Bonn.

viii Connotation and cultural associations

Connotation is concerned with the associations which a word or expression has.

A

Now that you are at an advanced level of English you need to become more aware not only of what words mean but also of what their connotations are. **Connotation** is the term which linguists use to refer to the associations which words have for speakers of a language.

For example, the word cowboy, as used in an expression like **cowboy builders** or **cowboy plumbers**, has associations of dishonesty and unreliability.

The connotations which words have are often exploited in advertisements. For example, an advertisement for an Indian firm of builders took the slogan:

You've tried the cowboys. Now try the Indians.

This slogan draws on two sets of connotations – the *cowboy* association mentioned above and the association of *cowboys and Indians* as from Wild West films. It neatly suggests that Indians, as the traditional opponents of cowboys, embody as builders the opposite characteristics of honesty and reliability.

B

Very often connotations may be quite personal. Someone who had a bad experience of dogs in childhood may think of a dog as being fierce and frightening, whereas for others dogs may represent loyalty and friendship. It may help you to learn words if you keep your own personal connotations in mind as you try to memorise them.

For example, imagine that you want to learn the three words below. What personal associations do they have for you? Close your eyes and imagine these things in your own personal context as you try to learn the words.

a shark **a scar** **a diamond**

Some connotations, however, are shared by all or most members of a language group and you need to appreciate what such connotations are in order fully to understand much of modern writing, in particular journalism. What are the connotations of *shark, scar* and *diamond* for English speakers in general?

C

Connotations used in journalism may be quite short-lived. The phrase **The Iron Lady**, for example, used to refer to Mrs Thatcher when she was Prime Minister of Britain in the 1980s, (the image being of a strong, hard and unyielding woman), soon lost any strong associations for most people when she lost office. Sometimes connotations are not the same for all native speakers of the same language but may vary from one geographical area to the next. **Black cats**, for example, have associations with *good luck* in Britain but with *bad luck* in the USA. Good modern dictionaries will give you information about widely shared connotations.

D The connotations which words have in English may be the same in your language too. Can you match the colours with their connotations in English? Are any of these the same in your language?

1 blue	purity
2 green	evil
3 yellow	miserable
4 red	inexperienced
5 white	danger
6 black	a coward

In this book we shall refer to connotations whenever they are relevant. Be aware of them also in your own reading and listening. Make notes of any interesting examples you encounter.

1 Abbreviations and acronyms

A

Abbreviations are simply the shortening of words and expressions.

Some common abbreviations come from Latin:

e.g. for example, from *exempli gratia*
i.e. that is, from *id est*
NB note well, from *nota bene*
AD the year of Our Lord, used to count years since the birth of Christ, from *Anno Domini*

Some come from shortened words:

bedsit: one room which is a **bed**room and a **sit**ting room
sitcom: short for **sit**uational **com**edy (a kind of TV programme)
sci-fi: science fiction

Some are pronounced as individual letters:

EU European Union
BC Before Christ, used to count years before the birth of Christ
ID identity document
asap as soon as possible

Some abbreviations are **acronyms**, i.e. they are formed from the first letters (or occasionally syllables) of a word or series of words and are pronounced as a word:

AIDS /eɪdz/ acquired immune deficiency syndrome
NATO /ˈneɪtəʊ/ North Atlantic Treaty Organisation

Some can be pronounced both as an acronym and as individual letters:

VAT value-added tax, pronounced /væt/ or /viː eɪ tiː/
UFO unidentified flying object, pronounced /ˈjuːfəʊ/ or /juː ef ˈəʊ/

B

Sometimes abbreviations can have more than one meaning.

AA Alcoholics Anonymous [an organisation helping people with alcohol-related problems] *and* **the AA** the Automobile Association [a UK motorists' club]
PC personal computer *or* Police Constable [the lowest rank of police officer in the UK] *or* politically correct [avoiding expressions which may suggest prejudice and cause offence]
m metre, mile, million, male, married **p** per, pence, page

C

Some abbreviations are particularly common in writing.

RSVP reply please [used on invitations, from French, *répondez s'il vous plaît*]
PTO please turn over
FAQ frequently asked question [found mainly on websites]
These abbreviations are increasingly common in electronic text messages:
FYI for your information **AFK** away from keyboard **LOL** laughing out loud
BTW by the way **R** are **C** see **U** you **EZ** easy **4** for **2** to, too, two

D

Abbreviations are often used in newspaper small ads for accommodation.

£300 **pcm excl:** rent is £300 per calendar month excluding payment for gas, electricity, etc.
£60 **pw inc:** rent is £60 per week including gas, electricity, etc.
f/f: fully furnished **s/c:** self-contained [has all it needs within itself]
suit n/s prof female: would suit a non-smoking woman in a professional job
all mod cons: all modern conveniences, e.g. washing machine
ch: central heating **d/g:** double garage **o.n.o.:** or nearest offer
Note that you may see different punctuation for these expressions – **c/h, c.h.** and **ch**

Exercises

1.1 **Insert the correct Latin abbreviations from A into the gaps.**

1 This antique vase dates from 1500 ....
2 Fruit, ... the usually sweet part of a tree or bush which contains seeds, is normally delicious to eat.
3 .... fruit cannot be taken across the border into the USA.
4 Fruits, ... lemons, pears and grapes, are sometimes added when cooking poultry.

1.2 **How are the abbreviations in these sentences pronounced? What do they stand for?**

1 If he can't kick the habit on his own, he should try joining AA.
2 Read pp.10–22 for homework.
3 Cars must not exceed 30 mph in a built-up area.
4 The film gives a convincing depiction of life BC despite some curious anachronisms.
5 Do you believe in UFOs?
6 Write back asap.

1.3 **What do these abbreviations stand for? Choose from the words in the box. Use each word once only.**

1 WHO 2 UNESCO 3 IMF 4 OBE 5 GMT 6 IOC 7 RSPCA 8 EST

Animals	Educational	International	Organisation	Standard
British	Empire	Mean	Organisation	Time
Committee	Fund	Monetary	Prevention	Time
Cruelty	Greenwich	Nations	Royal	United
Cultural	Health	Olympic	Scientific	World
Eastern	International	Order	Society	

1.4 **Translate this mobile phone text message into standard English.**

c u 4 t at 3, OK? BTW K's going 2 b here 2.

1.5 **As requested in the note below, write an advert to appear in the small ads column of the local newspaper. Use D opposite to help you and be as brief as possible.**

Could you prepare an advert for a girl to rent the third bedroom in our flat? We want someone who doesn't smoke and it would be nice to have a teacher or a nurse or someone in a reasonably reliable job. The advert had better mention that the flat is fully furnished and centrally heated and has all the kitchen appliances she might need. Don't, of course, forget to say that she would have to pay £220 a month, not including bills.

1.6 **Write an advert for someone to rent your own house or flat.**

1.7 **Sometimes the exact name of an organisation is chosen so that its acronym has a humorous or memorable effect. For example, ASH stands for Action on Smoking and Health. Here are some more examples. What do you think the other letters stand for?**

1 DUMP Disposal of .... Medicines and ....
2 NOW National .... of Women
3 UNITE .... of National Income Tax Employees
4 CALL Computer Assisted .... Learning
5 AAAAA American .... for the .... of Abbreviations and Acronyms

2 Prefixes: creating new meanings

A Preposition-based prefixes: different meanings

Over- may indicate (a) an excess of something, or (b) something that covers or dominates something, or (c) the crossing of some kind of barrier.

(a) EXCESS That film was **overrated** in my view. [people said it was better than it really was]
It was a bad restaurant, with an **overpriced** menu. [too high prices]

(b) COVER In this program, you can choose to **overwrite** the existing file or to save it as a new file. [cover/replace the old text with the new text]
Our garden is **overshadowed by** the block of flats next door. [the flats cast a shadow over our garden]
She always felt **overshadowed by** her older, more successful, sister. [metaphorical use, felt less important than]

(c) CROSS He **overstepped** the mark when he said that. [crossed a barrier into offensive/unacceptable behaviour]
Will you be staying **overnight**? [from one day to the next]

Under- may indicate (a) less than the desired amount, or (b) something below another thing, or (c) some kind of negative behaviour.

(a) LESS Don't **underestimate** the time it will take. [think it will be less than it really is]
The company is seriously **understaffed**. [lacking staff]

(b) BELOW It's quite wet **underfoot**. Did it rain last night? [on the ground, beneath your feet]
The **underlying** question is a very difficult one. [the deeper question]

(c) NEGATIVE I wish you would not **undermine** everything I do. [attack, weaken]
He did it in a very **underhand** way. [secretly and possibly dishonestly]

Up- can suggest a change of some kind, often positive.
The airline **upgraded** me to business class. [changed my ticket to a better class]
There has been an **upturn** in the economy. [sudden change for the better]

Cross- (from *across*) usually indicates a link between two separated things.
Cross-border cooperation has led to a number of arrests of drug smugglers. [across the frontiers of two or more countries]
Cross-cultural misunderstandings often happen. [between people of different cultures]

B Less frequent prefixes

Con-/com- often suggests mixing things together. It often occurs in verbs of communication.
converse **commiserate** **condolences** **congeal** **contaminate**

E- can give the idea of something coming out of something.
They were **ejected** from the restaurant for bad behaviour. [formal: thrown out]
The machine **emitted** a loud noise and then stopped working. [formal: gave out]

A(d)- often means adding something to something or that things are connected. Sometimes the 'd' is replaced by doubling the following consonant.
The building **is adjacent to / adjoins** the hotel. [formal: is next to]
She gave me an **annotated** edition of Shakespeare's works. [with notes added]

Pro- can often suggest pushing something forward or increasing it.
promote **proliferate** **procrastinate** **procreate**

Exercises

2.1 **Decide which of the meanings of *over-* and *under-* are most obvious in the words in bold. Use the labels (a), (b) or (c), as in A opposite. Circle the correct letter. Use a dictionary if necessary.**

1 I really think she **overstated** her case, and lost a lot of sympathy.	a	b	c
2 The plane's **undercarriage** failed to open and it crashed.	a	b	c
3 A detailed list of awards is given **overleaf**.	a	b	c
4 He has a very **overbearing** personality.	a	b	c
5 The project was **underfunded** from the outset.	a	b	c
6 During the cruise, a child fell **overboard** and drowned.	a	b	c

2.2 **Rewrite these sentences using words from the opposite page.**

EXAMPLE Cooperation across the frontier has been very good.
Cross-border cooperation has been very good.

1 The hotel gave me a luxury room instead of the ordinary one I'd booked.
2 Would you like to spend the night there or come back the same day?
3 The problem that lies under the surface is a very serious one.
4 Misunderstandings between cultures are, sadly, very frequent.
5 I think this hotel charges too much.
6 It's slippery walking just here. Be careful.
7 The company experienced a rise in popularity since it changed its name.
8 I felt that what she said was critical of my position and weakened it somewhat.
9 It would be a mistake to think Frances was less intelligent than she really is.

2.3 **Which of these words may be used with the prefix *a(d)-* as in B opposite? Circle YES or NO. How is the prefixed word written? Use a dictionary if necessary.**

EXAMPLE fix	(YES)	NO	affix
1 locate	YES	NO	....
2 verse	YES	NO	....
3 state	YES	NO	....
4 mission	YES	NO	....
5 pertain	YES	NO	....
6 minister	YES	NO	....
7 drain	YES	NO	....

2.4 **Write sentences to illustrate the meaning of these words. Use a dictionary if necessary.**

1 promote 2 proliferate 3 procrastinate 4 procreation

2.5 **What is the approximate meaning of the prefixes highlighted in the following words? Use a dictionary if necessary.**

1 **ab**dicate **ab**scond **ab**duct
2 **a**blaze **a**float **a**drift
3 **extra**terrestrial **extra**neous **extra**curricular
4 **inter**related **inter**departmental **Inter**net
5 **intra**venous **intra**departmental **intra**net

3 Suffixes: productive suffixes and word classes

A Productive suffixes

Some suffixes are **productive** [used to create new words]. You therefore need to understand their meaning if you are reading contemporary English. You might also feel adventurous enough to try **coining** [creating] some words of your own! The meaning of the example words below is clear from the meanings of the root and the suffix. (In the word **washable**, **wash** is the root and **able** is the suffix.)

-**able** can be used productively, whereas *-ible* never is. It combines with verbs to form adjectives. Note that **-able** means 'can be': a **washable** jacket is one that can be washed. **disposable** nappies, **predictable** results, **avoidable** problems, a **manageable** situation

-**conscious** combines with nouns to form adjectives that describe people who consider one aspect of their lives especially important: **health-conscious** person, **class-conscious** society, **safety-conscious** company, **time-conscious** workforce

-**esque** combines with the names of famous people to form adjectives that describe something or someone similar in style: **Picassoesque** paintings

-**free** combines with nouns describing something undesirable to form adjectives to describe nouns without that undesirable aspect: **stress-free** life, **tax-free** shop, **additive-free** food

-**rich** combines with nouns (often chemical or organic substances) to form adjectives to describe nouns with a lot of that substance: **fibre-rich** diet, **calcium-rich** foods

-**led** combines with nouns and nationality adjectives to form adjectives describing things that are controlled or influenced by the original noun or nationality:
community-led initiative, **student-led** protest, **worker-led** uprising

-**minded** combines with adjectives or nouns to form new adjectives describing people with particular characters, opinions or attitudes: **like-minded** friends [with similar interests], **career-minded** young women, **money-minded** managers

-**proof** combines with nouns to form adjectives describing things that can resist the damage or difficulty caused by that noun: **ovenproof** dish, **waterproof** jacket, **soundproof** room, **idiot-proof** instructions

-**related** combines with nouns to form adjectives to describe one thing as connected with another: **stress-related** absence from work, **age-related** earnings, **tobacco-related** illness

-**ridden** combines with nouns to form adjectives describing people or things with a lot of that noun: **guilt-ridden** person, **crime-ridden** city. Note that if a person is **bedridden**, they have to stay in bed because they are ill.

-**worthy** combines with nouns to form adjectives that describe people or things that merit whatever the original noun refers to: **newsworthy** incident [worth reporting in the news], **praiseworthy** action/pupil [deserving praise]

B Different word classes

-**ly** is not only an adverb ending, it also forms quite a few adjectives: **lively** children [full of energy], **costly** holiday [expensive], **leisurely** walk [relaxed], **miserly** man [mean with money]

-**ant** is most familiar as an adjective ending (**relevant** information, **distant** hills) but it can also make nouns from verbs to describe a person: an **applicant** for a job, an insurance **claimant**, a police **informant**, a quiz **contestant**, an **occupant** of a house

-**en** makes adjectives from nouns (**woollen** jumper, **golden** hair) but it also makes verbs from adjectives: **to moisten** your lips, **to sweeten** tea, a situation **worsens**, a face **reddens**

Exercises

3.1 **Complete the table below with your own examples.**

suffix	*new example in phrase*	*suffix*	*new example in phrase*
-able	a debatable issue	-minded	
-conscious		-proof	
-free		-related	
-rich		-ridden	
-led		-worthy	

3.2 **Match each adjective on the left with the two nouns it best collocates with in the box.**

EXAMPLE student-led *rebellion, demonstration*

1 additive-free
2 avoidable
3 disposable
4 guilt-ridden
5 high-minded
6 newsworthy
7 oil-rich
8 ovenproof
9 soundproof
10 stress-related

knives and forks income drinks mistake room ~~rebellion~~ delay foods criminal story illness expression glove booth speech dish country ~~demonstration~~ problems personality principles economy

3.3 **Which of the suffixes in A opposite could combine with the words in the box below to make new words? Note that there is more than one possibility for each word.**

age dust Byron sugar work

3.4 **Rewrite the sentences using the suffix given in brackets.**

EXAMPLE The weather can't be predicted. (-able) *The weather is unpredictable.*

1 Poisonous mushrooms can be easily identified. (-able)
2 He thinks so much about his career that he has no time for his family. (-minded)
3 The new phone boxes are supposed to be indestructible by vandals. (-proof)
4 During the Civil War, the country was totally overcome by terror. (-ridden)
5 The soil on that farm contains a lot of nutrients. (-rich)
6 The bank decided that he did not have enough income to allow him credit. (-worthy)

3.5 **Using a suffix from A make up words with the following meanings.**

1 operating in the style of the current President of the USA
2 food for vegetarians must be this
3 connected with class
4 containing a lot of vitamins
5 can be dry-cleaned
6 very aware of people's clothes
7 initiated by the government

3.6 **Are the following words adverbs, adjectives or verbs? Check in your dictionary.**

1 dampen
2 friendly
3 dearly
4 silken
5 roughen
6 masterly
7 kindly
8 darken

4 Word-building and word-blending

Many literary or academic words in English are formed using ancient Greek and Latin prefixes and roots. Many English speakers are not aware of the meanings of the word parts listed here, but knowing them can help you to understand and remember new words.

A Common well-established word parts

*word part**	*meaning*	*example*
auto-	self	an **autonomous** country [self-ruling]
bio-	life, living things	**biodegradable** packaging [able to decay naturally]
cyber-	relating to computers and robots	a **cybercafé** [café where customers can use computers with the Internet]
de-	opposite action	to **decolonise** a country [remove colonists from]
-graph-, **-gram**	writing	a **monograph** [long article or short book on a subject that the writer has studied for a long time]
-gress-	step, walk, go	a **congress** [a conference, i.e. a meeting where people come together]
-ics	an area of study or knowledge	**obstetrics** [the study of childbirth]
-phon-	sound	**phonetics** [the study of human speech]
-ology	study	**criminology** [the study of crime]
pre- (opposite = **post-**)	before	**prepaid** postage [paid for in advance]
retro-	back, backwards	**retroactive** law [taking effect from a date in the past]
techno-	relating to advanced machines	**technophobia** [fear of using technological machines such as computers]
tele-	over a distance	**telepathic** experience [feeling something from a distance]

* The dash (-) in this column indicates whether the word part is usually found at the beginning, in the middle or at the end of a word.

Although these word parts above will help you to understand words, you cannot use them as freely to form new words as the productive prefixes and suffixes in Unit 2 and Unit 3.

B Blends

An interesting, if much less common, way of forming words is by combining two well-established words, e.g. **brunch** = a meal that is a combination of breakfast and lunch.

heliport: a place where helicopters can land and take off (helicopter + airport)
smog: polluted fog (smoke + fog)
motel: a roadside hotel for people travelling by car (motor + hotel)
Chunnel: tunnel linking Britain and France (Channel + tunnel)
guesstimate: an approximate calculation (guess + estimate; verb – to guesstimate)
docusoap: TV series about real people using hidden cameras (documentary + soap opera)
breathalyser: a device to find out how much alcohol a person has drunk (breath + analyse)

Exercises

4.1 **Using information from the table in A, explain the basic meanings of these words.**

EXAMPLE biography = *writing about a life*

1 telegram
2 telephone
3 autobiography
4 phonology
5 to retrogress
6 graphology
7 to destabilise
8 autograph

4.2 **Can you think of five more words using only those word parts listed in A and any other basic endings like *-ist* or *-ical*?**

4.3 **Look at the following prefixes. Use your dictionary to find two new words beginning with these prefixes and write them in your vocabulary notebook.**
Choose only words that use the prefixes studied in this unit. *Postman*, for example, clearly has not been formed using the prefix *post-*.

1 cyber
2 techno
3 retro
4 tele
5 auto
6 pre
7 post
8 phon

4.4 **Rewrite these sentences, replacing the underlined words with a word that includes the word part given. Use a dictionary if necessary.**

EXAMPLE I had to put off my trip to Japan. (POST)
I had to postpone my trip to Japan.

1 She asked the star for his signature on the back of her table napkin. (GRAPH)
2 She took a degree in the science of crime at Stockholm University. (OLOGY)
3 The novel is largely based on the writer's own life. (BIO)
4 It's an exhibition looking back at the painter's life and work. (RETRO)
5 He believes you can cure yourself by telling yourself you are cured. (AUTO)
6 Working at home and keeping in contact with the office by phone, fax and modem is becoming increasingly common. (TELE)
7 Some areas are now deliberately trying to become less industrial. (DE)
8 Crime committed through the Internet is a growing cause for concern. (CYBER)

4.5 **Rewrite these sentences, replacing the underlined word with an explanatory phrase.**

EXAMPLE Most of the time planes fly on autopilot.
Most of the time planes fly automatically, controlled by a computer rather than the pilot.

1 The firm makes job applicants do a graphology test.
2 Johnny loves his cyberpet.
3 Matt's a techno-wizard!
4 He's giving a paper at a pre-conference event in Spain.
5 Is it OK if I post-date this cheque?

4.6 **What words have been combined to make these blends? What do you think they mean?**

1 infomercial
2 edutainment
3 cybrary
4 vegeburger
5 swimathon
6 funtastic

5 Global contact and language enrichment

A

Read the texts about English vocabulary and note the words and expressions that are useful for talking about language enrichment.

When one language takes words from another, the new items are called **loan words** or **borrowings** – though neither term is really appropriate as the receiving language does not give them back. Whereas the speakers of some languages take pains to exclude foreign words from their **lexicons** [vocabulary], English seems always to have welcomed them. Over 120 languages are on record as **sources** [where something comes from] of its present-day vocabulary.

English has been enormously extended by each wave of invaders coming to Britain. Thus, for example, Viking and Norman invasions hugely **enriched** [made richer] the basic Anglo-Saxon **word stock** [set of words]. Scholarship then introduced many words **of classical origin** [from ancient Latin or Greek] at the time of the Renaissance. Moreover, English speakers' contact with the world as, for example, explorers, pirates, imperialists, convicts or fortune-seekers have all had **linguistic consequences** [results affecting language].

B

Here are just some examples of words coming into English from other languages.

language	*word*	*meaning*	*phrase*
Arabic	**amber**	yellowy-orange precious stone	an amber necklace
Dutch	**roster**	list of people's turns for jobs	the cooking roster
Farsi	**tabby**	female or stripy cat	our old tabby
German	**gimmick**	frivolous way of attracting attention	advertising gimmicks
Greek	**tonic**	medicine to make you feel more lively	take a tonic
Hindi	**cot**	child's bed with high vertical sides	sleep in a cot
Icelandic	**mumps**	a childhood illness	have mumps
Japanese	**hara-kiri**	type of ceremonial suicide	commit hara-kiri
Portuguese	**palaver**	unnecessary trouble	What a palaver!
Russian	**intelligentsia**	social class of intellectuals	19th century intelligentsia
Spanish	**hammock**	net hung and used as a bed	sleep in a hammock
Turkish	**turban**	type of men's headwear	wear a turban

C

Some English words may look like words in your language but have a different meaning. Such words are known as **false friends**, e.g. the German word *Gift* looks like the English word **gift** [(birthday) present] but actually means *poison* in German. The English word **sympathetic** resembles a word meaning, simply, *nice* in many other European languages, but in English **sympathetic** has a much narrower meaning [understanding and caring about someone else's suffering]. Note also that the pronunciation of a word borrowed into English may be quite different from its pronunciation in its language of origin.

Exercises

5.1 **What collocations other than those in the texts in A are there for these words?**

1 source of 2 enrich 3 classical 4 linguistic

5.2 **Which of the words in B do these pictures illustrate?**

1 ....

2 ....

3 ....

4 ....

5.3 **Fill the gaps with one of the words from B.**

1 The company will be committing economic .... if it agrees to such a proposal.
2 Most children these days are inoculated against .... when they are babies.
3 I have some lovely .... earrings. They match my yellow scarf perfectly.
4 A weekend beside the sea was just the .... we needed after the long winter.
5 Who's on the .... for the cleaning this week?
6 The clowns went out into the street as a .... to advertise their circus.

5.4 **Think of words that have come from your own language into English. Try to find words from these topic areas, which are particularly rich in loan words in English.**

- food and drink
- flora, fauna and landscape features
- industrial products and inventions
- clothing and the home
- politics and society
- the arts, sports and leisure activities

5.5 **Make a list of false friends for English and your own first language. Here is a list begun by a German speaker.**

word	*similar word in my language + meaning*	*meaning in English*
gift	*Gift = poison*	*(birthday) present*
sympathetic	*sympathisch = nice*	*understands and cares about others' problems*

5.6 **These words are said to have moved from English into a number of other languages. Which of them exist in your language?**

Thematic fields	**English source words**
food and drink	bacon, beefsteak, jam, pudding, sandwich
flora and fauna	bulldog, dog, mustang [wild horse], skunk
clothing and the home	blazer, cardigan, pullover, sweater, patio
political and social life	parliament, Tory, boycott, budget, inflation, strike
industry and inventions	car ferry, container, freight, computer chip, cable TV
arts, sports and leisure	ace [1 in playing cards], boxer, football, break dance

FOLLOW UP Make a list of words that have come from English into your language. The meaning and the pronunciation may well have changed in the move from one language to another. So check if this has happened and make appropriate notes beside the words in your list.

6 Similar but different: words easily confused

A Words similar in form and close in meaning

Some words not only look similar but are quite close in meaning.

The United Nations should **intervene** to stop the civil war. [step in; neutral in meaning]
She shouldn't **interfere** in things that don't concern her. [involve herself; negative and critical]
The phone's been ringing **continually**. It's driving me crazy. [very frequently; often negative]
(From a recipe) Stir the mixture **continuously** until it boils. [without stopping]
There's a new **series** on TV about space exploration. [set of related programmes]
I don't want to miss this week's episode of *Oliver Twist*. It's a **serial** – if I miss one I'll lose track of the story. [set of programmes where the story continues over different episodes]
We sat **in the shade of** a big oak tree. [out of the sun; pleasant connotation]
The evening sun cast long **shadows**. [dark areas or shapes]
They lived **in the shadow of** a chemical factory. [in a place dominated by; negative connotation]

B Words of different form but from the same area of meaning

The cake mixture should be **moist** but not sticky. [slightly wet]
The climate in the north is **damp** and rather cold. [slightly wet in an unpleasant way]
The **theme** of the festival was '1000 years of culture'. [the main idea that everything followed]
The **topic** of conversation soon changed from the weather to the latest gossip. [what the people talked about at any given moment]
The **security** officer at work said there had been a burglary. [concerned with protection of property, etc.]
The **safety** officer told him that he must wear a helmet. [concerned with prevention of accidents, etc.]

C Phrasal combinations

Sometimes, phrasal verbs have noun forms which may be in a different order and have different meanings.

verb	*noun*
Six prisoners have **broken out** of a high security jail.	There has been a **breakout** at a high security jail.
The disease has **broken out** in several villages in the north of the country.	There has been an **outbreak** of the disease in several villages in the north of the country.
Economists are **looking out** for signs of an end to the recession.	The **outlook** is not good. The economy seems to be stagnant.
He stood at the corner **looking out** for police cars.	He was the **lookout** while the others robbed the bank.

In some cases, there are two verb forms with the same words in a different order and with different meanings.

verb 1: particle second	*verb 2: particle first*
end up [finish]	**upend** [move into a vertical position]
hold up [delay]	**uphold** [confirm, support]
do out [decorate]	**outdo** [do better than]

Exercises

6.1 Circle the correct word in these sentences. Use a dictionary if necessary.

1 I have always tried not to intervene/interfere in things that are not my business.
2 The traffic was stationary/stationery for a few minutes, then it began to move again.
3 She paid me a nice compliment/complement; she said I was the most intelligent person she had ever worked with.
4 I'm sorry! I wasn't trying to evade/avoid you. I just didn't know you were here.
5 At the entrance there was a big signal/sign saying *No children*.
6 The teacher intervened/interfered to stop the argument between the two students.
7 The other benefits I received in the job were complimented/complemented by an excellent pension plan.
8 If you need stationary/stationery for your office, just ask the secretary.
9 He was continually/continuously complaining about something or other.
10 He was fined £20,000 for avoiding/evading taxes and failing to declare his income.
11 The signal/sign changed to green and the train moved away from the station.
12 You have to press the button continually/continuously until the red light comes on. Don't take your finger off it, or it won't work.

6.2 Decide whether the particle should go *before* or *after* the verb in these sentences.

EXAMPLE I don't think these shoes will ....out.... last .... till the end of winter. (OUT)

1 We .... ended .... the sofa and used it to block the doorway. (UP)
2 The cheetah is so fast it can .... run .... a sports car. (OUT)
3 She's always trying to .... do .... everyone. Why is she so competitive? (OUT)
4 The committee .... held .... her complaint, and she was awarded compensation. (UP)
5 The Beatles have .... lasted .... most other 1960s groups in popularity. (OUT)
6 We .... ended .... eating in a dingy café on the edge of town. (UP)
7 I'll leave on Monday. I don't want to .... stay .... my welcome. (OUT)
8 The radio's not working. The batteries have .... run .... (OUT)

6.3 Match the verbs on the left with a suitable object on the right.

1 rehearse	the batteries in the clock
2 revise	flowers in the garden
3 change	for an exam
4 alter	a friend at the airport
5 pick up	someone's suspicions
6 pick	a garment that's too big
7 rouse	an end-of-term play
8 arouse	someone who's sleeping

6.4 Choose a noun from the box that can be associated with the following sentences.

a lookout	an outbreak	a breakout	an upset	an outlook	a setup

1 There has been violence in the capital city.
2 My stomach was bad so I couldn't go to work.
3 He is very cheerful and positive about life.
4 They fooled him into thinking his car had been stolen, but it hadn't.
5 She made sure nobody was looking, while her husband did the shoplifting.
6 Four prisoners have escaped from a maximum security prison.

7 At work: colleagues and routines

A Colleagues

Look at this extract of someone talking about their job and their colleagues.

Well, Philip **is my opposite number** [has the same position/does the same job as me] in the company's New York office.

He and I have a good **working relationship** [how we communicate and work together]. Last month we got a new boss, who quickly established a good **rapport** [/ræp'ɔː/ communication/relationship] with everyone in the office. I do socialise with my **workmates** [informal: colleagues, especially in non-professional jobs] but we try not to **talk shop** [informal: talk about work].

The company is generally very **hierarchical** [/haɪər'ɑːkɪkəl/ has a structure with powerful and less powerful people]; there's a **pecking-order** [a system where some people have the right to get benefits/promotions before others] for everything. I **do a job-share** [we each have a 50% contract for the same job] with a woman called Rosemary. It suits us both as we each have children to look after.

B Daily work routines

Nancy gets to work at about 8.45. She has to **clock in** and **clock out** [use an electronic card to record the time she arrives and leaves each day]. She works fixed hours; she has a **nine-to-five job.** Brett can come in at any time from eight o'clock till ten in the morning; he **works flexi-time** / he's **on flexi-time**, but his core hours are 10.00 to 12.00 and 2.00 to 4.00. Archie doesn't go to the office at all. He works from home with his computer; he's a **teleworker.** Bert works different times each week; every third week he works nights; he does **shift work** / he's a **shift worker.** Mick has his own company; he's **self-employed** and works from home. His wife works for different companies at different times; she's **freelance** / she **works freelance.**

C During the day (different work-patterns)

Most of the day I do routine tasks, but occasionally there's a crisis or I have to **meet a deadline** [have something finished by a fixed day or time]. At certain times of the year I have a very **heavy workload** [amount of work I have to do] but at other times it can be quite **light.**

I start work at my machine at seven o'clock when I'm on the **day shift.** The job's very **mechanical** [you don't have to think about what you are doing] and **repetitive** [the same thing every day]. All I ever think about is **knocking off** at three [informal: finishing work]. The shift I hate most is the **night shift.** I start at ten and work all night till six in the morning. The job's a bit **monotonous** [boring because it never changes].

I have a **glamorous** job [very exciting, which everyone admires]. I'm a pilot. The hours are **irregular** and **antisocial** [do not enable one to have a normal social life], but I'm not **stuck behind a desk** [informal: sitting in an office all day] and there's a lot of variety. The **stress levels** can be quite high when you know people's lives depend on you. I feel sorry for people who are **stuck in a rut** [stuck in a job they can't escape from] or working in **dead-end jobs** [jobs with no prospects of promotion].

D Types of work

I have a lot of **paperwork** to do by tomorrow. [letters/reports to write, forms to complete]
My father did **manual** work all his life and was very fit. [hard and physical]
I think I'd like **vocational** work, like being a nurse or a teacher. [which helps people]

Exercises

7.1 **Correct the mistakes in this paragraph.**

I think I have a good work relationship with most of my colleagues. I tried to establish a good report with them from the very beginning. The person I like most is my opposite member in our office in Paris. Generally, when I socialise to my colleagues outside of work, we try not to talk about shop, but it's not easy and sometimes we have a good gossip about people who are not there.

7.2 **Give three adjectives which you think describe each of these jobs (for example, *stressful, glamorous, dead-end*). Think of words you would use in your own language, then try to translate them into English. Use a dictionary if necessary.**

1 assembly-line worker
2 shop steward
3 PR officer
4 bodyguard
5 lifeguard
6 trawlerman
7 private eye
8 refuse collector

7.3 **Use words and phrases from B and C on the opposite page to complete these sentences.**

1 I would get bored if I had a nine ....
2 When I arrive in the morning and leave the office in the evening I use this card to ....
3 I'm very tired; recently I've had a very heavy ....
4 I don't want an office job. I don't want to spend all day stuck ....
5 I can clock in any time between eight and ten and clock out between four and six; I'm on ....
6 I'd hate to feel trapped in my job and to be stuck in ....
7 He's not here this evening, he's working nights; you see, he does ....
8 I work for different companies at different times as it suits me. I'm ....
9 I used to work for someone else, but now I'm my own boss; I'm ....
10 I stopped working in the hamburger restaurant. It was just a dead-.................................... .
11 When I was working in the factory, all I could think of all day was the moment when I could knock ....
12 Being a nurse is a good job, but you can't go out much with friends. The hours are a bit ....

7.4 **Using a dictionary if necessary, give one example of ...**

1 a manual job
2 a vocational job
3 a job with great variety
4 a job with irregular hours
5 a job with routine tasks
6 a job with regular deadlines
7 a job with lots of paperwork

8 At work: career and promotion

A Getting a job

Look at this **job ad** (informal)/**advertisement** (formal) for the IT (Information Technology) industry.

> **Ambitious Achievers**[1]
>
> Up to **£30k**[2] **basic**[3]
>
> ***Money motivated, eager, looking to work in a dynamic, fast-moving industry?***
>
> We are looking for ambitious, dynamic sales professionals with the talent and **drive**[4] to develop a **rewarding**[5] career within the IT industry. You will work in **close-knit**[6] teams, maintaining and developing relationships with a **diverse**[7] range of clients.
>
> Ideally you will possess some previous IT **sales experience**[8] and a good knowledge of computers. Most importantly you will have a strong desire to succeed.
>
> If you **fit this description**[9] and are seeking a **lucrative**[10] career in IT sales then call Claire Walden or Graham Keen on 01960 479 6021.

1 people determined to succeed and achieve great things
2 thirty thousand pounds
3 guaranteed minimum salary without overtime or bonuses
4 strong motivation
5 giving you a lot back
6 working in a close relationship
7 of different types
8 experience selling things
9 have these qualities
10 producing a lot of money

The text has some words with similar meanings in connection with work; learn them in pairs:
motivated and **eager** (person) **dynamic** and **fast moving** (industry/profession)
to seek a career in ... and **to look to work in ...** (note look *to*, meaning consider or hope, not look *for*)

B During your working life

In some countries, women are allowed **maternity leave** and men **paternity leave** if they're having a child. [time away from work to have a new baby]
What **perks** (informal) / **(extra) benefits** (formal) do you get in your job? [extra things apart from salary, e.g. a car]
How important is **job satisfaction** to you? [the feeling that your job is worth doing and fulfils you]
What's your **holiday entitlement**? [number of days you have the right to take as holiday]
Do you get regular salary **increments**? [formal: increases/rises]
Most people don't want to **reach/hit a glass ceiling**. [reach a level where you cannot get further promotion, even if you deserve it]
Most people think they are **overworked and underpaid**. [often said together as a humorous fixed expression]

Exercises

8.1 Make these rather informal sentences more formal by using words and phrases from the opposite page.

1 Do you often look at the job ads?
2 I haven't worked in sales before.
3 There's a lot of money in selling computers. I made 70k last year.
4 We sell quite a mixed range of products.
5 I thought I would apply for the job since it sounded just like me.

8.2 Find expressions on the left-hand page which mean the *opposite* of the underlined words or phrases.

1 a very <u>loosely organised</u> team
2 a very <u>frustrating</u> job
3 to have <u>low motivation</u>
4 a rather <u>static and slow-moving</u> profession
5 a <u>drop</u> in your salary

8.3 Read the text and answer the questions.

1 Why does 'a career' sound better than 'a job'?
2 What are 'ambiguous' situations?
3 What expression means 'not depending on other people'?
4 What is the abstract noun that means 'your ability to find clever or imaginative ways of doing things'?
5 What mental quality do you need for this job?
6 What job do you think this advertisement is for?

An exciting outdoor career

If you're an out-of-the-ordinary person who is looking for more than just a job, we are offering a unique career that requires you to use your intelligence, self-reliance and responsibility. If you have an adventurous spirit, a strong, positive personality, a tough mind and a high level of personal integrity, and if you think you can deal with rapidly-changing, ambiguous and unpredictable situations that will test your resourcefulness to the limit, then contact us now.

Phone 070037652, or e-mail
personnel@leadership.com

8.4 Put these expressions into two groups: *usually negative* (–) and *usually positive* (+). Some of them are new expressions not on the opposite page.

1 to hit a glass ceiling
2 to have a lot of perks
3 to be snowed under
4 to be demoted
5 to be passed over for promotion
6 to get turned down for a job
7 to be short-listed for a job
8 to be a high-flyer

8.5 Some words here are not used correctly or in their usual way. Correct them.

1 I started studying French at university, but I didn't finish my career and left after one year.
2 My boss rose my salary with £2,000 a year. I was delighted.
3 I'm underpaid and overworked, like everybody! And I'm always stressed up.
4 My holiday titlement is four weeks a year.
5 He got maternity leave when his wife had a baby.

8.6 Imagine you are a careers adviser. What advice would you give to someone who is ...

1 money motivated and who is prepared to take risks?
2 a very talented musician who is not necessarily money motivated?
3 an achiever who has a background in IT and is a very confident person?
4 suffering from a lack of job satisfaction in their present job?

9 Business I

A Modern business techniques

When John left school he was desperate for a job so he took the first one he was offered – in **telesales**[1]. He thought **telemarketing**[2] sounded quite glamorous but soon found that most of the people he phoned hated **cold-calling**[3] and put the phone down when he tried the **hard sell**[4]. When he realised that the company made most of its money through the rather dubious techniques of **inertia selling**[5] and **confusion marketing**[6], he decided to leave and train as a hairdresser instead.

1 selling or marketing goods and services by phone
2 see note 1
3 phoning people who have not requested a call in order to try to sell them something
4 attempt to sell something by being very forceful
5 when a company behaves as if you agreed to buy something because you did not actually refuse it
6 selling products and services in a package, in a way that makes it very difficult to work out which company is cheapest

B Buying and selling

Supermarkets sometimes sell an item very cheaply just so that they attract a lot of people into the shop where they will also buy more profitable items – the item being sold very cheaply is called a **loss leader**.

If a company finds a **niche market**, it finds a specialised, small group of customers with particular interests that that company can meet.

People sometimes make a purchasing decision based on **brand loyalty**. [confidence in that particular make and a tendency always to choose it]

If you **shop around**, you try different companies or shops to see which offers best value.

If you buy something **on approval**, you have the right to return it if it is not satisfactory.

If you **have first refusal on** something, the seller promises that you will be asked if you would like to buy it first, and only if you do not want it will it be offered for sale to others.

If an item is said to **come/go under the hammer**, it is sold at an auction. [sale of goods or property where people make gradually increasing **bids** and the item is then sold to the highest **bidder**]

C A business career

Sally started her own catering business and this turned out to be very **lucrative**[1]. However, she got increasingly irritated by all the **red tape**[2] involved in business and when a larger company suggested **merging**[3], she was interested. The two companies did not agree immediately on all the details of the takeover but they managed to **reach a compromise**[4] and **hammer out a deal**[5] without too much delay. In some ways Sally was sad that her company had been **swallowed up**[6] but she is now quite glad to be free of the hassles of **entrepreneurship**[7]. She has used the money raised by the sale of her **capital assets**[8] to buy a large house in the south of France.

1 producing a lot of money
2 bureaucracy (negative)
3 joining together to form one new company
4 come to an agreement in which both sides have to give in a little bit on what they would have otherwise liked
5 talk seriously and in detail until a business agreement is made
6 taken over by a larger company (slightly negative)
7 involvement in business and taking financial risks
8 buildings and machines owned by a company

Exercises

9.1 **Match the two parts of these business collocations from the opposite page.**

1 loss	selling
2 capital	refusal
3 confusion	leader
4 first	tape
5 hard	marketing
6 inertia	loyalty
7 brand	assets
8 niche	sell
9 red	market

9.2 **Look at A and B opposite. Fill the gaps in these sentences.**

1 A unique painting will come .... the hammer in London tomorrow.
2 It's a sensible idea to shop .... a bit before buying a computer.
3 Jeremy has promised me that, if he ever decides to sell his motorbike, I can have .... refusal on it.
4 I don't mind trying a hard sell on a person who has already expressed an interest in our products, but I hate ....-calling.
5 I wasn't sure whether the desk would fit into my office so I bought it .... approval.
6 If you want to make a .... for something in an auction you first have to catch the auctioneer's eye.
7 If you work in telesales you spend most of your day on the ....
8 They produce special clothes for people who like to do yoga and have really captured this .... market.

9.3 **Replace the underlined words with a word or phrase from C with a similar meaning.**

1 As their business interests were really very similar, it did not take them very long to <u>come to an agreement</u>.
2 If you want to go into the import and export business, you had better be prepared for a lot of <u>bureaucracy</u>.
3 At the moment they are discussing the possibility of their companies <u>becoming one</u>.
4 Sportswear is a very <u>profitable</u> business to be in at the moment.
5 Only a few people have a real talent for <u>the risk-taking of opening a new business</u>.
6 A number of small companies have been <u>taken over</u> by that large multi-national in the last six months.

9.4 **Answer these questions about the words and phrases on the opposite page.**

1 Find three words or phrases that have negative associations – for most people at least.
2 Name two things that might count as capital assets.
3 Find three expressions that relate to ways of buying things.
4 Find three expressions that relate to ways of selling things.
5 Find three expressions that are based on a metaphor and explain what the metaphor is and why it is appropriate.

FOLLOW UP

The most useful business words for you to learn are those that relate to your own field. Go to the website <u>www.business.com</u>. This has links to sites organised according to a range of general and specialist business fields. Print out any useful pages and keep them in a special file.

10 Business 2

A

Here are some important words for talking about business agreements.

to **put in/submit a tender:** to supply a written offer to do a job for an agreed price
to **win a tender:** to be given a job, after submitting a tender
to **meet/miss a deadline:** to supply / fail to supply something by the agreed time
a **penalty clause:** part of a contract specifying what will happen if an agreement is broken
an **outstanding** account: an account that has not yet been paid
to **default on a payment:** to fail to pay something that had been agreed
to **acknowledge** receipt: to inform the sender when something is received
to **ship** an order: to send out goods that have been ordered – nothing to do with boats; what is sent is the **shipment**
to **expire:** to end – of something that was agreed for a fixed period; the noun is **expiry**

B

Reading humorous books about work can be a fun way of learning new words on the topic. Here is an example from a popular book which makes fun of the modern workplace.

Some Rules of Management
(from a Handbook for Managers)

- The problem is not a lack of resources, it's a lack of meetings.
- If you're talking, you're **communicating**[1].
- Low **morale**[2] is caused by character **flaws**[3] in your employees.
- If 10 people can complete a project in 10 days, then 1 person can complete the project in 1 day.
- **Teamwork**[4] is when other people do your work for you.

[1] this verb suggests that listeners understand what the speaker is trying to convey
[2] amount of confidence felt by a person or group
[3] weaknesses
[4] working together for a common purpose

C

Here are some things that people have said about business.

We demand that big business give the people a square deal; in return we must insist that when any one engaged in big business honestly endeavors to do right, he shall himself be given a square deal. (*Theodore Roosevelt*)

It is difficult but not impossible to conduct strictly honest business. What is true is that honesty is incompatible with the amassing of a large fortune. (*Mahatma Gandhi*)

The growth of a large business is merely the survival of the fittest [...] The American Beauty rose can be produced in the splendour and fragrance which bring cheer to its beholder only by sacrificing the early buds which grow up around it. (*John D. Rockefeller*)

The salary of the chief executive of the large corporation is not a market award for achievement. It is frequently in the nature of a warm personal gesture by the individual to himself. (*J. K. Galbraith*)

Accountants are the witch-doctors of the modern world and willing to turn their hands to any kind of magic. (*Lord Justice Harman*)

British management doesn't seem to understand the importance of the human factor. (*Charles, Prince of Wales*)

Exercises

10.1 Rewrite these sentences using the word in brackets.

1 Do you have many accounts which have yet to be paid? (outstanding)
2 Until what date is your contract valid? (expire)
3 Please let us know when you receive our payment. (acknowledge)
4 It is very important that you complete your work by the agreed time. (meet)
5 We would like to invite companies to send us proposals as to how they would do the job and what they would charge for it. (submit)
6 It is company policy to take legal action against customers who fail to pay their accounts. (default)

10.2 Look at B opposite. Complete the sentences using a word from the box.

employee	flaw	lack	morale	project	resources

1 Joanna is working on a very interesting .... at the moment.
2 Unfortunately, there's a .... in your reasoning.
3 What used to be called Personnel is now called Human ....
4 The new manager is doing his best to raise .... in the office.
5 Sadly our new product has met with a total .... of consumer interest.
6 We are extremely sorry to lose Matt as an ....

10.3 Which of the people quoted in C is making each of these points?

1 Top businessmen often award themselves bonuses regardless of their performance.
2 It is impossible to be both rich and honest.
3 Managers don't pay enough attention to the people who work for them.
4 Large businesses succeed by destroying small businesses.
5 Companies must treat customers fairly; then government will treat companies fairly too.

10.4 Match the parts of the collocations from C.

1 a chief	a fortune
2 a personal	of the fittest
3 a square	business
4 the survival	factor
5 an award	gesture
6 to turn	executive
7 the human	deal
8 to amass	your hand to
9 to conduct	for achievement

10.5 Choose one of the collocations from exercise 10.4 to fit each of these gaps.

Jack is now the .... (1) of a large company. He managed to .... (2) by designing some computer software which sold all over the world. He's a talented man, prepared to .... (3) any job that needs doing. He is good to his employees, always giving them .... (4) because he knows how important .... (5) is if you want .... (6) successfully. Last year he won .... (7) in business. In a remarkable .... (8), he gave his prize money away to his employees.

11 Cramming for success: study and academic work

A Study and exams

Before an exam you can **revise** or **cram**[1] for it. If the exam happens every year, you can look at **past papers**[2]. Some things can be **memorised** or **learnt off by heart**. But **rote-learning**[3] is not sufficient for most subjects. It is also possible to use **mnemonics**[4]. But tricks alone are not enough, and the best idea is to **bury yourself in your books**[5] until you **know the subject inside out**[6].

1 study intensively for a short time
2 exam papers from previous years
3 learning purely by repetition
4 [/nɪˈmɒnɪks/] tricks that help you remember something, for example: 'i' after 'e' except after 'c' is a mnemonic for English spelling (e.g. friend, but receive)
5 spend the maximum time studying
6 know it completely

B Written work for courses, etc.

word	*description*
composition	could be just 50–100 words, often used to refer to children's work
essay	longer than a composition, more serious, hundreds or even thousands of words
assignment	a long essay, often part of a course, usually thousands of words
project	like an assignment, but emphasis on student's own material and topic
portfolio	a collection of individual pieces of work, not necessarily written
dissertation	a long, research-based work, perhaps 10–15,000 words, for a degree or diploma
thesis	a very long, original, research-based work, perhaps 80–100,000 words, for a higher degree (e.g. PhD)

C The writing process and evaluation

It's a good idea to start with a **mind-map**[1] when preparing an essay. Always write a **first draft**[2] before **writing up** the final version. Your essay should be all your own work; **plagiarism**[3] is a very serious offence in most colleges and universities. There is usually a **deadline**[4]. After the essay is **submitted**[5], it will be **assessed**[6] and usually you can get **feedback**[7].

1 diagram that lays out ideas for the topic and how they are connected to one another
2 first, rough version
3 /ˈpleɪdʒərɪzəm/ using other people's work as if it was yours
4 date by which you must hand in the work
5 handed in (formal)
6 evaluated and given a grade
7 comments from the teacher/tutor

D Aspects of higher academic study

University academics **carry out** [less formal **'do'**] **research** and are expected to read **academic journals** [note: not ~~magazines~~], which publish **papers/articles** on specialised subjects. If a library does not have a book or journal, you can usually get it through **inter-library loan** [system where libraries exchange books/journals with one another]. Academic study can be very demanding and intensive, and some students **drop out** [leave the course before the end because they cannot cope], but the majority survive till **finals** [the last exams before receiving a degree].

Exercises

11.1 Correct the wrong usage of words to do with written work in these sentences.

1. His PhD assignment was 90,000 words long and was on the history of US place names.
2. Little Martha did her first dissertation in school today. It was called 'My family'.
3. We have to hand in an essay at the end of the course. It can consist of up to five different pieces of work.
4. The teacher gave us the title of this week's project today. We have to write 1,000 words on the topic of 'If I ruled the world' and hand it in next Monday.
5. At the end of this course you have to do a 5,000-word thesis which will be assessed, and the grade will contribute to your final degree.
6. I think I'll do a study of people's personal banking habits for my MSc composition. It has to be about 12,000 words.
7. I've chosen to do the portfolio instead of the two exams, because I like to do one single piece of work where I can research something that interests me personally.

11.2 Rewrite this short text using words and phrases from A instead of the underlined words.

When I'm preparing intensively for an exam, I don't see any point in looking up exam papers from previous years, nor is there any point in just learning things by memory. I know some people develop very clever memory tricks to help them remember the material, but there's no real substitute for re-reading and going over the term's work. It's a good idea to have some sort of diagram to organise your ideas, and memory-learning is useful, but in a limited way. At the end of the day, you just have to read a huge amount until you feel you know the subject 100 per cent.

11.3 Here are some idiomatic expressions about studying and exams which are not on the opposite page. Use the context to guess what they mean and choose the right answer.

1. It's very easy to fall behind with your studies if you miss even just a few classes.
   a) stay close behind other students b) find yourself far behind other students
   c) get ahead of other students
2. She seemed to just breeze through the exams. Everyone else was in such a panic and almost had nervous breakdowns.
   a) do them calmly and efficiently b) not take them seriously c) cheat in them
3. I just can't seem to get the hang of English prepositions. Just when I think I've learnt them I make new mistakes.
   a) memorise b) understand c) enjoy
4. When I sat down and looked at the exam paper my mind just went blank. Everyone else seemed to be writing away quite happily.
   a) became confused b) became very focused c) became empty

11.4 Answer these questions.

1. What do we call the first attempt at writing something, e.g. an essay?
2. What word means 'the date by which you must do something'?
3. What word means 'using someone else's ideas as if they were yours'?
4. What are more formal words for 'to hand in' and for 'to mark'?
5. What verb do we use when someone doesn't complete their course?
6. What is another word for an academic article? Where can you read them?
7. What is the name of the system for getting books from other libraries?
8. What word means 'the comments you get back from the teacher about your work'?

12 Education: debates and issues

A Opportunity, equality, etc.

Read the text and note the phrases and collocations in bold.

All education systems may ultimately be judged in terms of **equality of opportunity**[1]. This is not the same as the debates over **selective**[2] versus **comprehensive**[3] **schooling**[4]. It is rather a matter of whether everyone has the same opportunities for educational achievement or whether **elitism**[5] of one sort or another is **inherent in**[6] the system. **League tables**[7] for schools and colleges may actually help unintentionally to **perpetuate**[8] inequalities, while claiming to promote the raising of standards. Inevitably, league tables divide the world into good and bad, success and failure, resulting in a **two-tier system**[9], even if that is only how the public **perceives**[10] it. The ability of the **better-off**[11] parents and **well-endowed**[12] schools to push children towards the institutions at the top of the league may, in the long term, have the effect of **depressing**[13] opportunity for the **less well-off**[14] or for children from home environments that do not provide the push and motivation to **excel**[15].

1 when everyone has the same chances
2 pupils take exams for entry
3 everyone enters without exams
4 education received at school
5 when you favour a small, privileged group
6 existing as a basic part of something
7 lists of schools or colleges from the best down to the worst
8 make something continue forever
9 a system with two separate levels, one of which is better than the other
10 sees, considers
11 richer
12 receiving a lot of money in grants, gifts from rich people, etc.
13 reducing
14 poorer
15 achieve an excellent standard

B Other debates and issues

example sentence	*meaning of words in bold*
Some people think we should return to an emphasis on **the three Rs**.	reading, writing and arithmetic, the traditional, basic skills
Literacy and **numeracy** are skills no one can afford to be without.	– the ability to read – the ability to count / do basic maths
Curriculum reform is often done for political reasons rather than for good educational ones.	changes to the educational programme, e.g. the national syllabus
Nowadays, **lifelong/continuing education** is an issue, and creating opportunities for **mature students** is important.	– education for all ages – adult students older than the average student
Special needs education is expensive because class sizes need to be small or **one-to-one**.	– education for children who cannot learn in the normal way, because they have some disability – one teacher and one pupil, not a group
He was unhappy at his new school because the older boys were **bullying** him.	frightening or threatening

'Leadership and learning are indispensable to each other.' *(US President John F. Kennedy)*

Exercises

12.1 Complete the collocations by filling in the missing words according to the meaning given in brackets.

1 .... tables (lists of schools from best to worst)
2 .... education (entry to schools is decided by exam results)
3 equality of .... (when everyone has the same chances)
4 .... inequalities (making inequalities continue forever)

12.2 Change the underlined words, using more formal and more appropriate words from A. Make any other changes that are necessary.

1 Inequality is built into the education system.
2 Giving access only to privileged groups is bad for the country in the long term.
3 Education where everyone gets into the same type of school without exams is a basic political ideal in many countries.
4 A system where there are two levels of schools reduces the opportunities for children from poorer families and favours those from richer families.
5 Some private schools have lots of wealth and receive gifts of money, and this means they can have better resources.
6 All parents want their children to achieve the best possible results at school.
7 Emphasis on the three Rs is considered by parents to be the key to success.

12.3 Which words or expressions from B mean ...

1 the ability to read?
2 the ability to count and do basic maths?
3 changes made to the official programme of education in a country?
4 the traditional basic skills of reading, writing and maths?
5 a student who is older than the typical age, for example, in a university?
6 teaching with one teacher and just one pupil?

12.4 Answer these questions for your own country.

1 Under what circumstances do school closures occur?
2 What are typical discipline problems in your country? What do teachers do?
3 What special needs provision is there in typical schools?
4 What provisions are there for lifelong education?

12.5 Match the words on the left with the definitions on the right. The words refer to people involved in education. Use a dictionary if necessary.

A–Z

1 PTA	a) teacher who works in a school when needed (e.g. if someone is sick)
2 school governors	b) group consisting of teachers and parents who meet regularly
3 supply teacher	c) teacher who works in different schools and travels between them
4 peripatetic teacher /perɪpəˈtetɪk/	d) group which oversees all the business of the school

FOLLOW UP

To continue learning vocabulary about education, read *The Times Higher Educational Supplement*, the *Education Guardian* or a similar newspaper devoted to educational issues. Alternatively, you could visit their websites at www.thes.co.uk and www.guardian.co.uk/education

13 Talking about yourself

A

Chinese astrology organises years into cycles of twelve with each year named after an animal. The Chinese believe that the year you are born in affects your character.

animal	*year*	*characteristics*
RAT 	1972, 1984, 1996	Imaginative, charming, generous, quick-tempered, opportunistic[1]
BUFFALO 	1973, 1985, 1997	Conservative, methodical[2], conscientious, chauvinistic[3], a born leader
TIGER 	1974, 1986, 1998	Sensitive, emotional, tend to get carried away[4], stubborn, rebellious
RABBIT 	1975, 1987, 1999	Affectionate, obliging[5], gallant[6], sentimental, superficial[7]
DRAGON 	1964, 1976, 1988	Fun-loving, popular, perfectionist, gifted, may sometimes be tactless[8]
SNAKE 	1965, 1977, 1989	Sagacious[9], charming, intuitive[10], stingy, inclined to procrastinate[11]
HORSE 	1966, 1978, 1990	Diligent[12], independent, placid[13], friendly, can be selfish and cunning
GOAT 	1967, 1979, 1991	Elegant, artistic, always ready to complain, plagued by[14] worry
MONKEY 	1968, 1980, 1992	Witty, magnetic personality[15], can be self-seeking[16] and distrustful
ROOSTER 	1969, 1981, 1993	Industrious, shrewd[17], decisive, very extravagant, a flashy[18] dresser
DOG 	1970, 1982, 1994	Down-to-earth, altruistic[19], morose[20], sharp-tongued[21], a fault-finder[22]
PIG 	1971, 1983, 1995	Intellectual, tolerant, naïve[23], downfall[24] could be desire for material goods

1 using situations for own benefit
2 systematic, careful
3 too patriotic
4 become too excited and lose control
5 ready to help
6 (of man) polite to women
7 not caring about serious things
8 inclined to say things that upset or offend people
9 wise
10 understanding instinctively
11 delay doing something
12 hard-working
13 calm, does not easily become excited or angry
14 troubled or distressed by
15 personality that attracts people to you
16 wanting to gain advantage for oneself
17 having good judgement
18 expensive or impressive
19 thinking of others rather than oneself
20 gloomy
21 inclined to speak in a severe and critical way
22 critical person
23 without enough experience of life, trusting too easily
24 cause of destruction

B

Charming, witty, wise – recognise yourself? Stingy, selfish, sly – must be somebody else!

Some words in the chart above have positive associations, others negative ones. Here are some words from the chart together with other words that share some aspects of their meaning. The table shows which have positive and which have negative associations.

positive	*negative*	*positive*	*negative*
generous, unstinting	extravagant, immoderate	shrewd, astute	cunning, sly
resolute, dogged	stubborn, mulish	sober, serious	morose, sullen
thrifty, frugal	stingy, parsimonious	witty, pithy	sharp-tongued, terse
diligent, industrious	work-obsessed, (a) workaholic	tolerant, broad-minded	unprincipled, unscrupulous

Exercises

13.1 **Match the words on the left with their opposites on the right. Use a dictionary if necessary.**

A-Z

1 altruistic	unsystematic
2 diligent	generous
3 intellectual	thick-skinned
4 methodical	unhelpful
5 morose	flexible
6 obliging	low-brow
7 quick-tempered	selfish
8 sensitive	cheerful
9 stingy	placid
10 stubborn	lazy

13.2 **Answer these questions.**

1 Which animal represents you? To what extent do the characteristics apply to you?
2 Think of a friend and find their animal in the chart. Give examples of why you think each characteristic is appropriate or not.

EXAMPLE My friend is a rooster. I think he is industrious because he worked very hard to find a lot of information for a research project he had to complete at college. I don't think he is shrewd because someone tricked him into investing in a non-existent company.

13.3 **Arrange all the adjectives and descriptive phrases from A into three columns under the following headings.** *describe me* *might describe me* *do not describe me*

13.4 **Which people does the speaker have a positive opinion of and which a negative one?**

Let me tell you about my new colleagues. Pat, my boss, seems very astute and witty. I find her deputy, Vince, a bit parsimonious and work-obsessed. I share an office with Julie who's a bit sullen and mulish. I also do a lot of work with Sam who's very tolerant and generous.

13.5 **Now imagine that someone else is talking about the same people, but sees them in a different light. How might he or she describe them?**

EXAMPLE Pat is very sly and terse.

13.6 **What are the abstract nouns from these adjectives? Use a dictionary if necessary.**

1 altruistic	3 diligent	5 industrious	7 gallant	9 morose
2 parsimonious	4 placid	6 sagacious	8 terse	10 unscrupulous

13.7 **The words in 13.6 are more unusual words and are most likely to be found in writing. Give a synonym for each word that would be more likely to be used when speaking.**

EXAMPLE altruistic – unselfish

FOLLOW UP

Find some useful vocabulary for describing your own or others' personality by doing an Internet search on the word 'horoscopes' and following any links which interest you. On some websites it is possible to do personality quizzes to find out what sort of person you are.

14 Relationships: positive aspects

A Love and romance

When Tom met Lily it was **love at first sight**. [love began the first moment they saw each other]
She **fell head over heels in love** with him. [fell deeply and madly in love]
Nick **only has eyes for** Diana. He's not interested in other girls. [is only attracted to]
I've often seen David and Valerie at the cinema together, but it's purely a **platonic relationship**. [affectionate relationship between people of the opposite sex that is not sexual]
Nora was more than **infatuated with** [romantically obsessed with] Brian; she was completely **besotted with** [almost stupidly or blindly in love with] him.

B Friendships and other positive relationships

Anona and I **hit it off** immediately [liked each other the moment we met]. We're true **soulmates** [people who feel close to each other in spirit and who understand each other deeply].
Nelly was my mother's **lifelong companion**. [friend who was with her all her life]
The moment I met Rob I could see he was **a man after my own heart**. [someone you admire because they do or think the same as you; can also be **woman after one's own heart**]
Charlie and I **get on like a house on fire**. [have a very good, enjoyable relationship]
Jim and Tony have been **bosom friends/buddies/pals** for years. [very close, good friends]
Patricia and Carmen are **inseparable**. [always want to be together, very close]
There's always been a close **bond** between Kirsten and her aunt. [relationship or feeling of togetherness]

C General social relationships: collocations

The replies in these conversations are another way of saying what the first speaker says.

A: You seem to be very similar to Alan – the way you think and look at life.
B: Yes, we've always been **kindred spirits**.

A: What a nice wedding! Ian and Sally seem to be perfect for each other.
B: Yes, such a **well-matched** couple!

A: Our Spanish friends are always phoning their brothers and sisters.
B: Yes, well, I think **family ties** in Spain are much stronger than here.

D Nouns and adjectives

adjective	*noun*	*example*
affectionate	**affection**	He never shows much affection for his children.
amiable	**amiability**	She always treats us with great amiability.
considerate	**consideration**	'Have some consideration for the other students!' she said angrily.
faithful	**faithfulness**	Faithfulness is the key to a good marriage.
fond	**fondness**	Over the years she developed a fondness for Mario that went beyond a purely business relationship.
loyal	**loyalty**	He was a great team captain who inspired loyalty in the players.

Exercises

14.1 Match words on the left with words on the right to complete the expressions. Then use the expressions to complete the sentences below.

love	pals
head	it off
bosom	over heels in love
hit	spirits
kindred	at first sight

1 When Patrick met Andrea it was ....
2 Phil and Colin look at life in the same way. They're ....
3 Ever since they worked together, Lucy and Clare have been ....
4 They just looked at each other and fell ....
5 When Joss and I met, we immediately ....

14.2 Fill the gaps in these sentences.

1 Rachel only has .... for Mark these days. She's crazy over him.
2 They look such a .... couple. I wonder if they will get married?
3 Sheila and I have always got .... like a house ....
4 He's completely .... with her. I've never known him to be so much in love before. He's like a teenager. (two possible answers)

14.3 Complete the following tables with the correct noun or adjective forms. There are some words not on the opposite page. Use a dictionary if necessary.

noun	*adjective*
	loyal
consideration	
passion	
	devoted
	fond
	faithful

noun	*adjective*
respect	
affection	
	romantic
support	
	amiable
trust	

14.4 Now complete these sentences which include words from the table above, using the correct preposition. Use a dictionary if necessary.

1 She's absolutely devoted .... her mother and visits her every day.
2 I've always had a lot of respect .... my boss, and I do enjoy my job a lot.
3 She's been so loyal .... me all these years, I can't let her down now.
4 He's very supportive .... his colleagues; they're very lucky.
5 I'm quite fond .... Larry, but that doesn't mean I want to marry him.
6 He puts a lot of trust .... me, and I feel I can trust him too.

14.5 Answer these questions, giving a reason why.

Name someone in your life who ...
1 you feel a close bond with.
2 is a real soulmate for you.
3 is a person after your own heart.

15 Relationships: problems

A Friendship

I think we should all be more careful in the use of the word 'friend'. It does not, and should not, be applied to a **casual acquaintance**. There are **colleagues**, **allies** and **partners** – all of them pretending to be friends because it suits their purpose. **True friends** want nothing from you and don't expect any special favours. We should ask nothing from them except **loyalty**, despite our faults. They should speak well **behind our backs**. Such friends are hard to find ...

The text says a friend is not the same as a **casual acquaintance** [person you know, but not very well]. Friends should show **loyalty** [support for us in good and bad times]. They should not **talk behind our backs** [say bad things about us when we are not there].
Here are some qualities of friendship and their opposites:

quality	*opposite*
loyal (adj.) loyalty (noun)	disloyal (adj.) disloyalty (noun)
supportive [always supports you]	unsupportive, critical
honest, truthful	dishonest, untruthful

Other key words:
Russia and America were **allies** [countries which fight on the same side] in the Second World War.
We were **business partners** [people who own the same business] but now we're **bitter rivals** [people in competition with each other in an aggressive and negative way].

Examples of problematic friendships. Note the prepositions.
Terry has been **disloyal to** me on a number of occasions.
Jo's always very **critical of** her friends. I don't like that.
OK, I was **dishonest with** you. I'm sorry, but I didn't want to hurt you.

Note these collocations of some of the words in the table.
Jim has always been **scrupulously honest** in his dealings with us.
I would never expect **complete and unswerving loyalty** from a friend.
Monica has always been my **staunchest ally** at work. I can always rely on her to support me.
I was amazed that someone who called herself a friend could be so **deeply critical**.

B Breakdowns: expressions and collocations

Relationships can **break down** because of **genuine misunderstandings**.
A **rift** [serious disagreement that divides people] can develop between two people or groups.
There's been a lot of **discord** [disagreement and discontent] in the office lately.
My father and I **don't see eye to eye** [have different opinions] on most things.
His love affair with Anna has **turned sour** [become bad]. I think they'll **split up** [separate].
Our marriage **has had its ups and downs** [had good and bad moments], but basically we're OK.
a **bumpy relationship** [up and down like a car on a road with bumps]
a **broken home** [family split up by divorce]
a **family feud** /fjuːd/ [quarrel in a family causing bad feeling for many years]

Exercises

15.1 **Give the opposites of these adjectives. Some are from A opposite; some are new. Use a dictionary if necessary.**

1 loyal 2 truthful 3 honest 4 welcoming 5 contented 6 warm-hearted

15.2 **Some words in these sentences have been used incorrectly. Rewrite the sentences using the correct word from A.**

1 We both own the company: we're bitter rivals.
2 I've made several casual colleagues since moving to London, but no close friends yet.
3 Were Britain and the USA colleagues in the First World War too?
4 The two companies hate each other: they're acquaintances.

15.3 **Fill the gaps with suitable adjectives or adverbs from the opposite page.**

1 You need .... allies at work who won't let you down.
2 His .... honesty is a quality I greatly admire.
3 I don't know why she was so .... critical of him; it seemed very unfair.
4 Her .... and .... loyalty to him was a mistake. He betrayed her in the end.
5 Ray and Hilary were .... rivals at work, but seemed to get on well outside of the office.
6 When all my other so-called friends drifted away, Jack always remained a .... friend to me.

15.4 **Rewrite these sentences to give the *opposite* meaning.**

1 Rick and his sister shared the same opinion on a lot of things.
2 Her affection for Andrew has grown stronger lately. I expect they'll get engaged.
3 Our relationship stayed firm because we always understood each other.

15.5 **Use expressions from the opposite page to describe these situations.**

1 We both thought the other was going to pick up Roger. There was a ...
2 The kids have been unhappy since their parents divorced. They come from a ...
3 Her marriage has been both good and bad at different times. It has ...
4 The two union leaders have had a serious disagreement which has split them. A serious ...
5 Two of the brothers have not spoken to their other brother for twenty years because of something bad that happened. I think it's a ...

15.6 **Fill the gaps with a suitable preposition.**

1 I know I'm not perfect, but I've never been dishonest .... you.
2 She's very critical .... her colleagues.
3 Why are you always so disloyal .... me?

15.7 **Say what you think these expressions mean in your own words. Use a dictionary if necessary.**

1 to die of a broken heart
2 to hate someone's guts
3 to have it in for someone
4 to be on bad terms with someone

THE FAR SIDE® By GARY LARSON

Look. I just don't feel the relationship is working out.

16 Passions: reactions and emotions

A

Here are some verbs which refer to having a strong desire that is hard to control.

Pregnant women **crave / have a craving for** strange things like tuna and banana pizza!
I still **hanker after / have a hankering for** a bright red sports car. [**Hanker** is especially used about something you cannot have.]
Young children often seem to **thirst / have a thirst for** knowledge. [**To hunger for** can also be used in the same way as to **thirst for**.]
Sometimes my cousin just **yearns to** be on her own with no family responsibilities. [If you **yearn to do / yearn for / have a yearning for** something, it means that you want something that you do not have and, often, can never have.]
An Olympic gold is probably the most **coveted** sporting prize. [**To covet** something means to want to possess it very much.]

B

Here are some verbs describing ways of reacting to other people's emotions.

word	*meaning*	*example sentence*
defuse	make a dangerous or tense situation calmer	Jane tried to **defuse** the tension by changing the subject.
placate	stop someone feeling angry	Jim was very angry with his daughter and it took all her charm to **placate** him.
conciliate	end a disagreement between two people or groups by acting in a friendly way towards both sides	An independent advisor has been brought in to **conciliate** between the unions and the employer.
appease	end a disagreement by giving the other side an advantage that they are demanding (normally used in a disapproving way)	Although **appeasing** the enemy postponed the war for another year, it did not ultimately prevent it from happening.

A useful adjective from placate is **implacable**. (NB ~~placable~~ doesn't exist.) It is used about someone's opinions and feelings and means that they cannot be changed. I cannot understand the **implacable hatred** that he still feels for his old rival.

C

Here are some more words which refer to being extremely happy.

to rejoice: be extremely happy Everyone **rejoiced** at the news of her recovery.
exultant: feeling great pleasure and happiness, usually because of a success
Sarah was in an **exultant** mood for weeks after doing so well in her exams.
jubilant: expressing great happiness especially at a victory
There were **jubilant** shouts as the results of the referendum were announced.
rapture: extreme pleasure or happiness (adjective = **rapturous**)
He listened to the opera with an expression of pure **rapture** on his face.
bliss: perfect happiness (adjective = **blissful**) Note that the adverb **blissfully** collocates strongly with **happy, ignorant** and **unaware**.
They are **blissfully happy** even though they're poor.

There are a number of colloquial expressions which mean to be very happy.
You look **full of the joys of spring** today.
My daughter's just had a baby girl. We're **thrilled to bits** at the news.
I feel on top of the world. It's great to have a job again.
I've been **floating/walking on air** ever since I heard I got into drama school.
How did you feel when you scored the winning goal? – I was **over the moon!**

Exercises

16.1 **Choose one of the words below each sentence to fill the gaps.**

1 Since giving up smoking, I now find that I .... chocolate.
a) thirst b) crave c) hunger

2 Martha is very good at .... difficult situations.
a) placating b) appeasing c) defusing

3 Everyone is .... to bits that Joe was so successful in the competition.
a) blissful b) thrilled c) exultant

4 If he has a tantrum, you mustn't try to .... him. Don't give in!
a) conciliate b) appease c) defuse

5 When Lorna retires, there will probably be a lot of internal applicants for what must be the most .... job in the company.
a) yearned b) hankered c) coveted

6 Fortunately, her parents were .... unaware of what was going on.
a) rapturously b) blissfully c) exultantly

16.2 **Make a word from the same root as the word in brackets in order to complete the sentences. You may need a dictionary to help you.**

A–Z

1 Even after so many years away from the country where I was born, I still have a .... to return there some day. (HANKER)

2 Nick gazed .... at his neighbour's shining new motorbike. (COVET)

3 The lovers looked .... into each other's eyes. (RAPTURE)

4 Jean tried making some .... remarks which lightened the atmosphere a bit. (CONCILIATE)

5 Our local Member of Parliament is an .... opponent of all plans to extend the city. (PLACATE)

6 The mood of the negotiations was .... from the outset and a consensus was reached fairly rapidly to the .... of all present. (PLACATE; JUBILANT)

16.3 **Match the beginnings of the sentences with their endings.**

1 Sarah has been walking	on top of the world since finishing her thesis.
2 Beth is full	after a new computer.
3 Amanda seems to be	for children with AIDS.
4 Jill feels enormous pity	on air since she got engaged.
5 Sam is hankering	at his good fortune.
6 His parents rejoiced	of the joys of spring.

16.4 **Answer these questions.**

1 What sort of things might you say someone was blissfully ignorant of?

2 If a politician talks about appeasement, is he expressing approval?

3 Would people be more likely to be called jubilant or blissful if their team had won the World Cup?

4 Have you ever felt as if you were floating on air? When?

FOLLOW UP

You will find the language of passions and emotions in many different texts – e.g. in songs, in reviews, horoscopes or problem pages in magazines, and in literature. Make a note of any particularly expressive language that you come across. Write it down in a context that has some relevance for you. If you come across the phrase **to be on cloud nine** [to be very happy, colloquial], you might write down *I was on cloud nine when I heard I'd passed all my exams.*

17 Feelings: antipathies and aversions

A Antipathies and aversions

Antipathy is a feeling of strong, often active, dislike or opposition towards something or someone, e.g. **Antipathy** towards the government has increased as a result of the current crisis. The adjective with this meaning is not *antipathetic* but **hostile** or **unsympathetic**, e.g. a **hostile** crowd of protesters; an **unsympathetic** remark.
Aversion is a feeling of intense dislike or an unwillingness to do something, or it can also be the person or thing which causes that feeling. It is often used in the phrase **have/feel an aversion to**, e.g. I **felt an instant aversion to** the new manager. Arrogance has always been my **pet aversion** [the thing I dislike most of all].
Averse to means opposed to, usually used with **not**, e.g. I'm **not averse to** a good night out.

B More words for intense negative feelings

noun	*meaning*	*adjective*	*verb*
loathing	intense hatred	loathsome	loathe
abhorrence	intense disgust	abhorrent	abhor
scorn	lack of respect for something or someone felt to be worthless	scornful [showing lack of respect]	scorn
revulsion	strong disgust	revolting	revolt
repulsion	opposite of strong attraction	repulsive	repulse

C Adjectives with negative associations

Here are some words with strong negative connotations. Words marked * are informal.

word	*meaning*
bland	lacking taste, character or interest (food, etc.)
brash	too confident; too bright (clothes, etc.)
dowdy	dull in appearance or lacking style (clothes, person, especially of women)
fickle	changing opinions suddenly without reason
fuddy-duddy *	old-fashioned
grasping *	always wanting more money
nit-picking *	too concerned about unimportant details
obnoxious	unpleasant and rude
obsequious	too eager to praise or obey people

word	*meaning*
off-hand	showing rude lack of interest in others
officious	too eager to tell others what to do
ostentatious	displaying wealth or possessions in a vulgar way
pompous	too formal and showing that you think that you are more important than other people
pretentious	trying to appear more serious or important than you are
puerile	too silly and childish
sloppy *	not taking care in the way you work
squalid	very dirty and unpleasant
trite	lacking in originality; banal

Exercises

17.1 **Answer these questions about words in A and B.**

1 Name three foods that you find revolting.
2 Name three things that you loathe doing.
3 Name someone that you feel scorn for.
4 Are there any ideas that you find abhorrent?
5 Have you ever felt an instant antipathy to someone?
6 Do you have a pet aversion? If so, what is it?

17.2 **Make a word from the same root as the word in brackets in order to complete the sentences.**

EXAMPLE His books seem to me to reflect his own ....pomposity........ . (POMPOUS)

1 The parents are delightful but their children are .... (LOATHE)
2 Although Sal loves it, I find that painting of a woman with two heads quite .... (REPULSE)
3 The behaviour of some of the committee can only be described as .... (ABHOR)
4 You copied out the diagram very .... Please do it again. (SLOPPY)
5 .... is sometimes said to be more characteristic of women than men but I think that this is a false stereotype. (FICKLE)
6 After her contribution to the discussion, Nick looked at her so .... that she wished she had not spoken. (SCORN)

17.3 **Read the sentence below. Then write four sentences that express the same meaning, each using the given word.**

I loathe people who talk with their mouth full.

1 revolt 2 aversion 3 abhorrent 4 repulsion

17.4 **What words from C might you use to describe the following?**

1 someone who drives a pink Rolls Royce with fur seats
2 a girl who falls in and out of love with someone different every few weeks
3 someone who always laughs very loudly at the boss's jokes even if they're not funny
4 someone who never checks a piece of writing they have done and who never bothers to use a ruler to draw lines
5 a woman who only goes out with rich men because she is interested in their money
6 a flat with clothes all over the floor and dust on every surface
7 a piece of chicken cooked in water without any salt, pepper, herbs, spices or vegetables
8 a story that is full of clichés and has a predictable and sentimental plot

17.5 **Here are some words which express similar characteristics to those in C opposite, but show the characteristics in a more positive way. Find each word's pair in C. Use your dictionary if necessary.**

EXAMPLE nonchalant sloppy

1 traditional 3 meticulous 5 authoritative
2 childlike 4 casual 6 colourful

18 Observing others: appearance and mannerisms

A Words connected with size, weight and general appearance

word	*meaning*	*example*
scrawny	unattractively thin and bony-looking	He was too **scrawny** to be a football player.
lanky	very tall and thin, and usually moving awkwardly	A **lanky** teenager walked in.
gangling/ gangly	with long, thin arms and legs and rather awkward movements; often used of men and boys	A **gangling/gangly** youth approached him.
portly	with fat stomach and chest; often used humorously about older men	A **portly** figure stood near the ticket desk.
stout	with a quite fat, solid body; used of men and women	She's the **stout** woman wearing glasses, over there.
corpulent	fat (formal, literary word)	She introduced me to a rather **corpulent** gentleman.

B Aspects of facial appearance and complexion

I've noticed Robert has put on weight; he's getting a **double chin** [fat around the chin]. His hair always looks so **unkempt** [untidy; scruffy]. I don't know why he doesn't look after it. His sister is the opposite: **never a hair out of place** [her hair is always neat and tidy]. He has a rather **swarthy** [dark-coloured, used about skin] complexion. His sister's complexion is more **sallow** [yellowish and unhealthy-looking]. He works incredibly hard; he often looks **haggard** [his face shows tiredness and age, with the skin hanging in folds] and exhausted.

C Facial expression

Look at those models **pouting**[1] for the photographers! [positioning their lips in a sexually attractive way]
If she doesn't get what she wants, she **pouts** for the rest of the day. [positions her lips in a look of annoyance]
You don't have to **grimace**[2] every time I eat raw garlic. I happen to think it's delicious. [make an expression of pain or strong dislike]
I arrived late and she just **scowled**[3] at me. [gave a bad-tempered, angry look]
He was **leering**[4] at us. I felt very uncomfortable and wanted to leave. [looking in an unpleasant, sexually interested way]

D Mannerisms and actions with the hand

I asked him for advice but he just **shrugged his shoulders.** [lifted his shoulders up and down to show he didn't know or couldn't answer]
He **folded his arms** [crossed one arm over the other close to his body] and **crossed his legs** [crossed one leg over the other while sitting] and waited for me to speak.
She **bites her nails** and **picks her nose** all the time. It drives me crazy!
She **clenched her fist** and told him to get out of the room at once. [closed her hand as if to hit him]
He just **tapped his fingers** and waited. [made quick, light hitting movements, e.g. on a table]

Exercises

18.1 **From memory, put these words into two groups: 'fat' words and 'thin' words.**

stout corpulent scrawny portly gangling lanky

18.2 **Rewrite these sentences using one of the words from 18.1 instead of the underlined words. Use each word once only, and make any other necessary changes.**

1 She looks as if she needs a good meal; <u>her body is so thin and bony</u>.
2 Marian and Frank are very suitable for each other; they're both <u>very tall and thin</u> individuals.
3 A rather <u>round, overweight</u>, middle-aged man offered to show us the way.
4 A <u>very tall, thin, bony, awkward-looking</u> boy carried our bags for us.
5 She's become quite <u>fat</u> these days, ever since she stopped playing tennis.
6 A rather <u>overweight</u> gentleman ascended the stairs, red-faced and breathless.

18.3 **Use words from B opposite to write a sentence describing each of these pictures.**

1 
2 
3 
4 

18.4 **What are these people doing?**

EXAMPLE  *He is grimacing.*

1 
3 
5 
7 
2 
4 
6 
8 

18.5 **Answer these questions. Use a dictionary if necessary.**

1 The verb *to pout* had two meanings on the opposite page. What were they?
2 If someone scowls at you, how are they probably feeling?
3 What is the difference between a *swarthy* complexion and a *sallow* complexion?
4 What do we mean when we talk about someone's *gait*?
a) their way of looking b) their way of walking c) their way of talking
5 Give two reasons why someone might scratch their head.
6 Why might someone raise their eyebrows?
7 When would you clench your fists?
8 When do people normally shrug their shoulders?
9 What might you do with your fingers if you were nervous or impatient?
10 In what situations do you (a) fold your arms (b) cross your legs?

19 Observing others: character traits

A Visible behaviour: some useful adjectives

word	*meaning*	*example*
impetuous	acts on a sudden idea without thinking first; generally negative	He's so **impetuous**; I wish he would consider things first.
impulsive	similar to *impetuous*, but can be used in a more positive way	His **impulsive** generosity led him to give away most of his money.
effusive	gives exaggerated expression of pleasure, praise or gratitude	She always gives you such an **effusive** welcome.
excitable	easily excited by things	He's a very **excitable** child; he needs to calm down.
pushy	always selfishly promoting one's own position or interests (informal)	She's so **pushy**, it's typical of her to demand an interview for the new job.
garrulous	talks too much, especially about unimportant things	Freddie's so **garrulous**; it's impossible to get any work done.
taciturn	reserved or says very little (generally negative)	I thought he was rather **taciturn** when I first met him. He hardly spoke.

B Sociability

Jean's such an **introvert** [inward-looking and quiet], and her brother Mark is such an **extrovert** [outward-looking and sociable]. Strange, isn't it?
Mr Rogers is such a **diffident** man. [lacks confidence; has a low opinion of himself]
English people are traditionally thought of as rather **reserved.** [not immediately sociable]
Barbara tends to be rather **aloof**. I don't know if she's just shy. [unfriendly and not sociable]
My aunt Annie can be very **haughty** [unfriendly and thinks herself better than others] and **disdainful** [does not believe others deserve respect] at times, but she's lovely really.
I've always found Professor Mactoft very **unapproachable** [not easy to be sociable with or start a conversation with], but his colleague Dr O'Daly is very **approachable.**
Nancy is so **conceited** [thinks herself wonderful] and **self-important** [has an exaggerated sense of her importance], but Flora is such a **modest** person. [prefers not to exaggerate her own qualities]
My boss is such a **flirt,** though I would never call her that to her face. Nobody in the office is safe. [makes constant romantic approaches]

C Character traits

Joss is a somewhat **naïve** person; he thinks love can solve all the world's problems. [/naɪ'iːv/ willing to believe simple things perhaps because of inexperience]
Telephone salespeople often take advantage of **gullible** people. [easily deceived]
My father was a very **conscientious** man; he never took time off work unless he was really sick. [/kɒnʃi'enʃəs/ always took his work very seriously]
You are so **obstinate** [unwilling to change, despite persuasion] and **pig-headed!** [similar to *obstinate* but stronger, more disapproving] Why don't you listen when people give you good advice?
He's quite an **unscrupulous** character; I should be very careful if I were you. [lacking in moral principles, prepared to do very bad things]

Exercises

19.1 **Answer these questions.**

1 What is the opposite of *approachable*?
2 What word is a stronger way of saying *obstinate*?
3 If someone is *diffident*, do they have lots of or little self-confidence?
4 How could you describe a greeting that showed exaggerated pleasure?
5 Is *scrupulous* the opposite of *unscrupulous*? (Use a dictionary if necessary.)
6 Which tends to be more negative, *impetuous* or *impulsive*?

19.2 **Complete the following tables by writing the noun forms of the adjectives. Use a dictionary if necessary.**

A–Z

adjective	*noun*
excitable	excitability
disdainful	
impetuous	
obstinate	
modest	

adjective	*noun*
gullible	
reserved	
garrulous	
conceited	
pig-headed	

19.3 **Fill the gaps with adjectives from the opposite page. The first letter of each word is given.**

I remember my grandmother so well. Her i.. (1) generosity meant she was always giving money to beggars and other poor people. She was very a.. (2), never a.. (3), and would always chat to strangers; in fact she was quite an e.. (4) and would sing and dance at parties. But when it came to work she was very c.. (5) and never missed a day in forty years. She was a very determined person, indeed she could be quite o.. (6) and p.. (7), and could not be persuaded to do something she didn't want to. She was proud but never c.. (8) or s.. (9), talkative but never g.. (10), self-confident but never p.. (11), always wishing success for everyone else before herself. She was always d.. (12) of u.. (13) people, since she was a person of great moral principles.

19.4 **These sentences contain words from the opposite page, but in a different form. Rewrite the sentences using words from the opposite page. For example, use a noun instead of an adjective.**

1 She's a flirtatious sort of person, and doesn't care who knows it.
2 He's always had a tendency to be introverted.
3 Larry shows a lot of reserve, while his sister is known more for her approachability.
4 I'm a person who buys on impulse rather than thinking about what I really need.
5 He was a man of great garrulousness, and taciturnity is a word I would never associate with him.

FOLLOW UP

See how many words and expressions describing behaviour and character traits you can find in horoscopes in newspapers and magazines.

20 Birth and death: from cradle to grave

A

DOCTORS praised the fortitude of a mother yesterday who **made medical history**[1] when she gave birth to triplets, one of whom had grown outside her **womb**[2]. The surgeons **delivered**[3] the triplets by **Caesarean section**[4] last Friday after it was discovered that one of the babies had created its own **placenta**[5] outside the womb, putting the life of the mother at risk. Doctors had discovered that the mother was expecting triplets earlier in the pregnancy but it was not until the 28th week that they realised that Ronan had developed outside the **uterus**[6] and was the result of an **ectopic pregnancy**[7]. The mother had **conceived**[8] naturally and was not taking any fertility drugs. The majority of ectopic pregnancies result in **termination**[9].

1. did something medically very unusual
2. woman's organ where egg develops into a baby
3. helped mother to give birth
4. operation in which mother's stomach and womb are cut to allow baby to be born
5. tissue joining the **foetus**, i.e. the developing baby, to the mother and giving it food
6. medical word for 'womb'
7. when the egg develops outside the womb in the **fallopian tubes**, which link the ovaries to the womb
8. become pregnant
9. intentional ending of a pregnancy, usually by a medical operation (also called an abortion); a miscarriage is an early unintentional end of pregnancy

B

I come from a '**ripe old age**[1]' sort of family – I'm 70 now – and like the idea of living for a long time. I have an aunt, my **late**[2] mother's sister, who is 102. She lives in **sheltered accommodation**[3] but **has all her wits about her**[4]. Funerals used to be about people **mourning**[5]; now they are more likely to be a celebration of the person's life, which I think is much healthier. I haven't mentioned my funeral in my **will**[6] – I just want something absolutely plain and simple, a family-only **cremation**[7] service. I would like **my ashes**[8] **scattered**[9] on Ilkley Moor, near Leeds, where I spent a lot of time as a lad. I don't want any memorial stones. As for **obituaries**[10], I would just like them to be large. I just hope I don't die on the same day as a previous prime minister.

1. living well into old age; usually used in the phrase **to live to a ripe old age**
2. now dead
3. special housing, usually for old people, where care staff also live
4. is able to think and react quickly
5. expressing their sadness after someone's death (the mourners have been **bereaved**)
6. legal document saying what is to happen to your possessions after your death
7. service where a dead body is burned (as opposed to a **burial**, where the body is buried in the ground)
8. the remains of your body after cremation
9. thrown (people sometimes have their ashes scattered in a place which has special associations for them)
10. newspaper articles giving details about the lives of people who have died

C

colloquial expressions for being close to death – **to be at death's door, to be on one's last legs**
euphemisms for 'to die' – **to pass away, to pass on**
newspaper words – **fatalities** [dead people], **perished** [died], **slaughtered** [violently killed]
legal words – **the deceased** [the dead person], **to bequeath** [to leave something – **a bequest** – in a will], **to inherit** [to receive something – **an inheritance** – from someone who has died], to die **intestate** [without having made a will]

Exercises

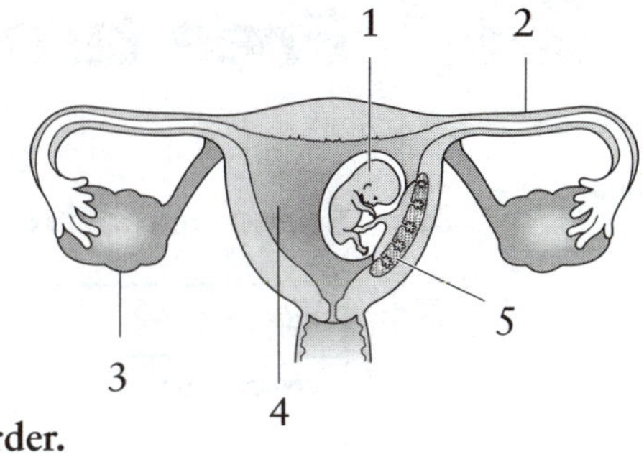

20.1 **Label the diagram with these words from A.**

uterus placenta fallopian tubes
foetus ovaries

20.2 **Put these stages in the development of a new life in order.**

conception delivery fertilisation labour pregnancy

20.3 **Correct these sentences which use the vocabulary in B and C.**

1 The whole country is in morning after the President's death.
2 I'd like my dust scattered at sea.
3 My extinct grandfather was a shepherd all his life.
4 I'm afraid her elderly godmother has just passed off.
5 My car is on its last leg.
6 My grandfather inherited me his gold watch in his will.
7 Mrs Wilson seems to have been at death's window for years.
8 Over two thousand people were perished in the earthquake.
9 It was amazing there was no fatality when the bridge collapsed.
10 My uncle left me a request of five hundred pounds in his will.

20.4 **Write sentences with the same meanings, using the word in brackets. In some cases you need to add a verb ending to the word given.**

1 Both my sisters are pregnant at the moment. (EXPECT)
2 Twins were born to Amanda Harrison last Monday. (BIRTH)
3 She has been taking medication to help her conceive. (FERTILITY)
4 All my grandparents lived to their 80s or 90s. (RIPE)
5 My grandmother is 90 but she is still very mentally alert. (WITS)
6 Unfortunately the deceased died intestate. (WILL)
7 John bequeathed £1,000 to each of his three nephews. (INHERIT)

20.5 **Choose words or expressions from the box to complete these texts.**

deceased	bequest	bequeathed	fatalities
inherited	slaughtered	perished	passed away

Yesterday was indeed a black day for our country. Twenty-five people .... (1) in an earthquake. There were ten road accident .... (2) and five more were .... (3) in a terrorist bomb attack. Among the .... (4) was one of our most popular young politicians.

I'm very sad to have to tell you that my grandfather .... (5) last month. He was very kind and .... (6) each of his grandchildren quite a large sum of money. I'd love to spend some of the money I .... (7) on visiting you. He also left a very large .... (8) to the university where he worked for most of his life.

21 Free time: relaxation and leisure

A Some adjectives to describe free time and leisure pursuits

adjective	*meaning*	*possible examples*
rewarding	gives you a lot of positive experiences	doing voluntary work, helping charities
fruitful	produces good results	collaborating/cooperating with someone in an activity
lucrative	makes a lot of money	selling your own arts or crafts, writing computer games
therapeutic /θerə'pjuːtɪk/	makes you healthy in body and/or mind	gardening, yoga, meditation
relaxing/calming	reduces stress, gives a peaceful feeling	reading, listening to music
time-consuming	takes a long time to do	being president of a club, being a member of a committee

I enjoyed being secretary of the sports club but it was very **time-consuming**. I had to give up two evenings a week to do it.
The conservation work I do is very **rewarding**. I feel I'm doing something good and useful.
Photography has been a **lucrative** pursuit for her. She often sells her pictures to magazines.
Painting is such a **therapeutic** activity. It makes me feel good, and teaches me patience.

B Some informal words describing the way people spend their leisure

Bob's a real **culture vulture**; he goes to every theatre and art gallery he can find. [big fan of anything cultural]
I'm a bit of a **couch potato**: I spend hours every day just watching TV. [physically very inactive person]
Mary's a bit of a **dabbler**: she does a pastime for a couple of weeks, then she gets bored and starts something different. [person who never keeps doing one activity for long]
Francis is a real **doer**. He never sits round for long and always has some project or other. [person who believes in acting and doing things, not just thinking]
Laura's a **shopaholic**. She buys all sorts of things she doesn't need. [person addicted to shopping; compare **alcoholic**: addicted to alcohol]

C Expressions and collocations connected with involvement in activities

Joe **is** heavily **into** downhill skiing these days. [informal: takes a great interest in / is very involved in]
I **went off** football and I started playing golf instead. [informal: stopped liking / lost interest in]
She **locks herself away** for hours in front of the computer and surfs the Internet every night. [isolates herself from the world]
He's totally **hooked on** motor racing these days. [informal: is addicted to]
What do you **get up to** at weekends, Michael? [informal: do]
Do you have a hectic social life? Yes, I have a pretty **full diary**. [a lot of commitments/activities]

Exercises

21.1 Fill the gaps with a suitable adjective from A on the opposite page.

1 I find writing poetry very .... It helps me to get a truer understanding of myself and gives me a good feeling inside.
2 I enjoy selling the pictures I paint, but it's not very .... I only made £300 last year.
3 Gardening is very .... It reduces stress levels and calms you down.
4 I've had a .... partnership with Jane for several years: she plays the piano and I play the violin. It's been very good for both of us.
5 Doing unpaid work at the hospital has been a .... experience for me.
6 I would like to be on the club committee, but I've heard it's very .... , and I don't have a lot of free time.

21.2 Solve these riddles, based on words in B on the opposite page.

1 I am a vegetable that sits where humans sit. What am I?
2 I seldom sit and talk, I always act. What am I?
3 I am a bird that eats the flesh of art. What am I?
4 I do some of this and some of that, but never all of this or all of that. What am I?

21.3 Answer these questions.

1 What kind of obsessions or addictions do you personally have?
2 What was the word on the opposite page that meant 'a person who is obsessed with going out and buying things'?
3 Using the same construction as in question 2 above, what could you call a person who is obsessed with, or addicted to, the following?
a) working all the time b) sport c) eating chocolate
4 What are you? Invent a word for your obsession(s).

21.4 In the text below, find ...

1 three expressions meaning 'time when you aren't working'.
2 an expression meaning 'divided equally'.
3 an expression meaning 'reducing the amount of work needed to do something'.
4 two words that mean 'getting machines to do work for us'.
5 an expression meaning 'making many articles/goods at once'.

This is how one expert on leisure time sees things changing over a long period.
- With the advent of agriculture 10,000 years ago, former hunters and gatherers gained ten per cent of their time off.
- By the 1770s, mechanisation increased leisure time to twenty-three per cent.
- By the 1990s, automation and mass production gave people forty-one per cent free time.
- By 2015, new technologies and labour-saving goods and services will split the week fifty/fifty between work and leisure.

21.5 Give more *informal* alternatives for the underlined words.

1 My daughter's <u>extremely interested in</u> folk music. She buys a lot of folk CDs.
2 He <u>isolates</u> himself in his darkroom and does photography for hours on end.
3 She's <u>totally addicted to</u> ice hockey these days. She watches every competition on TV.
4 I have a <u>long list of social appointments</u> for the rest of the month.
5 What do you <u>engage in</u> when you aren't working, Nigel?

22 All the rage: clothes and fashion

A

Read the newspaper article below about how different types of clothes are appropriate for different types of people and situations.

Karen Hyland, 22, a self-confessed '**scruff**[1]', about to graduate from the University of East Anglia this summer, is among those desperately seeking a speedy transition from the campus uniform of jeans, trainers and sweatshirts to smart suit and shoes, without resorting to the **pastel**[2], **power outfits**[3] favoured by New Labour's fresh female intake. Short skirts are to be avoided, as are Eighties shoulder pads, but no one wants to look **frumpy**[4] and the student budget is inevitably tight. 'I have to create a new image for my proposed career in television,' explained Karen. 'Money aside, choosing the right **outfit**[5] for my pending interviews is giving me nearly as much worry as my finals.' What Karen needed was The Interview Suit – something smart, young and modern, which would be suitable for most office **dress codes**[6], while being individual enough to convince prospective employers that she could bring personality and flair to the job.

1 dirty and untidy person
2 in pale colours
3 formal clothes to make you seem powerful
4 old-fashioned and boring
5 set of clothes for a particular occasion
6 accepted way of dressing in a particular social group

B

Here are some other words and expressions used in discussing clothes.

In offices many staff **dress down** on Fridays. [wear less formal clothes]
Sometimes an invitation or a restaurant or nightclub will ask people to dress in **smart-casual** clothes. [clothes that are informal but clean, tidy and stylish]
Clothes can be informally described as **dressy** [suitable for formal occasions], **skimpy** [close-fitting, using little material], **baggy** [loose, e.g. of sweater], **snazzy** [modern, stylish].
To be dressed to kill means to wear clothes intended to attract people's attention (sexually). Some rich people buy **designer (label) clothes** but most people prefer to buy clothes more cheaply **off the peg/rack** or **on the high street**.

C

Here are some more words and expressions relating to fashion.

A few years ago denim jackets were **all the rage.** [very fashionable]
They were dressed in **the height of fashion.** [an extremely fashionable way]
The magazine has **up-to-the-minute** fashion articles. [dealing with the most recent trends]
The film **has set a new trend** for the leather trousers worn by the heroine. [started a new fashion]
If you are **ahead of your time,** you have new ideas or opinions before they are fashionable.
If a fashion/trend **catches on,** it becomes popular.
A **slave of/to fashion** is someone who is strongly influenced by fashion.

D

Words and expressions connected with clothes are often used metaphorically.

to speak **off the cuff** [without having prepared anything]
to be hand in glove with someone [to have a close working relationship with someone]
cloak-and-dagger [involving secrecy and mystery]
to have/take the shirt off someone's back [someone's last possession]
to do something **on a shoestring** [spending as little as possible]
without frills [simple and plain]
to put someone in a straitjacket [restrict someone's freedom]

to wear the trousers (usually used of a woman) [to be the dominant partner in a marriage]

Exercises

22.1 Answer these questions about the text in A.

1 What did Karen mean by calling herself a 'scruff'?
2 What is the student 'uniform' said to consist of?
3 Is this 'uniform' typical for students in your country too?
4 Why does Karen want to change her style of dressing now?
5 What three things do newly-graduated students not want in their new clothes?
6 What does Karen want her 'interview suit' to be like and why?
7 What is the dress code in a workplace you are familiar with?
8 What sort of clothes do you think Karen should choose?

22.2 Fill the gaps with words or phrases from B.

1 Goodness me, you're dressed to ....! Where on earth are you going?
2 The sign outside the bar said: 'Dress .... – no jeans or trainers'.
3 I .... at work when I'm not meeting clients.
4 I can't afford .... clothes. I buy most of my outfits on the ....
5 That's a very .... shirt – those bright colours really suit you!
6 As soon as she gets home from work, she changes from her smart suit into tracksuit bottoms and a comfortable, ..., old jumper.

22.3 Answer these questions about current fashions.

1 What is all the rage in your country at the moment?
2 What was the height of fashion five years ago?
3 What do you think about people who are a slave to fashion?
4 How interested are you in being up-to-the-minute with fashion?
5 What sort of people start new fashion trends?

22.4 Use one of the phrases from D to rewrite these sentences.

1 I'm no good at speaking if I haven't had time to prepare what I want to say.
2 Although he's the head of a large company, his wife is the boss at home.
3 Have you any idea what all these secret and mysterious meetings at work are about?
4 Be careful what you say to Helen – she works very closely with the boss.
5 I wouldn't invite them to stay if I were you – they'll take everything you've got to give before you know where you are.
6 The new legislation has really restricted our freedom.

22.5 Here are more metaphorical uses of clothes words. Explain the literal and metaphorical meanings of the underlined words and expressions. Use a dictionary if necessary.

A-Z

1 The hotel provides a cheap, <u>no frills</u> service.
2 We wanted to leave but were <u>hemmed in</u> by the crowd and couldn't escape.
3 Phil's got so many books – his room is <u>bursting at the seams</u>.
4 The negotiations have been <u>cloaked in</u> secrecy ever since they began.
5 If she wins the prize again this year, it'll be a real <u>feather in her cap</u>.

22.6 Write a paragraph about the image you would like to convey through your clothes.

FOLLOW UP Find out about language relating to the latest fashion by going to the *Vogue* fashion magazine website at www.vogue.co.uk. Make a note of any useful vocabulary you come across.

23 Homestyles, lifestyles

A Homestyles

A **squat** /skwɒt/ is an empty building where people start living without the owner's permission.
A **hovel** /'hɒvəl/ is a very poor, dirty house or flat in a bad condition.
A **pied à terre** /pjeɪd/ɑː/'teə/ is a small flat or house in a city owned or rented by people in addition to their main home and used when they are visiting the city.
A **penthouse** is a luxury flat at the top of a building.
Council housing is provided by the state for people who cannot afford to buy their own homes.
High-rise flats are flats in a tall, modern building with a lot of floors.
A **granny flat** is a set of rooms for an elderly person, connected to a relative's house.

B Modern lifestyles

Today many people want to get out of **the rat race** [unpleasant way in which people struggle competitively for wealth or power] and live a less stressful or less conventional lifestyle.
Feng Shui: a Chinese philosophy which states that the position of buildings and the arrangement of objects in the home affects the health and well-being of people living there
minimalism: a style which involves using the smallest possible range of materials, colours, etc. and only the most simple shapes or designs
post-modernism: a style of architecture, the arts, etc. popular in the 1980s and 1990s which includes features from several different periods
New Age: a way of life and thinking which developed in the late 1980s and includes a wide range of beliefs and activities, e.g. astrology, alternative medicine, that are not accepted by most people and are a reaction against modern scientific and economic developments
subsistence farming: where people live by growing just enough food for their own family

C Idioms and metaphors relating to homes and lifestyles

expression	*meaning*	*example*
a household word/ name	something everyone knows	Nike has become a household name.
a drink on the house	a free drink	The restaurant owner offered us a bottle of wine on the house.
home truths	information that is true but not pleasant or welcome	It's time he was told some home truths about the way he's been behaving!
nothing to write home about	nothing special	The town is OK but nothing to write home about.
hit home	become fully understood or fully felt	The difficulty of managing without a regular salary is hitting home now.
That's the story of my life.	That's what always happens to me. (used humorously)	Everyone got a pay rise the week after I resigned. That's the story of my life!
have the time of your life	have a wonderful time	Paul's having the time of his life in Canada.
get a new lease of life	become more energetic and active than before	When Sue moved jobs she seemed to get a new lease of life.
a dog's life	a very unhappy and difficult life	Reg said he led a dog's life in the army.

Exercises

23.1 **Complete the following table about the types of accommodation in A.**

accommodation	*What kind of person lives there?*	*Would you like to live there? Why/Why not?*
squat	a homeless person or someone with very little money	I wouldn't like it because you never know when you might be evicted.
pied à terre		
council housing		
granny flat		
high-rise flat		
hovel		
penthouse		

23.2 **Which of the lifestyles in B might be illustrated by doing these things?**

1 ensuring no chairs have their back to a door
2 working in the office from 8 a.m. to 8 p.m. and at weekends
3 having all one's flat painted white with no more than one picture on any wall
4 owning a cow and growing all the vegetables you need
5 living in a caravan, using traditional herbs for medicinal purposes and planning your life in accordance with an astrological chart

23.3 **Look at the words describing trends in modern lifestyles in B. What kind of people do you think would be attracted by these lifestyles? What do you think of them yourself?**

EXAMPLE Feng Shui principles would appeal to people who are strongly aware of their surroundings and the influence that they have on them. The principles sound nice to me but I am sceptical about whether they are really true and I don't think I could be bothered rearranging all my belongings.

Now choose three words from B and write your own paragraphs.

23.4 **Look at C. Fill the gaps in these sentences.**

1 Because it was my birthday, the barman offered me a drink on the ....
2 Mandy's so selfish, she deserves to be told a few ....
3 The party was all right, I suppose, but nothing to .... home about.
4 The handsome new man at work is already married but that's the .... of my life!

23.5 **Choose one of the idioms from C to replace the underlined words in these sentences.**

1 We <u>had the most marvellous time</u> on holiday this year.
2 As soon as spring comes I feel as if I'm <u>becoming energetic and active again</u>.
3 The problems caused by the floods are only <u>making themselves fully felt</u> now.
4 I imagine that being a servant in the past was <u>very hard and tedious</u>.
5 All over the world <u>everybody knows about</u> McDonald's.

24 Socialising and networking

A Socialising

Socialising implies simply spending leisure time with other people. This can be done in lots of formal and informal ways. Here are some different ways in which people socialise.

a housewarming (party): a party to celebrate moving to a new house or flat
a launch (party): a party to celebrate the publication of a new book or product
a fancy dress party: a party where everyone dresses up in costume as other people
a stag party: a party before a wedding for the future husband and his male friends
a girls' night out / a hen party: an evening just for female friends spent at a restaurant, theatre or club, perhaps; a hen party is usually just before one of them gets married
a reception: a formal party, e.g. after a wedding or to meet an important visitor

Note that the phrase, **the wedding party**, usually refers to the main group of close family and friends at a wedding, rather than to the reception after the wedding.

A **black tie** or a **white tie** event suggests a formal party at which men have to wear black bow ties or white bow ties respectively.

B Networking

Socialising is meeting people purely for pleasure but **networking** is making contacts that will be useful to one's business or career. In the past career networking in England usually happened simply through the **old school tie** or **old boy network** [contacts made by the children of the traditional ruling class while at expensive private schools]. Now people are perhaps rather more **pro-active** [taking action yourself rather than waiting for something to happen] in trying to make useful contacts. They may try to **put themselves about** [informal: make themselves visible in the hope of being noticed by someone important and, thus, help themselves to **climb the career ladder**]. Networking involves such things as **exchanging (business) cards** and promising to **do lunch** sometime.

To hobnob is usually used with rather negative associations meaning to be friendly with someone who is important or famous.

I saw Dick **hobnobbing** with the boss after work yesterday.

To rub shoulders with is an informal expression meaning to mix socially with people who are famous. I hear **you've been rubbing shoulders with** royalty!

C Informal expressions

Here are some of the many informal expressions connected with socialising.

I don't like the people Rick **hangs out with / knocks around with**. [spends social time with]
Would you like to come to **a bash/do/get-together/booze-up** we're having on Saturday? [a party; the last expression is very colloquial and suggests that a lot of alcohol will be drunk]
(Said to your host) I hope I'm not **outstaying my welcome**. [staying too long]
Sandy's a real **party animal** [someone who loves going to parties] but her boyfriend can be a bit of a **party pooper** [someone who spoils parties by being disapproving or miserable].
Do you fancy going **clubbing** this evening? [going to one or more nightclubs]
Let's go out **on the town**. [enjoy the entertainments in a town, e.g. the bars, pubs and clubs]
Mandy's very **chummy/pally** with the boss's wife. [friendly]
I hate it at my new job – everyone's so **cliquey**. [a **clique** is a disapproving word for a small group of people who spend time together and do not allow others to join them]
Are they really **an item**? [having a romantic relationship]
If he ever **stood me up** [failed to turn up for a date], I'd **drop him** [end our relationship].
They've **gone on a pub crawl**. [gone to spend an evening going to several different pubs]

Exercises

24.1 Look at A and decide what kind of party you might be invited to if ...

1 a friend of yours is about to get married and is having a party before the wedding.
2 you are going to help a friend celebrate on the day of their wedding.
3 some friends have just moved into a new flat.
4 a friend has just had a book published.
5 your local council is arranging for important people in the area to meet a visiting dignitary.
6 you have friends who love dressing up as characters from famous films.

24.2 Rewrite these sentences by replacing the underlined words from B and C with an expression that means the same thing.

1 It's always good to see Hugh but somehow he always manages to outstay his welcome.
2 You wouldn't believe it but Helen and Mark are now an item!
3 I don't really approve of the way Erica puts herself about, but I'm sure it'll help her to make a success of going freelance.
4 Don't forget your old friends when your film becomes a hit and you're rubbing shoulders with the rich and famous.
5 I'm going to a birthday bash this weekend. Should be fun.
6 We must invite Jane to our do. She's a real party animal!
7 Mike'll want to go on a pub crawl as soon as his exams finish.
8 Let's have a night on the town as the children are with their grandparents tonight.

24.3 Answer the following questions relating to the expressions on the opposite page.

1 Who would you call a party animal and who would you call a party pooper and why? Which of these are you more likely to be called and why?
2 Does the old school tie network have any significance in your country?
3 If not, are there any other networks which can help people up the career ladder?
4 In which sort of careers do you think it is important to network?
5 It's Friday night. Would you prefer to go clubbing or to go on a pub crawl?
6 Which of the types of party listed in A have you personal experience of? How did you enjoy them?
7 If you describe an atmosphere as cliquey, do you like the atmosphere? Why / Why not?
8 Have you ever been stood up? What happened?

24.4 Complete the text by filling each of the gaps with one word.

Jeremy in our marketing department didn't go to a .... (1) school so he didn't have access to any of the privileges offered by the old .... (2) network. The people he .... (3) about with when he was at school mostly took quite menial jobs or had long periods of unemployment. However, Jeremy spent a few months doing work experience in a large bank. There he became .... (4) with several people who later helped him to further his business career. He also became very skilled at .... (5) himself about and this has also stood him in good stead over the years. He's very good at organising get- .... (6) at his home for influential people. He seems to get a kick out of rubbing .... (7) with important people.

FOLLOW UP You can hear people making small talk in English language films and TV. This website www.joblo.com/moviescripts.htm contains the scripts of a wide range of films. Choose one that interests you and note down any useful phrases you come across.

25 The performance arts: reviews and critiques

A Useful adjectives for describing works and performances

adjective	*meaning*	*example*
overrated	not as good as people say	It's an overrated film/play.
hackneyed	done so often it is boring	The plot was so hackneyed!
impenetrable	complex and impossible to understand	His films are impenetrable.
disjointed	unconnected and not in a clear order	The play was disjointed and difficult to follow.
far-fetched	impossible to believe	The film *Green Aliens from Mars* was a bit far-fetched.
risqué /rɪˈskeɪ/	slightly immoral and likely to shock some people	The play was a bit risqué, and some religious leaders criticised it.
gripping	exciting and keeping your attention the whole time	It was a gripping film from start to finish.
harrowing	extremely upsetting	It was a harrowing documentary about war and refugee camps.
moving	making you feel strong emotion, especially pity or sadness	It's a moving story about a child whose mother dies.
memorable	you remember it long after	That was a memorable performance.
understated	done or expressed in a simple but attractive style	The whole ballet is really understated.

B Success and failure

His latest opera was **panned** [very negatively criticised] by the critics, which is strange, since all his previous works have been universally **lauded** [highly praised].
The play **bombed** in London's West End, but was more successful in New York. [was a failure]
Her latest CD has won three **awards.** [prizes/honours, e.g. 'Best CD of the Year']
Anthony O'Donnell won the award for 'Best **up-and-coming** actor' of 2001. [likely to become very famous or successful]
The critics generally agree that her new symphony is a **masterpiece.** [very great work of art]
Novak **was** definitely **miscast** as the father in that film. [was the wrong person for the role]
She has become **typecast** as a middle-aged mother. [always associated with that type of role]
He was given several **encores** for his performance of the violin concerto. [/ˈɒŋkɔːz/ calls from the audience to repeat it]
She got a **standing ovation** for her performance of Juliet in *Romeo and Juliet*. [the audience stood up and applauded]

C Nouns relating to performing

I liked her **interpretation** of the song 'Yesterday'. [way of understanding and performing it]
I prefer the original **version** by the Beatles. [one of several performances that exist]
He gave an excellent **rendition** of Hamlet's speech. [performance on a specific occasion]
The actor's **portrayal** of the mother in the film was very tender. [the picture she created]

Exercises

25.1 **From memory, give an adjective from A which is *opposite* in meaning to the following words.**

1 credible/believable
2 original/novel
3 underrated
4 exaggerated
5 coherent/smooth-flowing

25.2 **Now use other adjectives from A instead of the underlined words in these sentences. Make any other changes that are necessary to produce a correct sentence.**

1 The musical shocked some people because they thought it was immoral and was attacked by several politicians and religious figures.
2 Her performance was one of those you will never forget, simply marvellous.
3 I can't remember the last time I saw such a film that keeps you in suspense and totally absorbed all the time.
4 It was a play that aroused very deep emotions in me.
5 It's a film that is difficult to watch without getting very upset.
6 Some of his films are absolutely impossible to understand because they are so dense and obscure.

25.3 **Answer these questions.**

1 Would you like to go to a play that was universally lauded by all the critics? Why / Why not?
2 Good performers deserve an encore. True? Would you give one?
3 Would you like to see a film that was panned by the cinema critics? Why / Why not?
4 What are the top Hollywood awards for films normally called? What is their more correct name?
5 Do most actors like to become typecast? Why / Why not?
6 A standing ovation shows that the audience disliked the performance. True? Why / Why not?

25.4 **Read the text and underline the words or phrases that match the eight definitions. Use a dictionary if necessary.**

1 the way an actor creates a picture of a person
2 he/she is the wrong actor for that part
3 a film/book/play that keeps you in suspense
4 keep you in suspense / constantly excited
5 up-and-coming
6 a film which huge numbers of people will go and see
7 a police or crime theme
8 a very great work of art

Cliffhanger not to be missed

In this latest blockbuster cops-and-robbers movie from the Holdart Studios, budding Hollywood star Florida Packline plays country-boy Ricky Smart, who gets involved with a gang of criminals intent upon stealing ten million dollars from a Chicago bank. However, their plans are spoilt by the discovery of a dead body in the tunnel they are digging through to the bank. Who is the mystery dead woman? Is she a stranger, or someone from Ricky's own past? Packline's portrayal of the confused boy from a small town caught up in big city crime is convincing, but Julia Fischer as his long-lost sister is somewhat miscast. Not a masterpiece, but it will certainly keep you on the edge of your seat.

26 The plastic arts

A

Read this extract from an article about the British public's attitude to modern art.

You have heard it so often, that all those modern artists are only **pulling the wool over** the public's **eyes**[1], and it is easy to laugh, in a superior kind of way, both at the more extreme examples of contemporary art and at the apparent **philistinism**[2] of its **detractors**[3]. But, almost by stealth, the British public has discovered it perhaps does like modern art after all. Has the public **wised up**[4], or has the art **dumbed down**[5]? If people find that contemporary art is not so difficult or complicated or highbrow and impenetrable as they once thought, it could also mean that art is somehow becoming less intelligent, less sophisticated than it was.

1 deceiving
2 inability to appreciate art or culture (disapproving)
3 critics
4 become more sophisticated
5 become less intellectual (usually to appeal to a mass audience)

B

The same article puts the attitudes to contemporary art in a historical perspective.

The current enthusiasm for modern art – there are more people visiting **Tate Modern**[1] every week than there were people in Florence at the height of the **Renaissance**[2] – appears to be more than a **fad**[3]. If people got nothing from what they see there, they would **vote with their feet**[4]. At the end of the 19th century a lot of people had problems with **Impressionism**[5], and, later, when confronted with **cubist**[6] paintings, the gallery-going public had problems with those too. The **surrealists**[7] were often **deemed**[8] mad, but liking **surrealism**[9] is perfectly sane and acceptable, and it appears everywhere, from posters to advertising campaigns. As a result, we are all now more **visually literate**[10] than before, more **immune to**[11] shocks, **inured to**[12] surprises.

1 new modern art gallery in London
2 period of new interest in the arts in Europe in the 14th to 16th centuries, especially in Italy
3 a short enthusiasm for something (disapproving)
4 stop coming
5, 6, 7, 9 types of artist and schools of art of the last 150 years
8 considered (formal)
10 educated with regard to art
11, 12 not affected by

C

Here are some words that can be used to comment on art. The opposites are in brackets.

highbrow: intended for educated, intelligent people, disapproving (**lowbrow**)
impenetrable: extremely difficult to understand (**transparent**)
sophisticated: showing advanced skills and understanding (**primitive**)
challenging: demanding considerable effort to be understood (**undemanding**)
dazzling: inspiring great admiration because it is brilliant in some way (**pedestrian**)
evocative: calling up images and memories (**uninspiring**)
exquisite: having rare beauty or delicacy (**clumsy**)
intriguing: interesting because it is strange or mysterious (**dreary**)
peerless: better than any other (**run-of-the-mill**)
tongue-in-cheek: not intended to be taken seriously despite appearing serious (**earnest**)

D

Words whose first association is with the arts are also often used metaphorically.

The writer **paints** his hero in a fascinating **light**. Minor characters are more **shadowy** but they are also **depicted** quite powerfully even though the **focus** is, inevitably, on the two central characters. These are **portrayed** with great sensitivity. The heroine is particularly **colourful** and we see how her character is **shaped** and **moulded** by events. Some say the author **illustrates** his **motifs** in a **black-and-white** fashion but the **images** he creates to **illuminate** the evils of slavery will remain with me forever.

Exercises

26.1 Are the following statements true or false according to the texts in A and B?

1 Most modern art is amusing.
2 Attitudes to modern art are changing in Britain.
3 People may be becoming more sophisticated or art may be becoming simpler.
4 Not many people visit modern art exhibitions in London these days.
5 People have often found it hard to accept new trends in art.
6 People don't have so much exposure to art these days.

26.2 Choose a word or phrase from A or B to complete these sentences.

1 Although some people liked the exhibition there were far more .... than enthusiasts among the reviewers.
2 When the price of cinema tickets doubled, the public simply .... and audiences declined dramatically.
3 Politicians have accused TV companies of .... their news broadcasts with the result that there is less public interest in political issues.
4 Every year there seems to be some new food .... that is quickly forgotten when the next thing comes on the scene.
5 Rick managed to .... his wife's .... for several years before she found out about his affair.
6 After spending such a long time camping, they have become .... to the discomfort of living in such a confined space.

26.3 Look at the twenty adjectives in C. Divide them into categories:

usually positive associations *usually negative associations* *negative or positive associations*

26.4 Choose one of the words from each pair of opposites in C and think of a work of art (of any kind) that you could apply it to. Write a sentence explaining why you think it applies.

EXAMPLE I think that the poetry of the 17th century English poet, John Milton, could be called highbrow because you need to be able to understand his classical allusions.

26.5 Circle the correct underlined word to complete these sentences.

1 I think that the artist's cartoons are usually rather highbrow/dreary/lowbrow as they are intended to appeal to a mass audience.
2 When an artist sent in an ordinary red brick to an exhibition, no one was sure whether it was impenetrable/run-of-the-mill/tongue-in-cheek or intended as a serious statement.
3 Although these cave paintings were made thousands of years ago they are in some ways very primitive/pedestrian/sophisticated.
4 I find those painter's pictures of dull grey street scenes rather dreary/peerless/dazzling.
5 The design on that china plate is earnest/exquisite/transparent – however did they manage to paint such fine detail?
6 Although his photographs are quite challenging/evocative/intriguing, it is worth making the effort to understand them.

FOLLOW UP

This website gives you a wealth of links to art galleries and museums worldwide: www.museumspot.com. Visit this site and follow up any links that interest you. Note any useful vocabulary you come across.

27 Talking about books

A Blurbs

A **blurb** is a short text usually printed on the back cover of a book describing what the book is about and sometimes including quotes from critics. Here are some examples.

◆ *Woman of Snow* is a **poignant chronicle**[1] of childhood in a small American town. Nora Delaye is the youngest child in a ...

Barass's third novel, this is a **compelling tale**[2] of mystery, love and betrayal in a **lugubrious setting**[3] reminiscent of the ...

A **page-turner**[4] full of brilliant moments of insight and an unparalleled depth of feeling, this is an **enigmatic tale**[5] that unfolds in ...

A **macabre**[6] and **chilling**[7] account of an unsolved murder that tears a village apart ...

A **breathtaking achievement**[8], a journey of self-discovery that enchants and saddens, with a combination of **wry humour**[9] and **evocative scenes**[10] of life in ...

1 /ˈpɔɪnjənt/ a moving and sad description of a sequence of events
2 powerful story that keeps you interested
3 rather dark and gloomy setting/situation
4 very interesting and engaging story
5 mysterious story
6 /məˈkɑːbrə/ often cruel or disgusting, concerned with death
7 causing great fear
8 amazing achievement
9 humour in the face of a bad situation
10 scenes which arouse memories or images

B Some less common types of books

type of book	*function/purpose*
journal	– a written record of what you have done each day – also means an academic publication containing articles reporting research, new theories, etc., published at regular intervals (e.g. every three months)
memoirs	written record of a person's own life, typically by a politician or military figure
anthology	collection of, for example, poems or short stories by different authors
compendium	collection of detailed, concise information about a particular subject
manual	usually a technical book with instructions, for example, a computer manual
logbook	book that records events and times, etc., for example, all the journeys made by a lorry or ship

C Other expressions for talking about books

I'm reading a book about the history of Ireland. It's **compulsive reading** [formal: difficult to stop once you've started]. *Or* It's one of those books you just **can't put down** [informal].

Bertram's latest novel is not a difficult book; in fact it's rather **lightweight** [not complex; slightly negative connotation]. It's good **bedtime reading** [nice to read in bed]. His last one was **heavy going** [difficult to read] and I just couldn't **get into** it [become involved/engage with].

Exercises

27.1 **Which names for types of books or other reading material from the opposite page would best fit these statements?**

1 It's by General Rogers who led the allied forces during the recent war.
2 It's so badly written I don't know how anyone could learn how to use the video camera by reading it.
3 I recommend it. If you want to read a typical selection of English poets, it's excellent.
4 The latest issue contains a paper by Professor Colin Frith, in which he presents a new theory of the human mind.

27.2 **Now rewrite these sentences using words or phrases from C to describe the experience of reading particular books.**

1 I just could not seem to become involved in the story, so I stopped reading it.
2 It's not very serious, and it's easy to read.
3 It's dense and very difficult to read.
4 Take it to bed with you; it's just right when you're settling down at night. All the time I was reading it I just couldn't wait to get to the next page.
5 You find yourself wanting to read more, it's so fascinating.

27.3 **Fill the gaps in these sentences with appropriate adjectives from the opposite page, based on the meaning in brackets. Try to do it from memory.**

1 The story takes place against a rather .... background in 18th century London. (dark, mysterious)
2 It's full of .... comedy and satire. (humour despite a bad situation)
3 The book is a .... documentation of abuse in a prison. (frightening)
4 The novel is full of .... passages depicting life in Scotland at the turn of the 19th century. (arousing memories or images)
5 It's a very .... novel; you never really know what is happening until right at the end. (mysterious/puzzling)
6 The novel is a .... portrayal of life in a coal-mining community during the time of the General Strike of 1926. (moving and very sad)
7 John Farr's latest novel is a .... masterpiece. (very impressive/great)
8 *House of the Dead* is a .... story of torture and death in a medieval castle. (cruel and dark)

27.4 **Write about 50–60 words describing a book you have read recently. Use at least six of the new expressions you have learnt in this unit.**

27.5 **Match the list of words describing things you might find in particular kinds of books with an appropriate type of book from the list.**

1 section on 'troubleshooting' [problem-solving]	compendium
2 concise information about a subject	journal
3 record of a recent examination or test of a lorry	manual
4 day-to-day record of life during a war in 1776	logbook

27.6 **Here are some things famous people have said about books. What do you think they mean?**

1 'All books are divisible into two classes, the books of the hour, and the books of all time.' (*John Ruskin: British philosopher*)
2 'Some books are to be tasted, others to be swallowed, and some few to be chewed and digested.' (*Francis Bacon: British philosopher and essayist*)

28 We are what we eat

A

This article is about the language used to label food products.

As a food label is often nothing more than an advert to tempt you to buy the product, you should pay particular attention to the choice of words used. Always watch out for the word 'flavour', as this may mean that the product contains **synthetic**[1] ingredients. Chocolate-*flavour* topping, for example, will not contain chocolate, even though chocolate-*flavoured* topping will contain a small percentage – so read carefully. Many manufacturers also use a range of meaningless descriptions. Feel-good words, such as '**wholesome**[2]', 'farmhouse', 'original' and 'traditional' do not mean anything. Other words such as 'farm fresh' and 'country fresh' also intentionally blur the true nature of a product's source. 'Fresh egg pasta', for example, means that the pasta was indeed made with real and not powdered eggs, but maybe months ago. Words that you *can* trust are 'organic', '**wholemeal**[3]', 'natural mineral water', '**Fair Trade**[4]', '**free-range**[5]' and the 'V' vegetarian symbol.

Consumer pressure over **GM**[6] foods has led to better labelling but **loopholes**[7] still exist. GM product **derivatives**[8], such as starches, sugars, fats and oils where no genetically modified protein or DNA material still remains, still go unlabelled in many products such as cereal bars, fish fingers, jellies and vegetable burgers.

Take particular care over low-fat and low-sugar products. Guidelines state that 'low-fat' foods must not have more than 5 per cent fat, while 'reduced fat' means that the total fat content is 25 per cent less than the standard versions of the same product. The terms 'light' or 'lite' are meaningless since they could refer to texture, fat content, sugar content or even colour.

1 made from artificial substances
2 good for you, physically or morally
3 containing all the natural substances in the grain with nothing removed
4 refers to products such as coffee, tea or chocolate marketed in such a way that the small farmers in developing countries who produce them get the profits rather than large multinational companies
5 relating to farm animals that are not kept in cages
6 genetically modified, i.e. the genes (DNA) of a natural product have been altered in some way
7 ways of getting round regulations (usually because they have not been written in a precise enough way)
8 things produced from

B Food metaphors

Inviting Joe and his ex-wives to the same party was a **recipe for** disaster. [situation sure to lead to]
The film has **all the ingredients of** a box office hit. [all the necessary characteristics]
Let's invite lots of friends to our wedding to **dilute** the relatives a bit. [make less dominant]
I'm not going to call him. I'm going to let him **stew** for another few days at least. [worry or suffer especially about something you think is his fault]
The police **grilled** the suspect for hours, but eventually let him go. [asked a lot of questions]
I'm sure this is going to be another of his **half-baked** schemes that never comes to anything. [unrealistic or not thought through properly]
Let's hire a karaoke machine – that'll **spice up** the office party. [make more lively]
Rick has started hanging around with some **unsavoury** characters. [unpleasant, morally offensive]
They started their business with high hopes but things soon **turned sour.** [went wrong]
Let's go for a coffee and you can tell me all the **juicy** gossip. [exciting and interesting]

Exercises

28.1 **Answer these questions about the text in A. You may need a dictionary to help you with some of your answers.**

1 Are food labels meant to provide information or to advertise the products?
2 Why do manufacturers try to hide the fact that foods contain synthetic ingredients?
3 In the phrase *fresh egg pasta*, does *fresh* refer to *egg* or *pasta*?
4 What do *organic*, *wholemeal* and *vegetarian* mean when describing food?
5 What does GM stand for? Explain what it means.
6 What is DNA?
7 *Cereal bars*, *fish fingers* and *vegetable burgers* are all types of fast food. Describe them.
8 This text is from a British magazine, so what does the word *jelly* mean? What would it mean in a US text?
9 How much fat would there be in *low-fat* cheese? And how much would there be in *reduced fat* cheese?

28.2 **Which do you think would be tastier and why?**

1 strawberry flavoured yoghurt or strawberry flavour yoghurt
2 orange drink or orange juice
3 raspberry jam or raspberry flavoured jam
4 farmhouse chicken or free-range chicken

28.3 **As pointed out in the text, *light* is an ambiguous word, i.e. it can be understood in different ways. Explain these phrases. Where possible, suggest an opposite to *light*.**

1 light coloured hair
2 a light wind
3 a light comedy
4 a light sleeper
5 to light a fire
6 a light aircraft
7 the light of my life
8 Got a light?
9 to light on the solution
10 In the light of the reports ...

28.4 **Explain the literal meanings of the words used metaphorically in the sentences in B.**

EXAMPLE recipe – *instructions for cooking a dish*

28.5 **Rewrite these sentences using the metaphors from B.**

1 My mother asked me a lot of very searching questions about where I had been last night.
2 Let's make the evening more interesting by organising some party games.
3 What's been happening while I was on holiday? You must fill me in on all the interesting gossip.
4 Don't tell her that her briefcase has been found. Let her suffer for a bit longer – perhaps she'll be more careful with it in future.
5 It might be a good idea to make these investments a bit less dominant in your portfolio by exchanging some of them for others in a different line of business.
6 They lived together happily for many years, but things changed for the worse when his mother came to live with them.
7 Patience combined with interest in your pupils is bound to lead to success for a teacher.
8 Lance's ideas are never thought through properly.

FOLLOW UP Find more food vocabulary at this site www.bbc.co.uk/food, which is an archive of recipes. Choose a recipe that interests you and note down any vocabulary that is new to you.

29 Dinner's on me: entertaining and eating out

A Paying the bill

We'll **split the bill**, shall we? [each person will pay for him/herself]
Lunch **is on me** today. [informal: I am paying for you]
Will you **join us** [come with us] for dinner at the City Plaza hotel? We'd like you to **be our guest.** [formal: we will pay]
Let me **get this.** [informal: pay the bill this time]
I was **wined and dined** every night by our New York office. [invited out to restaurants]

B Describing service

A new Italian restaurant called Bella Roma has just opened in the High Street, and we went there the other night to try it. I couldn't help comparing it to the Casa Italia, where we ate last week. In the Bella Roma, the service was **impeccable**[1] and quick; at the Casa Italia it's always a bit **sluggish**[2]. In the new place the waiters are **courteous**[3] and friendly without being **overbearing**[4]. In the other place they tend to be **sullen**[5] and the service is rather **brusque**[6], which I find very **off-putting**[7]. But at Bella Roma they'll **go out of their way**[8] to give you what you want.

1 perfect, cannot be faulted
2 rather slow
3 polite
4 too confident / too inclined to tell people what to do
5 bad-tempered / unwilling to smile
6 quick and rude
7 makes you feel you do not want to go there again
8 do everything possible

C Food preferences

I **have a sweet tooth** and can never say no to cakes or biscuits. [love sweet things]
I won't have dessert, thanks. You're lucky being so slim; but I'm afraid I have to **count the calories** / I have to be a bit **calorie-conscious** these days. [be careful how many calories I eat]
I like to end the meal with something **savoury** like cheese. [salty in flavour or with herbs]
Ben's a bit of a **fussy eater.** [person who has very particular demands when eating]
No, thanks, I won't have wine. I'm **teetotal.** [never drink alcohol]
Before I book the restaurant, do you have any particular **dietary requirements**? [formal: special needs or things someone cannot eat]
I won't have any more wine thanks. I don't want to **overdo it.** [eat or drink too much]

D Entertaining at home

A: Why not come home and eat with us? You'll have to **take pot luck.** [eat what we're eating, nothing special]
B: Thank you. Shall I **bring a bottle**? [usually means a bottle of wine]

A: Should I wear a suit on Friday?
B: No, no, it isn't a **dinner party** [rather formal dinner with guests], it's just an **informal get-together.** [informal group of people meeting for a meal/drinks/etc.]

A: Does anyone want **seconds**? [a second helping/serving of a dish]
B: Oh, yes please. It was delicious.

A: Can I pour you some juice? **Say when.** [tell me when I have served enough]
B: **When!** [That's enough, thanks.]

A: Help yourself to some **nibbles.** [things like nuts, crisps, etc., before a meal]

A: We leave at six. We can **grab a bite to eat** on the way. [have a quick meal]
B: Or we could get a **takeaway** when we get there. [ready-cooked meal bought to take home]

Exercises

29.1 Rewrite the underlined parts of these sentences using expressions from A.

1. No, please. Put your credit card away. <u>I'm inviting you for dinner</u>. (Use an informal expression.)
2. Let me <u>pay for this one</u>. You can pay next time. (Use an informal expression.)
3. Visitors to the company's head office in London are always <u>taken out to</u> the best restaurants. (Use a phrase with two words which rhyme with each other.)
4. <u>Fancy coming with us</u> for lunch tomorrow?
5. When we eat out as a group, <u>each person usually pays for their own food and drink</u>. (Use a shorter expression meaning the same.)
6. <u>I'd like to pay for you</u> at the theatre tomorrow night. (Use a formal expression.)

29.2 Rewrite the underlined parts of these sentences using expressions from the opposite page to describe food and drink preferences.

1. I <u>never drink alcohol</u>. (Use an adjective.)
2. I <u>don't really like sweet things</u>. (Use an idiom.)
3. <u>Are there things you can't or mustn't eat</u>? (Use a formal/polite expression.)
4. Just a small portion for me, please. I don't want to <u>eat too much</u>. (Use an expression that means the same.)
5. She's become <u>very careful about how many calories she's eating</u>. (Give two different ways of saying the same thing.)
6. Sasha is such a <u>choosy person when it comes to food</u>. It's difficult to find things she likes. (Use an expression that means the same.)

29.3 Give words from the opposite page which contrast with or are the opposite of ...

1. a sweet dish
2. a friendly waiter
3. a formal gathering
4. rude staff
5. quick service
6. dreadful service

29.4 Which expressions on the opposite page mean ...

1. eat whatever your hosts are eating at home, not a special dish for you?
2. tell me when I've poured enough in your glass?
3. get a quick meal or some other food that does not take a long time?
4. small items you eat before a meal, or perhaps at a reception?
5. another portion of what you have just eaten?
6. a semi-formal party or reception in someone's house, probably not a meal?

29.5 Make sure you know what all the words mean on these invitation cards.

Mr W. and Mrs B. Ogilvy
cordially invite you to a ball to celebrate the wedding of their daughter
Cassandra
to
Major Derek Littlebrain
at Barnet Hall on 21st March
7pm for 8pm
Black tie *RSVP*

Aaron and Sally
invite you to come along and
toast the launch of their new CD
at Frontiers Music store
88, Fleece Street
6 November at 5.30pm
aperitifs
admission by invitation only

30 On the road: traffic and driving

A UK driving and traffic regulations

Note the collocations.

- You must **give way** at a **give-way sign**. On a roundabout, traffic coming from your right **has the right of way** [is allowed to go before other traffic]. **Sounding/hooting/tooting your horn** is prohibited except in emergencies. **Jumping** [not stopping at] **a red light** is a serious offence. **Reckless driving** [very dangerous driving, without any care for others] is also a very serious offence.

- **Drink-driving** may result in a heavy fine or imprisonment. You may be asked to take a **breathalyser** [instrument you breathe into to measure alcohol level] test. **Hit-and-run** [running over or into someone and not stopping] accidents are extremely serious and could result in a **ban** [removal of one's driving licence] for several years and/or imprisonment. Less serious offences may result in **penalty points** [negative points on your licence which are added up over time]. **On-the-spot fines** [given at the scene of the offence] may be issued for careless driving and other offences.
- **Exhaust emissions** [waste gases produced by the vehicle] must meet government standards, and the car must be **roadworthy** [in a condition that it can be driven safely], which includes a minimum depth of **tyre tread** [the depth of the grooves in the tyre rubber].

B Traffic problems

Note the words in bold in these comments by people talking about driving problems they have experienced and other events on the road.

It was the rush hour, and there was a long **tailback** on the motorway. [line of slow or stopped traffic]

There was a **pile-up** [crash between several or many cars] involving ten cars, because of the fog, so the road was closed and we were **diverted** [directed away from our road] on to a narrow country lane.

I had stupidly parked in a **towaway zone** and came back to find my car had gone! [area where your car may be taken away if you park illegally]

I just parked for a few minutes outside the station, but when I came out my car had been **clamped**. [fitted with a metal device on the wheel to prevent it from moving]

I saw two men fighting next to their cars. I think it was a case of **road rage**. [anger or violence between drivers because of difficult driving conditions]

The road was wet and I **skidded** on a bend and almost crashed. [lost control of the steering]

There was a **head-on collision** [two vehicles hitting each other directly in the front] on the main road between here and the next village last night. Luckily, both cars had **air bags** and the drivers survived.

There was an accident at the junction between the A476 and the A53 this morning involving a lorry carrying a load of glue. Traffic has been stuck there for the last three hours. (*Radio announcement*)

Exercises

30.1 **Fill the gaps in these sentences using words and phrases from the opposite page.**

1 We can't park here; it's a .... zone.
2 There was a five-mile .... on the motorway because of road works.
3 Fog caused a number of ...., one of which involved 15 cars.
4 If it's a .... sign, you don't have to stop if the road is clear, but if it's a stop sign, then you must always stop.
5 Who has the .... at a corner in your country? Cars or pedestrians?
6 It was a .... accident, but the police have a description of the car.
7 The permitted level of .... is to be lowered in an attempt to reduce air pollution in big cities.
8 He was given a .... test and it was discovered he had consumed a huge amount of alcohol. He was charged with .... and fined £500.
9 In some countries drivers .... their .... just because they get frustrated. As a result, the city streets are incredibly noisy.

30.2 **Respond to these comments as in the example, so that your response explains the meaning of the underlined words. Use words from the opposite page.**

EXAMPLE A: I came out and saw a big metal thing on my wheels.
B: Oh, so your wheels had been clamped!
A: Yes. I had to pay £100.

1 A: As I drove round the corner there was some ice on the road and I lost control of the steering.
B: Oh, so ....

2 A: The two women were obviously having an argument about the way one of them had driven. Then suddenly they started hitting each other!
B: Oh, I guess it was a case of ....
A: Yes. It's happening more and more these days.

3 A: The policeman looked at my tyres and said they were illegal.
B: Oh, so you didn't have the minimum depth of ....?

4 A: The road was closed. Two lorries had come straight at each other and crashed.
B: Oh, so it was a ....

5 A: The policeman fined me £100 there and then. I have to pay it within seven days.
B: Oh, really? I didn't know they could give ....
A: Yes. You have no choice. They just give it to you and you can't dispute it at the time.

6 A: The man at the garage said my car wasn't in a fit condition to be driven legally.
B: Oh, so it's not ....

30.3 **What do you think the underlined expressions mean? Write their meaning in your own words. Use a dictionary if you cannot work out the meaning from context.**

1 There were three separate accidents in the city centre during the rush hour and soon there was total gridlock. It took about two hours to clear.
2 I've spent six hours behind the wheel today, and now all I want to do is rest. I never want to see another motorway.
3 The police car made me pull over and they checked my lights.
4 I had a minor bump yesterday. It wasn't serious, but one of my lights got smashed.
5 My car conked out on the motorway and I had to ring for assistance. It cost me £50.
6 He's a bit of a back-seat driver, so don't be surprised if he criticises your driving.

31 Travel and accommodation

A Booking travel and holidays

Here are some choices you may make when booking travel/holidays:

By air
- **scheduled** flight
  - **first, business** or **economy** class
  - **route** (e.g. via /ˈvaɪə/ Amsterdam)
  - **fare type** (e.g. **Apex**, **Budget**)
- **charter** flight
  - inclusive/all-in **package**
  - **flight only**
  - **extras** (e.g. airport taxes/insurance)

A **scheduled flight** is a normal, regular flight; a **charter flight** is a special flight taking a group of people, usually to the same holiday destination. **Apex** fares normally have to be booked a fixed number of days in advance and they offer **value for money. Budget** fares are usually cheaper but may have **restrictions** (e.g. you can only travel on certain days) and are usually **non-refundable** [you can't get your money back] or if you cancel, you may have to pay a **cancellation fee.** Some tickets allow a **stopover** [you may stay somewhere overnight before continuing to your destination]. **All-in packages** normally include accommodation and **transfers** [e.g. a bus or coach to and from your hotel].

Sea travel is normally on a ferry, and the journey is called a **crossing,** but you can have a holiday on the sea if you **go on a cruise**. For some people a luxury cruise is **the holiday of a lifetime** [one you will always remember].

You may decide to book a **berth** in a **shared cabin** [a bed in a cabin with other people], or to have a single or double cabin. For more money, you can often get a **deluxe** cabin, perhaps on the **upper deck** [the higher part of the ship, which is often bigger and more comfortable]. Cruises often go to **exotic** [unusual or exciting] islands where you can **get away from it all** [escape your daily life and routines].

Car hire is another way of **getting around** [informal: travelling to different places]. When you book it, you normally choose whether you want **unlimited mileage** [/ˈmaɪlɪdʒ/ you can travel as many miles as you like for the same price]. There may also be **extras** to pay such as accident insurance. If you hire a car it gives you the freedom to **go as you please** [go where you want when you want].

B Accommodation

Some people prefer hotels. Others prefer **self-catering** [where you do your own cooking] accommodation, such as a holiday apartment or **chalet** [/ˈʃæleɪ/ small cottage or cabin specially built for holiday-makers]. In Britain and Ireland, **guest houses** [private homes offering high standard accommodation] and **inns** [similar to pubs, but also offering accommodation; usually beautiful old buildings] offer good accommodation which is often cheaper than hotels, and there are many private homes offering bed-and-breakfast [often called **B and B**]. Some types of accommodation offer **half board** [usually breakfast and one other meal] or **full board** [all meals].

Exercises

31.1 **Use vocabulary from A opposite to express these sentences more briefly, as in the example.**

EXAMPLE It was a regular flight which the airline runs every day.
It was a scheduled flight.

1 I hate those special flights where everyone is booked to the same holiday destination.
2 It was a ticket you had to book 30 days in advance to get the cheaper fare.
3 The ticket allowed us to spend up to three nights in Singapore on the journey from London to Sydney.
4 You can get a bed on the ferry in a little room with three other beds.
5 We hired a car, with as many miles as we wanted free.
6 When you get there, the bus or taxi to your hotel is included in the cost of the holiday.
7 It was a special cheap fare, but there were some things you were not allowed to do.

31.2 **Match the words on the left with their collocations on the right.**

1 bed	catering
2 full	for money
3 self-	mileage
4 unlimited	island
5 exotic	and breakfast
6 value	board

31.3 **Which expressions in the box do you associate with each of the holidays below? Use a dictionary if necessary. Each expression may go with more than one type of holiday.**

to rough it	an exhilarating experience	to be out in the wilds
to lounge around	to keep on the move	to sleep under the stars
a real learning experience	to be your own boss	to just drift along
a cosy atmosphere	to go as you please	to spend a fortune on entrance fees

1 self-catering holiday
2 camping trip
3 staying in an inn or a guest house
4 skiing holiday
5 trekking holiday
6 cruise
7 sightseeing holiday
8 holiday with car hire

31.4 **Use the correct expressions from 31.3 in these sentences.**

1 It was a lovely cruise; we just .... all day.
2 I prefer self-catering because I like to ....
3 Camping is OK if you don't mind ....
4 Skiing is always such ....
5 Sightseeing's great but it's easy ....
6 The guided tour of the ancient ruins was ....
7 Inns and guest houses usually have quite ....

31.5 **Here are some pictures associated with holidays. Using vocabulary from the opposite page, and in your own words, what kind of holiday do you associate them with?**

1 
2 
3 
4 
5 

32 Tourism

A General descriptions of tourist destinations

FOR TOURISTS YEARNING to **escape the crowd**[1], **wander off the beaten track**[2] and **get back to nature**[3], Suriname increasingly looks **a promising choice**[4]. Nobody in Suriname claims that the country **boasts**[5] the best sand, sea and sun in the Caribbean. But that, in a way, is precisely the point: there aren't **hordes**[6] of people either.

As Henk Essed, director of the Suriname Tourism Foundation, observes: We don't really need masses of tourists like we have in the rest of the Caribbean. Instead, Suriname's modest **tourism sector**[7] focuses on what makes the country different. The biggest attraction for visitors **seeking something out of the ordinary**[8] is the **wealth of**[9] wildlife. Large **tracts**[10] of the country are still covered by **virgin**[11] rainforest, home to a huge range of **flora and fauna**[12].

There is great potential to develop **eco-tourism**[13] as one of the major sources of income in the near future, says Harold Sijlbing, managing director of Stinasu, an organisation which promotes conservation of wildlife and ecological awareness.

1 go where there are not many people
2 go to places tourists don't normally go
3 live a natural, rural style of life
4 a choice which could be a very good one
5 this use of *boast* is for listing the good qualities of a place (formal)
6 crowds, in a negative sense
7 tourist industry (formal)
8 common collocation: looking for something different/unusual
9 large amount of (formal)
10 areas of land, collocates with *large*, *vast*, *huge*
11 original and natural
12 plants and animals (Latin); a fixed phrase
13 holidays that respect the environment

B Travel advertisements

Unwind[1] in Estera, **recharge**[2] in Postalia, all from under £500

Guided tours for the **discerning**[6] traveller. Ancient sites in modern comfort.

Rambles, hikes and **treks**[10] **Unrivalled**[11] programme Send for our brochure

Taste of **the bush**[3]: all travel in air-conditioned **4x4**[4] vehicles

Stunning[7] locations. **Unbeatable**[8] prices. Phone now.

Waterfront[5] villas, self-catering, sleep up to six

Awe-inspiring[9] national parks

Savour[12] the renowned landscapes in our heartland[13]

1 /ʌn'waɪnd/ relax, reduce your general level of stress
2 get back your energy (like recharging a battery)
3 a term for the wild, tree- or grass-covered areas of Africa or Australia
4 pronounced four by four; vehicles with driving power on all four wheels
5 on the edge of the sea or of a river
6 who knows what he/she wants in terms of good quality
7 extremely beautiful
8 no other company can offer cheaper ones for the same service
9 it fills you with a sense of the power and beauty of what you are looking at
10 These three words represent a scale of length and difficulty. A **ramble** is a long, pleasant walk, not too demanding. A **hike** is more demanding, suggesting more difficult terrain. A **trek** is usually of several days over wild country.
11 no other holiday programme can match this
12 a word typically used in advertisements meaning enjoy
13 the inland areas furthest away from the sea or from borders with other countries

Exercises

32.1 Complete the expressions and collocations in these sentences, using words from A.

1 Malaysia .... some of the loveliest beaches in Asia.
2 The tourism .... is very important to the economies of many developing countries.
3 It is vital that tourism should not damage the flora and .... of beautiful areas of wildlife.
4 Most tourists like to feel free to .... off the .... track.
5 Nobody likes to travel to a place where there will be .... of other tourists.
6 People who spend all their time in big cities often like to .... back to .... when they go away for a holiday.
7 If you're .... something out of the .... why not try a snowboarding holiday? It's certainly different!
8 When I travel I always try to .... the crowd and find somewhere quiet.
9 There are vast .... of unspoilt land in the north of the country, with .... rainforests and a .... of wildlife.
10 We've studied the brochures and Tasmania looks a .... choice for this year.

32.2 Look at these extracts from travel and tourism advertisements and, in your own words, say what they mean. Use a dictionary if necessary.

1 Itinerary includes three shore excursions and 10 nights at sea
2 Flights subject to availability
3 Single room supplement £30 per night
4 For instant bookings or quotations, call 01785 67844532
5 Fly-drive option available on request

32.3 Use words from B opposite to fill the gaps, based on the words given in brackets.

1 This company is excellent and their prices are .... (RIVAL)
2 You should go into the .... to see the true culture of the country. (HEART)
3 There are some absolutely .... beaches to the north. (STUN)
4 I think Suntravel is .... when it comes to cheap destinations. (BEAT)
5 The mountains were so .... Many were over 5,000 metres high. (AWE)
6 We rented a .... villa. It was nice to be so near the beach. (WATER)
7 I just want somewhere quiet and relaxing to .... for a week. (WIND)
8 Everyone needs to .... their batteries now and again. (CHARGE)

32.4 Answer these questions.

1 Order these words from the most physically demanding to the least physically demanding: ramble, trek, hike
2 What verb might you find in travel advertisements meaning enjoy?
3 What adjective can be used with *traveller* to mean one who knows exactly what he or she wants in terms of quality and value?
4 Where would you find the bush?
5 How do you say this and what does it mean? 4×4

FOLLOW UP

If you have access to the Internet, look up the names of your favourite countries and try to find their tourist information web pages. For example, you can find information in English on Ireland at www.irelandtravel.co.uk, and on Spain at www.tourspain.es

33 Describing the world

A Climate

On a journey from north to south across this huge region, you would pass through a fascinating series of hot tropic landscapes. Plenty of rain falls in the far south, whereas the **arid**[1] northerly region is **prone to**[2] serious **drought**[3]. (*West Africa*)

1 dry
2 tending to have a particular negative characteristic
3 period without rain

B Vegetation

About one third of the landscape of Canada lies within the Arctic Circle and can remain frozen for up to nine months of the year. In these cold areas, known as the **tundra**[1], any **vegetation**[2] is limited. However, further south, large areas of land are covered by dense, **coniferous**[3] forests, known as taiga. Towards the border with the USA lie the mixed, temperate forests and the grasslands of the **prairies**[4]. (*Canada*)

1 area in north with no trees and permanently frozen ground
2 plant life
3 trees that are **evergreen** [green all year round] and produce cones, unlike **deciduous** trees, which lose their leaves in winter
4 flat grasslands in Canada and northern USA (similar to steppes in Asia or pampas in South America)

C Agriculture

In the south the main crop is rice, though tea, cotton, fruit and vegetables are also grown. The rice is planted in flooded **paddy fields**[1]. Two crops of rice and one of vegetables are harvested in a good year. In the north and west, which is drier and hillier, farmers grow a single crop of **cereals**[2] and **tend**[3] sheep and cattle. (*China*)

1 fields planted with rice growing in water
2 type of grass cultivated to produce a grain, i.e. a food plant like rice, wheat or maize
3 take care of animals

D Industry

One of the world's leading industrial nations, France has large **manufacturing**[1], steel and chemical industries and stands **at the forefront**[2] of engineering and technology. The country is a major producer of cars and aircraft. France has a large nuclear industry which **generates**[3] about 75 per cent of the country's electrical power. (*France*)

1 producing goods in large numbers
2 in an important position
3 produces

E Population

THE POPULATION of Brazil is a mixture of peoples. Some **are descended from**[1] native Indians who have always lived in Brazil, others from the Portuguese who ruled there for 300 years. Many Brazilians have African **ancestors**[2] who were brought over in the 17th century to work as slaves on sugar plantations. During the 20th century large numbers of European **migrants**[3] **settled**[4] in the south. (*Brazil*)

1 are related to
2 relatives from earlier times: we are our ancestors' **descendants**
3 people who move to live in another country (an **emigrant** is someone who leaves a country and an **immigrant** is someone who moves to live in a country – emigrants from Britain currently outnumber immigrants coming to live here)
4 made their homes

Exercises

33.1 **Some of the expressions from the opposite page are strong collocations. Match them.**

1 coniferous	plantation
2 industrial	industry
3 paddy	forest
4 chemical	field
5 sugar	nation

33.2 **Here are some other words which collocate with the words in the right-hand column in exercise 33.1. There are three for each of the above five words. Can you find them?**

coffee	deciduous	dense	civilised	manufacturing
oil	pharmaceutical	rain	ripe	rubber
tea	textile	wheat	independent	sovereign

33.3 **Complete the sentences using a word from the box.**

descendants	ancestors	migrants	emigrants	immigrants

1 I believe my .... came to Britain from France in the 17th century.
2 Many .... left Russia for France after the Revolution in 1917.
3 The USA has traditionally welcomed .... from all over the world.
4 Our largest cities are full of .... looking for work and a better life.
5 Some Scots are said to be the .... of 16th century Spanish sailors ship-wrecked off the Scottish coast.

33.4 **Use the words in brackets to complete each sentence. Then decide which country each sentence refers to. The countries you need are given in the box below the exercise.**

1 About 80% of the .... lives in or around cities along the .... where life is easier than in the .... towns and farms of the ....
(coast, outback, population, remote)
2 400 years ago it was the .... of the Inca .... that .... the .... of South America.
(centre, length, stretched, Empire)
3 Two thirds of the .... is under water but .... so, because the .... are .... to grow rice.
(flooded, deliberately, farmland, fields)
4 To the .... of a long, narrow .... more than a hundred islands .... the rest of the ....
(country, east, make up, peninsula)
5 Much of the land is ...., dotted with ...., but parts of the .... are more ....
(coastline, desert, fertile, oases)
6 A line of ...., many still ...., dominates the .... of this small country and ...., once rich with cedar, mahogany and oak, have been cut down for farmland.
(active, forests, landscape, volcanoes)

Oman	Vietnam	Peru	Australia	El Salvador	Denmark

34 Weather and climate

A Weather conversations

Here are some more unusual but still useful words about weather so that you can have typical weather conversations where you agree with someone by using a synonym. In these examples B replies using more informal language.

A: Bit **chilly** today, isn't it?
B: Yes, it's **freezing/nippy**, isn't it?

A: It's **hot**, isn't it?
B: Yes, it's **boiling/sweltering/roasting**!

A: It's a bit **windy** today!
B: Yes, really **blowy/breezy**, isn't it?

A: What **oppressive/sultry** weather!
B: Yes, isn't it **stifling/heavy/close**?

A: What a **downpour/deluge**!
B: Yes, it's **chucking it down/it's pouring**!

A: Isn't it **humid** today?
B: Yes, horribly **muggy/clammy**.

B Climate and metaphors

Climate metaphors are often used, particularly in written English. The word **climate** can refer to the general atmosphere or situation in society.

His dishonest policies towards the workers created a **climate of distrust.**
The government reforms have created a **climate of change**.
The words, **cultural, current, economic, financial, moral, political, social** and **prevailing** all collocate strongly with **climate** in this social sense.

She has a very **sunny disposition** – she's hardly ever miserable.
Job prospects are **sunny**.

Unfortunately, our plans met with a **frosty** reception.
'You lied to me, didn't you?' she said **icily**.
I'm **snowed under** with work – I'll never get through it all in time.

After the company accounts were examined, the manager left **under a cloud** of suspicion.
Don't let your love for him **cloud your judgement**.

The soldiers were hit with a **hail of bullets.**
The Prime Minister was greeted with a **hail/storm of abuse.**

After the long flight I was **in a haze** for a day or two.
I've only a **hazy idea** what you mean.

The truth is hidden **in the mists of** history.
She looked at him **misty-eyed** – clearly in love.

The article sparked off a **whirlwind** of speculation.
They had a **whirlwind romance.**

The horses **thundered** down the race track.
Thunderous applause followed his speech. (Note that **thundery** is used to describe stormy weather while **thunderous** describes a loud noise.)

The **winds of change/discontent/democracy** are blowing across the country.

Exercises

34.1 **Respond to these statements about the weather. Agree using slightly more formal language like that of speaker A in the dialogues opposite.**

1 It's a bit nippy outside, isn't it?
2 What a sweltering day!
3 Isn't it muggy here?
4 It's blowy, isn't it?
5 Close today, isn't it?
6 It's chucking it down!
7 It's clammy today, isn't it?
8 What a stifling day!

34.2 **What is the link between the literal and metaphorical meanings of these words from B opposite?**

EXAMPLE sunny – *pleasant and positive*

1 frosty
2 icily
3 snowed under
4 whirlwind
5 hail
6 under a cloud
7 in a haze
8 to thunder

34.3 **Find collocations for these words. You will find some on the opposite page, but use a dictionary to find more if necessary.**

1 ....
.... climate
....

2 prevailing ....
....
....

3 to cloud ....
....
....

4 the winds of ....
....
....

5 a frosty ....
....
....

6 a hail of ....
....
....

34.4 **Read the text below and find words in the text which mean the following.**

1 average
2 dry
3 height above sea level
4 distance from the equator
5 rain and snow
6 rays from the sun
7 make less extreme
8 situated very far from the sea
9 differing weather conditions at different times of the year

Schemes for dividing the Earth into climatic regions are based on a combination of indices of mean annual temperature, mean monthly temperature, annual precipitation totals and seasonality. The climate of a place is affected by several factors. Latitude affects the amount of solar radiation received, with the greatest in equatorial regions and the least in polar regions. Elevation affects both temperature and precipitation; mountainous areas are generally cooler and wetter. Location close to the sea or to large bodies of water moderates temperature; continental areas are generally more arid and more affected by extremes of temperature.

34.5 **Are climate and weather words used metaphorically in your own first language or in other languages that you know well? If so, do specific weather features evoke the same images in other languages as in English?**

35 Buildings in metaphors

A Buildings

Note how **cement** is used both to make buildings stronger and to make relationships stronger. It can be used in this way both as a noun and a verb: Let's have a drink together **to cement** our partnership.

Brick wall used metaphorically means a barrier: When I tried to find out what had happened to my tax claim, I **came up against a brick wall.**

Ceiling can be used to suggest a limit to something: They put a **ceiling** of twenty thousand pounds on the redundancy payments.

The **glass ceiling** is a phrase used to refer to an invisible barrier that stops people, especially women, from rising to top positions at work.

Roof as a metaphor: The **roof** fell in on my world on the day he died.

Notice how the colloquial phrase **go through the roof** has two different meanings. If prices go through the roof, they increase in a rapid, uncontrolled fashion. If, however, a person goes through the roof, he or she loses their temper.

Hit the roof, similarly, can be used about prices but it is far more commonly used to mean lose one's temper: The teacher will **hit the roof** when she sees the mess we've made of this work.

As a very tall building, **tower** conveys an idea of distance from ordinary people. If someone lives in an **ivory tower**, he or she does not know about the unpleasant and ordinary things that happen in life: Academics are often criticised for living in their **ivory towers.**

If a person is a **tower of strength**, they are extremely strong (in an emotional rather than a physical sense): Our friends were a **tower of strength** when our house burnt down.

If a person or thing **towers above** something or someone else, they are either outstandingly tall or outstanding in some other positive way: Jack **towers above** all his classmates although he is actually one of the youngest pupils.

B Entrances

Gateway is used metaphorically in the phrase be a **gateway to**, meaning provide access.
A degree in law is a **gateway to** a well-paid job.

Door can also be used in a similar way to gateway above, but it is also used in many other metaphorical phrases as well: Failing his final exams **closed/shut** a lot of **doors** for him.
Knowing several languages **opens doors** when it comes to finding work.
The new century gives us the opportunity to **close the door on** our past and make a fresh start.
Doing something **through/by the back door** suggests doing it unofficially: Joe came into the business by the back door – the manager knew him from university.

Key can be used as a noun or an adjective to suggest the importance of something:
This research may **provide/hold the key to** developing a cure for cancer.
Knowing the right people is **the key to success** in that country.
The **key figures** in the government all went to the same universities.
As an adjective **key** collocates strongly with:

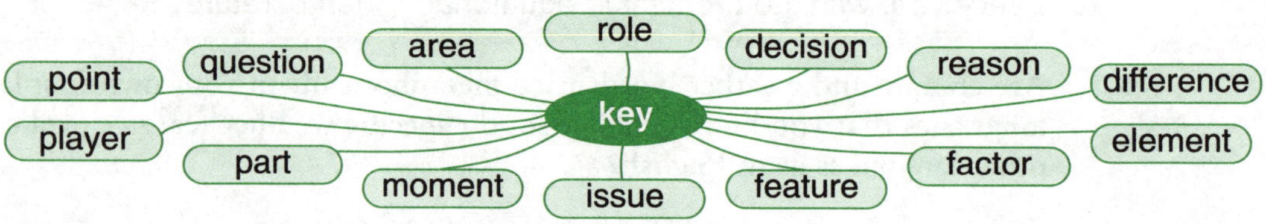

Exercises

35.1 Match the words on the left with those on the right to make metaphors. Explain what each metaphor means.

1 glass	door
2 ivory	feature
3 brick	ceiling
4 back	tower
5 key	wall

35.2 Complete these sentences by inserting the necessary verb.

1 The boss .... through the roof when she saw Robert arriving late again.
2 We hope that this scientist's work may .... the key to solving the problem.
3 A degree in economics .... the door to a number of interesting job opportunities.
4 Whenever you try to initiate something in this company you find that, sooner or later, you .... up against a brick wall.
5 Jan's father .... the roof when he saw that she'd dyed her hair purple.
6 Bill .... over all the other lawyers in his firm. He is by far the most able.
7 Her argument with the board last year has, unfortunately, ... a lot of doors for her in this company.
8 The roof .... in on their world the day that war was declared.

35.3 Rewrite the underlined parts of these sentences using one of the expressions on the opposite page.

1 My brother is always enormously supportive whenever I have a problem.
2 I would be reluctant to work for a company that does a lot of business in an unofficial way.
3 The fee for this work will depend on the time it takes but cannot be more than twenty thousand dollars.
4 The cost of petrol has risen dramatically in the last six months.
5 Having children often makes a marriage stronger.
6 Vancouver is the ideal place for starting to explore Western Canada.
7 The most important decision we have to take now is where to locate our business.
8 The professor has spent all his life in one university or another and really finds it very difficult to cope in the real world.

35.4 Here are some more metaphors based on aspects of buildings. Can you guess what the underlined expressions mean and rewrite them?

1 The company has been locked in a legal battle for several years now.
2 The speaker's request for questions was met with a wall of silence.
3 Working on this project together should help to lay the foundations for a good relationship in the future.
4 Her eyes were locked on mine as she told me she was planning to go abroad.
5 When Jack returned to this country he found his marriage in ruins.
6 This government should clean up its own back yard before criticising other countries.

35.5 Which of the metaphors in this unit also work as metaphors when translated literally into your own language? Look at exercise 35.4 as well as the opposite page.

36 Trees, plants and metaphors

A

Here are some metaphors based on parts of trees and plants.

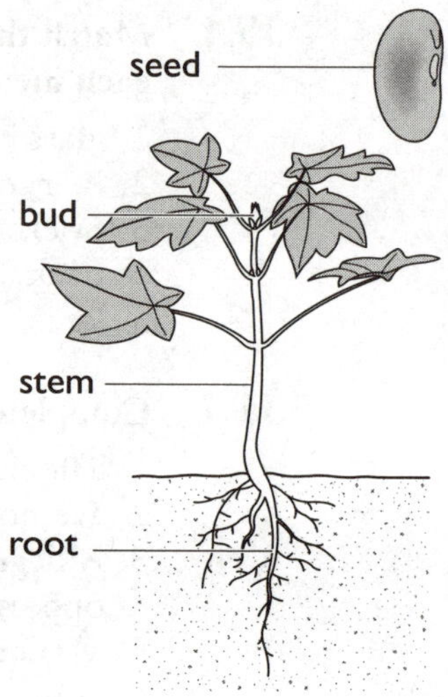

Seed(s) is often used to talk about the start of an idea or feeling: **the seeds of success, the seeds of discontent, the seeds of revolution.**

Root(s) is used to suggest the origins of something. You can talk about **going back to your roots**, for example, meaning going back to the place where your family came from. You can also talk about **the root of a problem** or **the roots of a tradition.**
Putting down roots means settling down and making your home in one place: After travelling the world for a couple of years, I was ready to go home and **put down some roots.**
When an idea becomes known or accepted, it can be said to **take root.**
Deeply and **firmly** collocate with **rooted** as in, for example:
Its origins are **firmly/deeply rooted** in the nineteenth century.
The **grass roots** of an organisation or society are the ordinary people in it, not the leaders.

Stem is used as a verb to signify that something originates in something else:
Her discontent **stems** from a traumatic experience she had last year.

A branch is something that grows off or **branches out** from a main organisation. So we talk about **branches of a shop** or a **business branching out into new directions.**
We haven't a blue sweater in your size, but you could try our Oxford Street **branch.**

Bud [flower before it opens] is used in the expression **nipped in the bud** [stopped before it develops into something].
He's showing signs of neglecting his work – we'd better **nip that in the bud.**
The adjective **budding** can also mean showing promise of future development:
She's a **budding** young actress.

B

Here are some metaphors based on verbs connected with plant growth and gardening.

The new boss is planning to **weed out** older or less experienced staff. [get rid of]
The government will probably have to **prune back** its proposals. [cut/limit]
At last she **is reaping the reward of** all her years of study. [is getting results from]
The journalists **have dug up** some interesting facts. [have discovered]
The idea **was germinating** while we were on holiday. [was beginning to develop]
Out-of-town shopping centres **have been sprouting** all over the country. [have been appearing quickly in large numbers]
Our business **is flourishing.** [is doing very well]
A deciduous tree **sheds** its leaves. [loses]
People can **shed employees/traditions/worries/inhibitions/weight.**
Plants **fade, wither, shrivel** and **wilt** when they die. These verbs can all be used metaphorically:
Hopes of finding survivors are **fading.** [becoming smaller]
High inflation means that our savings are **shrivelling.** [becoming less]
It was so hot in the classroom that the students were starting to **wilt.** [lose energy]
A **glance/look/remark** can **wither** or **be withering.** [make the recipient feel scorned]
She gave him a **withering look.**

Exercises

36.1 Match the beginnings of the expressions with their endings.

1 nipped	of the problem
2 a budding	root
3 grass	poet
4 the root	of discontent
5 to reap	roots
6 to take	in the bud
7 the seeds	rewards

36.2 Fill the gaps in these sentences.

1 Alec has spent most of his life in London, but he is keen to .... back to his roots when he retires.
2 The business is firmly .... in the west of England.
3 The idea took some time to .... root but it's very fashionable now.
4 His grandfather sowed the .... of the business's success.
5 The US bookshop chain is opening a number of .... in the UK.
6 It's about time she .... down some roots.
7 The idea for her novel .... from her interest in mountain climbing.
8 The St James's Drama College turns out a hundred .... actors every year.

36.3 What is the link between the literal and metaphorical meanings of these words from B?

1 fade	3 flourish	5 germinate	7 prune back	9 reap
2 shrivel	4 sprout	6 weed out	8 wilt	10 wither

36.4 Suggest three nouns that each of these adjectives could describe.

1 budding
2 flourishing
3 withering
4 fading
5 deeply rooted

36.5 Answer these questions.

1 What would you like to *shed* at this point in your life?
2 Can you think of a situation where you *reaped the rewards* of something you did?
3 What in your life is *flourishing* at the moment?
4 When did you last feel that you were *wilting*?

36.6 Here are some further metaphors based on plants. Answer the questions and use a dictionary if necessary.

1 If you are **the apple of** your teacher's **eye**, does your teacher like or dislike you?
2 If something, for example new houses, is said to be **mushrooming**, what is happening?
3 If someone **lives in clover**, do they live very poorly or very luxuriously?
4 What kind of person is a **couch potato**?
5 If discussions are **fruitful**, what are they like?

37 Animals and birds

A Describing animals and birds

word	*definition and/or examples*
mammal	animal that gives birth to live babies, not eggs, and feeds them on its own milk (e.g. cat, cow, kangaroo)
rodent	e.g. mouse, rat
reptile	e.g. snake, lizard
carnivore	animal that eats meat (e.g. lion, tiger)
herbivore	animal that eats grass/vegetation (e.g. deer, cow)
predator	animal that hunts/eats other animals (e.g. eagle, lion, shark)

B Describing typical animal behaviour

word	*meaning*	*example*
docile	behaves very gently	Our old cat is a very docile creature.
tame	not afraid of humans	These birds are so tame, they will sit on your hand.
domesticated	lives with or is used by humans	Dogs and cats became domesticated thousands of years ago.
wild	opposite of domesticated	There are wild cats in the mountains.
savage	extremely violent or wild	A savage wolf killed three of the farmer's sheep.
fierce	behaves aggressively	A fierce-looking dog stood in the doorway.

C Where animals and birds live

As more buildings and roads are constructed the **natural habitat** for these animals is shrinking. [preferred natural place for living and breeding]
Some wonderful animals can be seen if you visit the big **game reserves / game parks** in Africa. [areas of land where animals are protected from hunting, etc.]
A **bird sanctuary** has recently been opened on the coast, ten miles south of here. [protected area where birds can live and breed]
We went to the local **animal shelter** to ask if we could have a dog. [place where cats, dogs, horses, etc. which have no home are given food and a place to live]

D Human exploitation of animals and birds

Many people are opposed to **blood sports** such as foxhunting, cock fighting and bullfighting. [sports whose purpose is to kill or injure animals]
Nowadays, a lot of people refuse to wear coats made of natural animal fur since they are opposed to **the fur trade.** [the hunting and selling of animal furs for coats, jackets, etc.]
Poachers [people who hunt animals illegally] kill hundreds of elephants every year to supply **the ivory trade** [the buying and selling of ivory from elephants' tusks].
Animal rights activists often demonstrate outside this factory because animals are used in experiments there. [people who actively campaign for the protection and rights of animals]

Exercises

37.1 **Rewrite the underlined expressions in these sentences using more technical terms.**

1 There are dozens of different types of <u>squirrels, mice and things like that</u> living in the woods.
2 A whale isn't a fish, it doesn't lay eggs. It's actually <u>an animal that gives birth directly</u>.
3 There are some interesting <u>turtles and crocodiles and that sort of thing</u> near the river.
4 Everyone thinks these animals <u>eat meat</u>, but in fact they <u>only feed on certain kinds of leaves</u>.
5 The mother bird protects her eggs from <u>animals that attack them</u>.

37.2 **Fill the gaps in these sentences using adjectives from B on the opposite page to describe gentle or aggressive behaviour, or the relationship between animals and humans.**

1 Sheep are generally rather .... animals, but the other day one attacked our dog.
2 The lions look very .... with their huge teeth and large heads.
3 Elephants are .... in several countries in Asia, and they work hard carrying heavy weights.
4 The dolphins are very .... and will swim along with human beings.
5 I don't think .... birds should ever be hunted. They should be left in peace in their natural surroundings.

37.3 **Here are the beginnings and endings of some words related to animals and birds. Can you fill in the missing letters? You are given a clue as to the meaning.**

1 h..................................t (natural home)
2 s..................................y (protected place)
3 r..................................e (protected area, often for big game)
4 s..................................r (place for homeless animals)

37.4 **Answer these questions.**

1 What do we call sports that deliberately injure or kill animals for pleasure?
2 What name is given to the activity of buying and selling elephants' tusks?
3 What do we call people who illegally hunt or catch animals or fish?
4 What arguments would animal rights activists have against the fur trade?

37.5 **Complete the following table. Do not fill the shaded boxes. Use a dictionary if necessary. In the noun and adjective columns, mark which part of the word is stressed.**

noun	*verb*	*adjective*
carnivore		
herbivore		
predator		
poacher		

38 Environment and conservation

You probably already know a lot of words for talking about the environment, pollution, and so on. In this unit we look at words that are often used together (collocations). Try to learn some of these expressions and use them in your writing.

A Threats and potential threats to the environment

Shrinking habitats[1] are a threat to both plants and animals, and **endangered species**[2] need legal protection if they are to survive. Meanwhile, **global warming**[3] will produce rising sea levels and **climatic changes**[4], and **carbon dioxide emissions**[5] from the burning of **fossil fuels**[6] are contributing to the **greenhouse effect**[7]. In addition, population growth **exerts severe pressure on**[8] **finite resources**[9], and the **ecological balance**[10] may be upset by uncontrolled **deforestation**[11]. **Demographic projections**[12] suggest the world population will grow before it begins to stabilise. One of **the worst case scenarios**[13] is that there will be no tropical forests left by the year 2050. Our only hope is that **pristine environments**[14] such as Antarctica can be protected from development and damage.

1 places where animals live and breed which are decreasing in size
2 types of animals/plants which are in danger of no longer existing
3 steady rise in average world temperatures
4 changes in the weather/climate
5 carbon dioxide gas from factories, cars, etc.
6 coal, oil, etc.
7 warming of the Earth's surface caused by pollution
8 formal: puts pressure on
9 limited resources
10 balance of natural relationships in the environment
11 destruction/clearing of forests
12 forecasts about the population
13 the worst possibilities for the future
14 perfectly clean/untouched/unspoilt areas

B Responses to environmental issues and problems

Look at these newspaper headlines and note the useful phrases.

GOVERNING PARTY IN BID TO IMPROVE GREEN CREDENTIALS*

* reputation for positive support of the environment

PROPHETS OF DOOM AND GLOOM* SHOULD LISTEN TO SCIENTIFIC EVIDENCE, SAYS PRIME MINISTER

* people who always make the most depressing or pessimistic forecasts for the future

SUSTAINABLE DEVELOPMENT* THE ONLY ANSWER FOR EMERGING COUNTRIES, SAYS UN COMMISSION

* development of industry, etc. which does not threaten the environment or social and economic stability

PIECEMEAL CONSERVATION* INEFFECTIVE – NATIONAL POLICY NEEDED, SAYS NEW REPORT

*carrying out conservation one bit at a time, with no overall plan

Exercises

38.1 **Make these sentences formal by using words and phrases from A opposite instead of the underlined words. Make any other necessary changes to produce a correct sentence.**

1. All that carbon-what's-it-called gas put out by cars and factories is a major problem.
2. These flowers here are a type there's not many left of, so it's illegal to pick them.
3. A lot of wild animals have to survive in smaller and smaller areas where they can live.
4. Most of Patagonia is a completely spotless area that's never been touched.
5. We have to look after the things we use on this planet because they won't last forever.
6. If the cutting down of trees continues, there will be no forest left ten years from now.
7. Burning coal and oil and stuff like that causes a lot of pollution.
8. The sea will get higher if this heating up of the world continues.
9. Increasing population puts really big pressure on economic resources.
10. The way things all balance one another in nature is very delicate.

38.2 **Complete the following table, using a dictionary if necessary. Do not fill the shaded boxes.**

noun	*verb*	*adjective*	*adverb*
climate			
demography			
	project		
	sustain		

38.3 **Correct the mistakes in this paragraph.**

Profits of boom and gloom are always saying that we are heading for an environmental catastrophe, and that unless we adopt a policy of attainable development we will cause irreparable damage to the planet. The worst place scenery is of a world choked by overpopulation, the greenhouse affect and traffic gridlock. Much of what is claimed is exaggerated, but politicians are influenced by such voices and are always trying to improve their green potentials in the eyes of the voters.

38.4 **An American newspaper recently published these statistics. Read them and answer the two questions below.**

1. There is one word in the picture for a type of animal not mentioned on the opposite page. What does this new word mean? Use a dictionary if necessary.
2. Which phrase in this unit means the same as threatened species?

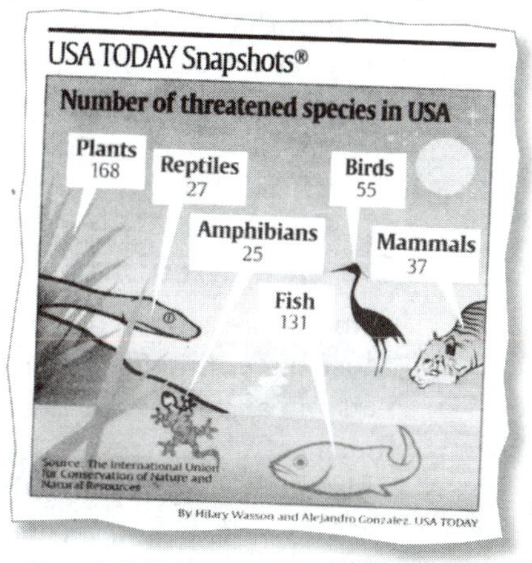

FOLLOW UP To get more vocabulary connected with environment and conservation issues visit the websites of major conservation organisations such as the World Wildlife Fund (WWF) at www.worldwildlife.org or Friends of the Earth at www.foei.org

39 Here to help: service encounters

A Good service

Look at these comments by someone about a company they recently used.

They're a good company. They always make sure you get a **prompt** [quick, without delay] reply to any **query** [/ˈkwɪəri/ question or enquiry about service] and they're very **responsive to complaints** [they listen, take them seriously and act]. When I rang to ask if I could change the delivery date, they were very **accommodating** [willing to understand and help] and **got back to me** [called me with an answer to my query] within ten minutes with a new date. Whenever I ring I get **impeccable** [100% perfect] service; they're always very helpful and **obliging** [willing and happy to do things for you], whatever the problem is.

B Bad service

adjective	*meaning*	*example*
incompetent	failing through insufficient skill, knowledge or training	It wasn't just bad service; they were completely **incompetent**.
impersonal	lacking a personal element	I find supermarkets so **impersonal**.
shoddy	poor quality (of service or of goods)	They repaired my car but the work was very **shoddy**.
substandard	below the standard expected (often used about actions)	It was a **substandard** performance altogether for such a big company.
uncooperative	not supportive, unwilling to work together	The secretary was very **uncooperative**. So I ended up doing it myself.

There's a huge **backlog** of orders and they can't deliver for three weeks. [number which are waiting to be dealt with]
They never seem to have any **sense of urgency** when you ring them. It's exasperating. [feeling that your request is important or urgent]
They have a **helpline** [telephone number where you can get help if you have problems], but it's useless; they always **put you on hold** [make you wait] every time you ring.
My TV broke down but it was still **under guarantee/warranty** so I didn't have to pay to get it repaired. [having a written promise by a company to repair or replace a faulty product]

C Service encounters on the Internet

Some expressions you might find when using Internet websites for goods and services:
Most big companies on the Internet offer a **secure site** [web address where no outside person can read your details] and have a **privacy policy** guaranteeing **safe transactions** [business exchanges which protect, e.g. your credit card from use by someone else].
This site has a very good **FAQ** [(pronounced as initials) frequently asked questions] link where you can find answers to the most important questions.
This Internet bookshop is excellent: you can **browse** and it has a very good site index. [look at the list of goods/services offered before buying]
Most large Internet shopping sites offer **immediate dispatch** [goods will be sent at once] and a **nationwide** service [covering the whole country].

Exercises

39.1 **Fill the gaps with appropriate words or phrases from the opposite page. There may be more than one possible answer.**

1. I rang to complain and they put me .... for about 15 minutes. Then I spoke to someone who promised to ring me again, but they never got .... me. I'll have to call them again.
2. They promised immediate .... of the goods I ordered, but I've been waiting over a week now, and nothing has arrived.
3. I've always found the company very .... to complaints and inquiries.
4. I was expecting a .... reply to my letter, but I've been waiting two weeks now, and still haven't had an answer.
5. I asked why they hadn't dealt with my order yet and they said there was a .... of orders which had built up over the Christmas holidays.
6. In my opinion, the goods and the service were both pretty .... I would have expected better quality from such a famous firm.
7. Staff in that shop are so .... ; they are genuinely helpful.
8. I rang the .... , but they couldn't solve my problem.

39.2 **Answer these questions for yourself.**

1. Do you have a backlog of anything at the moment?
2. Have you had any recent experience of someone being very accommodating towards you?
3. What sort of companies or services usually have a helpline? Have you ever rung one? If so, what for, and was it successful?
4. Has anyone who has served you been uncooperative recently? What was the situation?

39.3 **Here are some buttons taken from current Internet shopping and service sites. Match them with the list of functions.**

1. more hot deals
2. browse our categories
3. log in now
4. check availability
5. at a glance
6. killer bargains
7. online auction
8. site index
9. privacy policy

a) with one look you can see the whole range
b) look through the range before buying
c) rules for protecting your personal details
d) sale where you can offer a price for something
e) a further range of special offers
f) see if the goods you want can be supplied
g) list of all the goods/services available
h) the best special offers possible
i) enter the website straight away

40 Authorities: customs and police

A Entering and leaving: customs

On arrival in most countries as a foreigner you have to show your passport, a **landing card**[1] and often a **customs declaration form**[2]. You may need a visa and a **vaccination certificate**[3], depending on the **entry restrictions**[4]. Customs carry out **spot checks / random checks**[5] on people's luggage. They use **sniffer dogs**[6] to search for drugs and explosives. In most cases, you have to **clear customs**[7] at the **port of entry**[8]. Genuine refugees may try to seek **political asylum**[9]. Customs officers also look out for illegal immigrants, some of whom may be **economic migrants**[10].

1 form with your personal details and date of arrival
2 form showing how much money and what goods you are carrying
3 paper proving you have had the necessary health injections
4 rules about who can enter a country and for how long
5 checks done without warning
6 specially trained dogs who can smell drugs and bombs
7 take your bags through customs
8 the port or airport where you first enter a country
9 /ə'saɪləm/ permission to stay in another country to avoid political persecution back home
10 people who try to enter from poorer countries just to get work

B Police, traffic wardens, etc.

Look at this extract from an information leaflet for students coming to study and live in an English-speaking country. Note the collocations.

For some traffic **offences**[1] you have to pay a **fixed penalty**[2], and this may be an **on-the-spot fine**[3]. **Parking tickets**[4] for illegal parking are issued by police and/or traffic wardens.

If there has been an accident, the police may ask drivers to take a **breathalyser**[5] test and to **make a statement**[6] at a police station.

Police have limited **stop-and-search**[7] powers. **Surveillance cameras**[8] operate in many public areas.

A police officer cannot normally enter your home against your wishes without a **search warrant**[9].

1 *offence* is a formal word for an illegal action
2 fixed sum payable for a particular offence
3 fine payable at the time and place that you commit the offence
4 papers placed on driver's windscreens fining them for illegal parking
5 an instrument which you blow into that shows if you have consumed alcohol recently
6 say what happened and sign a copy of it
7 power to stop people and search them in the street
8 cameras that record everything that happens
9 official permission from a judge or magistrate to search your house

C Other types of policing

name	*definition*
security forces	often a name for the army and police together enforcing the law
plain clothes/undercover police	police who do not wear uniform
paramilitary police	police who are more like soldiers than civilian police officers
drug squad	police specially trained to fight the illegal drug trade
anti-corruption squad	police specially trained to discover and fight bribery/corruption

Exercises

40.1 **Rewrite these sentences using phrases and collocations from A instead of the underlined words.**

1 You'll have to show a paper proving that you have had injections for tropical diseases when you enter the country.
2 People entering from war-torn countries often ask for permission to stay to avoid political oppression in their own country.
3 You have to take your baggage through customs if you arrive on an international flight at San Francisco airport, even if you are flying on within the USA.
4 You have to fill in a paper saying how much money you're bringing into the country before going through customs control.
5 Some of the people were people who were poor and travelling hoping to find jobs, rather than genuine political refugees.
6 *Passenger to airline cabin attendant:* Could you give me one of those papers for filling in my passport number and personal details before we arrive, please?
7 At the airport the security guards had those special dogs that can smell drugs.
8 You'll need a visa; the rules about who can enter the country are very strict.
9 You have to fill in the city where you first entered the country in this box here.

40.2 **Give possible reasons for the circumstances in which the police might do the following (based on your own country or your own experience). Some of the things are not on the opposite page. Guess their meaning or use a dictionary if necessary.**

A-Z

1 carry out spot checks on lorries
2 charge someone with drink-driving
3 tap someone's telephone
4 use their powers of stop and search
5 carry out a surveillance operation on someone's house
6 set up a roadblock
7 publish a photofit picture
8 ask you to make a statement

40.3 **What do we call ...**

1 a police officer who does not wear uniform?
2 a police force that are more like soldiers than police officers?
3 police officers engaged in combating bribery in public institutions?
4 the official paper you sometimes find stuck on your windscreen when you park illegally?
5 the police unit that fights against the illegal drug trade?
6 the police and army considered as a single body?

FOLLOW UP

If you have Internet access, look up information concerning entry and immigration formalities for different countries, which are often available in English, and note any new vocabulary.
For example, for regulations about Great Britain, see www.homeoffice.gov.uk/ind/hpg.htm or for Australia, see www.immi.gov.au

41 World views: ways of thinking

A People in relation to their beliefs

person	*definition*	*related words*
adherent (of)	a person who supports a particular idea or party	adherence, to adhere to
convert (to)	someone who has taken on a new set of beliefs	conversion, to convert
fanatic	(disapproving) someone with a very strong belief	fanaticism, fanatical
radical	someone who believes there should be extreme political change, either of a left- or right-wing nature	radicalism
reactionary	(disapproving) someone opposed to change or new ideas	reaction
bigot	(disapproving) someone with strong unreasonable beliefs who thinks that anyone with other beliefs is wrong	bigotry, bigoted

B A definition of one world view

Feminism: The modern feminist movement stems from the middle of the 1960s in North America. Basically the movement seeks equal political and social rights for women. The main theoretical **assumption**[1] shared by all branches of the movement **derives from**[2] the belief that there has been a historical tradition of male exploitation of women. Feminists are anxious to **eradicate**[3] this exploitation. Feminism is a fairly general label attached not to a set of universally accepted **postulates**[4] but to a range of beliefs with little in common, save a desire to raise **consciousness**[5] and to **usher in**[6] a more equal society.

1 unquestioning acceptance that something is true
2 has its origins in
3 abolish or get rid of
4 basic principles (verb **to postulate**)
5 awareness
6 introduce

C Other words and expressions relating to believing

credible: believable The schoolboy produced a barely **credible** excuse for arriving late.
credulous: too willing to believe what you're told
He's a **credulous** fool to believe what the management says.
incredulous: not wanting or able to believe something
I was **incredulous** when he told me he was quitting his job to go to New Zealand.
credence: (formal) acceptance that something is true
This document **gives/lends/adds credence to** Professor Ray's hypothesis.
gullible: easily tricked into believing things that may not be true a **gullible** person
ingenuous: trusting, sincere, often in a way that seems foolish
It was rather **ingenuous** of Anna to ask a complete stranger to share a taxi with her.
(im)plausible: (un)convincing a **plausible** argument an **implausible** excuse
If you (formal) **ascribe** or **attribute** something **to** someone or something, you consider something to be caused, created or possessed by that person or thing.
Many scholars **ascribe/attribute** this anonymous poem **to** Dante.
a tenet: one of the principles on which a belief is based the main **tenets** of liberalism
give someone the benefit of the doubt: to accept that someone is telling the truth even though it is not certain We should **give her the benefit of the doubt.**
If you **take something with a pinch of salt,** you do not totally believe what you are told.
You should **take** what he says **with a pinch of salt** – he's inclined to exaggerate.
If you don't believe what someone is saying you can say informally:

I don't buy that!	**What d'you take me for?**	**Pull the other one!**
A likely story!	**I wasn't born yesterday!**	**I'll believe it when I see it!**

Exercises

41.1 **Write the name of one person you know who could be described by each of the words in A.**

EXAMPLE *an adherent of the Liberal Party – my Uncle Jim.*

41.2 **Find words and expressions in the text in B meaning:**

1 has its origin in (find two expressions)
2 wants to achieve
3 very much want to
4 totally
5 variety
6 not sharing much

41.3 **Look at C and circle the correct word in the sentences below.**

1 A gullible person believes everything even if it is plausible/implausible.
2 I don't find his story at all credible/credulous.
3 When marking exams, try to give candidates the advantage/benefit of the doubt.
4 A likely/probable story! I don't believe one word you said.
5 That may be your view, but I don't buy/sell it.
6 It is better to take his promises with a pinch of salt/pepper.
7 The discovery of some ancient pieces of pottery lends consciousness/credence to the theory that there was once a Roman settlement there.
8 The play has been assumed/attributed to Shakespeare.

41.4 **Choose the best words from the box to fill the gaps in the sentences below.**

adherents	ascribe	converts	credence	eradicate
ingenuous	pinch	postulate	tenets	

1 The party claims that its primary aim is to .... poverty.
2 It has been said that .... to a religion can often be much more active supporters of the religion than people who were born into it.
3 It was rather .... of him to suggest that many criminals would hand in their illegal weapons if they were promised an amnesty.
4 One of the basic .... of Marxism is that economic relationships determine the nature of society.
5 Many of the self-professed .... of this philosophy have never even read its basic texts.
6 Historians .... the origins of this philosophy to Ancient Greece.
7 These findings lend .... to the case put forward by the government.
8 Advances in modern technology have enabled contemporary physicists to .... new theories about the origins of the universe.
9 I take anything said by an election candidate with a .... of salt.

41.5 **Write six of the words and phrases in C in a sentence that is personally meaningful for you.**

EXAMPLE *You shouldn't be so gullible and believe everything sales people tell you.*

FOLLOW UP

Use an Internet search engine such as Google www.google.com to look up a world view that interests you, e.g. feminism, Marxism, humanism, Buddhism or any -ism that you want to research. Make notes about (a) the origins of the -ism, (b) what its basic tenets are, and (c) what differences there are between its different branches (if it has them).

42 Festivals in their cultural context

A Describing festivals

Look at these short extracts about Chinese cultural festivals.

The Taipei Lantern Festival is held at the time of China's traditional Lantern Festival, which falls two weeks after the Chinese New Year and features children parading about the streets at night carrying homemade lanterns. Lanterns remain the focus of the festival. The most spectacular of all is the theme lantern at the Chiang Kai-shek Memorial Hall.

Chinese New Year's Day will normally fall between January 10 and February 19. It is the grandest holiday for all Chinese around the world and is celebrated in many ways during the course of the season, depending on your age, sex, and marital status. It celebrates the birth of a new year, a time for renewed hope.

noun	*verb*	*adjective*
There are big **celebrations** on New Year's Day.	New Year's Day **is celebrated** in many ways. The festival **celebrates** the New Year.	It was a public holiday and everyone was in a **celebratory** mood.
The festival is a time of **renewal**.	Each year, the festival **renews** the national spirit of the people.	The success of the cancer drugs gave her **renewed** hope.
The **festival** is held in March. [special day(s)/event] The **festivities** go on for days. [enjoyable activities]		There was a **festive** mood in the village during the spring holiday.
The parade in the town square was a very colourful **spectacle**.		The parade is always very **spectacular**.
Many customs have their origin in pagan **ceremonies**.		A **ceremonial** procession is held through the streets of the city.

B Other useful words and phrases connected with festivals

A lot of people are very **superstitious**, especially about numbers and colours. [have illogical beliefs about hidden forces in nature]

The festival celebrated the **centenary/bi-centenary** of the country's independence. [100th anniversary / 200th anniversary]

In some cultures, traditional festivals celebrate the end of periods of **penance** [actions to show you are sorry for bad deeds] and **fasting** [not eating for a long period].

The Rio de Janeiro carnival is always a very **flamboyant** [extremely colourful and exaggerated] and **raucous** [very noisy] event.

The Festival of the Dead was very **sombre** [serious, heavy and sad] and **atmospheric** [had a special feeling or atmosphere].

The annual holiday **commemorates** all those who died in the country's civil war. [formal: respects and remembers officially]

Exercises

42.1 **Use words and phrases from A opposite to rewrite the underlined words. Use the word-class indicated and make any other necessary changes to the sentence.**

1. For Christians, Christmas *is a celebration of* the birth of Jesus Christ. VERB
2. The *festival events* included parades, sports and musical gatherings. NOUN (plural)
3. There was a *feeling of celebration* about the whole weekend. ADJECTIVE
4. For the country people, the spring festival *symbolically renews* the fertility of the land. NOUN
5. There was an atmosphere of *ceremony* as the military bands marched round the main square. ADJECTIVE
6. People tend to be in a mood *for having a festival* when the harvest is successfully completed. ADJECTIVE
7. You should go and see the lantern festival. It's always *very spectacular*. NOUN

42.2 **Here is an extract of someone talking about a festival using rather informal language. Write it as a more formal description, using words and expressions from the box instead of the underlined words, and making any other necessary changes.**

parade	atmospheric	focus	be believed to	associate
pagan	symbolise	sombre	superstitious	flamboyant
raucous	trace			

Well, it's called the Festival of Flowers, and it's *all to do with* the coming of spring, after the *dark, serious* winter months. It *all started with* a religious tradition of taking flowers to the church to offer them to God. Spring flowers are the main *thing in* the festival, and there's always a *big gang of people marching through the streets* dressed in traditional costumes. It's all very *lively and extremely colourful* and *rather noisy*, and it *has a great feeling about it*. The flowers *mean* new life, and *people thought they would be guaranteed* a good harvest later in the year if they were offered to God. Nowadays most people *don't have such funny beliefs about nature*, but there's still a *really old, pre-Christian* atmosphere about it all ...

42.3 **Which of these important days are celebrated in your country? Make sure you can describe what people do on these days in English. Use a dictionary or encyclopedia if necessary.**

A-Z

Mother's Day   Independence Day   May Day   Valentine's Day

FOLLOW UP

Use the vocabulary of this unit to write a description for tourists of an important festival in your country, religion or culture. Try to answer the following questions: When does it fall? What does it symbolise or commemorate? What is its main focus? What does it feature? What are its origins? When does it date back to? What sort of atmosphere does it have? Remember to alternate your vocabulary to avoid too much repetition.

43 Talking about languages

A Some major world language families

Indo-European [major group of languages in Europe and parts of Asia]

family name	*examples*
Slavic	Polish, Russian, Bulgarian
Germanic	Swedish, English, Dutch
Romance	Spanish, Romanian, French
Indo-Arian	Hindu, Romany (gypsy language), Farsi (spoken in Iran)
Celtic	Welsh, Irish, Breton (spoken in Brittany, France)
Semitic	Arabic, Hebrew
Austronesian	Malay, Tagalog (spoken in the Philippines), Maori (spoken in New Zealand)

B Some technical terms for talking about your language

Syntax: the grammar and word order
How does your language express **modality**? [meanings such as possibility and necessity] English does it with **modal verbs** like *must*, *could* and *should*.

Phonology: the sound system, i.e. pronunciation and intonation
How many vowel **phonemes** does your language have? [different sounds that distinguish meanings] English has 12 and 10 **diphthongs**. [sounds made by combining vowels, such as æ and ei]

Lexicon: technical term for vocabulary
The Germanic languages have many **compounds** [words formed by combining words, e.g. *software*]. English has a mixture of **Graeco-Latin** [originally from Greek and Latin] words and **Anglo-Saxon** [language of England from 500–1000 AD] words.

Orthography: technical term for writing systems
The English alphabet has 26 **characters** [letters or symbols]. Some writing systems, such as Chinese, are not alphabetic but have **pictograms** [characters representing pictures] or **ideograms** [characters representing ideas/concepts].

Morphology: how words are formed
There are three **morphemes** in *unthinkable*: *un*, *think* and *able* [units of meaning]. The Romance languages are **inflected** [words have endings to show tense, person, etc.], while the Chinese languages are **isolating** [each word has only one morpheme].

Written accents

accent	*name*
embaraçar (Portuguese)	cedilla /sɪˈdɪlə/
für (German)	umlaut /ˈʊmlaʊt/
être (French)	circumflex /ˈsɜːkəmfleks/

accent	*name*
tomé (Spanish)	acute /əˈkjuːt/
prière (French)	grave /grɑːv/
mañana (Spanish)	tilde /ˈtɪldə/

Exercises

43.1 Say which language family these languages belong to.

1 Russian	3 Hebrew	5 Malay	7 Hindu
2 Welsh	4 Dutch	6 Spanish	8 Bulgarian

43.2 Spell these non-English words aloud in English, as in the example.

EXAMPLE coupé
You say: C-O-U-P-E acute (accent)

1 puño (Spanish)	3 grâce (French)	5 siège (French)
2 gären (German)	4 facção (Portuguese)	6 café (French)

43.3 Rewrite these sentences using more appropriate technical terms from B on the left-hand page instead of the underlined words.

1 The writing system of Burmese is quite difficult for a foreign learner.
2 Japanese uses several different writing systems with hundreds of letters and symbols.
3 The vocabulary of a language like English is constantly changing. A lot of new technical words are based on roots from Latin and Greek, rather than words from the period pre-1000 AD.
4 Unlike English, some world languages have very few vowel sounds and no combinations of vowels.
5 This ancient and beautiful alphabet uses symbols that evoke pictures to express meaning.
6 *Windscreen* is a noun made from two nouns.
7 Meanings connected with probability and obligation are expressed in different forms in different languages.

43.4 Complete the word formation table below. Use a dictionary if necessary. If your dictionary gives pronunciations, mark any differences in stress between the noun form and the adjective form.

noun	*adjective*	*change in stress?*
orthography		
lexicon		
modality		

FOLLOW UP

Make sure you can describe your own language and its main features in English, using the terms given in this unit. For information about most of the languages in the world and for learning more vocabulary for talking about languages, see *The Cambridge Encyclopedia of Language*, by David Crystal, published by Cambridge University Press.

44 History

A

Here are some terms which are useful for talking about history, especially about power in history. The meanings of the words in bold should be clear from their context.

Lord Acton said, 'All power corrupts but **absolute power** corrupts absolutely.' Historically, power in Britain rests with the monarchy. Kings and queens **succeed one another to the throne** according to the **laws of succession.** A new monarch **accedes to the throne** as soon as his or her predecessor dies. The eldest son of the current monarch is the **heir apparent** with other close relatives said to be, say, **second, third** or **fourth in line to the throne**. If the eldest son is too young to reign, then a **regent** may take his place until he reaches a suitable age. There have been times in history when a **pretender** has **laid claim to** the throne, saying that it should rightfully belong to him, rather than to the person **proclaimed king**. In other words, he is trying to **depose** that king and to **seize power** for himself. His opponents would say that such a pretender is trying to **usurp power.** If he succeeds, then the person whose place he takes can be said to **fall from power.** A person who does not use power well can be said to **abuse power.**

B

Here are some words which you will meet when reading about the past in history books or literature. They may be fairly unusual concepts for the modern world but they are all still very familiar words which are also sometimes used metaphorically about life today.

Periods

feudal: relating to a social system strictly organised according to rank, typical of e.g. Europe in the Middle Ages
medieval: of or from the Middle Ages i.e. 1000–1500 AD
Renaissance: period of new growth of interest and activity in the arts especially in Europe in the 14th to 16th centuries
Victorian: relating to the period 1837–1901 when Victoria was Queen of Britain – associated with values of self-control, hard work, loyalty, strong religious beliefs

Military

infantry: soldiers on foot
cavalry: soldiers on horseback
legion: Roman army
(**suit of**) **armour:** metal protective clothing worn by soldiers

Transport

chariot: two-wheeled vehicle pulled by a horse and used in ancient times for racing and war
galleon: large sailing ship with three or four masts used in trade and war in the 15th to 18th centuries
stagecoach: covered vehicle pulled by horses that carried passengers and goods on regular routes
cart: open vehicle with two or four wheels and pulled by an animal

People

serf: person working on the land who legally belongs to his master
jester: person who entertained people in the Middle Ages with jokes
minstrel: person who entertained people in the Middle Ages with music and poetry
highwayman: man on horseback who robbed travellers on roads

Exercises

44.1 **Look at A. Choose six of the expressions in bold that you would particularly like to learn and use them in sentences about the history of a country you know well.**

44.2 **Which of the words described in B do these pictures represent?**

1 

2 

3 

4 

5 

6 

44.3 **Here are some of the words from B used in a metaphorical way in a modern context. Read the sentences and answer the questions about the underlined phrases. The literal meanings of the words in B should help you to work out their metaphorical implications.**

1 The princess swept into the room like a galleon in full sail.
Was the princess (a) small and awkward or (b) large and stately?
2 Offering him the job before the interview is rather like putting the cart before the horse.
Is this doing things in (a) the right order or (b) the wrong order?
3 He's a very reserved person and you'll probably find it hard to penetrate his armour.
Is the person described likely to be (a) thick-skinned or (b) self-contained and retiring?
4 The company was quite feudal in its organisation.
Was the company (a) hierarchical or (b) democratic?
5 The reasons why I would never take such a job are legion.
Does the speaker have (a) a few or (b) many reasons?
6 The Chancellor is a kind of modern highwayman with his road tax.
Does the speaker (a) approve or (b) disapprove of the Chancellor's tax?
7 There has recently been a renaissance of interest in the harp.
Has interest (a) increased or (b) decreased?
8 The party is urging a return to Victorian values.
Is the party in favour of (a) hard work or (b) more women in power?

44.4 **Answer these questions about the history of your own country.**

1 Has anyone ever had absolute power in your country?
2 Has anyone ever fallen from power in a dramatic way?
3 Has anyone ever tried to usurp power?
4 Which of the words describing historical periods in B could be used about your country?
5 Did soldiers in your country wear armour and, if so, what was it like?
6 Which of the transport words in B would be most useful in talking about the history of your country? Give reasons for your answer.
7 Which of the people in B do you think you might have liked to be? Give reasons for your answer.

FOLLOW UP

For some interesting and varied articles on different aspects of history try the History Channel website at www.historychannel.com. Try, for example, the link there which allows you to discover what historical events happened on your birthday and make a note of any useful new vocabulary that you come across.

45 Poverty: the haves and the have nots

A World poverty

DEFINING POVERTY **Absolute poverty** is defined according to an absolute minimum standard, often called the 'poverty line'. **Relative poverty** means that you are poor in relation to those around you. **Income poverty** ('less than a dollar a day', for example) means that you are poor if you have less money than the defined poverty line for your country. **Human poverty** takes into account other factors, such as life expectancy, infant **malnutrition**[1], **illiteracy**[2] and lack of food or clean water.

THE RICH In 1960, the 20% of the world's people who live in the richest countries had 30 times the income of the poorest 20%; now it is 82 times. The world's 225 richest people have a combined wealth of over $1 million million. Only four per cent of this wealth – $40 billion – would be enough for basic education and healthcare, adequate food, and safe water and **sanitation**[3] for all the world's people.

• the 15 richest people have assets that exceed the total **Gross Domestic Product (GDP)**[4] of sub-Saharan Africa.

• the assets of the 84 richest people exceed the GDP of China, which has 1.2 billion inhabitants.

AIDING THE POOR The UN has set the target for overseas aid at 0.7% of a country's **GNP**[5]. Only the Netherlands and Sweden currently meet this target and the US aid budget is the lowest of all. Overall, the average aid provided by richer countries is 0.22% of GNP. If it had stayed at its 1992 level of 0.33%, it would today be $24 billion more than it is.

The majority of aid is not spent on direct **poverty alleviation**[6]. Some is 'tied' to trade deals, or **debt servicing**[7]. In 1997, debt-service payments from sub-Saharan Africa amounted to 80% of aid. Only 24.3% of overseas aid goes to the poorest countries.

1 ill health caused by inadequate food
2 inability to read or write
3 systems for taking dirty water and waste from homes to ensure good hygiene
4 the total value of all the goods and services produced in a country in one year, excluding income received from abroad
5 Gross National Product is GDP plus money earned from abroad by companies based in that country
6 reducing the level of poverty
7 paying back money owed on loans

B Other words and expressions relating to poverty

A number of artists who only became famous after their deaths spent their lifetimes in **penury.** [the state of being extremely poor]

It's a very poor country – over 60% of the population live **on** (or below) **the breadline.** [having the level of income of an extremely poor person]

The charity's main aim is to improve healthcare in **impoverished** areas of the world. [poor, without much money to live on]

Everywhere in the city you see **destitute** people living in shop doorways or under bridges. [without money, food, home or possessions]

Unfortunately the number of **deprived** children in the world is growing, even in so-called rich countries. [not having the things necessary for a pleasant life – food, home, money]

When we were first married we were **living from hand to mouth**, so it's nice to be able to spend a bit more now. [having just enough money to live without suffering]

Ever since I lost my job, **money has been tight.** [there has not been much money]

Exercises

45.1 **Do these statements reflect the points made in the article in A? Mark each one *True* or *False*. If the statement is false, correct it.**

1 Income poverty takes health factors into account as well as money.
2 If the 225 richest people in the world each gave up 4% of their wealth, there would be no poverty problems in the world.
3 15 people each have wealth that is worth more than the GDP of sub-Saharan Africa.
4 The US gives 0.7% of its GNP to overseas aid.
5 The proportion of GNP given as overseas aid is increasing.
6 More than three quarters of aid is used to pay back previous loans from richer countries.
7 Just over a quarter of overseas aid actually goes to the poorest countries.

45.2 **Choose one of the words in the box to complete each of the sentences below.**

absolute	alleviation	Domestic	malnutrition
relative	sanitation	servicing	National

1 The figure for a country's Gross .... Product will be larger than that for its Gross .... Product.
2 In countries where food is scarce, ... is inevitably a major problem.
3 Using overseas aid for debt .... does not directly help any people who are suffering through poverty.
4 The amount of money earned by someone suffering from .... poverty will be greater in a rich area than in a poor area, whereas .... poverty does not take account of a person's immediate environment.
5 The Child Poverty Action Group does all it can for the .... of poverty among children in the United Kingdom.
6 Temporary refugee camps usually have rather poor .... facilities.

45.3 **Match the two halves of the collocations. They are all used in the text in A.**

1 poverty	poverty
2 life	deal
3 overseas	servicing
4 minimum	aid
5 debt	standard
6 infant	expectancy
7 trade	line
8 income	malnutrition

45.4 **Choose the best word to complete each of these sentences.**

1 A person who sleeps in a cardboard box on the street and begs for money can best be described as <u>impoverished/destitute</u>.
2 Without my husband's income, we were very much living from hand to <u>mouth/foot</u>.
3 When we were children, money was always <u>small/tight</u>.
4 Even children with rich parents can be <u>deprived/destitute</u> in terms of love and affection.
5 An increasing number of people live below the <u>penury/breadline</u>.

45.5 **Write a paragraph about the issue of poverty in your own country.**

46 British politics

A

This text from an incisive commentator on British politics and society, Anthony Sampson, uses many words and expressions which are useful when talking or writing about politics.

Behind the public debates of parliament, the hidden pressures on government influence **legislation**[1] much more than speeches. Growing numbers of Members of Parliament (MPs) are themselves well-paid to represent commercial or special interests, sometimes more assiduously than their own **constituents**[2]. But the most powerful **lobbies**[3], like the big **corporations**[4] or the **Institute of Directors**[5], do not bother much about Members: they can go straight to **ministers**[6] and **civil servants**[7]. [...] **Lobbyists**[8] reach their annual climax when the **Chancellor of the Exchequer**[9] is preparing his **annual budget**[10] and receives **petitions**[11] from business interests pressing for **tax concessions**[12].

1 law-making (person = a **legislator**; verb = **legislate**)
2 people who elected one MP (as a group = **constituency**)
3 interest groups who try to influence MPs (verb = **lobby**)
4 large companies (adjective = **corporate**)
5 organisation of top business people
6 MPs with top responsibilities, e.g. for health, education
7 people employed in government departments (the Civil Service)
8 people who lobby (see note 3)
9 finance minister (in the UK)
10 yearly financial plan (of tax rates, etc.)
11 formal requests often signed by lots of people
12 reductions in taxes (verb = **concede**)

B

In this text Anthony Sampson looks at the relative strengths of different types of lobbyists.

The interests of **producers**[1] – **centralised**[2], **close-knit**[3] and **well-funded**[4] – inevitably win over the **consumers**[5], who are scattered and **fragmented**[6], and the most powerful pressures of all, like the road-and-car lobby, change the face of the country through backstairs pressures which are concealed from any public debate. Gradually non-commercial lobbies have also become much better organised, like **Friends of the Earth**[7] or the **Child Poverty Action Group**[8], some with hundreds of thousands of **paid-up members**[9]. Others relentlessly lobby Members of Parliament with mass-produced letters and **deputations**[10] to intimidate and encircle them. [...] They have done much to **counter**[11] big-business pressures with the help of effective publicity; but they cannot take account of **grievances**[12] of the individual, who can only **appeal to**[13] his own Member of Parliament.

1 manufacturers; a person or business that makes something (note words from same root – **product, productive, mass-produced,** etc.)
2 concentrated in one central organisation (noun = **centralisation**)
3 with close ties to each other
4 with plenty of financial support
5 people who use/buy products
6 separate; not centralised
7 large environmental organisation
8 large organisation helping children
9 people who have paid their membership fees, i.e. committed members
10 people sent to speak for a group
11 oppose
12 complaints about unfair treatment
13 request support from

Exercises

46.1 **Are these statements about the texts true or false?**

1 Parliamentary debates are the main influence on legislation.
2 Some MPs do more for big business than for their constituents.
3 The most powerful business organisations approach ministers directly.
4 Business is influential partly because it is well-organised and has money.
5 The public is well-informed about all the different lobbies.
6 Non-commercial organisations are getting better at influencing MPs.
7 The individual can do nothing if he or she has a grievance.

46.2 **Read the texts opposite and find three examples of:**

1 nouns denoting people (Text A)
2 adjectives that can be used to describe social organisations (Text B)
3 verbs that can have a strong political association (Text B)

46.3 **Find words from the texts formed from the same roots as the words in the box.**

1 commerce	3 constituency	5 consumption	7 legislate
2 mass-produced	4 petitioner	6 pressurise	8 representative

46.4 **Now match the words in the box in 46.3 to their meanings below.**

1 person standing for the interests of a group
2 person signing a formal request
3 made in large quantities
4 to make laws
5 area represented by one MP
6 to try to force someone to do something
7 amount purchased, used or eaten
8 all the activities associated with business

46.5 **Explain the meanings of these words from the texts and put them in a typical phrase.**

Text A: influence assiduously a climax press for
Text B: close-knit backstairs relentlessly intimidate encircle

46.6 **Which word from A or B also has the meaning in italics and fits the gap in the sentence?**

EXAMPLE *polite* His behaviour was ......civil......, but not particularly friendly.

1 *place where customers stand to buy things in a shop or drinks in a bar.*
Customers are requested to queue at the other end of the ....
2 *the entrance hall of a house/building* Let's meet in the hotel .... at 8 p.m.
3 *be attractive to someone* That kind of music doesn't .... to me at all.
4 *vicar* Jo married a .... and had lots of work to do helping in his parish.
5 *not criminal* Divorce cases are heard in .... courts.
6 *round piece in a game* Each player takes it in turn to move his or her ....
around the board.

46.7 **Answer these questions about politics in your own country.**

1 What processes lead to legislation in your country?
2 What is the role of debate in government in your country?
3 How powerful are (a) big-business and (b) non-commercial lobbies in your country?

FOLLOW UP

Find more political vocabulary by visiting these websites: www.number-10.gov.uk for the UK and www.firstgov.gov or www.whitehouse.gov for the US.

47 The language of law

A Legal verbs

to abrogate a law/treaty: to bring a law/treaty to an official end
to bend the law/rules: to break the law/rules in a way that is considered not to be harmful
to contravene a law: to break a law
to impeach a president/governor: to make a formal statement saying that a person in public office has committed a serious offence
to infringe someone's rights: to prevent a person doing what they are legally allowed to do
to lodge an appeal: to make an official appeal
to uphold/overturn a verdict: to say that a previous decision was correct/incorrect
to pervert the course of justice: to put obstacles in the way of justice being done
to quash a decision/conviction: to change a previous official decision/conviction
to set a precedent: to establish a decision which must, in English law, be taken into account in future decisions
to award/grant custody to: to give one parent or adult the main responsibility for a child, especially after separation or divorce
to annul a marriage/agreement/law: to declare that it no longer exists and never existed

B Crimes

crime	*meaning*	*verb*	*criminal*
discrimination	unfair treatment on grounds of sex, race or nationality	discriminate (against)	
embezzlement	stealing money that is in your care or belongs to an organisation that you work for	embezzle	embezzler
harassment	making a person feel anxious and unhappy (sometimes for sexual reasons, sometimes to get, say, a debt repaid)	harass	
insider trading/dealing	illegal buying and selling of shares by someone who has specialist knowledge of a company	do/practise insider dealing/ trading	insider trader/dealer
joyriding	driving around for enjoyment in a car you have stolen	joyride	joyrider
money laundering	moving money obtained illegally so that its origin cannot be traced	launder money	money launderer
perjury	lying when under oath	commit perjury	perjurer
trespass	go onto someone else's land without permission	trespass	trespasser

C Legal adjectives

Matters relating to, say, divorce are of course dealt with in a **civil** court rather than a criminal court. More serious criminal offences are said to be **indictable** /ɪn'daɪtəbl/, i.e. they are tried by indictment /ɪn'daɪtmənt/ in a higher level of court, while **summary** offences are less serious and can be tried in a lower level of court. If a worker feels that his or her **statutory** rights have been infringed, then he or she may take the case to a tribunal, where an arbitrator has **discretionary** powers to rule on the dispute. The arbitrator's decision is **binding** on both sides – they have to abide by his or her decision.

Exercises

47.1 Choose the correct verbs from A to fill the gaps. Put the verb in the correct form.

1 Presidents Nixon and Clinton of the USA were both ....
2 The prisoner decided to .... an appeal against the court's decision.
3 The appeal court .... the verdict of the lower court and the prisoner was released.
4 In English law any previous legal decision .... a precedent for future decisions.
5 Judges almost always .... custody to the mother rather than the father.
6 I'm not asking you to break the rules, just to .... them a little.
7 You .... my legal rights by not allowing me to vote.
8 Witnesses charged with perjury are accused of .... the course of justice.
9 The marriage was .... because the man had never properly divorced his first wife.
10 The Supreme Court .... the murder conviction and the man was freed.

47.2 Which of the crimes in B might each of these people be charged with?

1 A camper who spent a night on a farmer's land without asking permission.
2 A businessman who diverted funds from the account of the company he worked for into his own personal account.
3 Two boys who hot-wired a car and drove it around town before abandoning it. [to hot-wire means to start without using a key]
4 A witness who gave false evidence in court.

47.3 Answer these questions about the adjectives in C.

1 If someone sues you because they tripped on the stairs in your house, would the case be heard in a criminal or a civil court?
2 Would murder be an indictable or a summary offence?
3 If a contract is binding what does that mean for the signatories, i.e. the people who signed it?
4 How could a fine or other punishment be described if a magistrate is free to decide whether to award it or not?

47.4 What are the nouns associated with these words? Use a dictionary to help you.

From these verbs – abrogate contravene impeach infringe pervert
From these adjectives – indictable discretionary statutory

47.5 Choose one of the nouns you found in exercise 47.4 to complete each of these sentences.

1 The .... is read out to the accused at the beginning of a trial.
2 The magistrates can choose the most appropriate penalty at their own ....
3 Some people consider .... of others' rights as being as serious a crime as theft.
4 Many rules relating to employment are set by ....
5 The trial was criticised by many as a .... of justice.

FOLLOW UP
Find out more about the law in the UK at this website: www.leeds.ac.uk/law/hamlyn/toc.htm. Note down at least ten more useful legal words and expressions.

48 War and peace

A Changes in attitudes to war

One area in which great changes occurred in the twentieth century is in the public attitude to war and peace. The vocabulary in which war is spoken about has ceased to be one of courage, **patriotism**[1] and pride, and has instead become one of failure or of unimaginable disaster. The 'War Office' has in general become the 'Ministry of Defence'; the greatest destructive weapons ever invented have become '**deterrents**'[2]. Most people went out of the century with a view of the military 'virtues', of the place of war in a civilised society, fundamentally different from that of the nineteenth century and earlier.

The inventor of dynamite at the end of the nineteenth century believed that his invention would **outlaw**[3] war, since the devastation it could produce would make any major outbreak destructive beyond imagination. After **1918**[4] the same view was held about **aerial warfare**[5]. My childhood was dominated by the conviction that a major war would end up wiping out the cities of the industrial world. Since **1945**[6], the possibility of **nuclear annihilation**[7] has seemed to make war between the **great powers**[8] an act of collective suicide. These factors alone have contributed to a **revulsion against**[9] large-scale military operations among thinking people in all nations – though the world is unquestionably still full of national, ethnic and political **causes**[10] whose supporters see a resort to bullets and bombs as the only means of **gaining their ends**[11].

New Internationalist 1999

1 loyalty to your own country
2 ways of discouraging people from doing something because of the negative results
3 make war illegal or impossible
4 end of the First World War
5 fighting a war using aeroplanes
6 end of the Second World War
7 total destruction by nuclear weapons
8 most important political powers (used about the USA and the Soviet Union from the 1940s to 1990s)
9 feeling of total disgust towards
10 movements, organisations
11 achieving their aims

B Other words and expressions relating to war and peace

to wage war: to fight a war
hostilities: acts of war **hostilities begin / break out / end / cease**
to besiege: to attack a place by surrounding it (noun = **siege**)
to ambush: to attack unexpectedly from secret positions (noun = **ambush**)
a truce: an agreement during a war to stop fighting for a time
a ceasefire: agreement between two armies or groups to stop fighting
to rout: to defeat totally (noun = **rout**)
peacekeeping troops: neutral soldiers engaged in keeping the peace in a divided society
an international observer: outside, neutral person or body
a campaign: planned group of military activities to **plan/organise/launch a campaign**
an incendiary device: bomb They may be **placed / set off / thrown.**
germ/biological warfare: using germs to cause disease among enemy soldiers or crops

C The metaphor of warfare

The government **is waging war on** drunken driving.
Paparazzi **are besieging** the Princess's home.
A major advertising **campaign** was planned to launch the new cosmetics range.
The Brazilian football team **routed** all the others in the World Cup.
The companies **are battling to** win market supremacy.
We have **a major fight** on our hands if we are to save the company from bankruptcy.
It's time to **rally the troops** and get them to do some overtime. [call together people/workers]

Exercises

48.1 Answer these questions about the text in A.

1 How had people's view of the place of war in civilised society changed by the year 2000?
2 The inventor of dynamite was the Swedish scientist Alfred Nobel, who also founded the Nobel prizes. How does the text help to explain why he made one of those prizes a Peace Prize?
3 What twentieth-century changes in the nature of warfare does the text mention?
4 What is the connection between these changes and the general attitude to war?
5 What kind of people do not share this general attitude to war?

48.2 Complete the word formation table below based on words used in A.

	verb	*noun*	*adjective*
1		deterrent	
2		warfare	
3	outlaw		
4		power	
5			nuclear
6		revulsion	
7		annihilation	
8		cause	

48.3 These nouns in the text in A can also have rather different meanings or be used in different contexts. Write a phrase which reflects their use (a) in the text and (b) in one other context. Use a dictionary if necessary.

EXAMPLE ends – *to gain your ends; The ashtray was full of cigarette ends.*

1 area	3 society	5 outbreak	7 act
2 operations	4 cause	6 resort	8 means

48.4 Write sentences using eight of the words and expressions about war in B.

48.5 Choose a word from the box to complete the sentences below.

ambush truce bomb explode siege

1 I heard Nick .... with laughter when he saw Tom trying to dance.
2 Jane decided to .... Sam on his way out of the office and invite him to have a drink with her on his way home.
3 The winning football team have been under .... from photographers.
4 Surely we've been arguing for long enough. Let's call a ....
5 If we .... along the motorway we'll be there in under an hour.

FOLLOW UP Find out about how the UN presents its peacekeeping role by going to this website: www.un.org/peace. Note down any useful vocabulary that you see there.

49 Economy and finance

A International aid, debt and development

In a public question-and-answer session on the Internet in 1999, Clare Short, the Minister responsible for Britain's international development policies and activities, gave this answer to a question from someone in Harare, Zimbabwe.

Question: Are the UK and Europe tired of trying to **encourage real and lasting development projects** in Africa?

Answer: It may surprise you to learn that there are many **encouraging signs** in Africa. Over the last three years, 31 African countries **achieved economic growth** of more than 3% per year. Foreign direct investment, although still too small, has been rising. Africa's share in world trade has shown signs of **recovering from its long decline**. Some countries, such as Mozambique, Côte d'Ivoire, Uganda and Mauritius, have done much better than this.

But some 250 million people in Africa still live in **deep poverty*** and we must do better. With other development agencies we are committed to supporting those African governments which are **following policies** to **reduce poverty** and **improve access to** better health, education and clean water.

* **abject poverty** is also a typical collocation

Useful collocations for *debt*:

DEBT: to repay, burden, to alleviate, to incur, debtor countries, to ease, to cancel

Development grants are often given to poor regions. [money to help economic development]

Sustainable development is the most important goal for most countries. [development that does not destroy the economy/the environment, etc.]

B Trade and cooperation

Free trade agreements often cause disputes between countries, especially when one country thinks the other is engaged in **restrictive practices**[1]. Occasionally, **trade wars** erupt, and **sanctions**[2] or **embargoes**[3] are **imposed** on countries, and may not be **lifted** for long periods. On the other hand European countries closely related economically and enjoying good relations have entered into **monetary union** and have a **single currency**.

[1] the placing of unfair restrictions, e.g. limiting imports
[2] restrictions on what a country may import/export
[3] total prohibitions on importing/exporting certain goods

C Economic difficulties and negative practices

If an economy is badly affected by war, we may refer to it as a **war-torn** economy. Economies in a bad state are often referred to as **ailing** economies.

Devaluation/revaluation of the currency may be necessary. [reduction/increase in value against other currencies]

Economies may **go into recession** and not **come out of / emerge from recession** for several years. A country may suffer from a **slump in prices** for its goods [serious fall/collapse in prices]. **Fiscal measures** [measures concerning taxes, etc.] may be used to **boost the economy** [give the economy a lift] when it is in recession.

Exercises

49.1 Try to recall from memory the collocations highlighted in A. Fill the gaps in these sentences.

1 Development is important, but it should be .... development, not the kind that destroys the environment and social structure.
2 The government is .... a policy of giving aid only where it is used to .... poverty.
3 There have been some .... signs that development aid is working in many countries.
4 Millions of people still live in .... poverty. (Give two answers.)
5 The economy has .... from its decline and is now doing well.
6 The struggle to .... economic growth in developing countries is a constant one.
7 It is important to encourage .... development projects, not just short-term ones.
8 The goal should be to improve .... to better health and education for the poor.

49.2 Rewrite these sentences about international debt using more appropriate language from the opposite page to replace the underlined words.

1 Over a period of five years, the country <u>got</u> huge debts which it could not <u>pay back</u>.
2 <u>Countries in debt</u> are completely at the mercy of the rich nations.
3 <u>The weight of debt</u> is so great in some countries that their economies are collapsing.
4 Richer countries could do a lot to <u>make</u> the debt of poor countries <u>less heavy</u> (give two answers), and indeed, in some cases, could <u>forget</u> the debt altogether.

49.3 Vocabulary quiz

1 What kind of war can break out between countries concerning imports and exports?
2 Which two verbs are used with *sanctions* and *embargoes* to mean (a) 'placing' and (b) 'removing'?
3 What is the name for activities which make free trade difficult or impossible between countries?
4 What kind of union is it when two or more countries decide to share a single currency?
5 What do we call sums of money given to poor regions to assist development?
6 What can we call an economy that is devastated by war?
7 What adjective beginning with the letter 'a' can be used to describe an economy in a bad state?

FOLLOW UP

If you have access to the World Wide Web, try doing a search with the words *international aid* and see how many articles in English you can find to read. If you do not have Internet access, look in the financial pages of any English language newspaper.

50 Personal finance: balancing your books

A Cash, cheques and cards

I was **broke/skint** at the end of last month. [had no money left; broke = informal, skint = very informal]
I'm **rolling in it** this month; I got a cheque for £3,000 for some work I did. [informal: have a lot of money]
It's difficult to **make ends meet** sometimes with three children and only one parent working. [to survive financially]
Things are a bit tight at the moment. [informal: my finances are not good]
I was **strapped for cash** and had to borrow money from my parents. [informal: needed cash and had very little]
She gave me a cheque for what she owed me but it **bounced**. [the bank refused to pay it]
Who shall I **make** this cheque **out to**? [What name shall I put on it?]
Shall we **put/stick** this meal **on** my credit card? Then we can forget it. (informal)
Could you **charge** it **to** my credit card please? (formal)
The **APR** for this credit card is 23%, that's two per cent lower than my other card. [annual percentage rate of interest]
My card **expires** 05/04. [is not valid after]
Credit card fraud has increased in recent years. [illegal use of someone's card or account]

A: Is this a credit card or a **charge card**? [card where you must pay back the whole debt each month]
B: Actually it's neither. It's a **store card**. [credit card issued by a store/shop for that store]

B Savings, pensions, etc.

The words in bold in these newsclips refer to longer-term aspects of personal finances.

Victims of last year's rail crash will receive **lump sum**[1] compensation payments following a High Court decision today.

A **golden handshake**[2] of one million pounds was paid to the boss of one of Britain's biggest companies today.

Mr Carslow had taken out an **endowment**[3] ten years earlier to pay for his son's education.

The thieves stole Mr and Mrs Freal's **life-savings**[4], which they kept under their bed in a metal box.

People with well-managed **share portfolios**[5] have done better than individuals who buy stocks and shares privately.

1 single, large payment
2 large payment to someone on leaving a job
3 combined insurance and savings plan that pays out after a fixed period
4 money saved over many years
5 combination of stocks and shares of different kinds

Exercises

50.1 Complete these sentences using vocabulary from the opposite page.

1 This is a credit card. If you want one that you have to pay off each month, then you should get yourself ....
2 She never used her card on 4th September. But someone did and bought hundreds of pounds of goods. It was a case of ....
3 I haven't got enough cash to pay for this meal, but they take credit cards; shall I just .... ?
4 You'll take a cheque, will you? Good. Who should I .... ?
5 He wrote me a cheque, but he had no money in his account so it ....
6 I'm sorry, I can't lend you anything at all. I'm absolutely .... (Give two answers.)
7 I couldn't really afford it as I was a bit ....
8 I have to be very careful how I spend my money; right now things are a ....

50.2 Look at these new words and phrases which are connected with personal finances. Match them with an appropriate definition below. Use a dictionary if necessary.

A–Z

excess	loan shark	pension plan	premium	mortgage	health cover

1 The amount you pay each month or year for an insurance policy.
2 A person who lends money at extremely high interest rates to people in financial difficulty.
3 Money you borrow to buy a house or flat.
4 Money you have to pay up to a certain level if you make an insurance claim.
5 Insurance you pay against illness.
6 A scheme to provide you with an income when you retire.

50.3 Complete these sentences.

1 She got a huge golden .... when she left the company.
2 My old aunt Jessie is .... in it. Every time I go to see her she gives me £100.
3 My father got a .... sum when he retired, so he bought a weekend cottage.
4 She put her .... -savings into an Internet company and lost everything when it collapsed.
5 The bank tried to persuade me to put my money into a share .... , with shares at different levels of risk, but all managed as one package.
6 Most students find it difficult to make .... and have to take evening or weekend jobs.

50.4 Answer these questions for yourself.

1 Look in your wallet or purse. What different types of cards do you carry?
2 Give the date on which one of your cards expires.
3 What kinds of store cards do you own? Which ones would you like to own?
4 Approximately what is the current APR on your credit card?

FOLLOW UP

Go into a bank and look at what kinds of services they offer (pick up some leaflets, perhaps). Test yourself on whether you can say all the things the bank does in English.

51 The media: print

A Typical sections found in newspapers and magazines

"One thing I always read in the paper is the **obituaries**[1]; it's so interesting to read about the lives of well-known people. I also usually read the **leader**[2] (or **editorial**); it helps me form my opinion on things. Although national newspapers give you all the important news, I find that if you just want to sell your car or something, the **classified ads**[3] in a local paper is the best place. But at the weekend I just love the Sunday papers. Most British Sunday papers have **supplements**[4] with articles on travel, food and fashion and so on, and that keeps me occupied for hours. Last week there was a **feature**[5] on new technology in one of them; it was fascinating. My teenage daughter prefers magazines, especially the **agony columns**[6]. I just can't imagine writing to an **agony aunt**[7]. It amazes me how people are prepared to discuss their most intimate problems publicly."

1 descriptions of the lives of famous people who have just died
2 an article giving the newspaper editor's opinion
3 pages of advertisements in different categories
4 separate magazines included with the newspaper
5 an article or set of articles devoted to a particular topic
6 sections in a paper or magazine that deal with readers' private emotional problems
7 person, typically a woman, who answers letters in the agony column

B Some types of printed material

name	*description/definition*	*example sentence*
pamphlet	small book with a soft cover, dealing with a specific topic, often political	The Conservative Party published a **pamphlet** on the future of private education.
leaflet	single sheet or folded sheets of paper giving information about something	I picked up a **leaflet** about the museum when I was in town.
brochure	small, thin book like a magazine, which gives information, often about travel, or a company, etc.	Do you have any **brochures** about Caribbean holidays?
prospectus	small, thin book like a magazine, which gives information about a school, college or university, or a company	Before you choose a university, you should send away for some **prospectuses**.
flyer	single sheet giving information about some event, special offer, etc., often given out in the street	I was given a **flyer** about a new nightclub which is opening next month.
booklet	small thin book with a soft cover, often giving information about something	The tourist office has a free **booklet** of local walks.
manual	book of detailed instructions how to use something	This computer **manual** is impossible to understand!

Exercises

51.1 **Without looking at the opposite page, test your memory for words that mean ...**

1 the small advertisements in different categories found in newspapers
2 a person you write to at a magazine to discuss intimate emotional problems
3 the section of a newspaper which has tributes to people who have just died
4 an article in a newspaper which gives the editor's opinion
5 a separate magazine that comes free with a newspaper
6 an article or set of articles devoted to a special theme

51.2 **Fill the gaps in these sentences with appropriate words from B.**

1 I've decided to do my own car maintenance, so I've bought the .... for my particular model.
2 Someone was giving out .... in the town centre today about a demonstration that's going to take place on Saturday.
3 I love looking through holiday .... and dreaming about flying off to exotic places.
4 I never read political .... ; they're so boring.
5 This .... gives the opening times for the art gallery.
6 I've got this really useful .... with details of all the local sights.
7 I've read the .... and I like that university; I think I'll apply.

51.3 **Sort this group of eight vocabulary items into two sets of four, one connected with *books*, the other with *magazines*. Use a dictionary if necessary.**

spine jacket subscription foreword issue binder edition quarterly

51.4 **From the context guess the most likely meaning of the expressions in bold.**

1 There's a new autobiography of the footballer Micky Rawlings, but it was written by a **ghost writer.**
a) someone who didn't have Rawlings' permission b) someone who wrote it on his behalf c) Rawlings wrote it but he used a different name
2 We've decided to go into **desktop publishing** for our sports club's newsletter.
a) published by a school or college b) published only on the Internet c) published using a home computer to design it
3 This book is a **facsimile** of an original edition published in 1693.
a) an exact reproduction in every detail b) a modernised edition c) a copy made on a fax/photocopying machine

51.5 **Here are some expressions in bold not on the opposite page, which refer to how newspapers, manuals, brochures, etc. present their information. Match the sentences with the source where you would be most likely to find them. Use a dictionary if necessary.**

1 It **lists** all the requirements for entry.	a) a political pamphlet on poverty
2 It **exposes** serious problems in the industry.	b) a guarantee leaflet with a new camera
3 It **draws attention to** the fundamental issues.	c) a university prospectus
4 It **gives you the lowdown on** accommodation.	d) a newspaper article
5 It's **packed with** useful tips.	e) a tourist brochure
6 It contains a lot of **small print.**	f) a booklet about buying a house

52 The media: Internet and e-mail

A The pros and cons of Internet use

Here is a list of some possible advantages (pros) and disadvantages (cons) of the Internet.

pros	*cons*
e-mail, **instant messaging**[1], **chat rooms**[2], **newsgroups**[3]	**ISP**[9] charges can be high for heavy users
e-commerce[4] (e.g. Internet banking, travel booking)	**downloading**[10] and **uploading**[11] times can be slow
ability to send files as **attachments**[5]	**spam**[12] can be annoying
fun of just **browsing**[6] and **surfing the Web**[7]	**cookies**[13] track your activities on the Web
ability to transmit **graphic images**[8] and sound files	many sites contain pornography and other **offensive material**[14]

1 a kind of e-mail where both people are online at the same time
2 an online conversation between a group of people on topics chosen by them, where you can enter or leave the 'room' at any time
3 a website where people with shared interests can get news and information
4 all kinds of business done on the Internet
5 files you send at the same time as e-mail messages
6 looking at different websites, with no particular goal
7 moving from one website or one web page to another, usually looking for something
8 technical term for pictures, icons, diagrams, etc.
9 (pronounced I-S-P) Internet Service Provider: a company that offers users access to the Internet and services such as news, e-mail, shopping sites, etc., usually for a monthly fee
10 bringing files to your computer from the Internet
11 sending files from your computer to the Internet or to another Internet user
12 unwanted advertisements and other material sent to you by e-mail from companies
13 a kind of program that is sent from the Internet to your computer, often without your knowledge, which can follow and record what you do, which websites you visit, etc.
14 material such as pornography, or extreme political views, or material that encourages hate and violence against people

B E-mail and Internet communications

I've **bookmarked** the CNN home page as I use it regularly to get the latest news. [put it in a list of websites I can access immediately]
If you **subscribe to** newsgroups, you often get hundreds of messages. [become a member of]
Some ISPs allow you to **screen out** unwanted mail. [prevent from reaching you]
Our **server** [central computer that distributes e-mail and other services to a group of users] at work was **down** [not working] yesterday so I didn't get your message till today.
Someone **hacked into** our company server and destroyed all our files. [accessed it illegally]
Do you have good **anti-virus software**? It's worth updating it frequently. [protection against computer viruses]
She must have changed her e-mail address – the e-mail I sent her **bounced.** [came back to me]
That file you sent me as an attachment was unreadable. The text was completely **garbled.** [just a series of meaningless letters and numbers]

Exercises

52.1 Match the words and phrases on the left with the explanations on the right.

1 attachment	Internet site where people with common interests can e-mail each other online
2 cookie	unwanted web pages (e.g. advertisements) sent to you via the Internet
3 spam	company that gives you access to the Internet and offers news pages, shopping, etc.
4 chat room	program sent to your computer from the Internet, used to follow your activities
5 ISP	file sent at the same time as an e-mail message

52.2 Some of these pairs of opposites exist in the language of Internet/computer communications, others do not. Tick the box for 'exists' or 'doesn't exist'.

	word	*opposite*	*exists*	*doesn't exist*
1	delete	undelete		
2	download	upload		
3	update	downdate		
4	inbox	outbox		
5	online	offline		
6	install	uninstall		

52.3 Use the correct words from the table above to fill the gaps in these sentences. You are given a paraphrase of the meaning in brackets.

1 I sent a photo of my house by e-mail to my friend in Canada, but it took ages to .... (transfer from here to there) and I spent 20 minutes .... (connected to the Internet).
2 I've had your message in my .... (a place where unread e-mails are stored) for two days but haven't had time to read it yet.
3 I had a lot of trouble trying to .... (add to the programs already on my computer) that new software I bought.
4 How do I .... (restore something accidentally rubbed out) on this computer?
5 I write my e-mails .... (while disconnected from the Internet) and then connect to send them.

52.4 Look at these expressions taken from magazine articles and advertisements for computers and Internet services. In your own words, say what the words in bold mean.

1 A new law has given **e-signatures** the same legal status as handwritten ones.
2 **E-learning** will become more and more common as an alternative to traditional learning.
3 We have **e-enabled** everything you need to study on the Internet.
4 **E-books** are beginning to seriously compete with traditional books.
5 The **dotcom** economy has attracted hundreds of new businesses hoping to make a fortune.

FOLLOW UP

Make sure you know how to read web addresses aloud. For example, for BBC news you can access http://news.bbc.co.uk/ which is read as *H-T-T-P, colon, double-slash, news-dot-BBC-dot-co-dot-UK, forward-slash*. Note that 'co' is read as /kəʊ/, 'org' and 'com' are normally read as /ɔːg/ and /kɒm/.

53 Advertising

A

Advertisers like language that suggests their product is of *especially high quality.*

Buy our latest CD player – many **innovative** features. [original and interesting]
The design of our beds is **unsurpassed.** [the best there is]
Our cars **leave other cars standing.** [are much better than other cars]
Use our exam courses – they will **put/leave other candidates in the shade.** [make candidates from other courses seem insignificant]

B

Advertisers like language that suggests *value for money.*

Rock-bottom prices in our sale. [extremely low]
Prices **slashed!** [dramatically reduced]
Bargains galore! [a huge number of products on sale at ridiculously low prices]

C

Advertisers like language that suggests *luxury and comfort.*

Pamper yourself with our new perfume. [treat yourself to something luxurious]
Indulge yourself with the best. [allow yourself something enjoyable]
Enjoy a **sumptuous** meal in **opulent** surroundings. [Both adjectives mean rich and special: sumptuous collocates most strongly with words relating to food and furnishings, and opulent with words relating to lifestyle.]
Live **in the lap of luxury** for two weeks. [in a very luxurious way]

D

Advertisers like language that suggests *scientific backing* for their product.

Vacuum cleaner **scientifically designed** to help you exercise as you use it.
Health drink medically **proven** to boost energy levels. [shown by research]
All our computers are **state-of-the-art.** [use the very latest technology]

E

Advertisers like language that suggests their products *make us more attractive.*

Our ties will make you **stand out in the crowd.** [be noticed]
Our new lipsticks are **tantalisingly** appealing. [temptingly]
Have **fetching** feet and **alluring** ankles in our summer sandals. [both adjectives mean attractive]

F

Advertisers often use rhyme and **alliteration.** [repetition of a sound]

Women's World – Wonderfully welcome every Wednesday.

It's much less fuss to catch the bus.

G

Here are some different kinds of advertising that are common in contemporary life:

magazine and newspaper advertisements/adverts; classified ads; TV commercials; posters; **billboards** [very large boards used for advertising]; **flyers** [sheets of printed information advertising something]; **trailers** [brief excerpts from a film, TV or radio programme which are used to advertise it]; sports sponsorship; banners; **sky-writing** [words written in the sky using smoke from a plane]; **sandwich boards** [advertising posters hung at the back and front of a person who then walks around a busy area]; brochures; carrier bags; logos on clothing and other products.

In addition, personalities often use TV interviews to **plug** [advertise] a new book or film.

Exercises

53.1 **Look at A to F opposite. Complete each of these sentences with one missing word.**

1 Enjoy a weekend in the .... of luxury.
2 Don't just follow the herd – take the chance to stand out in the ....
3 Don't miss the .... bottom prices in our special May Day sale.
4 For the best in state-of-the -.............................. equipment, come to Jones and Sons.
5 Why not pamper yourself this Christmas .... our new foam bath?
6 Treat yourself .... a special taste experience.
7 Our cosmetics .... all others in the shade.
8 You'll find bargains .... in our new discount superstore.

53.2 **Here are some more phrases that are typical of advertising language. Which of the categories, A to F, do they fit into? Some of them may fit into more than one category.**

1 colossal discounts
2 fit for a king
3 eye-catchingly elegant
4 go on – spoil yourself
5 developed by a team of international experts
6 we outshine the best of the rest
7 flatteringly fashionable
8 outstanding value

53.3 **Look at G opposite. What are these examples of?**

1 

2 

3 

4 

5 

6 

7 

8 

53.4 **Look at this text of an advert. What comments can you make on its language?**

Radiance renewed

VITATONIC deep skin refresher

VITATONIC is a remarkable new cream which will nourish your skin so effectively that it becomes as soft and smooth as a child's. A special blend of natural herbs and life-giving oils, it will dramatically revitalise the texture of your skin, restoring the freshness and glow of youth. Massage in with your fingertips morning and evening and you will soon be enjoying compliments on your complexion.

53.5 **Write an advert for one of these products – a lipstick, a car or a school. Try to make use of all the features in A to F. Use some of the new vocabulary from this unit.**

54 The news: gathering and delivering

A Gathering the news

JOURNALISTS gather news in a number of different ways. They may get stories from **pressure groups**[1] which want to **air their views**[2] in public. They **seek publicity**[3] for their opinions and may hold **press conferences**[4] or may **issue a statement / press release**[5]. A person who especially wishes to attract news attention will try to include a **sound bite**[6] in what they say. It is particularly hard for journalists to get material in the **silly season**[7].

Journalists also get stories by **tapping useful sources**[8] and by **monitoring**[9] international news agencies like Reuters. The more important a story is, the more **column inches**[10] it will be given in the newspaper. Journalists of different political persuasions often **put their own gloss/spin on a story**[11] and some journalists gather stories by **muck-raking**[12].

1 people trying to influence what other people think about a particular issue
2 express their opinions
3 want to reach a wider audience
4 meetings to give information to and answer questions from the press
5 give a formal announcement to the press
6 short memorable sentence or phrase that will be repeated in news bulletins and articles
7 time of year, summer in the UK, when there is not much happening and trivial stories end up on the front page
8 making use of people or organisations which regularly provide news
9 regularly checking
10 space
11 present a story in a particular way
12 collecting scandal (informal and disapproving)

B Delivering the news

A **rag** is an informal word for a newspaper and it suggests that it is not of very high quality. The **gutter press** is a disapproving term used about the kind of newspapers and magazines that are more interested in crime and sex than serious news. A **glossy** is an expensive magazine printed on good quality paper.

Journalists produce **copy**, which has to be ready for a **deadline**. When everything is ready the newspaper **goes to press**. A very important story that comes in after going to press may find its way into a **stop press** column. A very new newspaper or story can be said to be **hot off the press**.

A story that is only to be found in one newspaper is an **exclusive**. A **scoop** is a story discovered and published by one newspaper before all the others. A major story can be said to **hit the headlines** on the day it is published. At that time the **story breaks** or becomes public knowledge. If it is an important story it will **receive a lot of coverage** or space in the press. A newspaper may be taken to court for **libel** or **defamation of character** if it publishes an untrue story that harms a person's reputation. If you are doing research into a news event, you may want to get hold of some previous issues of newspapers, or **back copies**, and you may wish to make a folder of **cuttings** from the papers about the event. ■

Exercises

54.1 **Match the two parts of the collocations used in the text in A opposite.**

1 air	groups
2 issue	conference
3 muck	bite
4 press	season
5 pressure	raking
6 silly	sources
7 sound	a statement
8 tap	your views

54.2 **Fill the gaps with words from B.**

I started my career as a journalist working as a reporter on the local .... (1) in my home town. The first thing I had to do was to take over the role of agony aunt. This was quite difficult for an eighteen-year-old boy straight out of school! Still, I managed to produce enough .... (2) and in time for my first .... (3). When that first column of mine .... (4) to press, I felt extremely relieved and was so proud that I stayed up all night so that I could get half a dozen copies .... (5) off the press for all the members of my family! I still have a copy of that first article of mine in a folder where I keep .... (6) of all the work that I am especially proud of.

54.3 **Answer these questions about the language in the text in B.**

1 Would you write to a chief editor asking for a job on 'his rag'? Why / Why not?
2 What do you think about newspapers if you refer to them as the gutter press?
3 What is it very important for journalists not to miss?
4 Can you give an example of a famous fashion glossy?
5 What two words might describe the kind of story that a journalist dreams of getting?
6 What two expressions refer to the moment of publication of a big story?
7 Which two crimes are mentioned in the text and what do they consist of?
8 What might a film star keep in her scrapbook of press cuttings?

54.4 **Rewrite these sentences so that they mean the same thing, using the word in brackets.**

1 Every newspaper inevitably gives its own particular view of events. (SPIN)
2 I have to find some articles from some previous editions of *The Times*. (BACK)
3 Read all about the royal divorce! Only just published. (HOT)
4 The floods took up more space in the papers than any other story this week. (COLUMN)
5 Politicians are always ready and willing to give their opinions to the press. (AIR)
6 The story about the scandal surrounding her uncle broke on her wedding day. (HIT)
7 Any newspaper does all it can to prevent being sued for libel. (CHARACTER)
8 Muck-raking is a characteristic activity of an inferior kind of newspaper. (PRESS)

FOLLOW UP

Here are the websites for two of the main British national quality papers. Use their search facilities to find articles on any subject that is of particular interest to you.
The Times www.thetimes.co.uk *The Guardian* www.guardianunlimited.co.uk

55 Health and illness 1

A Phrasal verbs and verb-preposition collocations for health and illness

I'm **fighting off** a cold at the moment. [trying to get rid of]
Marge isn't in today; she's **gone down with** flu. [has caught, usually a non-serious illness]
I won't be going today. I've **come down with** a dreadful cold. [with *I* we say *come down* not *go down*]
I had a virus last week, but **I got over it** quite quickly. [got better/recovered]
My sister's **recovering from** a major operation. [getting better: used for more serious illnesses]
Harry **suffers from** hay fever and sneezes a lot if he is near grass or flowers. [used for more long-term problems]
He **died of/from** lung cancer. [*Not*: He ~~died with~~ lung cancer.]

B Health systems

In Britain, **healthcare**[1] is paid for through taxes and **national insurance**[2] payments taken directly from wages and salaries. The government decides how much will be spent on the **National Health Service**[3], but a lot of people feel they do not spend enough. Hospital treatment and visits to a **family doctor** (or **GP**)[4] at a **surgery**[5] or **clinic**[6] are free, but there is a **prescription charge**[7]. Dentists and opticians charge fees. Private healthcare is available and a large number of insurance schemes exist to enable people to **'go private'**[8].

1 general expression for all of the services offered by hospitals, clinics, dentists, opticians, etc.
2 tax paid by most adults which covers the costs of healthcare for everyone
3 British name for the service that covers hospitals, clinics, dentists, etc.
4 doctor who looks after people's general heath: GP means *general practitioner*
5 small centre with just two or three doctors
6 large centre with several doctors and kinds of services
7 charge for the medication the doctor prescribes, which you pay at a pharmacy
8 choose private healthcare

C Serious illnesses and health problems

Here are some serious illnesses, with the word-stress underlined. Make sure you know the stress-pattern when learning longer words or phrases. It is a good idea to make a note of it.

dia<u>be</u>tes: disease where the body does not properly absorb sugar and starch
bron<u>chi</u>tis: inflammation in the breathing system, causing you to cough
<u>heart</u> disease: serious illness connected with the heart which can lead to a heart attack
<u>skin</u> cancer / <u>lung</u> cancer / <u>breast</u> cancer: harmful tumours in those areas
T<u>B</u> (or **tubercu<u>lo</u>sis**)**:** infectious disease in the lungs
<u>cho</u>lera: an intestinal disease that can be caused by bad drinking water
hepa<u>ti</u>tis: inflammation of the liver
<u>ty</u>phoid: fever, with red spots on the chest and abdomen
<u>heart</u> attack/failure: when the heart fails

Exercises

55.1 Which is the odd one out in each group, in terms of the main word stress? Use a dictionary if you are not sure about words which are not on the opposite page.

EXAMPLE tablets medicine prescription (answer: prescription; stress on second syllable)

1 diabetes bronchitis cholera
2 heart attack sore throat lung cancer
3 hepatitis typhoid tuberculosis
4 illness disease sickness
5 consultant doctor surgeon
6 hospital ambulance transfusion
7 heart disease surgery TB

55.2 Sort these everyday phrasal verbs and expressions connected with health and illness into two groups, depending on whether they have *positive* or *negative* meanings with regard to health. Use a dictionary if necessary.

be poorly	feel a bit under the weather	be over the worst	fight off
be on the mend	be back on one's feet again	get over	come down with

Now fill the gaps using the expressions above.

EXAMPLE [Nurse to visitor in a hospital] 'I'm sorry, Mr Pickering is rather ....poorly.... today and we're not allowing visitors.'

1 [Someone speaking to a colleague just returned to work after an illness] 'Hello, Frank, good to see you ....'
2 [Person ringing their place of work] 'Jo, I won't be in today, I've .... a cold.'
3 [Person in hospital, just beginning to get better, talking to a visitor] 'Oh, I'm OK. I'm .... now. I still feel bad, but I should be out within a week or so.'
4 [Parent to a child with a cold] 'Don't worry, darling. Everyone has a cold now and then. You'll .... it.'
5 [Someone to their partner, who is worried about them] 'Don't worry. It's nothing serious. I'm just feeling .... , that's all.'
6 [Someone ringing a workmate] 'I'm trying to .... the flu, but nothing seems to help. I don't think I'll be in work tomorrow.'
7 Hilary was quite ill last week, but she's .... now and should be back at work next week.

55.3 Which of these collocations are normal, and which are not normal? Correct the inappropriate ones.

1 Her mother died with skin cancer.
2 Is there a prescription price in your country?
3 In Britain, national security is a separate tax from income tax.
4 Healthcare is the biggest item in the nation's budget.
5 Are there insurance societies for private healthcare in your country?
6 Private dentists charge very high fees.
7 She suffers of a severe allergy and can't be in a smoky room.

56 Health and illness 2

A Minor ailments and ways of talking about minor problems

Note that **hurt** is different from **ache**:
My arm **hurts** where I banged it against the car door. [gives pain caused by an injury]
My wrists **ache** from too much typing at the computer.

The fixed expression (**the usual**) **aches and pains** is often used to refer in a non-serious way to minor problems.
A: How've you been keeping recently, Mona?
B: Oh fine, you know, just the usual **aches and pains**. (~~Just the usual pains and aches~~)

The fixed expression **cuts and bruises** can refer to minor injuries.
A: I hear you fell off your bicycle. Are you all right?
B: Yeah, fine, just a few **cuts and bruises**, nothing serious. (~~Just a few bruises and cuts~~)

Some other kinds of physical discomfort:
My hand is **stinging** since I touched that plant. [sudden, burning pain]
My head is **throbbing**. [beating with pain]

I have a **stiff neck** from turning round to look at the computer screen all day. I'll have to move the monitor to a better position. [pain and difficulty in moving your neck round]
I feel a bit **dizzy**. I think I should sit down. [a feeling that you are spinning round and can't balance]
She was a bit **feverish** this morning, so I told her to stay in bed. [with a high temperature]
I had a terrible **nauseous** feeling after taking the medicine, but it passed. [/'nɔːsiəs/ feeling that you want to vomit]
He was **trembling** all over; I knew it must be something serious. [shaking]
My nose is all **bunged up** today with this horrible cold. [blocked]

Other informal expressions that mean 'not well, but not seriously ill':
You look a bit **off-colour** today. Are you all right?
I was feeling a bit **under the weather**, so I stayed home that day.
I'm just feeling a bit **out of sorts**, it's nothing to worry about. I'll be fine tomorrow.

B Alternative medicine

Nowadays a lot of people prefer alternative medicine (different from typical western systems). For example:

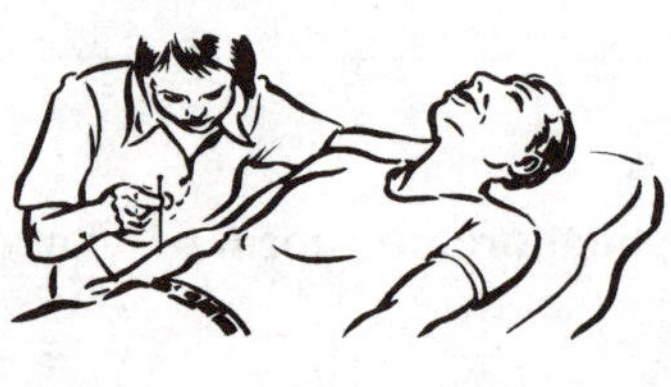

acupuncture /'ækjʊpʌŋktʃə/

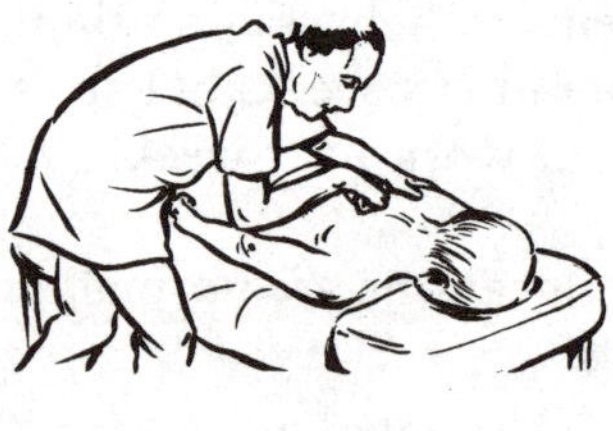

chiropractic /kaɪrəʊ'præktɪk/

herbal medicine

homeopathy /həʊmi'ɒpəθi/: taking tiny amounts of natural substances to treat an illness
aromatherapy /ərəʊmə'θerəpi/: using aromatic oils and massage

Exercises

56.1 **Correct the mistakes in these sentences.**

1 She was feeling out of the weather and a bit fevering so she took the day off.
2 I felt really off my colour yesterday and my head was throwing, so I took a tablet.
3 I felt a bit off the sorts and seemed to have more pains and aches than usual.
4 My arms are hurting after carrying that heavy suitcase of yours.

56.2 **Rewrite the underlined parts of these sentences using words and phrases from A.**

1 I was feeling quite as if I had a high temperature.
2 The drugs always gave her a feeling that she wanted to vomit.
3 I felt as if my head was spinning and went and lay down for an hour.
4 My nose was blocked so I got a spray from the chemist.
5 I got a pain in my neck from driving a long time in an awkward position.
6 Joanna was shaking and looked unwell, so I asked her if she needed help.

56.3 **Complete these sentences with words from the box. Use a dictionary if necessary.**

A–Z

dosage	prescription	allergic to	medication	symptoms	vaccinations	sick note

1 I can't take penicillin; I'm .... it.
2 Before you take those pills, read the label to see what the correct .... is.
3 I'm going abroad next month so I have to get the necessary ....
4 If you consult a new doctor you should tell him or her if you are already on any ....
5 Did the doctor give you a .... ? Do you want me to take it to the chemist's for you?
6 I told the doctor my .... , but I don't think she was listening.
7 The doctor gave me a .... for my employer. I was off work for two weeks.

56.4 **What do we call the type of alternative medicine which ...**

1 uses herbs and other natural plants?
2 uses oils which smell nice and are rubbed into your body?
3 uses needles to stick into specific parts of your body?
4 uses tiny amounts of substances which cause the illness the doctor is trying to cure?
5 manipulates your spine and bones to ease backache and other pains?

56.5 **Here are four pictures of things to do with health and medicine which are not on the opposite page. Can you match them with the labels?**

1
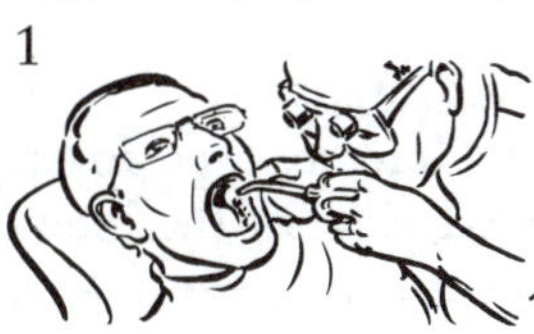
2
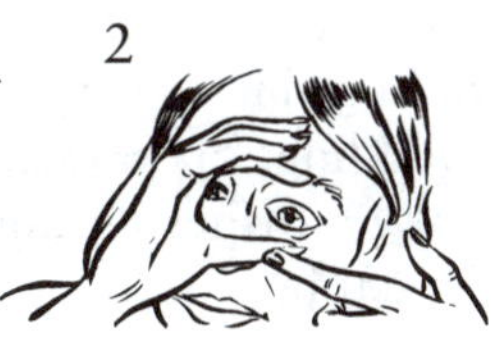
3
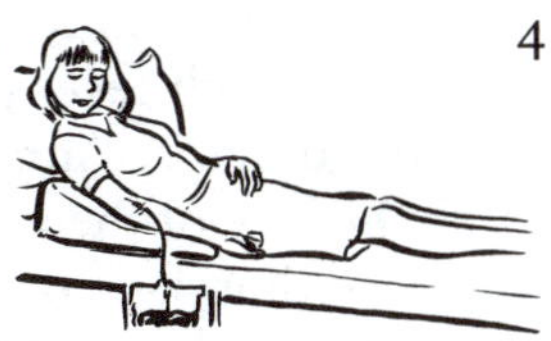
4

a) donate blood
b) have physiotherapy
c) get contact lenses
d) have a filling

57 Health and illness 3

A Medical information leaflets

Read these extracts from a leaflet contained in a packet of headache pills.

If your answer to any of the following questions is YES, then you should tell a doctor or pharmacist before taking these pills.

- Are you pregnant or breastfeeding?
- Are you sensitive to any of the ingredients in these pills?
- Do you suffer from liver, kidney or heart problems?
- Do you suffer from haemophilia [problems with your blood not **clotting**[1] properly]?
- Are you taking any other medicines – particularly for blood pressure, anticoagulants for thinning the blood, antidepressants, cortico-steroids, anti-epileptic drugs?
- Are you asthmatic?
- Are you suffering from **dehydration**[2]?
- Do you suffer from or have you suffered from a stomach **ulcer**[3]?

WARNING:
DO NOT EXCEED THE STATED DOSE

Medicines may cause unwanted **side effects**[4] in some people. If, after taking this medicine for the first time, you have an asthma attack or bronchiospasm (difficulty in breathing), gastro-intestinal haemorrhage (vomiting of blood or passing of dark, tarry **stools**[5]), stop taking these pills and consult a doctor or pharmacist.

1 forming a partly solid lump
2 not having enough water in your body
3 painful infected area on the skin or inside your body
4 unwanted effects in addition to the intended one
5 medical term for (formal) **excrement** or (informal, childish) **pooh**

B Medical metaphors

Problems and bad situations in society or other aspects of people's lives are often talked about as if they were illnesses.
The word **symptom** is often used when talking about problems in society.
The current spate of car thefts is a **symptom** of a deeper underlying problem.
This behaviour is **symptomatic** of his general lack of self-confidence.
The causes of a problem can be **diagnosed** and the outlook for a situation can also be referred to as the **prognosis** in the same way as we talk about the prognosis of an illness [how experts expect it to develop].

Here are some other examples of medical metaphors:
an **ailing** organisation [one that has a lot of problems] The economy has been **ailing** for some time, but it is hoped that the new government will improve things.
a rash of burglaries [a number of similar things happening at the same time]
World Cup **fever** election **fever** [great excitement]
at **fever pitch** to reach **fever pitch** [a point of very high intensity]
With a week to go before Anne's wedding, preparations had reached **fever pitch.**
Experts in the history of the area take a rather **jaundiced** view of the likely success of the peace talks. [unenthusiastic or sceptical because of previous bad experiences]
to **carry the scars of / be scarred by** [be permanently affected by a negative experience]
I'm afraid that children will always **be scarred by** having experienced war at so young an age.

Exercises

57.1 Complete the word formation table. Use a dictionary if necessary.

verb	*noun*	*adjective*
		pregnant
breastfeed		
		sensitive
clot		
	drug	
	dehydration	
	ulcer	
	effect	

57.2 Replace the underlined expressions with one of the metaphors from B. Make any other necessary changes.

1 Excitement grew extremely strong as the day of the final match dawned.
2 Unfortunately, a number of our investments are weak at the moment.
3 There has been a sudden large number of car thefts in our part of town.
4 Unfortunately, she is still affected in a negative way by her divorce.
5 Ralph's jealousy is a characteristic feature of a person with general low self-esteem.
6 What do you think the prospects are for the peace talks?

57.3 The medical words in the box below can also be used in a metaphorical way. Fill the gaps in the following text using these words. Use a dictionary if necessary.

paralysed	ailing	fatal	rash
disease	prognosis	fever	contagious

The country has been .... (1) by the latest rail strike, with no rail services at all running today. The railway service has been .... (2) for some time, but if today's action is prolonged it may prove .... (3) to the rail industry. The Minister for Transport commented, 'The country has been suffering from a .... (4) of local strikes since the first one in Nortown last month. It was .... (5) and one strike led to another. Things reached .... (6) pitch last week and we can only hope that this .... (7) will come to an end soon.' The minister's .... (8) is that things will only start to improve once people appreciate the seriousness of the situation.

FOLLOW UP

Learn more medical vocabulary by going to the following website which provides information on behalf of the UK National Health Service: www.nhsdirect.nhs.uk

58 Diet, sport and fitness

A Cholesterol and health

Cholesterol[1] only becomes a problem when you have too much of it and it starts to promote the production of a fatty **plaque**[2] that can clog the arteries. Interruption of blood flow to a main heart vessel can cause a heart attack; a blocked blood vessel on the way to the brain could cause a stroke.

Some say that cholesterol-rich foods such as eggs, shellfish and **offal**[3] should be banished from the diet, but these foods don't significantly raise cholesterol levels. The cholesterol in them is broken down quite efficiently and then **excreted**[4], so they are fine to eat in moderation.

Fibre[5] produces substances that help to clear the blood of bad cholesterol and acts as a '**buffer**'[6], so less fat is brought into contact with blood vessels and less is absorbed. Fibre also keeps bad cholesterol within the **gut**[7] from where it can be excreted.

1 fatty substance found in the body tissue and blood of all animals
2 unwanted substance that forms on the surface of the arteries
3 organs from inside animals which are eaten as food (brains, heart, kidneys, liver)
4 got rid of from the body
5 substance in food that travels through the body as waste, helping digestion
6 something (or someone) that helps protect from harm
7 tubes that carry food from the stomach

B Running and calories

Running, or swift walking, uses the major muscle groups, making it the most efficient form of **cardiovascular**[1] exercise. It has been shown to have a positive effect on blood fats by reducing cholesterol levels. It also lowers blood pressure and helps **diabetics**[2] by improving **glucose**[3] tolerance and reducing **insulin**[4] resistance.

Running is a very efficient way to burn calories. Converting your weight into **pounds**[5] and then multiplying the result by 75 per cent will give you the amount you burn per mile. The average is about 500 calories for every three miles. If you did this three times a week, you'd lose $\frac{1}{2}$ lb a week, 2 lb a month or 24 lb a year.

This all-round form of exercise is used in the treatment of mental illness and depression, because it is thought to raise levels of the **mood enhancer**[6], serotonin.

1 affecting the heart and blood circulation
2,3,4 people suffering from diabetes, an illness in which the body cannot cope with **glucose** [sugar] because it does not produce enough **insulin** [hormone that controls the level of sugar in the body]
5 measure of weight, 1 pound (lb) = 454 grams
6 hormone that makes you feel happier

C Sport and fitness metaphors

I **scored an own goal** when I told my boss it had only taken me a day to write the report. Now she wants me to write several a week. [made things worse rather than better]

My boss always seems to be **moving the goalposts**, which makes it very difficult to know what he wants. [changing the rules]

The new EU laws aim to provide a **level playing field** for all member states. [fair situation]

He's too young to be **in the running** for such a job. [seriously considered]

The two main parties in the election are still **neck and neck** in the opinion polls. [level with each other and equally likely to win]

Politicians often **skate around** a subject. [don't talk directly about]

The students all **sailed through** their exams. [passed very easily]

Exercises

58.1 **Answer these questions about text A.**

1 What two health problems may be caused by too much cholesterol?
2 Plaque can also form on teeth. Do you try to encourage or prevent this?
3 What do eggs, shellfish and offal have in common?
4 What sorts of food contain fibre?
5 Why is fibre useful?

58.2 **Answer these questions about text B.**

1 For what three conditions might doctors recommend running as a form of exercise?
2 How far on average does someone have to run to use up 500 calories?
3 In what way does this vary from person to person?
4 What mental health problem is also improved by running?
5 Why does running help with this problem?

58.3 **Suggest opposites for the underlined words using vocabulary from A and B.**

1 can unblock the arteries
2 glucose intolerance
3 to lower serotonin levels
4 a mood depressant
5 gentle walking
6 gain 2 lbs a week

58.4 **What sports do each of the metaphors in C come from?**

58.5 **Rewrite these sentences using metaphors from C.**

1 Sarah passed her exams without any difficulty at all.
2 I wish he'd get directly to the point.
3 I've been told that they are seriously considering me for the job of supervisor.
4 Although he meant it as a compliment, Rick didn't improve his chances with Helen when he told her she looked as if she had put on some weight.
5 The situation is hardly fair when 18-year-olds take the same exam as 15-year-olds.
6 It's hard to know what to do when the regulations seem to be constantly changing.

58.6 **These words from texts A and B can also be used in contexts different from diet and fitness. Write them in example sentences showing their use in different contexts. Use a dictionary if necessary.**

A-Z

1 interruption
2 banish
3 efficiently
4 buffer
5 vessels
6 tolerance
7 resistance
8 convert
9 burn
10 depression

58.7 **Write five pieces of advice relating to diet and fitness. In each sentence use at least one vocabulary item worked on in this unit.**

FOLLOW UP

Find a magazine article on the theme of diet and fitness. Read it and write a summary of it.

59 Aspects of industrialisation

A Processes and practices

expression	*explanation*	*opposite expression*	*explanation*
heavy industry	e.g. steel works, shipbuilding	**light industry**	e.g. manufacturing car parts, TV sets
manufacturing industry	making things; e.g. consumer goods	**service industry**	serving people; e.g. tourism, banking
high-technology (informal: **high-tech**)	involving computers; e.g. software industry	**low-technology** (informal: **low-tech**)	involving little or no computer technology
privatisation	e.g. selling off state railways to private companies	**nationalisation** or **state ownership**	when industry is owned by the government

Many big industries are run as **public–private partnerships.** [partly state-owned, partly owned by private industries or businesses]

The car industry receives huge **subsidies** from the government. [money/grants which enable it to stay in profit]

Foreign companies are often given **sweeteners** by the government to persuade them to open factories in poor or underdeveloped areas. [money/grants or tax benefits to encourage them to open a factory or business]

The government tries to encourage **inward investment.** [investment from foreign companies]

B Industrial practices

example	*explanation*
Most of the factory workers are **on piecework** which puts them under great stress.	they are only paid for the amount they produce
Child labour is a serious problem in some developing countries.	the employment of children to do adult jobs
In many countries, the right to **trade union representation** has only come after long struggles.	the right to have a union that negotiates wages and conditions
Many cheap electrical goods are produced in **sweatshops** in poorer countries.	factories where people work very long hours for low wages
The company became a **lame duck** and collapsed after five years.	weak business that loses money
The **big multinationals**[1] often close factories as a **cost-cutting exercise**[2] and **relocate**[3] and **switch production**[4] to countries where labour and costs are cheaper.	1 big companies with operations in many different countries 2 effort to reduce their costs 3 move the company's offices to a different place 4 move the centre of manufacturing to a different place, often where labour is cheaper
Industries cannot grow successfully if there is too much **red tape**.	bureaucracy, i.e. government rules and regulations
Retraining and reskilling are necessary when an economy is modernised.	training people for new jobs and teaching them new skills for things they have not done before

Exercises

59.1 **Use the expressions from the table in A to rewrite these sentences with more appropriate vocabulary instead of the underlined words.**

1 The economy cannot depend only on things like restaurants and hotels. We need to encourage industries that make things we can sell.
2 In this area there are a lot of industries that use computers and things, while in the north, they depend more on industries that don't use such up-to-date technology.
3 The idea that everything should be owned by the government is not very popular any longer, and selling industries off is the typical pattern all over the world now.
4 Industry with big factories producing things like steel and so on has declined, and now we're more dependent on industry that makes things like bicycles and furniture.

59.2 **Give words or expressions which mean:**

1 a payment or tax benefit to a company to persuade it to open a factory somewhere
2 a combination of state ownership and private ownership
3 payments or grants from the government which enable loss-making industries to continue
4 investment in a country by foreign companies
5 a weak industry that is losing money and cannot be rescued
6 bureaucracy and rules and regulations that restrict industry
7 an economy that depends on factories producing large quantities of cheap goods based on long hours and low wages
8 to change the location where goods are produced (two expressions)

59.3 **Here are some more expressions relating to problems in industry. Make sure you know what they mean, then use them to fill the gaps in the sentences below. Use a dictionary if necessary.**

black market · copyright infringement · industrial piracy · industrial espionage · money laundering

1 .... is a serious problem in many parts of the world, with factories producing illegal copies of top brand names.
2 It was a serious case of .... The designs for the new aircraft were photographed illegally and sold to a rival company.
3 .... is a problem for people who make a living writing books. Illegal editions mean that the author receives no payment.
4 .... is a huge international problem, as police and banks try to trace money from the illegal drugs trade and terrorism.
5 There is a big .... in the importation of untaxed luxury cars in some countries.

59.4 **Write a short composition of about 100–150 words describing the pattern of industrial practices in your country. Describe the labour situation, trade union rights, the right to strike, minimum wage, the role of multinationals, and so on, using as much vocabulary from the opposite page as you can.**

60 Technology and its impact

A Technical advances affecting daily life

technology	*examples of uses/applications*	*example sentence(s) with connected key words*
digital technology	digital photography, video and sound recording; digital broadcasting	The sound quality of a **digital** tape recorder is superior to that of an **analogue** [non-digital] one.
satellite communications	satellite navigation systems; mobile phones	She has an in-car **GPS** [global positioning system] navigation system, so she never loses her way.
biotechnology	genetic modification of plants	Biotechnology companies are experimenting with new, **disease-resistant** crops for farmers. [with a high level of protection against diseases]
artificial intelligence (AI)	automatic translation; identification systems	**AI** scientists are hoping to create computers that will be more and more like the human brain.
ergonomics	efficient design of human environments	This car has **ergonomically designed** seats; they're very comfortable on long drives. [designed to give maximum comfort and efficiency]

B The New Millennium Techie*

[* person who loves acquiring all the new technology]

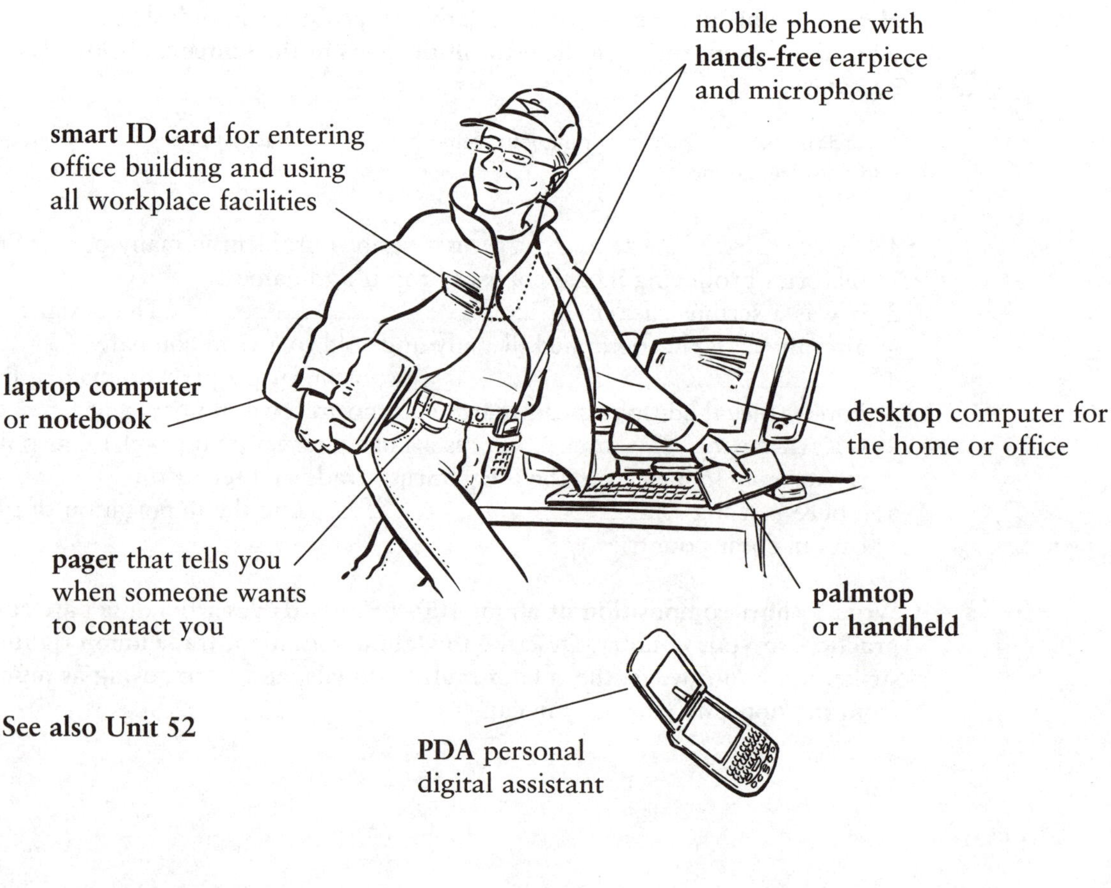

See also Unit 52

Exercises

60.1 Which type of computer is appropriate in the following sentences?

1 I've got all my friends' addresses on my .... I can just pop it into my shirt pocket; it's so convenient.
2 I've bought a new .... It's about the size of an A4 sheet of paper and it only weighs 3 kilos.
3 .... computers are small and light but the screen and keyboard are not very big and can be awkward to use.
4 I can't imagine not having a .... computer at home; I've got so used to it. It's like another piece of furniture now.

60.2 Here are some other words and phrases connected with computers. Not all of them are on the opposite page. Fill the gaps in the sentences. Use a dictionary if necessary.

A–Z

computer nerd	analogue	thumbnail	icon
screensaver	trackpad	techie	footprint

1 There are some good pictures of the Olympic Games on that sports website. You can look at .... pictures and then click on them to see the full-size version.
2 My younger brother's a real .... He never goes out, and all he ever thinks about is computers, computers, computers.
3 I'm a bit of a .... really; I love getting the latest mobile phone or the newest digital camera.
4 .... video cameras cannot match the versatility and quality of digital cameras.
5 He has a really cool .... which is a picture of planets, comets, stars and things all rushing towards you.
6 This new printer's got a smaller .... than the one I had before, which is good, since my desk is not very big.
7 Just click on that .... there to open the program.
8 I don't really like this .... on my laptop; I'd prefer a proper mouse.

60.3 Based on A on the opposite page, what types of technology would you associate with the following?

1 a round the world yachtsman/woman trying to establish his/her exact position
2 a designer creating a new type of computer keyboard which would be more efficient
3 a scientist producing a new type of wheat which does not need to be sprayed against insects
4 a camera that does not use film
5 a computer that could make decisions for itself

FOLLOW UP

The language and terminology connected with computers changes very quickly. If you want to keep up with it, read computer advertisements in newspapers and magazines, or else visit the websites of well-known hardware and software manufacturers, and note any new vocabulary and how it is used.

61 Future visions

A Technology

Some things we might see more of in the future:

smart buildings	computer-controlled buildings where things like lighting, heating, security, etc. are completely automatic; the adjective **smart** can be used for anything that is fully automatic, making its own decisions (e.g. a watch, a credit card, a camera, dishwasher, cooker)
virtual reality	computer-generated experiences that feel like the real thing; the adjective **virtual** can be used for any experience you can have without leaving your computer (e.g. a **virtual university/supermarket**)
interactive TV	TV set where you can choose exactly what to watch and when, and which can also be used as a computer for the Internet, etc.; the adjective **interactive** can be used for anything where the communication between you and the machine is two-way (e.g. **interactive video**: you do not just watch it, you can also send your own pictures)
interplanetary travel	travel to planets in outer space
e-commerce	doing business via the Internet

B The environment and nature

A **doomsday scenario** for the environment sees a world choked with pollution where many plants and animals have become extinct. [the worst possible prediction]
Traffic in cities may become **gridlocked.** [unable to move at all]
Genetic modification may be used to change fruit and vegetables so that they grow better. [changing genes] However, many people object to the idea of **genetically modified** (or **GM**) **food.** [food created by changing the genes of the ingredients]
Genetic engineering [making artificial changes to the genetic structure of organisms] and **gene therapy** [changing genes in order to prevent disease or disability] will be used to eradicate diseases, thanks to our knowledge of **the human genome** [the 'map' or index of all the genes in a human being].
Designer babies may be possible. [babies whose genetic characteristics are artificially created]
Cloning of animals, and even human beings, may become common. [making a genetically identical copy]

C Society and people

The breakdown of the traditional family structure has already occurred in some countries. In future, the **nuclear family**[1] may no longer be the main type of family unit, and more loosely defined relationships will develop. Communications and trade will be **globalised**[2]. Globalisation will also affect our relationships, how we mix and work with other people, and the world will become a **global village**[3]. We may even make contact with **extraterrestrial beings**[4]. The **gulf**[5] between rich and poor nations will widen if we do not do something about it.

1 family with father, mother and one or two children
2 cover the whole world
3 a single community covering the whole world
4 creatures from other planets
5 gap/difference

Exercises

61.1 **Match the words in the left-hand column with those in the right to make common collocations.**

1 gridlocked	reality
2 genetic	village
3 human	traffic
4 virtual	genome
5 global	modification

61.2 **What do we call ...**

1 food which has been grown by interfering with plant genes?
2 an identity card that holds every possible kind of personal information about you?
3 the experience of near-reality you can get with certain computer programs?
4 an exact genetic copy of something?
5 creatures from other planets?
6 the process of altering human and animal genes?
7 the process of treating defective genes to get rid of diseases?
8 a baby whose genetic features have been chosen by its parents?

61.3 **Rewrite the underlined words in these sentences using expressions from the opposite page.**

1 The <u>worst possible prediction</u> for human society is that we will destroy ourselves with nuclear weapons.
2 <u>Travelling to other planets</u> may become normal in the coming centuries.
3 <u>Doing business via a computer</u> will become more and more normal.
4 The team of scientists is doing research into <u>the index of all the genes in a human being</u>.

61.4 **Which words or phrases from the opposite page are associated with these sentences?**

1 These tomatoes will stay fresh for several months.
2 A typical family is often said to consist of husband, wife and 2.4 children.
3 This sheep is identical in absolutely every respect to the sheep standing next to it.
4 Doctors will be able to cure most diseases within the next one hundred years.
5 The world is becoming a very small place in terms of economics and communication.
6 Soon you'll be able to decide what you watch and when you watch it on TV.

61.5 **Only one of the following ideas is actually <u>not</u> true. Can you guess which one?**

1 A Canadian businessman is developing a way of breaking up and melting Arctic icebergs so that he can sell very pure mineral water.
2 Russian scientists want to put a vast mirror into orbit that will be half as bright as the moon, to light up dark parts of the earth (e.g. Siberia in the winter).
3 Small, low-lying islands in Florida will be raised on huge metal stilts to protect them from rising sea-levels due to global warming.
4 Computer scientists are developing fully-functioning computers that can be worn on the wrist like a watch.

61.6 **Write a short composition (about 100–150 words) entitled *My vision of the future*. Consider the future in terms of technology, the environment and society.**

62 Space: expanse and confinement

A Things occupying a lot of space

word	*typical contexts of use*
extensive	Edinburgh has extensive traffic-free routes. The building contains extensive educational facilities.
spacious	a spacious garden The city of Washington is spacious and green.
roomy	a roomy car The house was roomy.
rambling	a large, rambling building a rambling family mansion

Other words and phrases connected with occupying a large amount of space:
I like Canada because I love **wide open spaces.** [large areas without buildings or trees]
Little white cottages **were scattered** across the landscape. [covered a wide area]
The problem with this university is that the buildings are rather **spread out** and it takes a long time to get from one place to another. [not close to one another]

B Insufficient space or things occupying too small a space

word	*typical contexts of use*
cramped	cramped hotel rooms living in small, cramped apartments
poky (informal)	two poky little rooms a poky little flat
congested	tanker traffic on the congested waterway the congested streets (full of traffic, people, etc.)
compact	a tiny, compact refrigerator a compact, low, white villa

C Other words and expressions

I saw her at the carnival, but I couldn't get to her because I was **hemmed in** by the crowds. [surrounded by people and not able to move]
There **isn't enough room to swing a cat** in his flat. [informal: the flat is very small]
We were **packed in like sardines** on the bus. [informal: too many people in a small space]
The government offices are an absolute **labyrinth.** [/'læbərɪnθ/ vast and complex]
Do you suffer from **claustrophobia?** [klɔːstrə'fəʊbiə/ fear of confined spaces] My brother's the opposite; he suffers from **agoraphobia.** [ægərə'fəʊbiə/ fear of open spaces]

In these conversations, speaker B paraphrases what speaker A says. Note the verbs in bold.

A: There were 16 of us in a minibus that seated 10, and it was a long journey.
B: Yes, we were all **crammed into** that tiny space for over five hours!

A: There's not much room, is there? Can I sit between you and Mark?
B: Yes, you can **squeeze in** between us.

A: We felt as if we were in prison in that youth hostel, didn't we?
B: Yes, we all felt as if we'd been **incarcerated** for some terrible crime!

A: Shall I put all those old papers into this rubbish bag?
B: Yes, just **stuff** them all **in** and we'll take it away later.

Exercises

62.1 **Choose the most likely word from the box to fill the gaps, based on the typical contexts given in A and B opposite.**

compact	cramped	spacious	poky	extensive	roomy

1 Me live in that .... little flat! Not on your life!
2 I'd prefer a .... car on a long journey.
3 This camera is nice and .... ; you can hide it in your pocket and not look like a tourist.
4 Her mother lived in a rather .... apartment near the park.
5 The city centre is beautifully .... with many wide open squares.
6 The capital city has a(n) .... underground railway network.

62.2 **How (not) to sell a house. Imagine you are an estate agent, writing a description of a house for sale. Decide which of the underlined words is most suitable to persuade someone to buy the house. Use a dictionary for any words you are not sure of.**

Kingsmead House, Letchwood.

The property is rambling/spacious/a labyrinth, with a cramped/compact/poky garden, and is situated only ten minutes away from the bustling/congested/crowded town centre. There are excessive/extensive/expensive leisure facilities nearby. Shops, banks, restaurants and other services are located in the pleasantly designed neighbourhood. Viewing by appointment. Offers in the region of £220,000.

Ref 023DW446

62.3 **Rewrite the sentences using the words in brackets.**

1 The kitchen is so small you can hardly move in it. (CAT)
2 I feel dizzy when I'm in small, crowded spaces. (SUFFER FROM)
3 I couldn't get out of my space in the office car park the other day. (HEMMED)
4 Holidays in Australia are great if you love vast landscapes without any towns. (OPEN)
5 I hate the London Underground during rush hour. Everyone is pressing against one another in the trains. (SARDINES)
6 I dropped a glass and tiny pieces went all over the floor. (SCATTER)
7 The buildings in the holiday complex cover a wide area. (SPREAD)
8 The train was very full but I just managed to get on before the doors closed. (SQUEEZE)

62.4 **Using words from B and C opposite, rewrite these sentences.**

1 Hundreds of people spent years as prisoners in the cells of this dark, damp castle.
2 I quickly put a few clothes and a couple of books in a rucksack and set off at once.
3 She has an irrational fear of open spaces.
4 We'll all have to try and fit into my little car; Larry hasn't got his with him today.
5 I always get a terrible feeling of being trapped in a small space when I'm in a lift.
6 I don't think we should try and fit everything into one suitcase. Let's take two.

FOLLOW UP

If possible, read some descriptions of properties for sale or to rent in an English-language paper or on the Internet. Note what words are used to describe spaciousness or compactness. Alternatively, look at descriptions of buildings and landscapes in tourist literature in English.

63 Time: sequence and duration

A Colloquial expressions relating to time

We only meet **once in a blue moon.** [very infrequently]
He's spent **all his born days** in the village. [all his life]
I'll be with you **in a mo / in a sec / in a tick / in less than no time / in a jiffy**. [very soon; **mo** and **sec** are short for 'moment' and 'second']
Joe's been working here **for yonks / for donkey's years / since the year dot.** [for a long time]
We can talk about this **till the cows come home / till hell freezes over** but I'm not going to change my mind. [forever]
Are you sure he gave you the book **for keeps**? [to keep forever]
He turned up just **in the nick of time** – he very nearly missed the train. [only just in time]
He was a famous athlete but now he's **over the hill / past it.** [too old]
She was a child film star but was already a **has-been** by the age of twenty. [person who is no longer famous]
Sue did her homework **in a flash / at a rate of knots.** [very quickly]

B Adjectives relating to the passing of time

adjective	*meaning*	*collocations*
fleeting	brief or quick	glimpse/visit/smile/moment/appearance
transient	lasting for only a short time (formal)	effect/population/feeling/pleasure
persistent	lasting for a long time or hard to stop or get rid of	cough/problems/rumour/smell/ accusations/critic/offender/failure/gossip
inexorable	continuing without hope of being stopped (formal)	rise/slide/decline/pressure/ advance of time
incipient	just beginning (formal)	frustration/rage/illness/rebellion/wrinkles
pristine	unchanged from its original condition (formal)	condition/beach/image
protracted	lasting for a long time or made to last longer (formal)	negotiations/discussions/argument
lingering	taking a long time to leave or disappear	perfume/kiss/smile

C Quotations relating to the theme of time

Time is like a river made up of the things which happen, and its current is strong; no sooner does anything appear than it is carried away, and another comes in its place, and will be carried away too. (*Marcus Aurelius*)

The illimitable, silent, never-resting thing called Time, rolling, rushing on, swift, silent, like an all-embracing ocean-tide, on which we and all the Universe swim like exhalations, like apparitions which are, and then are not. (*Thomas Carlyle*)

There is no past, present or future. Using tenses to divide time is like making chalk marks on water. (*Janet Frame*)

Time is a great teacher but unfortunately it kills all its pupils. (*Hector Berlioz*)

Exercises

63.1 Put the words in the correct order to make sentences.

1 since / They've / same / living / the / house / year / the / been / in / dot
2 airport / the / the / time / to / of / We / nick / just / got / in
3 to / keeps / Sarah / it / John / for / gave
4 no / we / time / in / Together / get / less / can / done / it / than
5 never / all / He's / his / been / than / nearest / born / town / further / days / in / the
6 nick / We / hospital / got / in / to / time / the / of / the

63.2 Which of the adjectives in B would you be most likely to use to describe the following?

1 a scent that remains in the room after its wearer has left
2 a feeling of joy that is short lived
3 criticism that seems to go on and on
4 a headache that is beginning
5 sheets that are beautifully clean and starched
6 the never-ending ageing process – you can't stop its progress
7 a grin that lasts only for a moment
8 an investigation that takes a long time to complete

63.3 Match the adjectives on the left with the words on the right to make collocations.

1 lingering	beach
2 fleeting	population
3 incipient	kiss
4 inexorable	smell
5 persistent	peace negotiations
6 pristine	appearance
7 protracted	wrinkles
8 transient	advance of time

63.4 List all the words in the quotations in C which have associations with water.

63.5 Explain what each of the quotations means in simple non-metaphorical language. Then comment on why these quotations are more effective than their simplified explanations.

63.6 Rewrite these sentences using the word in brackets so that they keep the same meaning.

1 Jo's worked in the same office since the year dot. (DONKEY'S)
2 We'll be ready to leave in a mo. (LESS)
3 Most of the members of the band may be in their fifties but they're certainly not past it. (HILL)
4 You can argue with him till hell freezes over, but he'll never see sense. (COWS)
5 My grandmother's lived all her life in the same house. (BORN)
6 Kit promised he'd get here at a rate of knots and he kept his word. (FLASH)

63.7 Answer these questions.

1 Would you like to work for the same company for donkey's years?
2 What could you personally happily do till the cows come home?
3 Do you think it's a good thing to spend all your born days in one place?
4 Can you think of one thing that you do once in a blue moon?
5 What sorts of things do you do at a rate of knots and what sorts of things do you do **at a snail's pace** [very slowly]?

64 Motion: nuances of pace and movement

A

verb	*type of movement*	*reasons for type of movement*
limp	uneven	one leg hurts
hobble	awkward	shoes too tight, feet hurt
stagger	unsteady	drunk, ill
stumble	nearly falling	uneven surface
lurch	sudden or irregular	drunk, ill, walking on moving ship, etc.
tiptoe	quiet and on toes	not to be heard
amble	easy, gentle	pleasure or relaxation, no special aim
stride	long steps	purposeful
strut	proud, chest held out	to look important
tramp	firm, heavy steps	walking for a long time
trample	pressing repeatedly with feet	often wishing to destroy
stamp	pushing foot down heavily	anger, or just heavy-footed
trudge	heavy, slow, with difficulty	tired
chase	quickly	wanting to catch something or someone

B

Many of the words above can be used in metaphorical [non-literal] ways too.

The maths lesson **limped** to a conclusion and everyone thankfully left the room.
Tony's business **staggered** on for a few years and then finally collapsed.
Jane did **staggeringly** well in her exams. [amazingly]
The government has **lurched** from one economic crisis to the next.
Maria **takes** everything that life throws at her **in her stride.** [takes … calmly]
Parents and teachers should try not to **trample** on children's dreams.
If the Campbells don't pay their bill this week, you'll have to **chase** them.
Although the economy seemed to be **stumbling** last year, it has made a perfect recovery now.

C

Words used about the movement of water can be used about the movement of people.

Crowds of tourists **flowed** across the square all day long.
As soon as the school doors opened, children **spilled** out into the playground.
People **streamed** into the lecture hall and soon there was standing room only.
People have been **pouring** into the exhibition all day.
A **trickle** of people had already appeared outside and by midday a crowd had gathered.
We **meandered** round the town, window-shopping to our hearts' content.
Refugees have been **flooding** across the border since the start of the war.

D

Here are some adjectives often used with **taking (a) step(s)** in a metaphorical context.

backward big critical decisive first giant
major significant unprecedented [never having happened before]

Exercises

64.1 The walking verb in each of these sentences is incorrect. Which verb would be a better choice for each sentence? Look at A to help you.

1 The tramp strutted wearily homeward, his shoulders hunched in the rain.
2 The mother trudged across the bedroom, doing her best not to wake the baby.
3 Those tight shoes with their ridiculously high heels are making her amble.
4 Ever since he had an accident last year, he has stamped a bit.
5 The drunken men strode unsteadily out of the pub at closing time.
6 Please try not to stumble on the daisies – they look so pretty in the grass.
7 The little dog tramped after the postman and caught his trouser leg in his teeth.
8 The sea was so rough that even the sailors were tiptoeing around the decks.

64.2 Answer these questions about the sentences in B opposite.

1 How successful and enjoyable was the maths lesson?
2 Did Tony's business come to a sudden end?
3 Did people expect Jane to do so well in her exams?
4 Did the government seem to take each crisis smoothly and in its stride?
5 What kind of person do you think Maria is?
6 What do parents and teachers do to children's dreams, if they trample on them?
7 How exactly might this person chase the Campbells?

64.3 Look at the water words in each of the example sentences in C. What does the word suggest about the way the people in those sentences are moving?

64.4 Use the water words in C in sentences that illustrate the movement of water or liquid.

64.5 Complete these sentences in any appropriate way.

1 Rudi took his first steps towards becoming a doctor today when he ....
2 .... was a very significant step for humankind.
3 Yesterday the British government took the unprecedented step of ....
4 It was a big step for me to ....
5 I think you took a backward step when you ....
6 The business took a critical step today when it ....

64.6 Here are some more verbs of movement. Complete a table for them like the one used in A opposite. Use a dictionary if necessary.

verb	*type of movement*	*reason for type of movement*
file		
saunter		
sidle		
glide		
mill around		

64.7 Which of the verbs in exercise 64.6 would these people probably do?

1 graceful dancers
2 guests at a cocktail party
3 schoolchildren going into class
4 someone who is irritatingly anxious to make you like them
5 tourists exploring in a relaxed way

65 Manner: behaviour and body language

A Manners

When I was a child, gentlemen used to raise their hats to female acquaintances on the street and I was taught to **mind my Ps and Qs**[1] and to give up my seat for my **'elders and betters'**[2] on the bus. Now I am grown-up, no one either raises their hat to me or offers me a seat on a crowded bus. It's as if **courtesy**[3] itself is now a thing of the past! Some might call it **prim** or **starchy**[4] to hanker after an old-fashioned code of **etiquette**[5], but things must somehow have been pleasanter when people tried to behave in a **gentlemanly** or **ladylike**[6] way. I don't believe that people observed the **social graces**[7] just because they were anxious about doing **the done thing**[8]; it was more a matter of being considerate to others and **oiling the wheels of**[9] social interaction. So, let's stop being **offhand**[10] with each other and **stand on ceremony**[11] just a little bit more.

1 make an effort to be polite
2 people older than you
3 politeness (adjective = **courteous**)
4 very formal and correct; without humour (other words for this are **strait-laced** and **prissy**)
5 formal rules of behaviour
6 polite in a rather formal way
7 polite behaviour
8 informal phrase for 'socially acceptable behaviour' (opposite = **not the done thing**)
9 making easier
10 casual, slightly rude
11 insist on formal behaviour

B Body language

Research shows that we communicate more through body language than we are aware. Here are some examples of how we indicate emotion through body language.

verb	*what it indicates*	*comment*
flutter your eyelashes	flirting	used of female behaviour towards a man
raise your or others' eyebrows	surprise or shock (either showing or causing)	either a person or behaviour can raise eyebrows
twitch	nervousness	repeated small movements with part of the body
flinch	pain or fear	sudden small movement
squirm	embarrassment or nervousness	move from side to side on your chair in an awkward way
smirk	self-satisfaction	smile (negative associations)
beam	happiness	broad smile (positive associations)
sniff at something	disapproval	you also sniff when you have a runny nose
snort	disgust or great amusement	make an explosive sound by forcing air quickly up or down the nose
titter	nervousness or embarrassment	small laugh

Exercises

65.1 **These adjectives from A in the box below have either *positive* or *negative* associations. Write them down in two lists – positive and negative.**

prissy	offhand	gentlemanly	ladylike	starchy	strait-laced

65.2 **Match the words on the left with the words on the right to make collocations.**

1 code	graces
2 elders	thing
3 give up	on ceremony
4 mind	the wheels
5 oil	your seat
6 social	and betters
7 stand	your Ps and Qs
8 the done	of etiquette

65.3 **Look at B and answer these questions.**

1 *Priscilla fluttered her eyelashes at Rob.* Why might she do this?
2 *Joe was twitching all evening.* Do you think he was relaxed?
3 *Jane sniffed at every comment I made at the meeting.* How did Jane feel about my comments?
4 *Jack flinched when I touched his arm.* Why do you think he flinched?
5 *The children's language on the bus raised a few of the other passengers' eyebrows.* What must the children's language have been like?
6 *Look at the photo. Meg's smirking and Tanya's beaming.* Who does the speaker think looks nicer – Meg or Tanya?
7 *There was an occasional titter at the comedian's jokes.* Do you think the comedian was pleased at how his jokes were received?

65.4 **Circle the best of the two underlined words to complete each of these sentences.**

1 Willy sniffed/snorted with laughter all through the play.
2 Whenever I'm tired or nervous, my eyelid starts to twitch/flinch.
3 Sit still and don't squirm/smirk like that.
4 Who's Mary fluttering her eyebrows/eyelashes at now?
5 The dentist stopped drilling as soon as he felt me flinch/snort.
6 Please don't titter/sniff – here's a box of tissues!

65.5 **Here are some more verbs associated with manner. What does each set have in common? Use a dictionary to help you.**

A–Z

1 snigger, chortle, guffaw, giggle
2 glower, scowl, frown, glare
3 gawp, ogle, scan, leer
4 whimper, sniffle, sob your heart out, grizzle

FOLLOW UP

Find out more about social situations and rules of etiquette and the language used to describe them at www.bartleby.com/95/. Note down any interesting vocabulary items you find there.

66 Sound: from noise to silence

A Adjectives indicating lack of sound and their collocations

word	*definition/explanation*	*example*
silent	without noise or not talking; used for people and things that are perhaps unexpectedly or surprisingly quiet	They asked him several questions but he remained **silent**. The house was completely **silent**. Note also: **silent films/movies** [films made before sound was introduced]
quiet	without much noise or activity, or not talking much	It's very **quiet** here at night. [no noise] I had a **quiet** day at the office. [not much activity] My father was a **quiet** man. [didn't speak a lot]
noiseless	without noise; usually used as an adverb in formal or literary style	He closed the door noiselessly behind him. [with no sound at all]
soundless	without sound; usually used as an adverb in formal or literary style to indicate an unexpected lack of sound	The object vanished **soundlessly** into the night sky. Was it an alien spacecraft?

B Less common verbs for specific noises

The door **slammed** in the strong wind. [closed with a loud bang]
My bike wheel is **squeaking**. I'll have to put some oil on it. [high, irritating noise]
We could hear the disco music **pounding** through the walls. [dull, beating sound]
The old wooden door **creaked** as I opened it. [noise of friction of wood and/or metal]
The sausages **sizzled** in the frying pan and smelt delicious. [sound made by frying]
A shot **rang out** and the bird fell from the sky. [typically used for the sound of a gunshot]
From our cottage, we could hear the waves **crashing** on the beach in the distance. [loud, heavy noise, typically used for waves]
He always **hoots/toots** his horn to let us know he's arrived. [sound made by a car horn]
In Rio you can hear police car sirens **wailing** all night. [making a rising and falling sound]
She **hammered** at the door but nobody answered. [knocked very loudly and repeatedly]

C Some expressions for noise and silence

There was an **eerie** silence in the old church. [rather scary]
The noise of the aircraft engines was **deafening**. [extremely and painfully loud]
He has one of those **grating** voices that gets on my nerves. [unpleasant, irritating]
She let out a **piercing** scream and fled as fast as she could. [high noise that hurts the ears]
Molly has a very **high-pitched** voice; it can be a bit irritating at times. [a constantly high level]

D Some fixed expressions connected with noise and silence

Everyone was so shocked and silent **you could have heard a pin drop**. [there was total silence]
Hey you kids! Be quiet! **I can't hear myself think!** [said when people are making too much noise]
I need **peace and quiet** after a busy day at work. [calm and quiet period, after a noisy time]
You're **as quiet as a mouse**! I didn't hear you arrive at all. [very quiet indeed]

Exercises

66.1 **Fill the gaps with appropriate forms, adjectives or adverbs, of the words *silent*, *quiet*, *noiseless* or *soundless*. Only *silent* may be used more than once.**

1 He closed the jewel-encrusted box .... and left the room without waking the two sleeping figures in the bed.
2 It's very difficult to find a .... place to live nowadays, even in the countryside.
3 Charlie Chaplin's .... films are as funny today as they were in the 1920s.
4 The great bird flapped its wings and rose .... into the evening sky.
5 The women kept up a .... protest in front of the laboratories.

66.2 **Write a sentence which could come immediately before the following sentences, using verbs from the box and the word(s) in brackets, as in the example.**

~~slam~~	pound	creak	crash	sizzle	ring out	toot	squeak	wail

EXAMPLE (door) The door slammed loudly.
The wind must have blown it shut.

1 (shot) ....
Somebody was firing at the birds on the lake.
2 (door) ....
It was very old, made of oak and difficult to open.
3 (music, walls) ....
It was as if the musicians were playing in our bedroom.
4 (chicken, frying pan) ....
The sound and the smell made me even more hungry.
5 (rusty door hinges) ....
I think they need some oil.
6 (horn) ....
I looked out of the window and saw her car parked outside.
7 (waves) ....
It was wonderful to be so near the sea.
8 (police sirens) ....
There must have been an accident, or perhaps a robbery.

66.3 **Which adjective can describe the following? (One letter from the correct answer is given.)**

1 An extremely loud noise, e.g. very loud music ....f..........
2 A strange, almost scary silence ....r..........
3 A high noise that hurts your ears ....c..........
4 A harsh, irritating kind of voice ....g..........
5 A voice that always sounds very high ....p..........

66.4 **Complete these expressions.**

1 It was so quiet you could have ....
2 I've had some noisy, hectic days with all those kids, now I'm looking forward to some ....
3 Turn that music down! I can't ....
4 I don't even notice that Jack is in the flat sometimes. He's ....

67 Weight and density

A Synonyms for heavy

There are a number of adjectives similar in meaning to *heavy*. Note their typical contexts.

adjective	*typical contexts*	*example*
weighty	abstract and physical things; usually includes the idea of 'seriousness'	a **weighty** tome [large book] discuss **weighty** issues
unwieldy	abstract and physical things; usually includes the idea of 'difficult to handle'	**unwieldy** discussions an **unwieldy** object [e.g. a big box]
cumbersome	often used for machines and equipment that are difficult to handle; also used for systems, structures, etc.	a **cumbersome** weapon a **cumbersome** procedure
burdensome	usually used of abstract things	a **burdensome** duty
ponderous	usually used of abstract things, 'serious', but with more of a negative connotation	a **ponderous** tone of voice a **ponderous** thesis
lumbering	usually used of physical things; often suggesting 'heavy movement'	a **lumbering** truck **lumbering** reptiles

B Phrasal verbs with weigh

I hate being **weighed down** with heavy suitcases when I travel. [carrying very heavy things]
She looked tired and **weighed down** with problems.
We'll have to **weigh up** the alternatives before deciding. [consider and compare]
She **weighed out** a kilo of nuts and put them in a bag. [weighed a quantity of loose goods]
I have to confess something to you. It's been **weighing on me** for ages. [troubling my mind]
The discussion was getting heated, and then Jean **weighed in** with some uncomfortable financial arguments. [added more points to the argument]

C Making things more/less dense

You can put some flour in to **thicken** [make thicker] the soup, but you should **sift** it [shake it in a sieve to separate the grains] first, or it will go **lumpy** [have solid pieces in it].
The soup has been in the fridge so long it's all **congealed**. [become thick and solid]
This curry powder is years old. It has completely **solidified** in the packet. [become solid]
Do you have some white spirit? I need to **thin** this paint. [make thinner]
This fruit juice is very strong. I could **dilute it / water it down** a bit, if you like. [add water]
As the rush hour ended, the traffic began to **thin out**. [become less dense]
The hairdresser **thinned** my hair **out** and it feels much lighter now. [made it less thick]

D Adjectives connected with density

The jungle was nearly **impenetrable**, so progress was slow. [impossible to move through]
The bomb shelter has an **impermeable** barrier that protects the occupants from radiation. [no liquid or gas can pass through]
This glue works even on **impervious** materials like glass and steel. [liquid cannot pass through]

Exercises

67.1 **Based on the typical contexts in A, use the words in the box below to fill the gaps in the sentences.**

lumbering	cumbersome	weighty	unwieldy	burdensome	ponderous

1 It's a rather .... system. I wish they would simplify it.
2 He gave a very .... lecture on economic history that just bored everyone.
3 They spend hours drinking coffee and discussing .... political matters.
4 A great .... horse and cart was blocking the road, and no one could overtake it.
5 She had so many .... obligations; her life was not her own.
6 The advancing troops were slowed down by their ...., old-fashioned equipment.

67.2 **Fill the gaps in these diagrams with a word from A that could collocate with all three nouns.**

1 .... dinosaur / vehicle / goods train

2 .... fax machine / procedure / suitcase

3 .... encyclopedia / topic / issue

4 .... tone of voice / sermon / narrative

67.3 **Correct the wrong uses of phrasal verbs with *weigh* in these sentences.**

1 I weighed on a kilo of the flour and then added water to it.
2 He's very irritating. When you're trying to have a rational discussion, he always has to weigh through with his own selfish point of view.
3 I owe Gerry £150; it's been weighing over my mind for weeks. I must pay him.
4 We were weighed up with huge suitcases and bags, and the airport was terribly crowded; it was a nightmare.
5 I have to weigh in the various options before I decide which job to accept.

67.4 **Answer these questions.**

1 What does a hairdresser use *thinning-out* scissors for?
2 If there is dense fog, then it gets even denser, what verb could you use to describe the change?
3 What happens if you leave some coffee in the bottom of your cup for about a week?
4 What does 'Do not use undiluted' mean on the instructions on a bottle of medicine? What must you do before taking it?
5 What could you use a sieve for in cooking?
6 If someone is impervious to insults, is it easy to upset them by calling them stupid?
7 Is aluminium permeable or impermeable?
8 If someone says a book is 'impenetrable', what do they mean?
9 What do you think it means to say that someone's philosophy is 'rather lightweight'?
10 Which verb can be used to describe a situation where heavy traffic is becoming less?

68 Colour: range and intensity

A Words and expressions for specific colours

pitch black: intensely black, used about darkness, night, etc. (**pitch** is an older word for tar)
jet black: intensely black, used about hair, eyes, etc. (**jet** is a black semi-precious stone)
scarlet: brilliant red, the colour of traditional British letter boxes
crimson: strong deep red
shocking pink: an extremely bright pink
ginger: orangy red, used about hair and cats
navy: dark blue, used about clothes, not eyes
turquoise: greenish blue, used about fabrics, paint, sea, etc. but not usually eyes
beige: a light creamy brown
mousy: a light not very interesting brown, used only about hair
chestnut: a deep reddish brown, used about hair and horses
auburn: a red-brown colour, usually used about hair

B Words for talking about colour

Red, blue and yellow are **primary colours**, by mixing them together you can make other colours. **Pastel colours** are pale shades of colour – pink, **mauve** [pale purple] and pale yellow, for example. **Strong colours** are the opposite of pastels. **Vivid colours** are strong, bright colours like scarlet or turquoise. **Fluorescent** colours are very bright colours which seem to glow in the dark. **Electric** blues or greens are extremely bright blues or greens. If white has a **tinge of** green, there is a very slight shade of green in it. If something is **monochrome**, it uses only one (or shades of one) colour, e.g. black, white and grey. The suffixes **-y** and **-ish** show that a colour is partly present, e.g. **bluey green, reddish brown.**

C Colour metaphors

blue = depression (to **feel blue**); pornographic or indecently referring to sex (**blue movie, blue joke**); physical or unskilled (**blue-collar workers**)

red = anger (to **see red** = to be very angry); danger (**red alert**, a **red flag**); special importance (The royal visitor was given **red carpet** treatment. The day we met will always be **a red-letter day** for me.); left-wing in politics (**red point of view**)

green = nausea (to **look green**; People who are seasick often **turn/go green** and sometimes vomit.); envy (She turned **green with envy** when she saw her friend's diamond engagement ring.); care for the environment (**green tourism**; the **Green Party**)

black = depressing or without hope (a **black future**); anger (to look **as black as thunder**); illegality or incorrectness (**black market, black sheep of the family, black mark**).
During the war people bought many goods on the **black market**. If I don't finish this report in time, that'll be another **black mark** against my name.
My brother was the **black sheep** of the family and left home at seventeen.

grey = lack of clarity (a **grey area**); brains (**grey matter, grey cells**)

white = purity (**white as snow, whiter than white**); being pale (She was afraid and went **white as a sheet**; a **white knuckle** [terrifying] ride at a theme park); office workers (**white-collar workers**)

Exercises

68.1 Look at A and answer these questions.

1 Which four of these colours can be used to describe hair?
2 Which three of these colours might be used to describe an animal?
3 Which of the shades of red would you be most likely to use about the sky at sunset?
4 Which four of these colours are the most vivid?
5 Which of the blue and brown colours are used about shoes?
6 What colour is the traditional London bus?
7 Would you prefer to have mousy hair or auburn hair? Why?
8 When you are outside at night and you can't see, how can you describe the darkness?

68.2 Look at C. Match the situation on the left with the response on the right.

1 That child looks a bit green.	No, they make me feel sick.
2 He's always in a blue mood these days.	Yes, it's not at all clear what we should do.
3 That TV programme always makes him see red.	Yes, but they need qualifications.
4 It's a bit of a grey area, isn't it?	I think he's going to be sick.
5 They seem to be trying to blacken his name.	Yes, they want to do their bit for the environment.
6 Do you like white knuckle rides?	Yes, he can't stand the presenter.
7 White-collar workers earn more.	Yes, ever since his wife left him.
8 They're going to vote for the Greens.	I wonder what they've got against him?

68.3 Look up the colours below in an English learner's dictionary. Write down any new and useful expressions in example sentences of your own.

black white red blue yellow green

68.4 Advertisers often use exotic words with special associations to indicate colour. Look at the words in the box and answer the questions. Use a dictionary if necessary.

magnolia	strawberry	violet	ruby	emerald
burgundy	forget-me-not	jade	amber	cornflower
poppy	sapphire	turquoise	lime	coral

1 Which of the words in the box refer to precious or semi-precious stones?
2 Which of the words in the box refer to flowers?
3 Which of the words in the box refer to food or drink?
4 Which of the words in the box would be used to describe pastel shades?
5 Divide the words in the box into the basic colours that they refer to:
pink/red *blue* *green* *other* (specify colour)
6 Which two of the precious stone words are most likely to be used to describe the sea?
7 Which two of the flowers words is a romantic novelist most likely to use to describe his heroine's eyes?
8 Which of the words are (a) purplish red (b) creamy white and (c) yellowy orange?

68.5 Choose ten words or expressions that you particularly wish to learn from this unit and write them down in sentences of your own.

69 Speed

A Going fast

These verbs suggest going somewhere very quickly on foot or by a means of transport – **race, dash, tear.** I **dashed/raced/tore** to the station just making it in time for the last train.

These verbs also suggest fast movement but are used mainly for going short distances – **nip, pop, zip, dart, whizz.** I **nipped/popped/zipped/darted/whizzed** into the post office to buy some stamps and came out only to see my bus disappearing into the distance.

The verb **bolt** also suggests fast movement over a short distance but it also has the added association of running away from something. The frightened horse **bolted** across the field.

The verb **career** suggests that something is moving rapidly and is out of control. The car skidded and **careered** down a bank. The company seems to be **careering** into financial ruin.

These verbs – **scamper, scurry, scuttle** – suggest small rapid steps, often of lots of small animals together. As we went into the dark shed, we saw mice **scampering** away and spiders **scurrying** into corners. Cockroaches **scuttled** into a crack in the floor.

These verbs emphasise the fact that speed is increasing – **speed up, accelerate. Accelerate** is used only about transport whereas **speed up** can also refer to movement on foot. Both verbs can be used figuratively. We'd better **speed up** if we're going to get there on time. The growth of the company has **accelerated** since it started exporting.

B Going up or down fast

These verbs suggest a downward movement as well as speed – **plunge, plummet.**
He put on a lifejacket and **plunged** into the icy water.
Notice that they are mainly used metaphorically. When export sales began to decline, our hopes of business success **plummeted.** After the death of his father, he was **plunged** into despair.

These verbs suggest a fast upward movement – **soar, rocket.** Notice that they are mainly used metaphorically and have strong associations with financial matters such as prices and share values. When export sales **rocketed** our hopes of success **soared.**
The primary association of **soar** is with birds and when it is used about people's feelings it provides associations of happiness and carefreeness.
My heart **soared** when I heard that he was coming home.
The opposite of **soar** and **rocket** in a financial context would be **slump** or **tumble.** Both suggest a rapid downward movement. Shares **slumped** on the stock market yesterday with telecommunication companies **tumbling** most dramatically of all.

C Going slowly

These intransitive verbs emphasise that the movement is slow – **crawl, creep.** They are often used metaphorically.
Prices have been **creeping** up since May. It was rush hour and the traffic was **crawling.**

Totter also suggests a fairly slow movement but it is one that is particularly unsteady as well. Mary **tottered** down the road laden with parcels and bags.

Sidle means to walk anxiously and nervously.
Sam **sidled up to** the boss's desk and coughed to attract his attention.

Dawdle means to move more slowly than is necessary. Don't **dawdle** on the way home.

Exercises

69.1 **Answer these questions.**

1 Would you be more likely to dash to the shops if you had plenty of time or if you were in a hurry?
2 If a car accelerates, does it speed up or slow down?
3 If you stop to look in shop windows, are you scampering or dawdling?
4 If traffic is said to be crawling, is it moving freely or is there a traffic jam?
5 If you plan to sell some shares, would you prefer their price to rocket or to tumble?
6 If a woman is wearing particularly high heels, is she more likely to scurry or to totter?
7 If a car slips on ice, is it more likely to be said to career or to dart across the road?
8 Who do you think is feeling more confident – a person who races up to greet you or someone who sidles up to greet you?
9 If you are thinking of buying your first flat, would you prefer the price of accommodation to be creeping up or to be soaring?
10 We sometimes say that people bolt their food. Does this mean that they eat fast or slowly?

69.2 **Would you be pleased or not to read the following headlines in your newspaper?**

1 Taxes rocket in new budget
2 Shares plunge in uncertainty over US presidency
3 Economy totters on the brink
4 Hopes soar for more Olympic medals
5 Profits plummet
6 Jobless figures creep up

69.3 **Which do you think is the best verb to fill each of these gaps?**

1 When the car suddenly swerved to avoid hitting the dog, it .... out of control and crashed into a tree.
a) popped b) bolted c) careered d) dashed
2 When she switched the bathroom light on she was horrified to catch a glimpse of cockroaches .... away into cracks in the tiles.
a) plummeting b) scuttling c) creeping d) nipping
3 I'm going to .... into town in my lunch hour. Can I get you anything?
a) bolt b) plunge c) totter d) nip
4 If you don't ...., you'll miss the bus and be late for school.
a) accelerate b) rocket c) speed up d) crawl
5 Meena's spirits .... when she learnt that she had won first prize.
a) plunged b) soared c) zipped d) tore
6 When the boy saw the fierce dog, he .... into the house.
a) darted b) careered c) tottered d) bolted
7 I'm just going to .... to the letter box to post these letters.
a) scurry b) totter c) plunge d) pop
8 Richard .... into the house, trying hard not to wake his parents.
a) soared b) crept c) scampered d) accelerated

69.4 **Do you notice anything about the form of these words – *race, dash, tear, nip, zip, pop, dart, bolt*? Can you suggest why this form fits the meaning?**

70 Cause and effect

A 'Cause' verbs and their collocations

The differences between these verbs is best learnt by observing their typical collocations.

Cause usually collocates with negative results and situations.
The new computer system has **caused** us a lot of problems.
His stomach cancer was **caused** by exposure to atomic radiation.

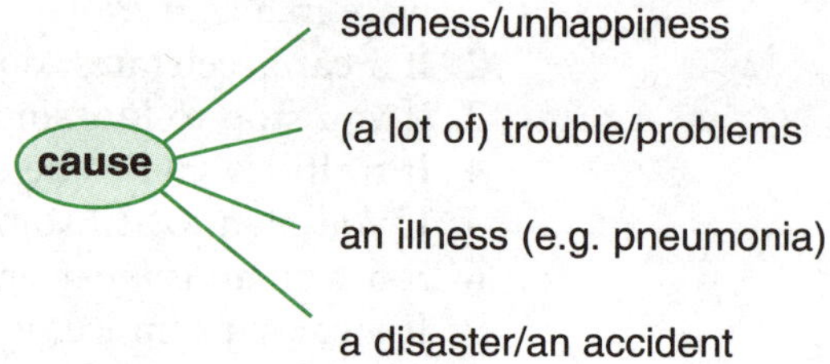

Produce is more neutral, and deals with more concrete results. It is used in formal contexts.
Scientists can **produce** statistics and figures that can prove almost anything.
In low light conditions, a fast film will **produce** the best photographs.

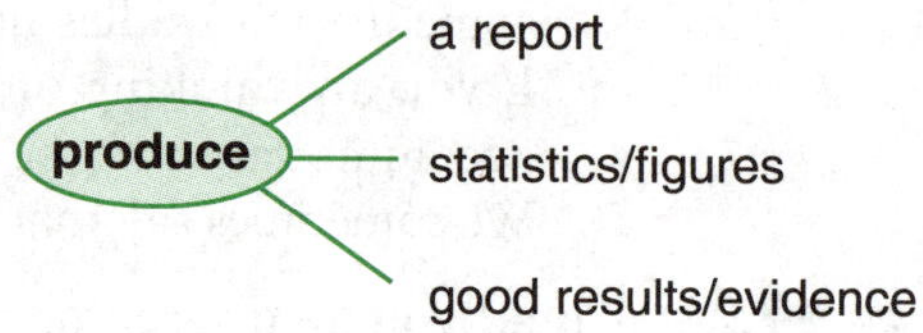

While *cause* usually collocates with negative situations, *give* can be used for positive or negative ones. *Give* is less formal than *cause*.
Our dog has **given** us a lot of pleasure over the years.
This car is **giving** me so much trouble, I'm going to get rid of it.

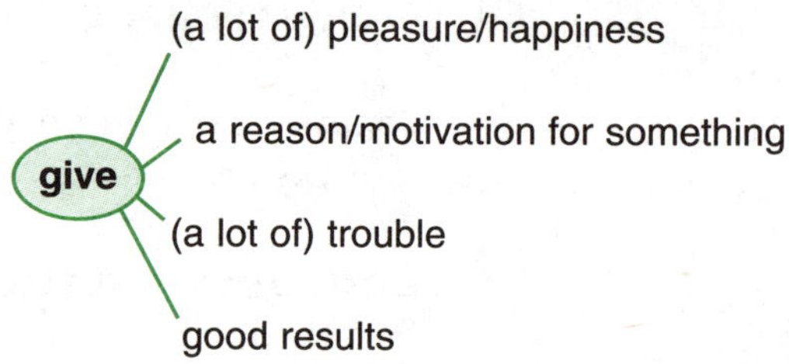

Generate is often used in contexts where people are forced to do more than usual, and in computer contexts. It sometimes has a rather negative feel. It is used in formal contexts.
It's going to be difficult to **generate** sufficient interest in the project.
The government will have to **generate** the extra funds somehow or other.

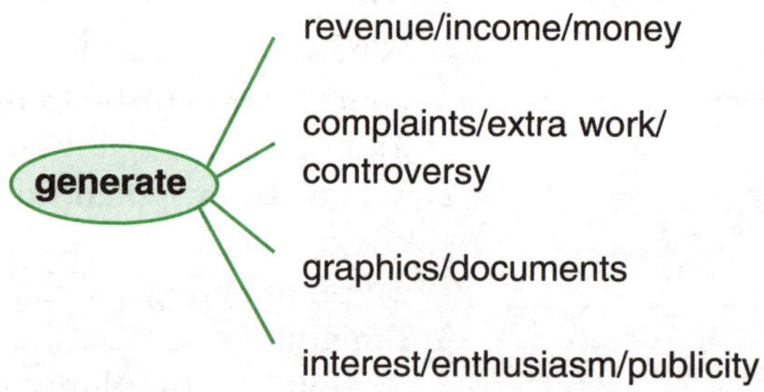

General comment: *Cause* and *give* are often used for things happening without people doing anything: The hurricane **caused** terrible damage.
Produce and *generate* usually suggest some sort of intervention by people:
His presentation **generated** a lot of interest in the project.

B Other 'cause' verbs

The news **provoked** a feeling of despair in everyone.
The events in the north **precipitated / sparked off** a political crisis. [quickly/suddenly caused]
The invention of the car has **brought about** great changes in our lives. [gradually produced]
Your action has **resulted in** a formal complaint from a member of the public. [produced]

Exercises

70.1 Decide which verb from the opposite page best fits each gap. There may be more than one possible answer.

1 The decision by the government to relax the regulations has .... a lot of investment in the poorer regions.
2 We need to .... a list of names and addresses by six o'clock tonight.
3 Her death was .... by a sign falling from a shop front in the heavy winds.
4 The Governor's remarks almost .... a full-scale war between the two regions.
5 His stupidity .... in none of us being able to get home that night.
6 Your letters have .... me so much pleasure. Please don't stop writing them.
7 The book .... a lot of anger amongst female readers.
8 I don't necessarily want to .... a crisis, but I have some bad news to tell you all.

70.2 Use a dictionary to look up these 'cause' verbs which are not on the opposite page. Write a sentence illustrating the meaning of each one.

incite   prompt   induce   breed

70.3 Rewrite these sentences using a more formal connecting expression from the box to replace 'because of'. There may be more than one possible answer.

thanks to	as a result of	owing to	due to	as a consequence of

1 Because of the crash on the motorway, all traffic is being severely delayed.
2 We got there in time, because of your advice.
3 My computer crashed, because of which I lost all the data.
4 Because of one bad decision after another, he's lost all his money.
5 The flight was cancelled because of bad weather.

70.4 Use any of the words and expressions from the opposite page to connect the events in the left-hand column with those in the right-hand column, as in the example.

EXAMPLE Scientists **have produced** statistics showing a direct link between smoking and cancer.

1 scientists	stunning images and graphics
2 the higher taxes	statistics showing a direct link between smoking and cancer
3 icy roads	the breakup of his marriage
4 a brave bank assistant	endless problems and involved me in a lot of expense
5 my old car	two robbers were in jail last night
6 this software	riots in three cities
7 jealousy	a number of serious accidents this week

70.5 Think of something in your life which has ...

1 caused you a lot of problems.
2 given you a lot of happiness.
3 provoked a feeling of anger in you.
4 resulted in embarrassment for you.

71 Comparison and contrast

A Talking about similarity

key word	*collocation*	*meaning*
affinity	I often feel there is a cultural **affinity between** London **and** New York. I **felt an affinity with** the writer as I read this novel.	closeness; feeling that different things/people have much in common
akin	Their music is more **akin to** that of the Beatles than to the Spice Girls.	similar in spirit/feel
analogy	To **use** a sporting **analogy**, middle-age is like half-time at a football match.	see similarities that help us understand something
correspond	The picture this news article paints **does not correspond to** the truth.	is not equal to/does not match
equate	It's a mistake to **equate** the price of something with its true value.	consider as the same
tantamount	She knew that to apologise would be **tantamount to** admitting she had failed.	the equivalent of (normally used in negative contexts)
interchangeable	The goals of the two sides in the war have become almost **interchangeable**.	so similar that they could be exchanged one for the other
indistinguishable	Mrs Burton's shop was **indistinguishable from** all the others in the street.	so similar you cannot see the difference

B Talking about difference: adjectives with di-

adjective	*contexts/comments*	*example*
diverse	used of different types of something	The **diverse** ethnic groups living in Malaysia give the country its cultural richness.
disparate	used of different types within a group, but emphasises separation and difference	The **disparate** regions of Spain all have unique customs and cultures.
dissimilar	very often used with *not*	This house is not **dissimilar** to the one I was born in.
divergent	often used of contrasting opinions or ideas	They have widely **divergent** opinions.
distinct	used to describe differences where one might be deceived by similarities	The Swedish and Norwegian languages are quite **distinct** from one another, even though they look similar when written.
discrete	different and separate, not overlapping	There are several **discrete** categories of verbs in English.

Exercises

71.1 **One of these words is followed by a different preposition from the rest. Which word is it and which preposition does it need?**

akin correspond dissimilar distinct tantamount

Now use the words above and their prepositions in these sentences.

1 The state of Maine in the USA is not .... parts of Scandinavia. They both have lakes and forests.
2 To pretend I didn't want to be with her would be .... telling a lie.
3 What you say .... what I've heard too. I am sure it's correct.
4 His life story is more .... a novel by Charles Dickens than a James Bond film.
5 The culture of the north of the country is quite .... that of the south, and it's a mistake to think they are the same.

71.2 **Fill in the missing words.**

1 There is a close affinity .... Singapore .... Hong Kong: both are crowded, vibrant cities existing in a confined space.
2 I just cannot feel any affinity .... his poetry; it's too dark and cruel.
3 This version of her essay is indistinguishable .... the first version. I can't see any changes.
4 It would be a great mistake to equate his shyness .... coldness or unfriendliness.

71.3 **How many words can you remember from B which begin with *di-* and which refer to differences? Can you complete the list?**

1 disp.. 3 diss.. 5 div..
2 div.. 4 dist.. 6 disc..

71.4 **Circle the more suitable alternative. Each word should be used only once.**

1 Japanese and Korean culture are quite diverse/distinct, even though, to the outsider, they often appear similar.
2 The way they weave carpets in this region is not dissimilar/divergent to the way they are made in neighbouring countries.
3 English verbs do not always fit very easily into dissimilar/discrete categories. For instance, is the verb *used to* an ordinary verb or a modal verb like *would*?
4 Seen from the widely disparate/divergent viewpoints of left and right, the problem either originates in too much freedom or in too much state control.
5 It would be very difficult to unite the disparate/discrete tribes and ethnic groups to form one coherent political force.
6 Her CD collection contains quite a divergent/diverse selection of music, with everything from classical to heavy metal.

72 Difficulties, dilemmas and hitches

A Nouns relating to difficulties

Fairly small difficulties: **a snag** **a hitch** **a setback** **a glitch**
Glitch usually refers to a technical problem of some kind. The other words are more general.

More important difficulties:
A **stumbling block** is something that prevents action or agreement.
A **pitfall** is an unexpected difficulty (often used in the plural).
An **obstacle** is anything that stops progress, either literally or metaphorically.
An **impediment** is something that prevents free action, progress or movement.
A **dilemma** is a situation where a difficult choice has to be made between two, sometimes unpleasant, alternatives.
An **ordeal** is a severe experience, which is very difficult, painful or tiring.

More formal words meaning difficulty: **adversity** **hardship** **affliction** **tribulation**

B Adjectives relating to difficulty

adjective	*meaning*	*collocations*
abstruse	difficult to understand	theory, argument, philosopher
arduous	difficult, tiring, needing much effort	climb, task, journey
complex	difficult to understand as it has many parts	issue, problem, theory, process
convoluted	unreasonably long and hard to follow	explanation, sentences, theory
gruelling	extremely tiring and difficult	journey, work, match, expedition
insufferable	difficult to bear as it is annoying or uncomfortable	behaviour, heat, boredom, pain
obstructive	causing deliberate difficulties	person, measure
stiff	difficult to beat	opposition, competition
tough	difficult to deal with or do	time, job, climate, decision
traumatic	shocking and upsetting	experience, past, childhood
wayward	changeable, selfish and/or hard to control	behaviour, child, person

C Colloquial expressions relating to difficulties

Oh dear, more homework! **What a pain! / What a drag!** [What a nuisance!]
What's eating him? / What's got into him? / What's bugging him? / What's (up) with him? [What's the matter with him?]
I can't face the **hassle** of moving house again. [situation causing trouble or difficulty]
My daughter keeps **hassling** me for a new bike. [pestering, asking again and again]
to slog (your guts out) / to grind / to graft / to flog yourself to death [to work hard]
in a fix / in a spot / in a hole / up against it / up to one's neck [in a difficult situation]
The company's in a **sticky/tricky** situation now the workers are going to strike. [difficult]
I think I'm **off the hook / in the clear / out of the wood(s)** now. [freed from a difficult situation]

Exercises

72.1 Choose the best word from the box to complete the sentences. Put the word in the plural if necessary.

dilemma	glitch	hardship	impediment
ordeal	pitfall	snag	stumbling block

1 Jane is caught in a terrible .... – should she go abroad with the man she loves or take the promotion she has at last been offered at work?
2 At first there were some .... with the software, but it's OK now.
3 Women in wartime also have to face a great deal of ....
4 The hostage is writing a book about his six-month ....
5 The proposal is very good. The only .... is that it is a little expensive.
6 Ian used to have a speech .... but he's overcome it and is now an actor.
7 The leaflet gives new businesses information about typical .... to avoid.
8 Negotiations were going well until the issue of sick pay became a major ....

72.2 Which of the adjectives in B might you use to describe:

1 a pupil who deliberately makes it hard for his teacher to continue with the lesson
2 opposition in an election that has very strong arguments and public support
3 an accident which affects the victim psychologically
4 a book that deals with very difficult ideas without simplifying them
5 a child who is very disobedient and self-willed
6 pain that is almost impossible to put up with
7 a speech that is very difficult to follow because the line of argument is very complex
8 an exhausting Arctic expedition

72.3 Fill in the gaps in this conversation using words from C.

A: What's got .... (1) you, Paul? You look really fed up!
B: Oh, I don't know. I've been slogging my .... (2) out at work and it's all getting too much. My wife says I should leave rather than go on flogging myself to .... (3). But I really can't face the .... (4) of looking for something else at the moment.
A: What a .... (5)! I'm also in a bit of a .... (6).
B: Why? What's up .... (7) you then?
A: I'm in a .... (8) situation at home. My landlord's threatening to put the rent up. It's so difficult to find anywhere else to live. Still, at least my Italian exam is over.
B: Great! How did that go?
A: Not bad. It's a great relief it's over. I hope you soon get through all your work and begin to feel off the .... (9) soon.
B: Thanks. I think I'll feel out of the .... (10) when this project is over.

72.4 Answer these questions about difficulties.

1 When have you been in a dilemma? What were the choices that were facing you?
2 Give an example of a project you were involved in that suffered a setback.
3 Can you name someone who has triumphed over adversity? Explain your answer.
4 What obstacles have you had to overcome in your life so far?

73 Modality: expressing facts, opinions, desires

A

Here are some useful expressions based on modal verbs.

I must admit/confess/say that I didn't enjoy the film.
You want me to lend you £1,000! **You must be joking!**
You **must have been frightened/worried/nervous/happy, etc.** when you heard the news!
Don't look so miserable – **it may/might (well) never happen!**
What, may/might I ask, was the point of throwing your pen on the floor like that?
I was just glancing out of the window when **who should I see but** the boss.

A: Why are you so gloomy? The interview didn't go that badly. **You still might** get the job!
B: **I should be so lucky!** [That is not likely!] All the other candidates were better qualified.

Don't worry about spilling the wine. **Accidents will happen!** [accidents are inevitable]
The car **won't start.** What can I do?
That'll be John making that noise. He always plays his music very loud.

B

Here are some ways of expressing probability.

The odds are he'll get the job. [it is likely that]
The odds are against her passing the exam. [it is unlikely that]
They **are bound to** get married in the end. [almost certain to]
He's **likely to** call round this evening.
It's **probable/likely/certain/inevitable** that they'll come and visit us at the weekend.
In all probability we'll get the job finished on time.
The chances are small that people will be living on the moon in the next decade.
There's every likelihood that the price of petrol will rise soon.

C

Here are some ways of expressing advice.

If I were in your shoes / in the same boat, I'd ...
[if I were in the same situation]
Let me give you a tip/hint/suggestion/some pointers.
I hope you'll take this in the spirit in which it is intended,
but you really should have checked the boat first.
It would be advisable/sensible/expedient/advantageous/prudent/wise to ... [formal]

D

Here are some ways of expressing obligation and lack of obligation.

It is **essential** that you (should) take strong footwear with you.
Wearing a safety helmet is **obligatory** in this area.
The road was blocked. We **had no option** but to turn back.
It is **compulsory** to put the lights out by ten o'clock.
We **have an obligation to** preserve the school's good name.
Some courses are **optional** but Maths and English are **compulsory.**

E

Here are some ways of expressing a desire to do something.

I am **determined/anxious/eager/resolved** to do whatever I can to help.
He **wishes/desires/yearns/longs** to return home.
She has **ambitions/aspirations** to become Prime Minister.

Exercises

73.1 **Look at A. Match the situations on the left with the responses on the right.**

1 Are you going clubbing tonight?	Shall I have a look at it?
2 I've just handed in my notice.	They must be very happy.
3 The car won't start.	You must have been terrified.
4 You might find buried treasure.	It'll be the Patels.
5 I'm afraid I've broken a cup.	What, may I ask, was the point of that?
6 Jane and Joe have just had twins.	I should be so lucky!
7 Someone's at the door.	You must be joking! I'm much too old.
8 I only just managed to escape.	Don't worry. Accidents will happen.

73.2 **Rewrite these sentences using the words in brackets.**

EXAMPLE Sandra'll probably get the job. (LIKELIHOOD) *In all likelihood Sandra'll get the job.*

1 You must put on a life jacket. (OBLIGATORY)
2 I expect that Harry'll take over his father's job. (ODDS)
3 You should apologise to him at once. (SHOES)
4 You must do what the police officer says. (OPTION)
5 I'm sure they'll settle down eventually. (BOUND)

73.3 **A friend of yours has an important job interview tomorrow. Complete these pieces of advice in any way you like.**

1 If I were ....
2 I hope you'll take this in the spirit in which it is intended ....
3 Let me give you one ....
4 It would be sensible ....
5 It would be wise to ....

73.4 **Write down four rules for a school using the words in brackets.**

1 (essential) ....
2 (compulsory) ....
3 (optional) ....
4 (obligatory) ....

73.5 **Complete these sentences using the appropriate form of the words in brackets.**

1 Jill caused her parents a lot of .... when she was a teenager. (ANXIOUS)
2 The town council expressed their .... to do what they could to help ease the traffic problems in the city. (DETERMINE)
3 The poem is about the poet's .... for his lost innocence. (YEARN)
4 Did you make any New Year's .... this year? (RESOLVE)
5 Her Majesty is .... that you attend her in the throne room immediately. (DESIRE)
6 Her .... to please is very touching. (EAGER)
7 She would have enjoyed her year abroad more had it not been for her .... for her boyfriend at home. (LONG)
8 There's no point in talking about what you might do if you went on a trip around the world. It's just .... thinking. (WISH)

74 Number: statistics and assessing quantity

A Some surprising numbers

- 3,000 = **recorded sightings**[1] of UFOs by military and civilian pilots
- 200,000,000 = the number of people who could be **sustained**[2] by the food eaten by the world's **rodents**[3] each year
- 450,000 = plastic containers flung into the world's seas every day
- $97,000,000 = hourly world **expenditure**[4] on military activity
- 4 = **factor**[5] by which nitrogenous fertiliser use increased between 1960 and 1981 in the USA
- 102 = the average **IQ**[6] of 7–8 year olds who were breast-fed
- 92 = the average IQ of 7–8 year olds who were not breast-fed
- 177 = estimated world population increase **per**[7] minute

1 times seen that have been officially written down
2 kept alive or supported
3 small animals including rats, mice, squirrels
4 spending
5 number by which another number or quantity is multiplied; here fertiliser use **quadrupled** (= ×4)
6 intelligence quotient (measure of intelligence; average IQ = 100)
7 for each (used when expressing rates, prices or measurements)

B Describing statistics and numbers

When the different amounts were added up, the **aggregate** was £600,000. [total]
I've **aggregated** all the figures. [added up all the different amounts]
The Chancellor said the July rise in inflation was only a **blip**. [temporary change]
The spectrum is a **continuum** of colour from red to violet. [something that changes gradually or in very slight stages, without distinct divisions]
There seems to be a **correlation between** mathematical and musical ability. [connection between facts or things which cause or affect each other]
For some reason the July figures have **deviated** from the norm. [moved away from the standard or accepted pattern]
There's a **discrepancy between** our figures and yours. [difference between two things that should be the same]
Share prices have been **erratic** this last month. [not regular and often changing suddenly]
The company's figures were found to be **flawed** and the accountant was fired. [inaccurate]
Sales **fluctuate** from day to day. [go up and down]
There's been a five-**fold** increase in exam enrolments. [multiplied by the stated number]
The teacher said that the quality of her students' work was **in inverse proportion to** its quantity – the shorter the essay the better. [in opposite proportion to]
Our data is **inconsistent with** yours. [not in agreement with]
Interest rates **seesawed** all year. [went up and down]

C Assessing quantity

Let me give you a **ballpark figure**[1] of how much money we expect to make this year. If I **tot everything up**[2], we begin to **run into six figures**[3]. There are a lot of **variables**[4] and our **projected figures**[5] may not be all that accurate. So I've **erred on the side of caution**[6] and I've **rounded things down**[7] rather than up in order to give you a **conservative**[8] estimate.

1 guess believed to be accurate
2 add everything up (less formal)
3 get a figure over 100,000
4 different factors that may change
5 planned figures
6 been cautious
7 make, say, 2.5 into 2 rather than 3
8 cautious

Exercises

74.1 Choose a word from A to complete each of these sentences.

1 Another .... of an Unidentified Flying Object was reported last night.
2 .... are small mammals with long, sharp front teeth.
3 Sales didn't double or even triple last year, they ....
4 Some psychologists believe that tests which claim to measure a person's intelligence .... are not a test of true intelligence.
5 Most countries' .... on the army is higher than that on schools.
6 There are said to be 554 people .... car in India.
7 His salary was not enough to .... his wife and five children.
8 Expenditure on disposable nappies is greater by a .... of seven per average British woman than per average Spanish woman.

74.2 Rewrite these sentences using the words in brackets so that they keep the same meaning.

1 The two reports of the accident appear to be inconsistent. (DISCREPANCY)
2 The value of the shares has quadrupled. (-FOLD)
3 There seems to be a negative correlation between job satisfaction and educational achievement. (INVERSE)
4 The water levels didn't go up and down as much as we'd expected last year. (FLUCTUATE)
5 I don't need to know all the individual figures – just give me the total. (AGGREGATE)
6 His moods change – one minute he's happy, the next he's depressed. (ERRATIC)

74.3 Answer these questions.

1 If you give someone a ballpark figure, is it (a) precise or (b) rough?
2 If you round up 68.7, does it become (a) 69 or (b) 68?
3 If you want to give a conservative estimate when forecasting profits, would you prefer to (a) underestimate or (b) overestimate your figures?
4 If your weekly wage (in dollars) has just run into four figures, how much do you earn?
5 If you tot up all the numbers between 1 and 10, what do you get?
6 Name two variables that might affect a soft drinks company's projected profits.

74.4 Complete the word formation table below. Do not fill the shaded boxes.

verb	*noun*	*adjective*
deviate		
	discrepancy	
		flawed
		inverse
		inconsistent
err		

FOLLOW UP

If you are interested in maths, follow up some links at this maths-oriented website. Try, for example, the Tower of Hanoi puzzle which you will find in the section of games and puzzles.
www.cut-the-knot.com/content.html

75 Permission and prohibition

A Permitting and agreeing that something may happen: verbs

All these verbs are formal and many are taken from newspapers. Note the prepositions in bold.

verb	*meaning*	*example*
accede	accept, but often associated with an initial unwillingness to accept something or give permission	The Prime Minister has **acceded to** demands to release secret documents about the recent war.
acquiesce /ækwi'es/	permit something to happen, but often associated with a degree of secrecy or conspiracy	The Foreign Minister **acquiesced in** the plan to restrict imports from certain countries.
assent	agree to something, often associated with plans, proposals, ideas, etc.	Britain has **assented to** a proposal to enlarge the European Union.
authorise	give official permission	The university has **authorised** the use of dictionaries during language examinations.
condone	approve or allow something which most people consider to be wrong	The judge **condoned** the use of reasonable force by the police officers who arrested the man.
countenance	consider giving assent or permission, often used in negative contexts	No government would ever **countenance** abolishing taxes altogether.
endorse	give official approval to something	The cabinet has **endorsed** a proposal to change the way universities are funded and managed.

B Permitting: phrasal expressions

The committee have been **given carte blanche** to investigate the problem and come up with a solution. [/kɑːt'blɑːnʃ/ formal: complete freedom to do whatever they think necessary]
The City Council has **given the go-ahead** for the new car park. [informal: given permission for the building to start] *Or:* The City Council has **given the green light** to the new car park.

C Prohibiting and disapproving: verbs

verb	*meaning*	*example*
bar	officially exclude; forbid someone access to something	Three students were **barred from** using the library because they had damaged books.
clamp down	use one's full power to prevent or limit something	The government has decided to **clamp down** on illegal immigration.
outlaw	make something illegal	Parliament has passed a bill **outlawing** the use of mobile phones while driving.
veto /'viːtəʊ/	use one's official power to forbid	The president has **vetoed** the plan to open membership of the club to the public.

Exercises

75.1 **Fill the gaps with a suitable verb which expresses the meaning in brackets. There may be more than one possible answer.**

1 The committee were in favour of the proposal but the president .... it. (used his/her official power to forbid it)
2 I would never .... the use of capital punishment, no matter how serious the crime. (approve or refuse to condemn)
3 The newspaper revealed that the Prime Minister had .... in the secret decision to sell arms to the dictator. (agreed to it, without openly admitting it)
4 The new bill going through Parliament will .... the use of unlicensed drugs by doctors. (make illegal)
5 The school governors have .... the use of detention after lessons as a punishment for bad behaviour. (used their official power to permit)
6 She has been .... from lectures because she disrupted one last term. (forbidden to enter/attend)
7 The President finally had to .... to demands for his resignation. (agree after being initially unwilling)
8 The police have announced that they are to begin to .... down on motorists who exceed the speed limit near schools. (take serious action to reduce the number of)

75.2 **Vocabulary quiz**

1 One expression on the opposite page has French words in it. Which expression is it and what does it mean?
2 Which permitting expression reminds you of traffic lights and why?
3 Which word in A is also a formal noun which means 'the expression on your face'?
4 Which expression connected with permission is formed using the word 'ahead'?

75.3 **Look at these headlines containing further words and expressions connected with permission and prohibition not on the opposite page. Match them with the news clips. Use a dictionary if necessary.**

1 GOVERNMENT TO LIFT EMBARGO ON COMPUTER IMPORTS

2 RAILWAY FRANCHISE EXTENDED FOR FIVE YEARS

3 POLICE TO ADOPT ZERO-TOLERANCE OF FOOTBALL HOOLIGANISM

4 NEW TRADE SANCTIONS ANNOUNCED

a The company will be allowed to run services through to 2009, provided all conditions ...

b The hope is that firms will benefit from less severe competition in domestic markets if imports are subject to ...

c ... at present, chips and processors must be home-produced or else ...

d ... anyone using threatening behaviour will be liable to immediate arrest ...

76 Complaining and protesting

A

Here are some expressions that are useful when complaining.

Note that the formality and strength of a complaint also depend on the speaker's stress and intonation. The expressions listed as 'neutral' here may become more informal if the speaker uses a particularly heavy stress or intonation pattern.

Informal: Look here! I've just about had enough of ...
Honestly! You can't possibly do that!
For goodness sake! I'm fed up with ...
You've got to do something about ...

Neutral: It just won't do!
I wish you would(n't) ...
Something will have to be done about ...
I'm not at all satisfied about ...

Formal: I wish to complain in the strongest terms about ...
I take great exception to ...
I really must object to ...
This is most unsatisfactory.

B

Here are some verbs and nouns relating to complaining, protesting and remonstrating.

verb	*meaning*	*noun*
complain (about)	express dissatisfaction or annoyance	complaint
protest (about) /prə'test/	strongly express complaint, disapproval or disagreement	protest /'prəʊtest/
object (to)	be against something or someone	objection
remonstrate (against)	formal: complain to someone or about something	remonstrance
find fault (with)	criticise or complain about even small mistakes	fault-finding
grumble (about)	complain in a quiet but angry way	grumble
gripe (about)	informal: to complain continuously	gripe
grouse (about)	informal: to complain, usually often	grouse
whinge (about)	informal: complain persistently	whinge, whingeing

C

British English speakers often complain or protest in a rather indirect way.

Expressions	*What is really meant*
It's **a bit** chilly in here.	I wish you'd close the window.
Your son **would be well advised to** work a bit harder.	Your son is very lazy.
Your work **would benefit from** some proofreading.	Your work is extremely careless.
Her appearance **is not her highest priority.**	She's scruffy.
The children **tend to be** a bit noisy.	You can't hear yourself speak.

TIP Collect more examples of the language of complaint by looking at the letters pages of newspapers. The letters often object to points made in previous articles or protest about current issues.

Exercises

76.1 **These statements are either very formal or very informal. Which are they? How might the same idea be conveyed at the other end of the register scale?**

1 Look here! I've just about had enough of your rudeness!
2 I am writing to remonstrate against some injustices in your regulations.
3 You've got to do something about the state of your desk.
4 I wish to protest in the strongest possible terms about the awful facilities at the station.
5 You can't possibly go out in that dress!
6 This behaviour is most unsatisfactory!

76.2 **Complete each of these sentences. Only one word is needed in each case.**

1 What's Janet whingeing .... now?
2 We .... great exception to the proposed plans.
3 Mr Sim objected .... our parking our caravan in front of his house.
4 He's always writing letters to the newspaper finding fault .... something or other.
5 Something will have to be .... about traffic problems in the city.
6 I wish people .... smoke in restaurants.
7 This standard of work just won't .... !
8 You would be .... advised to start looking for another job.

76.3 **How might you complain in the following situations?**

1 You are complaining to your flatmate about your noisy neighbours.
2 You're complaining in a fairly neutral way to your neighbours about the noise they make.
3 You're writing to the local newspaper about the problem of noise in the neighbourhood.
4 You're complaining to your boss about new and longer working hours.
5 You're complaining to your friend about having to work longer hours.
6 You're writing an official letter of complaint to the top level of management about having to work longer hours.

76.4 **Look at C opposite. What might a British person mean in the following situations?**

1 (walking into a room) 'It's a bit stuffy in here!'
2 (on a school report) 'Jack tends to complete his work rather too quickly.'
3 (in a reference letter) 'Punctuality is not Simon's highest priority.'
4 (at a work appraisal) 'You'd be well advised to re-assess your long-term plans.'
5 (commenting on a room) 'It would benefit from a lick of paint.'
6 (coming into a room) 'The TV seems to be a bit loud.'

76.5 **Look at C opposite. What might a British person say in the following situations if they wish to make their complaint in a rather polite and tentative way?**

1 A head teacher would prefer her staff to come to school dressed more formally.
2 A hotel guest is commenting to another guest about the smallness of the portions in the restaurant.
3 A passenger on a train wants to tell the ticket inspector that the trains are overcrowded.
4 A wife wants to tell her husband that he should take more exercise.

77 Apologising, forgiving and reconciliatior

A Apologies and excuses: collocations

adjective collocations	*noun*
sincere, heartfelt	apology
good, perfect, lame, flimsy, weak	excuse
cast-iron, convincing, perfect, phoney	alibi
flimsy, false	pretext

He offered his most **heartfelt apology** for having offended everyone. [most sincere apology]
It was a rather **lame excuse**, and nobody really believed it. [weak excuse]
The police questioned her about the murder, but she had a **cast-iron alibi**: she had spent the whole day teaching at the local primary school. [firm reason why she was innocent]
He got an interview with her on the rather **flimsy pretext** of being interested in her research. [weak and not very believable pretext]

B Expressions of apology/regret/forgiveness in legal contexts

As he was pronounced guilty of murder, Jesse Smith showed no **remorse**[1] whatsoever. He was sentenced to the electric chair. All three of his companions who were on trial with him were **acquitted**[2] of the crime and walked out of the courtroom free. Smith later **repented**[3] whilst in prison awaiting his execution. He was due to be executed at dawn on the 23rd of May, but he got a last-minute **reprieve**[4] from the Minister of Justice.

1 feeling of guilt or regret
2 declared not guilty
3 said he was sorry and asked for forgiveness
4 official order stopping or delaying punishment

Other examples:
The President issued a **posthumous pardon** for all the innocent men and women. [official forgiveness after someone's death for crimes they were unjustly convicted for]
The Committee of Inquiry **exonerated** the Minister from all responsibility for the disaster. [declared someone to be free of blame]

C Peace and reconciliation in the military context

type of agreement	*explanation and example*
armistice	agreement to stop war while peace discussions take place The generals from the opposing armies **declared/signed an armistice**.
truce	declaration (not necessarily written) that fighting will stop for a period The terrorists declared a Christmas **truce**.
accord	agreement not to fight, or to work together peacefully The two sides in the civil war **signed a peace accord**.
treaty	written agreement between countries agreeing to end a war or not fight The two nations signed a **peace treaty** in 1996.

Exercises

77.1 Fill the gaps with suitable adjectives. There may be more than one possible answer.

1 She had a .... excuse for not mowing the lawn: she was allergic to grass.
2 I thought he gave rather a .... excuse and I'm not convinced at all.
3 He got into the concert on the somewhat .... pretext of wanting to help the disabled people in the front row.
4 The police had to let her go free, since she had a .... alibi.
5 I want to offer you all my most .... apology for the trouble I've caused.

77.2 Can you guess which of the words in the box (in an appropriate form) was used in these quotations from famous poets and writers?

forgive	apology	excuse	repent

1 'Several .... are always less convincing than one.' (*Aldous Huxley*, English novelist, 1894–1963)
2 'How pleasant it is, at the end of the day, no follies to have to .... ; But reflect on the past, and be able to say, that my time has been properly spent.' *Anne Taylor*, English writer of children's books, 1782–1866)
3 'We read that we ought to .... our enemies but we do not read that we ought to .... our friends.' (*Cosimo de Medici*, Italian statesman, 1389–1464)
4 'It is a good rule in life never to .... The right sort of people do not want .... and the wrong sort take a mean advantage of them.' (*P.G. Wodehouse*, English writer, 1881–1975)

77.3 Correct the errors in these sentences.

1 The President granted him a repentance just an hour before he was due to be executed.
2 He was exonerated of murder in 1984, but two years later was convicted of armed robbery in the same courtroom.
3 She showed a complete lack of reprieve for her evil deeds and just laughed when the judge sentenced her.
4 The Public Inquiry pardoned him from all blame for the accident at the factory.
5 Most Christians believe that if you remorse your bad deeds just before you die, God will forgive you.
6 Ten years after his death, John Wilson was given a humorous pardon by the government when another man confessed to the crime he had been hanged for.

77.4 Rewrite the underlined parts of the sentences using words from C on the opposite page and fill the gaps with a suitable verb. Use a dictionary if necessary.

1 The two armies .... a period without fighting during the religious holiday.
2 Both governments .... to the terms of the document ending the war permanently and it was signed on 15th August, 1954.
3 The long-standing agreement to work together between the government and the unions is in danger of ....
4 The generals .... the agreement to end fighting while peace terms were worked out at midday on 25th February, 1968.

78 Complimenting and praising

A Collocations with compliment and praise

The boss would get better results if he **paid** his staff **compliments** occasionally.
He asked us what we thought of his suit, but he was really only **fishing for compliments.**
Take it as a compliment that he feels relaxed enough to fall asleep at your dinner party!
A **back-handed compliment** is one that seems to say something pleasant about someone but could in fact be taken as an insult, e.g. That dress makes you look quite slim.
A **double-edged compliment** is similar in that it has both a positive and a negative side to it, but does not seem to have the slightly malicious intention on the complimenter's behalf that often seems to be there with a back-handed compliment, e.g. He **paid** me the **double-edged compliment** of saying my driving was pretty good for a beginner.

The phrase **give praise to** is usually reserved for a god. An action or person that deserves praise is **praiseworthy** and people are **praised for** their actions.
Other common collocations are **widely/highly praised** **praised to the skies**
to sing someone's/something's praises **to shower/heap praise on someone/something**
To **damn someone with faint praise** is to praise with such a lack of enthusiasm that you give the impression of actually having rather negative feelings.

B Other expressions relating to praising

expression	*meaning*	*example*
pay tribute to	praise (formal)	At the memorial service I **paid tribute to** his kindness.
give someone a standing ovation	stand up and clap loudly for a long time	At the end of the concert, the audience **gave** the young pianist **a standing ovation**.
extol the virtues/ benefits of	praise highly (formal)	I'm fed up of listening to her **extolling the virtues of** her private tennis coach.
be the toast of	be admired for some recent achievement	A few months ago hardly anyone had heard of her but now **she's the toast of** Hollywood.
pat someone on the back / give someone a pat on the back	praise, often children	My teacher **patted me on the back / gave me a pat on the back** for my good marks in the maths test.
earn/win plaudits	get positive comments (formal)	The exhibition **earned plaudits** from all the major reviewers.
laud *	praise highly in official situations (formal)	The Prime Minister has **lauded** the new peace initiative.

* Related adjectives are **laudable** (of behaviour) and **laudatory** (of comments or remarks).

These mostly informal expressions imply praising someone for your own benefit.
to flatter **to make up to** **to crawl** **to suck up to** **to lick someone's boots**
Someone who behaves like this can be called **smarmy, slimy** or **a crawler** (all informal); or (more formal) **servile** or **obsequious.**

Notice how **flatter** can also be used more positively: That dress **flatters** her figure. [makes her figure look better than it really is] The noun **flattery** is often used in the phrase **Flattery will get you nowhere!** [insincere praise will not achieve anything].

Exercises

78.1 **Look at A and then fill the gaps in these sentences with one word.**

1 A: Do you like my new hairstyle? B: Don't .... for compliments.
2 At the meeting everyone was .... your praises.
3 He's not very good at .... people compliments.
4 Mr Biggs is always praising his own pupils .... the skies.
5 It may sound a bit double-edged but I think you should .... what he says .... a compliment.
6 He never knows what to say when fans .... praise on him.
7 I didn't enjoy the film but it has been very .... praised by the critics.
8 Look at this reference. It's really .... the candidate with faint praise.

78.2 **Look at the table in B. Match the beginning of each sentence with its ending.**

1 The performers were given	tribute to his predecessor.
2 In the speech the new manager paid	a pat on the back for her drawings.
3 They're always extolling	the toast of the tennis world.
4 Matt's design earned him	a standing ovation.
5 The teacher gave Becky	the virtues of living in the country.
6 The new young Czech player was	the highest plaudits from the judges.

78.3 **Look at the words under the table in B. Write each of the following sentences in four different ways. Indicate which of your sentences are particularly formal or informal.**

1 He's always sucking up to the boss. 2 I wish she wasn't so smarmy.

78.4 **Complete this word formation table. Do not fill the shaded boxes.**

verb	*noun*	*adjective*
compliment		
praise		
congratulate		
laud		
flatter		
crawl		
smarm		

78.5 **Choose one of the words from the table in 78.4 to complete these sentences.**

1 I've got some .... tickets for tonight's concert. Would you like to come?
2 Simon has got a bit of a reputation as a .... when he's around women.
3 After winning the prize he received many .... notes from friends.
4 Her actions were foolish but her motives were ....
5 I'd like to offer you my .... on your silver wedding anniversary!
6 There's no point saying how good I am. .... will get you nowhere!
7 Whilst we cannot but .... the skill of their actions we must express a certain disapproval of the risks they took.

79 Promises and bets

A Promises

If you **promise someone the earth/moon**, you promise them a great deal. It is usually implied that such a promise is unrealistic.

The afternoon **promises** to be interesting! [the speaker expects it will be interesting]
Promise can also be used to indicate positive future development:
The child already shows great **promise** as a violinist.
She's a **promising** artist although her style is still rather immature.

An **oath** is either a formal promise or an example of taboo language.
In court, witnesses are **put on/under oath** when they have to swear to tell the truth.
To **swear** is either to make a formal promise or to use **swear words / bad language**. [taboo expressions]

Notice how **swear** is often used in informal spoken English in expressions like these:
I **could have sworn** I left my purse on the table. [was absolutely certain]
I think she lives on Rose Street but I **couldn't swear to it**. [am not totally sure]
My mother **swears by** these vitamin pills. [uses them and thinks they are wonderful]

To **pledge** (**a pledge**) means to promise something, often friendship or money:
On the last day of term we all **pledged** eternal friendship.

To **vow** (**a vow**) is to make a determined decision or promise to do something: He **vowed** to discover who had killed his father. The couple **exchanged vows** in the marriage ceremony. Both **vow** and **pledge** are found more in written than spoken English.

New Year's resolutions are special promises **to turn over a new leaf** [to change one's behaviour for the better] at the beginning of a new year. **Resolutions** and **vows**, like **promises** or **pledges**, can be **made**, **kept** or **broken**.

B Bets

To **bet** (**a bet**) is to risk money on the unknown result of something in the hope of winning more money. People spend (and lose) a lot of money betting on horses, for example. The amount of money that you risk is your **stake**. You can **stake** a sum of money on something happening. A more formal word for **bet is wager**: She put a **wager** of £10 on a horse. Both words can be used in a non-literal sense: I'd **wager** that he will come to a bad end.

There are a number of colloquial expressions connected with betting.
Your best bet would be to look for a part-time job. [the best decision or choice]
You think Stuart'll win? **Don't bet on it!** [I think what you've just said is unlikely to happen.]
My granny enjoys **having a flutter** on the horses. [having a small bet]
I'd **put money / my life on** Jack getting the job. [I'm sure that Jack will get the job.]

C Famous promises or quotations about promises

I swear by Almighty God that the evidence I shall give in court today shall be the truth, the whole truth and nothing but the truth. (*in court of law*)

... to have and to hold from this day forward, for better for worse, for richer for poorer, in sickness and in health; to love and to cherish, till death us do part. (*part of Church of England wedding vows*)

Promises and piecrusts are made to be broken, they say. (*Jonathan Swift*, Irish writer, 1667–1745)

Exercises

79.1 Which sentence in each pair sounds more formal?

1 a) Ricky promised to love her always.
  b) Ricky pledged to love her always.
2 a) Tom swore he would take revenge.
  b) Tom vowed he would take revenge.
3 a) Lou wagered a lot of money on the result of the elections.
  b) Lou bet a lot of money on the result of the elections.
4 a) Lina made a resolution at New Year to give up smoking.
  b) Lina made a vow at New Year to give up smoking.

79.2 Fill the gaps in these sentences with one word.

1 He .... her the moon but they ended up in a tiny flat in the dingiest part of town.
2 In an English court of law you can opt to swear the .... on the Bible if you wish.
3 You can choose yourselves what topics you want to concentrate on for the exam, of course, but I think your .... bet would be to focus on Shakespeare and the Romantic poets. They always come up!
4 Dad's not a real gambler, but he does like to have the occasional .... on the horses.
5 Rob has certainly .... his promise to love his wife in sickness and in health as he nursed her devotedly through the years of her cancer.
6 Sue's bound to pass her driving test first time. I'd put my .... on it!

79.3 Rewrite these sentences using the word in brackets, so that they keep the same meaning.

1 I think you should see a doctor. (BET)
2 My mother takes these herbal teas and believes they are wonderful. (SWEARS)
3 John's been rather lazy with his homework but he has promised to try harder next year. (LEAF)
4 I was sure I locked the door when I went out. (SWORN)
5 The new production of the play sounds as if it will be most unusual. (PROMISES)
6 I'm sure that the Democratic Party will win the next election. (MONEY)
7 Do you ever bet on the horses? (FLUTTER)
8 Her mother disliked the film because it contained so much bad language. (SWEAR)

79.4 Answer these questions.

1 Look at what people promise one another during a wedding service. What wedding vows do people make in your country? Can you translate them?
2 What point is Jonathan Swift making, in your opinion, and how is his use of language effective?
3 Mark Twain said, 'To promise not to do a thing is the surest way in the world to make a body want to go and do that very thing.' (*Mark Twain*, American novelist, 1835–1910) Do you agree with him?

80 Reminiscences and regrets

A

Here are some clichés which are sometimes used when people reminisce.

In the good old days ...
Schooldays are the best/happiest days of your life.
We used to have to make our own entertainment in those days.
Life wasn't as easy then.
We didn't have it as easy as young people today do.
Things aren't what they used to be.
They don't make bikes/songs/trains, etc., like they used to.

B

Here are some other examples of the language people use when reminiscing.

A: It's great to see you again. It must be ten years since we were at school together! Do you **keep in touch with** any of our old teachers?

B: No, I wonder what happened to **whatsisname**? Er, I think he was called Mr Cain. I realise now how difficult things must have been for them, having to teach the likes of us! And **do you ever hear anything of** James?

A: No, I wonder whether he and Karen ever got married. And **whatever became of** Sal?

B: Mmm, and **I often wonder** what Sarah **ended up** doing. We did **have good times**, didn't we? **Do you remember how** we used to leave notes for each other in that hole in the wall?

A: Of course I do. **I'll never forget how** I used to look forward to checking what was there. I often wonder what would have happened if anyone else had looked in that hole and found our notes.

B: I must say that **what stands out in my mind** is the relative freedom we used to have.

A: Me too. When **I look back**, I appreciate how much things have changed.

B: Yes, though we probably see the past through **rose-tinted spectacles** rather than how it really was.

C

Sometimes people feel sorry about a situation. Here are some ways of expressing regret.

I wish I'd known you were arriving today.
I wish I hadn't given up learning the piano.
It's disappointing that the exam results are so poor this year.
I'm disappointed in you.
I regret not spending more time with my aunt when she was ill.
He showed no sign of remorse for what he had done.

Some more informal ways of expressing regret:

If only I hadn't spoken to her like that!
If I'd only known then what I know now.
If only we could have our time all over again!
It's a pity/shame we can't stay longer.
I'm sorry I forgot your birthday.
The team's behaviour was a disgrace.
He should never have done that – it's a scandal!

Some formal, rather literary ways of expressing regret:

I rue the day we ever met. [I regret very much that we ever met]
I lament the passing of time. [I feel sad that time passes]
I mourn my lost opportunities. [I feel sad about opportunities I had but did not take up]

Exercises

80.1 **Find one word to complete the following sentences.**

1 Things aren't what they .... to be.
2 Your .... are the happiest days of your life.
3 We didn't .... it as easy as young people do today.
4 Do you keep in .... with anyone from school?
5 People often see the past through .... spectacles.
6 I wonder what .... of that man who used to live next to the post office?
7 I appreciate now how difficult life .... have been for my grandparents.
8 What .... out in my mind is how hard we had to work.

80.2 **Look at C. Match the beginning of each sentence with its ending.**

1 I'm disappointed	my lost youth.
2 I rue the day	not apologising for what I said.
3 I feel a certain remorse	in my results.
4 I regret	I agreed to go into business with him.
5 I mourn	that we didn't make a go of it.
6 It's disappointing	for what I said to her.

80.3 **Complete these sentences in any appropriate way.**

1 Someone in an unhappy marriage may regret ....
2 They don't make .... like they used to.
3 Things were much safer in the .... days.
4 It's a shame you .... Jill to the party. I wanted to meet her.
5 If only .... I know now.
6 The boy .... to the old lady like that. It was very rude of him.
7 I wonder .... to those people who used to live next door to us?
8 I'll never .... Susan looked on her wedding day.
9 I'm .... I'm late.
10 It's a .... to go now. I'd have liked to have a longer chat.

80.4 **Answer these questions.**

1 What did you use to do when you were a child that you no longer do?
2 What do you regret doing?
3 What will you never forget doing?
4 Do you keep in touch with any of the friends that you knew at primary school?
5 Do you know what happened to the people you were at school with?
6 What stands out in your mind when you think about your own childhood?
7 What do you feel remorse for?
8 What have you found disappointing?
9 What do poets often lament?

80.5 **Write these sentences in more formal language. Use the word in brackets.**

1 I'm sorry that I didn't buy her a birthday present. (REGRET)
2 It's a shame that you won't play the piano for us. (DISAPPOINTED)
3 It's a pity that he is so unreliable. (WISH)
4 I wish we still had trams in our town. (LAMENT)
5 If only we were still young! (MOURN)

81 Agreement, disagreement and compromise

A Agreement – sharing views

verb + preposition	*meaning*	*example*
tally with	match or agree with	Her complaints **tally with** the comments we have received from other people.
concur with	share/agree with an idea/opinion	His opinion **concurs with** the general opinion of the experts on this matter.
be/find yourself in accord with	be in complete agreement with	The President found himself **in** full **accord with** the opposition.
coincide with	be the same as	Your views **coincide with** mine on the question of crime and punishment.
conform to	fit in with	His ideas do not **conform to** the general definition of civilisation.
approve of	think something is right or good	My parents **approve of** my choice of profession and support me fully.

Note the expression **to agree to differ**, which is used when people continue to hold different opinions but see no point in continuing to argue about them.
We couldn't reach a consensus at the meeting, so we just **agreed to differ.**

B Political and social disagreement

noun	*meaning*	*example*
dissent	opposition to the accepted way of thinking	There is a lot of **dissent** within the party on the issue.
discord	lack of agreement or harmony (suggests arguments and rows)	The political **discord** of the 1980s resulted in a five-year civil war.
rift	disagreement (with different groups/factions forming)	The growing **rift** in the Democratic Party over defence policy is now public.
split	when a larger group breaks up into two or more smaller groups because they disagree about something	A major **split** in the Conservative Party resulted in several ministers resigning.
division	more abstract and formal than split (can be used countably or uncountably)	There is (a) major **division** in the Socialist Party over economic policy.

C Compromise

The two sides have **reached a compromise** with regard to the plan to build the new road across a nature reserve.
The Minister was not prepared to **compromise on** the issue of raising university fees.
The government **made** several **concessions to** the protesters. [accepted some of the demands of]
The management and the union **reached a settlement** and the strike ended. [reached a decision/agreement]
In this particular case we should **exercise** some **discretion.** [be sensitive, use our judgement]

Exercises

81.1 **Fill in the prepositions which normally accompany the verbs in the table. Then use these expressions (except *agree with*) to fill the gaps in these sentences. Use each item once only.**

verb	*preposition*
agree	with
approve	
conform	
tally	
coincide	
concur	
compromise	
be in accord	

1 The list of principles .... to the normal idea of what a set of rules should be trying to achieve.
2 My view .... completely with yours. We think on exactly the same lines.
3 For once all the committee members .... with one another.
4 Her latest statement simply does not .... with her earlier ones. She is contradicting herself.
5 I .... of all the changes suggested, and hope they can be made to work.
6 This plan is in .... with the proposal made by the committee in 1998.
7 Even though I disagree, I'm willing to .... on your proposal to increase our expenditure.

81.2 **Match these newspaper headlines with the most suitable extract.**

1 **RIFT OVER PENSIONS POLICY GROWS**
2 **DISSENT MUST BE KEPT WITHIN LIMITS, MINISTER SAYS**
3 **PARTY SPLIT OVER TAX CUTS NO LONGER A SECRET**
4 **DIVISION IN EUROPE OVER RESPONSE TO AFRICAN CRISIS**
5 **RELIGIOUS DISCORD THREATENS SOCIAL HARMONY**

a) Approximately 50% of members think the proposals are wrong.
b) Intolerance is increasing and there have been isolated outbreaks of violence.
c) There is increasing pressure on the Minister to think again.
d) Several different approaches have emerged which could weaken unity.
e) To disagree is everyone's right, but a sense of responsibility is also important.

81.3 **Rewrite the sentences using a noun instead of the underlined word. Make any other necessary changes.**

1 The President has <u>conceded</u> that the opposition party should be allowed a place on the committee.
2 I think one should always be as <u>discreet</u> as possible when it is a question of people's private lives.
3 The landowners <u>settled</u> their dispute with the authorities over the route of the road.
4 The negotiating team were able to <u>compromise</u> and put an end to the long strike.

FOLLOW UP Read or listen to a news broadcast in English on radio, TV or the Internet and see how many words refer to agreeing and disagreeing in political and other contexts.

82 Academic writing I

Units 82 and 83 deal with vocabulary that is often used in academic writing in any subject.

A Presenting arguments and commenting on others' work

If you **advocate** something, you argue in favour of it: He **advocated** capital punishment.
If you **deduce** something, you reach a conclusion by thinking carefully about the known facts: Look at these sentences and see if you can **deduce** how the imperfect tense is used.
If you **infer** something, you reach a conclusion indirectly: From contemporary accounts of his research, we can **infer** that results were slower to come than he had anticipated.
If someone's work **complements** someone else's, it combines well with it so that each piece of work becomes more effective.
If someone's work **overlaps** with someone else's work, it partially covers the same material.

You might call someone's work: **empirical** [based on what is observed rather than theory] **ambiguous** [open to different interpretations] **coherent** [logically structured] **comprehensive** [covering all that is relevant] **authoritative** [thorough and expert]

B Talking about figures and processes

If figures or decisions are referred to as **arbitrary**, they are based on chance rather than a plan or any particular reason.
Figures that **deviate** from the norm are different from what is typical.
If statistics **distort** the picture, they give a false impression.
If you refer to the **incidence** of something (e.g. left-handedness), you are talking about how often it occurs in the population.
If something (e.g. the incidence of brown eyes) is **predominant**, it is the largest in number.
If things (e.g. stages in a process) happen **in sequence**, they happen in a particular order.
If you want to say that something happens in many places or with many people, you can say that it is **widespread**: **widespread outbreaks** of an illness, **widespread alarm**

C Words used instead of more everyday words in an academic context

academic verb	*everyday verb*
append	add (at the end)
conceive	think up
contradict	go against
convene	meet
demonstrate	show
denote	be a sign of, stand for
negate	make useless, wipe out
perceive	see
reside	lie, live
trigger	cause
utilise	use

academic word	*everyday synonym*
the converse	the opposite
crucial	very important
likewise	similarly
notwithstanding	despite this
somewhat	rather
thereby	in this way
whereby	by which (method)

Exercises

82.1 Which of the five verbs in A best fits in each sentence?

1 Although my brother and I are researching in similar areas, our work, fortunately, does not .... It has, however, often been said that what I do .... his work very well.
2 Look at the complete set of graphs and see if you can .... the rules governing the data from them.
3 This article .... a somewhat different approach to the problem than that which has been put forward by others in the field.
4 A great deal can be .... about the artist's state of mind from the content and style of his later works.

82.2 Which of the five adjectives in A best describes each of these things?

1 a textbook written by the most highly regarded expert in the field
2 research based on a survey of the population
3 a poem which can be understood in two quite different ways
4 an argument which is well-expressed and easy to follow
5 a textbook which gives a broad overview of an entire discipline

82.3 Answer these questions which use vocabulary from B.

1 If the incidence of asthma in children is increasing, what is actually going up: a) the seriousness of asthma attacks b) the number of asthmatic children
2 What are the next two numbers in the sequence *1, 4, 9, 16, 25, 36*?
3 If the average mark of schoolchildren in a maths test was 68% and James's mark deviated most markedly from that average, what do we know about James's mark?
4 If a historian distorts the facts, does he present them a) accurately b) clearly c) in a misleading fashion?
5 If a sociologist chooses the subjects of her research in an arbitrary fashion, is she being careful to get people from an appropriate balance of backgrounds?

82.4 Use vocabulary from C to rewrite these sentences in a more formal academic style.

1 We believe the information lies in archives that must not be opened until 2050.
2 He thought up his theory while still a young man.
3 Each of the signs in the phonetic alphabet stands for a sound rather than a letter.
4 This study went against what was previously held to be true and so started a great deal of discussion amongst specialists in the field.
5 Details of the experiment have been added at the end of the report for those who wish to see how we arrived at our data.

82.5 Rewrite this paragraph, using words from C, to make it sound more academic.

The study was initially **thought up** in order to validate a new method of enquiry **by which** genetic information could be **used** to predict disease. Our work **goes against** the findings of Hill (2001); indeed it would appear to **show** the **opposite** of what he claimed. We **see** our work as presenting a **rather** different view of the genetic factors which **cause** disease. **Despite this**, our work does not **wipe out** Hill's, as his studies served the **very important** purpose of devising symbols to **stand for** certain tendencies, **in this way** facilitating further research. We hope that Hill will **similarly** find our work to be valid and that when international researchers **meet** next April, they will concur that much of value **lies** in both our and Hill's studies. Our results are **added at the end**.

83 Academic writing 2

A Explaining, reinforcing, exemplifying

Look at these newspaper snippets and note the contexts in which the words in bold occur.

The Prime Minister **reiterated**[1] his concern that the debate should not be dominated by personal attacks. He also asked ...

The recent events **underscore**[4] the need for a better understanding of the environmental impact of biotechnology. If this phase in the ...

Mr Burns' comments **epitomise**[2] the attitude of many parents nowadays. He seems to be in the ...

Several historians have **posited**[5] a connection between the decline of the Roman Empire and the eruption of a far distant volcano ...

It was a philosophy first **expounded**[3] by John Ruskin in the nineteenth century. If human ...

In an attempt to **account for**[6] the lack of interest, political analysts have looked at past voting patterns. On the basis of ...

1 repeated, restated
2 are a perfect example of
3 developed, proposed
4 emphasise
5 suggested as a basic fact/principle
6 explain, find the cause of

B Categorising and including

Japanese visitors **comprised/made up** 70% of the hotel's guests last year. [70% consisted of]
The course **is comprised of** two elements: reading and writing. [is composed of]
These two approaches can be **subsumed** under one heading. [brought together / united]
The book **embraces** a number of issues, from economic to religious ones. [covers/includes]
Her philosophy is difficult to **categorise**. [label as belonging to a particular type or class]

C Structuring the text

Some words and expressions for ordering and arranging the parts of an essay.

function in the text	*example*
beginning	I should like to **preface** /ˈprefɪs/ my argument with a true story.
mapping out the text	I shall **return** to this point later in my essay.
connecting points	This **brings me/us** to my next area of discussion, which is finance.
focusing	I should now like to **address** the question of the arms race.
ordering points	The arguments are presented in **ascending/descending order** of importance.
quoting/referring	The ideas of several writers will be **cited** in support of the argument. The text **alludes to** several themes that need closer examination.
including/excluding material	Discussion of the roots of the problem is **beyond the scope of** this essay. It is impossible to **deal with** all the issues in this short essay. There will only be space to **touch upon** the big question of political responsibility.
drawing conclusions	We are **forced to conclude** that unemployment will always be with us.

Exercises

83.1 Look at these extracts from essays and use words from A opposite to improve their style, making the underlined words more formal.

1 The response from the public <u>really shows us</u> the importance of having a full investigation of the facts.
2 This view of the world was originally <u>laid out</u> by the Ancient Greek philosophers.
3 It is not easy to <u>find the reason</u> for the fall in population of these birds.
4 Economists have <u>said there might be</u> a link between exchange rates and a general lack of confidence in the European Union.
5 I should like to <u>say again</u> here that the issue is not one that can be easily resolved.
6 The recent events <u>are the best example of</u> the dilemma faced by politicians the world over.

83.2 Rewrite these sentences using the verb in brackets and making any other necessary changes.

1 70% of the landmass is mountain ranges. (COMPRISE)
2 A wide variety of subjects are dealt with in the book. (EMBRACE)
3 I think these three sections can all come under one heading. (SUBSUME)
4 Poems are not easily amenable to being put into different types. (CATEGORISE)

83.3 Complete the table with the noun forms of these verbs. Use a dictionary if necessary.

A–Z

verb	*noun*
categorise	
preface	
allude to	
cite	
reiterate	
epitomise	

83.4 Fill the gaps with words from C that express the meaning in brackets.

1 I shall .... to this issue later in this essay. (come back to)
2 The question of monetary union .... us to our next topic: the idea of a federal Europe. (means we've arrived at)
3 Smith just .... upon the subject of Internet policing but does not go into it in depth. (mentions only briefly)
4 I shall attempt to .... the problem of censorship later in this discussion. (attend to, consider)
5 Psychological factors in learning foreign languages are .... this essay. (outside of the topic area)
6 I shall discuss the poets in .... order, that is to say I shall comment on the least important ones first.
7 In the final analysis, we are .... that there is little hope of stamping out illegal drugs altogether. (have no choice but to believe)
8 This unit has attempted to .... a range of useful vocabulary for formal writing. (give all the necessary information about)

84 Writing: style and format

A Aspects of writing

If you're in a hurry, you can **scribble** a note to someone. [write quickly, without much care]
I'll just **jot down** (informal) / **make a note of** (more formal) your phone number before I forget it. [write something down to remember it]
I'll **copy out** the information on hotels for you. [copy in writing]
Some students **write down** everything the lecturer says. [copy in writing what is spoken]
She's **writing up** her dissertation at the moment, so she's very tired and stressed. [making a proper written text based on notes]
This isn't the final version; it's just a **first draft**. [first attempt at writing something]
She bought the **manuscript** of a famous poem at the sale. [original handwritten version]
She got so bored at the meeting she spent the whole time **doodling**. [drawing and writing irrelevant things on the paper in front of her]

B Typing, word processing and print

I've finished my book. I'm sending the **typescript/manuscript** to the publisher tomorrow. [typed text]
I've done the text, but I want to **format** it properly before printing it. [create the page as it will appear when printed]
I usually **cut and paste** or **copy and paste** bits of material from my notes when I'm writing an essay, then link them all together. [move text from one place to another using a word processor]

These words are in a **shaded box.**

These words are in bold, *these are italicised / in italics.*
These words are in a different font size from the rest, and these are in a different typeface.
- This sentence has a **bullet** in front of it.

** This sentence has two **asterisks** in front of it.

    This sentence **is indented.** [begins away from the normal margin]

"This sentence is in **double inverted commas / quotation marks.**" 'This one is in **single quotation marks / quotes.**'
Types of brackets: () **round** brackets < > **diamond/angle** brackets [ ] **square** brackets { } **chain/curly** brackets
CAPITALS or **UPPER CASE** (more technical) is the opposite of **small letters** or **lower case.**
This person has written her name in **block capitals:** MONICA FLATLEY

This is the first page of a typical academic book. Look at the structure and the names of the different elements.

> **English Grammar**[1]**:**
> **A new method of classification**[2]
> **Contents**
> *Chapter 1* Verbs[3]
> *1.1* Transitive verbs[4]
> *1.2* Intransitive verbs

1 title
2 subtitle
3 chapter heading
4 sub-heading (within a chapter)

Exercises

84.1 Correct the mistakes in these sentences.

1 Let me just jott in your e-mail address, or I'll forget it.
2 I'll just scramble a note for Jim to tell him where we've gone.
3 I spent the whole lesson just dawdling in the margin of my exercise book, I was so bored.
4 She's been writing down her PhD thesis for the last three months, that's why no one has seen her.
5 I'll send you a drift of the letter so you can suggest any changes before we send it.

84.2 Circle the correct answer to describe these sentences.

1	**I love the summer.**	upper case	bold	italics	
2	WILL YOU BE QUIET!	upper case	bold	italics	
3	*This is crazy.*	upper case	bold	italics	
4	Can you read this?	new typeface	new font size		
5	I've missed you	new typeface	new font size		
6	so i wrote to mr smith.	upper case	lower case	block capitals	
7	Name: ANNE TAYLOR	upper case	lower case	block capitals	
8	{See next page}	diamond	round	chain	square
9	[Not suitable for children]	diamond	round	chain	square
10	<johnjo@speedmail.com>	diamond	round	chain	square

84.3 Label the parts of the texts, as in the example.

The Last Wilderness — 1 *title*
A journey across Siberia — 2 ....
by Wanda Allova

Chapter 8 Feeding your dog — 3 ....
8.1 Regular meals — 4 ....
8.2 Quantities

5 .... — • Making an appointment* — 6 ....

84.4 Fill the gaps in these sentences.

1 Students may submit their essays in .... or in handwriting.
2 With the computer, I can .... the document before printing it, so that it looks professional. You can't really do that with an old-fashioned typewriter.
3 She works in the museum, conserving ancient ....
4 I need to improve the paragraphing of my essay. I'll try to cut and .... and move some sections around.

85 Lexical strategies for speaking

A

In spontaneous speech we make frequent use of rather vague words like **thing** or **get**. Here are some examples of how they are used:

That's **one of the things** I want to talk to him about. [**thing** = subject]
Anne **has got a thing about** mice. [She either really likes or dislikes them.]
Don't **make such a big thing of it!** [Don't make so much fuss about it!]
There **wasn't a thing** we could do about it. [a thing = anything]
For one thing, I haven't got time. **For another thing**, I can't afford it. [Firstly … Secondly …]
The thing is, I have to get the essay in by tomorrow morning. [used to introduce a topic or provide an explanation]
As things are at present ... [As the situation is]

I don't **get** it. [understand]
We must **get** that parcel in the post today. [send]
She had big plans to travel the world but she just never **got it together**. [took positive action or organised herself]
Jill will **get things sorted out** today. [organise things so that the problem is solved]
I hope I can **get her to myself** this evening. [be alone with her]

B

When we can't remember the word for something, we often replace it with a vague word:

for objects: **thingy** **thingummy** **thingumajig** **thingumabob** **whatsit** **whatchamacallit** **whatnot**
for people: **whatsisname** (for a man) **whatsername** (for a woman) **whosit**

I can't find the **thingy** we use for crushing garlic.
Did you see **whatsisname** today?

C

Certain quantifiers are common in speaking though rare in writing. For example, the following expressions mean a lot of:

bags of **loads of** **masses of** **buckets of** **oodles of** **a load of** **a mass of** **umpteen**

I'll help you – I've got **bags of** time.
They can afford to go on exotic holidays as they've got **oodles of** money.
I've tried phoning her **umpteen** times but she never seems to be at home.

These expressions mean a little or some: **a bit of** **a scrap of** **a touch of**

You've been sitting there all day but you haven't done **a scrap of** work.
Bill's got **a touch of** flu but he should be fine by next week.
I've got **a bit of** a headache.

D

Here are some expressions which we can use in speech to make what we are saying sound less threatening and potentially offensive to the person we are talking to.

It's not the most practical idea – and **I mean that in the nicest possible way**.
It's **not the most** practical/sensible/intelligent/appropriate thing you've ever done. [It's impractical / not very sensible / rather unintelligent / inappropriate.]
What a load of idiots – **present company excepted**, of course. [not including you or me]
I think a lot of the staff here, **myself included**, have not been working quite as hard as we should.
No offence intended, but I think you've misunderstood the basic problem.
If you don't mind my saying so, I think that you could have handled that better.
That's true up to a point, but I think it's basically giving a rather misleading picture.

Exercises

85.1 **Look at A. Explain what the expressions with *thing* and *get* mean in the following sentences.**

1 Don't make such a big thing about it. I'm only going for a few days.
2 Jorge has got a thing about Madonna. He plays her music all the time.
3 The thing is, I don't know when we'll get back.
4 Unless things change, we won't be able to get away for a holiday.
5 We've got a number of things to get through before lunchtime.
6 I don't get on with them very well. For one thing, we like different things. For another, I find them quite rude.
7 Did you get what the lecturer was saying? I didn't get a thing.
8 I hope we can get everything sorted out today. It's time we got it together!

85.2 **What words do you think the speaker is looking for in each of these sentences? Choose from the words in the box.**

colander	protractor	corkscrew
Leonardo DiCaprio	pliers	Leonard Nimoy

1 Where's the thingummy for opening wine bottles?
2 Look, isn't that whatsisname? The actor who was in *Titanic*.
3 I can't find the thingumabob for measuring angles.
4 Have you got a whatsit for pulling out nails?
5 Where's the thingy for draining potatoes?
6 The book is about Leonard whosit – the guy who was in that sci-fi series.

85.3 **Write out the sentences in exercise 85.2 again using a different vague word from the one used in the exercise.**

EXAMPLE *Where's the whatsit for opening wine bottles?*

85.4 **Look at C. Write these sentences in a more formal style.**

1 There's no need to rush – we've got oodles of time.
2 I've asked her out umpteen times, but she's always got some excuse.
3 He hasn't done a scrap of useful work here since he first got the job.
4 I've got a load of papers I want to get rid of.
5 Pat asked masses of people to her get-together at the weekend.
6 Sue's got bags of energy – don't know where she gets it all from!

85.5 **Look at D, then fill the gaps in this text.**

This is a very boring party, present .... (1) *excepted, of course. No one, myself* .... (2), *I suppose, seems to be making much of an effort to chat. No* .... (3) *intended, but don't you think you could have dressed a bit more smartly? If you don't* .... (4) *my saying so, I think you should have put on a bit of make-up. I mean that in the nicest* .... (5) *way, of course!*

85.6 **Look up *thing* and *get* in an English learner's dictionary. Make a note of any other good expressions that you find. Write them down in example sentences of your own.**

86 Speech: style and articulation

A Verbs denoting volume: from quiet to loud

Mumble and **mutter** are both usually negative: Stop **mumbling**! I can't hear what you're saying
He was **muttering** something under his breath, probably complaining, as usual.
Murmur can be more positive: They **murmured** their approval when he told them the plan.
The phrase **without a murmur** means without any protest or complaint or comment:
They accepted it all **without a murmur**. I was surprised. Normally they complain.

Raise one's voice can be used in positive or negative contexts:
You'll have to **raise your voice** a bit. She's a little hard of hearing. [speak louder]
'Don't you **raise your voice at** me!' [Do not speak in that loud, angry tone.]

Shout, yell, scream, roar and **shriek** are all followed by **at**: Don't **shout at** me.
Yell often conveys urgency, anger, frustration; it is also used when there is much surrounding noise: He **yelled** at the children to stop messing around with his computer.
'Stay where you are!' he **yelled** above the noise of the traffic.
Shriek means loud and very high-pitched. It can be used in negative and positive contexts.
'Oh, wow! That's fantastic!' she **shrieked**.
Roar suggests very loud volume, but deeper-pitched, like a lion. It is used in positive and negative contexts: As he kicked the ball into the goal, the crowd **roared**, 'Yes!'
'How dare you come in here!' he **roared**.

B Verbs describing episodes of speech and styles of conversation

Note how **away** is used to emphasise continuous/extended talk:

He's been **chattering away** on the phone all morning. [suggests light, non-serious talk]
Tom and Lily are always **nagging** (**at**) each other. [criticising faults or duties not done]
We always **gossip** about work when we go out together. [talk about people, rumours, etc.]
Stop **bickering** you two! Why can't you be friends? [arguing in an irritated way]
It took him a long time to realise they were **winding him up**. [/ˈwaɪndɪŋ/ informal: teasing/fooling him]
They spent all evening **slagging off** their colleagues. [informal: criticising]
I realised she was **buttering me up** for some reason. [negative: saying nice things to me because she wanted something from me]
Janet is always **whining** and **whingeing** about something. [informal, negative: complaining]

C Speech and articulation problems

problem	*example*	*meaning*
lisp	He speaks with a **lisp**. / He **lisps**. He says 'thing' instead of 'sing'.	difficulty in making an 's' sound and making a 'th' sound instead
stammer	He hates speaking in front of people because he's got a really bad **stammer**.	speak with abnormal pauses and repetitions
stutter	'I want to t-t-t-tell you something,' he **stuttered** nervously.	repeat sounds at the beginning of words
slurring	He was **slurring** his words because he had drunk far too much alcohol.	his words had a slow, lazy sound; difficult to understand
tongue-tied	I want to tell her I love her, but I **get tongue-tied**.	cannot say what I want to say; mix up my words

Exercises

86.1 **Without looking at the opposite page, can you remember the following?**

1 a verb meaning 'to argue in an irritated manner'
2 a phrase meaning 'without complaining'
3 a verb meaning that someone often makes a 'th' sound instead of an 's' or 'z' sound
4 three verbs meaning 'speak very loudly' that are followed by *at*
5 how the verb *roar* is different form the verb *shriek*
6 two verbs connected with talking about people, usually when they are not present, either about their private affairs or saying very negative things about them
7 a verb meaning to tease someone or fool them to make them look silly

86.2 **Fill the gaps with one word.**

1 'I want to c-c-c-c-come with you,' she .... nervously.
2 I got .... and said to her 'Your backet's dutiful' instead of 'Your jacket's beautiful'!
3 I wish you'd speak up and stop .... I can't hear a word you're saying.
4 I had to .... at him to be heard, the noise of the plane was so loud.
5 'I love you,' he .... softly.
6 I hate people who .... about their workmates. I never talk about other people.
7 The drugs had made her speech very incoherent. I couldn't follow what she was trying to say. She was .... all her words.
8 She speaks with a .... I thought she said she had too much *fun* on her holiday, but she was trying to say *sun*.

86.3 **Correct the mistakes in these sentences.**

1 They're always whineing and winging about everything. Take no notice of them.
2 I don't believe you. I think you're winding me.
3 Do you think Peggy was trying to banter me up for some reason? I wonder why she was saying all those nice things about me? I'm suspicious.
4 You're always nigging at me! Just leave me alone and let me watch TV!

86.4 **Complete the crossword.**

Across
3 people often do this on the phone for hours
4 rather low voice

Down
1 speak loudly
2 problem in speaking
5 make a loud, deep sound like a lion

87 Vague language expressions

A Vague expressions for numbers

He left a sum **in excess of** $1 million when he died. [more than; used in more formal contexts]
It'll cost you **somewhere in the region of** £600 a month to rent a flat. [less formal: **around/about** £600]
It'll take five hours **give or take** half an hour to drive there. [informal: could be 4.5 or 5.5 hours]
The second meeting is **approximately** two and a half months after the first one. [rather formal: could be a week before or after]
It'll take a week **or so** to get the computer repaired. [informal: more than a week, but unclear how much more]
Quite a few students hadn't registered. [a surprisingly or undesirably *large* number]
There was only a **smattering** of women authors among the prize winners. [small proportion]
Would you like a **dash** of chilli sauce with your kebab? [very small quantity]
I'd like a **dollop** of ice cream with my fruit salad; shall I just help myself? [usually a small amount, but we can also say **a large dollop**]
Even though we put on **lashings** of suntan lotion, we still got sunburnt. [very large quantities]
Every morning I have toast with **oodles** of butter. [very large quantities, usually of food]

B Making ideas and actions less precise in informal conversation

More or less is often used with verbs and adverbs to make things more vague:
I think we've **more or less** solved the problem with the computer now.
My English is **more or less** on the same level as the other students in the class.

A bit and **a bit of a** are used with adjectives and nouns to soften the meaning:
I'm **a bit** fed up with all the complaints I'm getting.
We were in **a bit of a** panic when we heard there was a strike at the airport.

Or whatever, or something and **things like that / that kind of thing** are useful expressions for referring vaguely to things and actions:
You could work Saturday then spend Sunday going to museums **or whatever.** [or similar activities]
If you don't want tea, have a lemonade **or something.** [any other kind of drink you want]
In the evenings we played quiz games **and things like that / and that kind of thing.** [different kinds of entertaining activities]
We need a big container made of plastic; a dustbin or **something along those lines** would do. [something fitting that description]
He said he was fed up with all the attacks and criticisms, **or words to that effect.** [or similar words expressing the same meaning]

Note: the words and phrases in this unit are mostly for informal conversation, except where indicated, and may sound inappropriate in more formal contexts.

Exercises

87.1 **Make the numbers in these sentences less precise, using expressions from A opposite.**

1 The company will invest £10.3 million in new technology over the next five years. (formal)
2 It will cost you £7,000 to have the whole house redecorated.
3 It could take six, seven or eight hours to drive to Aberdeen, depending on the traffic. (Give an informal *and* a more formal version)
4 27 students failed the exam. I was rather surprised and disappointed.

87.2 **These sentences contain some more vague language items used in conversation which are not presented on the opposite page. Underline the items that make the meaning less precise. Make a note of the grammar (i.e. is the item used with nouns, adjectives, etc?).**

1 Her hair's a sort of reddish colour, and I'd say she's, well, forty, forty-fiveish.
2 The garden was a bit on the big side, but it was very pretty.
3 There was a kind of elasticky thing that held the two parts together, and I've lost it.
4 They're good shoes. They're comfortable on long walks and that.
5 I've been to the doctor's and had treatments and suchlike and I'm sure it helps in one way or another.

87.3 **Fill the gaps in these sentences with a suitable word from A opposite.**

1 Mm! Look at those gorgeous desserts with .... of cream and chocolate sauce on them. I must have one!
2 Just a .... of milk in my coffee, please; I like it quite dark.
3 He put .... of hair gel on before going out to the disco.
4 Most of the people in the class were Spanish, with just a .... of other nationalities.
5 She put a .... of mayonnaise on her salad and mixed it all up.

87.4 **Put an appropriate adjective or noun in the gap. There will usually be more than one possible answer.**

1 It's a bit .... that she hasn't rung. I hope she's not ill.
2 The computer keeps crashing; it's a bit of a ....
3 It was a bit .... ; I couldn't remember his name. I'll apologise next time I see him.
4 If you don't want a big meal you could have a .... or something.
5 Make yourself at home. There are some magazines there, or you can just .... or whatever.
6 It's a sort of craft shop; they sell .... and things like that.
7 When you go on business trips, do you have time to go .... and that?

87.5 ***Thing*** **and** ***stuff*** **are useful vague words when we cannot remember the name of something. Write definitions for each item below using** ***thing*** **or** ***stuff*** **as in the example.**

EXAMPLE a toothbrush *a thing to clean your teeth with*

1 a tape measure
2 shoe polish
3 a corkscrew
4 a hammer
5 leftovers
6 suntan lotion

88 Types of idiom

A Verb-plus-object

idiom	*meaning*	*example*
ram something down someone's throat	impose one's ideas/views on someone	OK, so you're a Marxist; you don't have to **ram it down everybody's throat**.
draw the line at something	refuse to behave in a certain way because you think it is wrong	I do use some strong language sometimes, but I **draw the line at** using offensive words.
have second thoughts	change your opinion or begin to have doubts about it	I'm **having second thoughts about** accepting that job offer. The pay's not enough.

B Prepositional phrases (preposition plus noun phrase)

Our boss always keeps us **in the dark** about changes until the last minute. [uninformed]
Over 100 villagers were killed **in cold blood** by the soldiers. [deliberately, without emotion]
It just happened **out of the blue**. [completely unexpectedly]

C Compounds

idiom	*meaning*	*example*
a kick in the teeth	an insult or unfair act	Not giving her the new job was a real **kick in the teeth** for her.
a stumbling block	an obstacle	Their connections with terrorism have always been **a stumbling block** in the party's political progress.
open-ended	having no planned ending, can be developed in many ways	I'm not prepared to give an **open-ended** commitment; I would like to have an agreement in writing.
state-of-the-art	most modern, most technically advanced	He always has a **state-of-the-art** computer and the latest camera.

D Other types

type	*example*
binomial (word + word)	She always acts so **high and mighty**. [self-important, arrogant]
simile (**as** + adjective + **as** + noun)	I'm **as blind as a bat** without my glasses. [can hardly see]
conversational phrases	Hi, Mick, **long time no see**. [I haven't seen you for a long time]
sayings/maxims	**Every little helps**. [even a small contribution is helpful]
proverbs	**Don't count your chickens before they are hatched**. [do not rely on things in the future before they happen]

Exercises

88.1 **How many idioms of the type verb + object can you find in this text? Underline each one. Use a dictionary if necessary, especially a good dictionary of idioms.**

> I always try to make the most of any opportunity to make new friends, such as a party or a social event. But it's not always easy to break the ice, and when you don't know someone, it's so easy to put your foot in it by saying something insensitive or something which unexpectedly rubs someone up the wrong way. But if you keep an eye on what you say, play it by ear and just try to act naturally, it can make all the difference and you may find you stand a good chance of making a new acquaintance or even a good friend.

Now match each of the idioms you found above with their meanings from this list.

be watchful/careful about something
create a relaxed social atmosphere
get the maximum benefit from a situation
irritates someone
say or do something socially embarrassing
have a very positive effect
there is a strong possibility
don't plan in advance, just see how things go

88.2 **Complete these idioms using the following prepositions: *in, under, on, out, in, from, at.* Use a dictionary if necessary.**

1 We were talking .... cross purposes. I was talking about the exams, and you thought I meant the course as a whole.
2 I was a bit .... the weather last week, but I feel much better now.
3 I'm afraid we'll have to start .... scratch again. This system just isn't working.
4 We were kept .... the dark for weeks before anyone told us the truth.
5 Where we live now, we have great shops and everything we need .... our doorstep.
6 They were killed .... cold blood by rebel soldiers.
7 One day, ... of the blue, he left his job and emigrated to Australia.

88.3 **Rewrite each of these sentences using one of the idioms from exercise 88.2.**

1 I hate being uninformed about things at work.
2 The terrorists had no mercy and killed all the hostages.
3 The mountains and ski slopes are just a few miles away; we're so lucky.
4 Without any warning she received a letter from her long-lost brother.
5 I often find Jane and I have misunderstandings.
6 It looks as if they'll have to start all over again.
7 Keith's not looking too well these days, is he?

88.4 **Make combinations using a word from box A and a word from box B to complete the sentences. Use a dictionary if necessary.**

A	make	nitty	half	long	saving

B	hearted	winded	grace	believe	gritty

1 I feel we're not really getting to the .... of the issue.
2 The .... of the whole situation is that we will no longer have to spend money on a project that was doomed to fail anyway.
3 He lives in a .... world which is very different from reality.
4 It was a .... lecture which said very little.
5 She joined us in a rather .... way; you could see she really didn't want to be with us.

89 Idioms for situations

A When things go right

If something or things ...	*this means ...*
worked like a dream	a plan succeeded absolutely perfectly
went according to plan	they occurred exactly as intended
went/ran like clockwork	they went smoothly, with no difficulties
is/are up and running	it has / they have begun to work as planned
is/are falling into place	it is / they are on the point of starting to work well
is/are looking up	it is / they are looking very positive

B When things go wrong

Oh no! That's all we needed! [in response to news that makes current problems even worse]
That's the last thing I wanted to hear! [in response to news that fulfils your worst fears]
This is like a bad dream! [when one bad thing after another happens in quick succession]
It's a real nightmare. [used very generally, e.g. about traffic jams, computers going wrong]
What a pain! [very general: in response to any situation that causes you difficulty]
It's the calm before the storm. [when things are quiet, but you fear they are about to change]

C Confusing situations or situations you don't understand

When she said her name was Bloor it **threw me completely**. [I didn't know how to respond]
The meeting he organised was **a complete shambles**. [a totally disorganised and chaotic event]
It's a mystery to me how people know about my private life. [it's something I cannot understand]
I'm sorry, we must have **got our wires crossed**. I thought the meeting was at 11, not 10.30. [there must have been a miscommunication/misunderstanding]
It's as clear as mud. [in response to an explanation that only confuses you even more]
Let's not muddy the waters. [let's not confuse matters by introducing irrelevant things]
I'm not with you. / You've lost me there. [what you have said has confused me]
We can't see the wood for the trees. [too much detail prevents us seeing the overall situation]

D Resolving difficulty (or failing to do so)

It's nothing; **it's just a storm in a teacup**. [a lot of fuss / big argument that will soon be forgotten]
It would make life easier if you delayed it till next week. [it would help to solve the problem]
That was **a close call/thing**. [it was almost a disaster, but it turned out OK].
We solved the problem **at the eleventh hour** by sending a fax to his home number. [at the very last minute before disaster might have occurred]

It's just a storm in a teacup.

Nothing seems to have happened about the money that disappeared. It was all just **brushed under the carpet**. [all officially forgotten and never resolved; never mentioned again]

Exercises

89.1 Complete the idioms in these conversations.

1 A: Did everything go all right at the conference?
B: Yes, the whole thing went like ....

2 A: Did you take my advice?
B: Yes, and the whole thing worked like a ....

3 A: How are things at work? Still bad?
B: No, no, in fact things are really beginning to look ....

4 A: I'm afraid our idea of increasing the membership didn't really work.
B: Oh well, things don't always go according ....

5 A: Are you optimistic about your plans for the future?
B: Yes, I think things are beginning to fall ....

6 A: Have you started the new training programme you were planning?
B: Oh yes, it's up ....

89.2 Rewrite these sentences using an idiom based on the word given in brackets.

1 I can't understand how she can eat so much food and yet stay so slim. (MYSTERY)
2 The traffic in the city centre is very, very bad on Saturdays. (NIGHTMARE)
3 How inconvenient! We have to be at the airport at 5.30 a.m. (PAIN)
4 It's all very quiet; I'm sure it won't last. (STORM)
5 It was just a stupid row that blew up over nothing and then everyone forgot it. (STORM)
6 She asked me a question that completely surprised me and I didn't know how to answer it. (THROW)
7 This is an unbelievable series of bad events. (DREAM)
8 Oh no! I didn't want to be told that! (HEAR)
9 I'm sorry; there was a misunderstanding. (WIRES)
10 I'm sorry; I didn't follow what you just said. (LOSE)

89.3 What idioms are these pictures associated with?

1
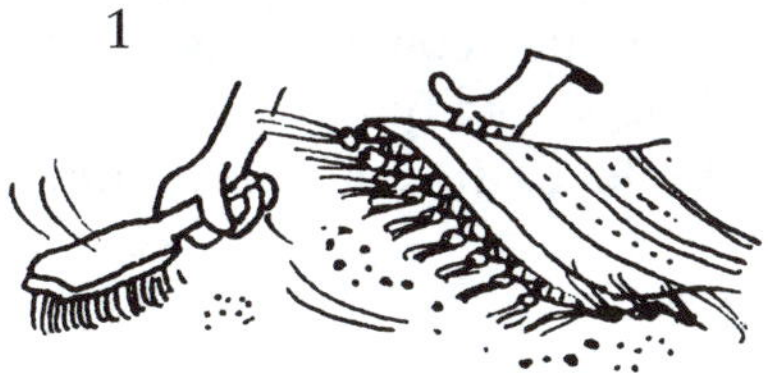
2
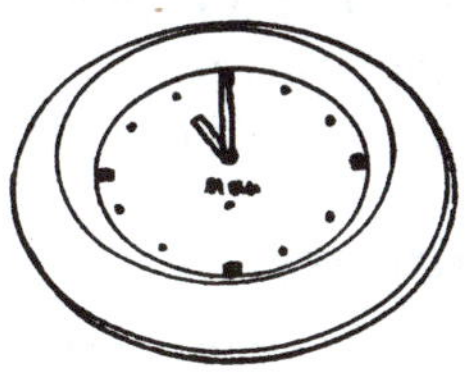
3

89.4 What idiom means ...

1 something completely disorganised and chaotic?
2 almost a disaster, but just avoided?
3 very unclear and confusing?
4 make something unclear and confusing by introducing irrelevant things?

90 Idioms that comment on people I

A Liking and disliking

Juliet **only has eyes for** Romeo. [is only attracted to]
Damian **loves** Anne **to bits.** [loves very much]
She is **the woman of his dreams.** He is **the man of her dreams.** [the perfect partner]
They immediately **fell head over heels in love.** [fell deeply in love]
They hadn't met before that holiday but they **got on like a house on fire.** [got on very well]
I **have a soft spot for** Kevin – he was always very kind to my grandma. [am fond of]
His rude behaviour really **gets up my nose / gets on my wick / gets on my nerves / gets my back up.** [informal: annoys me]

B Intelligence and knowledge

Jack's been in the business so long that he really **knows what's what.** [is an expert]
The new prof certainly **knows his stuff.** [is an expert in his field]
Although Sam is the manager, his wife is really **the brains behind** the company. [the most intelligent person in the company]
If you need help with the quiz, ask your grandfather. He's **a mine of information.** [a rich source of information]
You won't solve the problem if you don't use your **grey matter.** [intelligence, brains]
Milly **is nobody's fool** – she'll never believe such a poor excuse. [is very clever]
We **haven't a clue / the foggiest (idea)** what the bosses are planning. [have no idea]
I suspect Sue's **in the know** but she won't tell us anything. [has inside knowledge]
Pat **has the gift of the gab.** [talks well and persuasively]
My grandma **could talk the hind legs off a donkey.** [could talk for hours]
I can't stand Mark – he's such a **know-all / smart aleck.** [someone who shows off their cleverness in an irritating way]
Although his parents are both very bright, Neil **has got nothing between the ears / is as thick as two short planks.** [is extremely stupid]
Hugh is a bit **slow on the uptake** – you have to explain things to him several times.
Tim's dad **wasn't born yesterday** [is not stupid] – Tim won't be able to **pull the wool over his eyes.** [deceive him]
I **can't make head or tail of** what you're trying to say. [can't understand]
Rita is **one sandwich short of a picnic.** [stupid] You may come across other informal expressions following the same pattern and indicating stupidity:
He's **one cell short of a battery / one slice short of a loaf / several bricks short of a load.**

C Happiness and sadness

expression	*meaning*
to be on top of the world / on cloud nine / in seventh heaven / over the moon	to be extremely happy
to be in (your) element / to be made for	to be ideally suited for
to rave about	to be enthusiastic about
to look like the cat that got the cream	to look irritatingly pleased with yourself
to be down in the dumps / down in the mouth	to be depressed

Exercises

90.1 **Would you be pleased or displeased if someone said the following things to you?**

1 You certainly know your stuff.
2 You get on my wick.
3 You're nobody's fool.
4 You're two sandwiches short of a picnic.
5 You're such a know-all.
6 You're as thick as two short planks.
7 You're such a smart aleck.
8 You've got the gift of the gab.

90.2 **Correct the mistakes in the idioms in these sentences.**

1 It's no fun spending time with Jez and Sal as they only have an eye for each other.
2 Try to solve these problems by using your pink matter.
3 Most parents weren't born today – they have a good idea of what their kids get up to.
4 Maggie could talk the front legs off a donkey.
5 Mary's on cloud seven now she's at university.
6 They are head over feet in love.
7 I haven't the cloudiest idea what we should do about this letter.
8 Gilly has a soft place for Jim – she's always talking about him.
9 Ruth and Paul raved after the play.

90.3 **Complete the idioms in this text by filling each of the gaps with one word.**

Sarah has met the man of her .... (1). She loves him .... (2) bits. Fortunately he gets on like a house on .... (3) with her parents. I've known Tony for years and also have a .... (4) spot for him. He is a .... (5) of information. He works in a library where he is in his .... (6). He certainly knows what's .... (7) in libraries and can help anyone, even those people who are as thick as two short .... (8). Tony and Sarah have both been on .... (9) of the world since they met. I haven't a .... (10) when they will get married, but I am sure that they will marry as they are clearly head over .... (11) in love. Sarah's last boyfriend was very different. His behaviour really got her father's .... (12) up and I must admit he got up my .... (13) as well. He was such a know-.................... (14) even though I actually thought he had .... (15) between the ears. I can't understand why Sarah was so down in the .... (16) when they split up. Never mind, she's in .... (17) heaven again now.

90.4 **Look up these idioms in your dictionary. Do they fit best into A, B or C opposite?**

1 to put someone in the picture
2 to think the world of someone
3 to look as miserable as sin
4 to hit it off
5 to be walking on air
6 to let the cat out of the bag

90.5 **Choose one of the idioms in exercise 90.4 to replace the underlined phrases below.**

1 Amanda admires her father very much.
2 When I met my penfriend, we immediately got on like a house on fire.
3 I wanted to keep the present a secret but my little boy gave the game away.
4 Why have the children had such unhappy faces all evening?
5 If you come round this evening I'll explain everything to you.
6 I've been on cloud nine ever since I heard your good news!

91 Idioms that comment on people 2

A People's character

A: So, what do you think of your new colleagues?
B: Well, Miranda always seems **to be in a world of her own**[1]. Joe is **a rough diamond**[2] but it's worth putting up with his brusqueness. I quite like Sarah – she **never minces her words**[3]. Liz **is her own worst enemy**[4] – if she had a bit more confidence in herself, others would appreciate her more. Jill **is very much her own person**[5] – although all the rest of the family are teachers, she is determined to make a career in business. And Ben's **a soft touch**[6] – anyone can persuade him to lend them some cash.
A: Well, you are **a dark horse**[7] – I never thought you'd **get the measure of**[8] us so fast!

1 to be lost in a daydream
2 a good person with an abrupt manner
3 always says exactly what she thinks without trying to be diplomatic
4 behaves in a way that does not help her
5 is not influenced by others
6 can easily be persuaded
7 someone who hides their skills
8 gain a full understanding of

B People's feelings in particular situations

idiom	*meaning*
be/feel (all) at sea	feel lost or confused
want to curl up and die	feel terribly ashamed and embarrassed
turn (your) stomach	make (you) feel sick
be at a (complete) loss for words	not know what to say
be at the end of (your) tether	feel unable to deal with something because you are too tired, worried or annoyed
be full of beans	be full of energy
drive someone crazy / round the bend / nuts	make someone angry or mad
be dead on (your) feet	feel exhausted
put a brave face on it	pretend to be happy about something
go ballistic / blow a fuse / hit the roof/ceiling	react extremely angrily

C People's relationships

They had a terrible argument about their business plans and have **been at loggerheads** ever since [disagreed strongly]. I know there's been a lot of **bad blood** between them in the past but I thought things had improved now. [negative feelings, disagreements]
Susie **can twist/wrap her father round her little finger** – he'd do anything for her. In other words, she **has him eating out of the palm of her hand.** [can persuade him to do anything for her because she has so much control over him]
Don't trust him – he's **a snake in the grass.** [someone who pretends to be friendly but may do things that will harm you]
Tom has a knack of **rubbing me up the wrong way.** [irritating me without intending to]
He always **gives** his son **the benefit of the doubt.** [believes good rather than bad about him]

Exercises

91.1 Look at A and answer these questions.

1 Which two idioms would you most like to have used about you?
2 Which two would you least like to have used about you?

91.2 Look at B and then choose one of the idioms to complete each of these sentences.

1 The teacher .... when he saw the mess the children had made.
2 The children .... today – it must be the fresh sea air.
3 I .... when they rang up out of the blue and offered me a job.
4 I felt .... on my first day at work but I soon got used to it.
5 After a whole day of sightseeing in London, I ....
6 Mel's constant whingeing is ....
7 I .... when I realised that Melissa had heard what I said.
8 I'll just have to .... and hope no one sees I'm upset.
9 Just thinking of hot milk with a skin on it ....
10 I was .... when the children's mother arrived home. I think I'd really have lost my temper with them if I'd been on my own much longer.

91.3 Look at C and complete these idioms by adding a missing word.

1 He means well, but somehow he never fails to .... me up the wrong way.
2 Someone told me that the brothers have been at .... for over a year now.
3 Tess likes him but I wouldn't trust him. I think he's a .... in the grass.
4 You don't know that it was Nick that stole the money – I really think you should give him the .... of the doubt.

91.4 What idiom could you use to describe these people?

1 Your Aunt Vicky, who can easily be persuaded to give you some money.
2 Mike, who did not tell people of his plans to get married that afternoon.
3 Maria, who pretends to be your friend but is really planning to cause trouble for you.
4 A toddler, who is being very active and energetic.
5 Your mother, who did not know what to say about something you told her.
6 Yourself, on your first day in a new country where you do not know the language.
7 Helena, who is preoccupied by a daydream rather than reality.

91.5 Sometimes it can help you to learn and remember idioms if you know the literal meaning of all the words. What do the underlined words mean? Use a dictionary if necessary. Why do you think these idioms developed their meanings?

1 at the end of my tether
2 to curl up and die
3 to blow a fuse
4 a rough diamond
5 to go ballistic

91.6 Answer these questions.

1 Can you name two things that drive you nuts?
2 When did you last feel dead on your feet?
3 Can you describe an occasion when someone you knew hit the ceiling?
4 Have you ever been at loggerheads with anyone? If so, why?
5 Can you wrap anyone round your little finger?
6 Can you think of a situation when you had to give someone the benefit of the doubt?

92 Idioms that comment on stories and reports

A

Note how some idioms in the text below set the scene (1–3), some make the events more intense or exciting (4–8), and some comment on the events and draw conclusions (9–16).

One day, I was sitting at my desk in the office, **minding my own business**[1] and just **twiddling my thumbs**[2], when my colleague Tom Jessop came walking towards me. **I could feel it in my bones**[3] that something was going to happen. Suddenly, **out of the blue**[4], and **without so much as a by-your-leave**[5], he pulled the power cable out of the back of my computer, switching it off instantly. **Before I knew where I was**[6], he was switching it on again, and **in next to no time**[7], it was working normally. He explained that he had noticed out of the corner of his eye that I was just about to open an e-mail which he knew contained a dangerous virus, and he reacted quickly to stop me doing it. He explained that he had just opened the infected e-mail himself and that now his computer had completely crashed. **To cap/crown it all**[8], he had lost a long, important report he had almost finished. But, **would you believe it**[9], I had not saved my work for about an hour, and, **to cut a long story short**[10], by pulling out my power cable he caused me to lose a report I was writing too, even though he saved me from the virus! However, **as luck would have it**[11], I remembered later that I had a copy on my laptop, so everything **turned out all right in the end**[12], and **all's well that ends well**[13], at least for me. **I lived to tell the tale**[14], but poor old Tom lost everything on his computer. I know **it was just one of those things**[15], but still, **it just goes to show**[16] how you can never trust technology.

1 doing nothing special
2 feeling bored, with nothing to do
3 I could sense
4 completely unexpectedly
5 without asking permission or warning anyone
6 before I had time to be aware of what was happening
7 very quickly
8 as the worst event in a series of bad ones
9 said when one is about to tell a coincidence
10 to tell something briefly
11 purely by luck
12 finished well
13 said as a comment on a good ending to a series of bad events
14 I survived the events
15 it was an event that one just has to accept
16 used to state the moral or logical conclusion of the events

B Other expressions that occur in narratives

A: It turned out she went to the same school as my sister.
B: Well! **It's a small world,** isn't it? [said when a coincidence happens between people]

"So I said, I'm not afraid of animals, let me carry it. **Famous last words!** It was a six-foot snake!" [said when one later regrets something one has said]

A: I don't think I'll ever trust her again.
B: Well, **you live and learn,** don't you? [comment on events from which someone has learnt a lesson]

"So you're from Earth too? Small world isn't it!"

Exercises

92.1 **Complete the idioms in these sentences.**

1 I was just standing there, and then, out of .... , a man on a horse rode up to me.
2 I was in the office, minding .... , when I heard a bell ringing in the street.
3 I could feel .... that it wasn't going to be an ordinary day.
4 We were just twiddling .... , waiting for something to happen.
5 Then, without so much .... , he took my bike and rode off.

92.2 **Which idiom means ...**

1 to get quickly to the end of the story?
2 you usually learn something from a bad experience?
3 coincidences happen in this world of ours?
4 I survived all the bad things?
5 the events prove/demonstrate that ...?
6 the events were something you just have to accept?

92.3 **Match the beginnings and endings of the idioms below.**

1 as luck	that ends well
2 famous	believe it
3 in next	would have it
4 all's well	it all
5 to crown	last words
6 would you	to no time

92.4 **Match the underlined idioms with their definitions. Use a good general dictionary or a dictionary of idioms if necessary.**

A–Z

Idioms

1 I had a feeling of déjà vu.
2 So far so good, I thought.
3 One thing led to another.
4 If you can't beat them, join them.
5 You can't win them all.
6 I had nothing to lose, so I did it.

Definitions

a) A series of events all happened, over which the speaker had little control.
b) The speaker felt he or she had already experienced what was about to happen.
c) One always has to accept that bad things will happen as well as good.
d) Things were already bad, and the proposed action could not make them worse.
e) Things were going fine up to that point.
f) One is resigned to accept something that one has been struggling against.

FOLLOW UP

Look in the letters column of an English language magazine at the kind of letter where someone writes in to recount something unusual that has happened to them. Note any idioms of the kind illustrated in this unit.

93 Phrasal verbs 1

There are a great many phrasal verbs in English and the next three units cannot, of course, deal with them all. The aim of these units is to approach phrasal verbs in a number of different ways and to give you some tips to help you understand and learn them.

A

The best way to learn phrasal verbs is undoubtedly in context. Keep a section of your vocabulary notebook or file for phrasal verbs. When you come across one in a text that you are reading or listening to, note it down in a complete sentence or paragraph.

Here are a couple of useful points to remember about phrasal verbs.

- A verb + particle/preposition combination may have a number of different meanings. Look, for example, at these different meanings for **take off**: a plane **takes off** you can **take off** a coat/glasses/make-up a burglar may **take off** if he hears someone coming something is **taken off** a bill when a discount is allowed.
- You will probably find it best to concentrate first on understanding phrasal verbs rather than trying to use them. There is usually another English word you can use instead of a phrasal verb. For example, instead of saying the burglar **took off**, or 10% **was taken off** the bill, you can say the burglar **left hurriedly**, or 10% **was deducted from** the bill. Note that an alternative is not always possible. For example, it is not possible to find a synonym to replace **take off** when talking about **planes taking off** or **taking off clothes**.

B

Many phrasal verbs in English are based on verbs like **do, make, get, go, run, turn**, which have very little precise lexical meaning of their own, or verbs such as **stand**, which have several different meanings. One approach to learning phrasal verbs is to build a ripple diagram based round one of these verbs. For example:

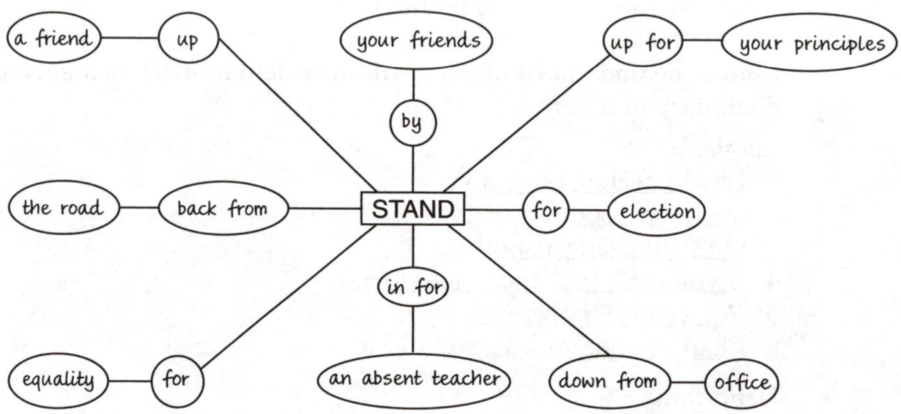

C

Such a diagram will be particularly useful if accompanied by sentences that illustrate the meanings of the phrasal verbs more clearly.

Ron waited an hour for Alice, then he realised he had been **stood up** and went home furious.
You should always **stand by** your friends when they are in trouble.
You should also **stand up for** your principles, even if it makes you unpopular.
The house **stands back from** the road, so you wouldn't notice it as you drive past.
There are three people **standing for** election in this constituency.
The party that I support **stands for** equality and improved social services.
I often had to **stand in for** other teachers who were absent.
After ten years as Mayor, Damian Taylor decided it was time to **stand down**.

Exercises

93.1 Complete these sentences containing *stand* in any way that seems appropriate to you.

1 The police asked people to stand back ....
2 When he was at school, John always used to stand up for ....
3 Michael Porter has decided to stand down ....
4 I always knew that Laura would stand by ....
5 The Socialist Workers' Party stands for ....
6 On my first day as a teacher I had to stand in for ....
7 I would never dream of standing .... up.
8 Masha is considering standing for ....

93.2 In the ripple diagram on the opposite page, you have two distinct uses of *stand for*. Use your dictionary to help you find two further ways in which *stand for* is used and then write one sentence to illustrate each meaning.

93.3 Here are some sentences based on phrasal verbs with *keep*, *tell*, *blow* and *pull*. Use your dictionary to help you complete the sentences by adding the necessary prepositions or particles.

1 The draught was so strong that it blew .... the candle.
2 He was very ill last year but, thank goodness, he pulled ....
3 The stress of his illness eventually told .... his wife and she fell ill too.
4 How do you plan to keep .... your English once this course finishes?
5 It is almost impossible to tell the original and the forgery ....
6 The papers are full of the scandal, but in a few days it will all have blown ....
7 The bus pulled .... sharply at a red light and I lost my balance and fell over.
8 Sara walks so fast that I can't possibly keep .... with her.
9 Wages have been kept .... for far too long even though prices have gone up.
10 An argument blew .... at the end of the meeting and it ended on a sour note.
11 The teacher told the boy .... for chewing gum in class.
12 The invigilator wouldn't have realised Sue was cheating if Amy hadn't told .... her.

93.4 Rewrite these sentences using a phrasal verb based on the verb in brackets. Use a dictionary if necessary.

1 Please don't walk on the grass. (KEEP)
2 Sam is going to the dentist to have a tooth extracted this afternoon. (PULL)
3 This is such a lovely photo. I'd like to have it enlarged and framed for my wall. (BLOW)
4 Rod's going to apply for the job, but the fact that he has so little experience will make it less likely for him to get it. (TELL)
5 Her idea for a new business is brilliant. I just hope she can succeed. (PULL)
6 Do you think that Ken might not be telling us the whole truth? (KEEP)

93.5 Make ripple diagrams to help you learn both the verbs you have been working on in exercises 93.3 and 93.4 and other phrasal verbs based on *keep*, *tell*, *blow* and *pull*.

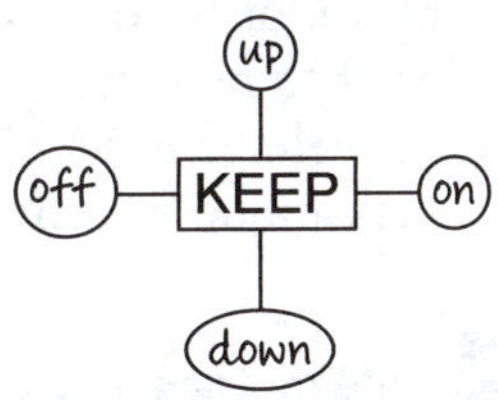

93.6 Rewrite the example sentences in C without using any phrasal verbs.

94 Phrasal verbs 2

A

In Unit 93 we looked at some phrasal verbs based on basic verbs like *stand*, *keep* and *tell*. In this unit, we look at phrasal verbs based on more unusual verbs or verbs which do not give rise to so many different phrasal verb constructions. The phrasal verbs are grouped according to their preposition or particle.

* marks the phrasal verbs that are more informal.

away

The boy tried to escape from his country by **stowing away** on a passenger liner. [hiding on ship, plane or other form of transport]
Taxes have been **whittling away** at our savings for some time now. [gradually destroying]
I've been **slogging away*** at this report for hours. I'm really fed up with it. [working hard]

down

A: What's the weather like with you?
B: It's **pelting down***. You'll get soaked if you go out without an umbrella. [pouring with rain]
There have been many complaints that universities are **dumbing down** their degree courses in order to attract more students. [making less intellectually demanding]
The government had made a serious mistake but, of course, they did what they could to **play it down.** [make it seem less important]

off

The police would never have caught the burglars if a rival gang hadn't **tipped them off.** [passed on secret information]
It was so hot in the sun that I **dozed off.** [fell asleep]
The anaesthetic is **wearing off** and my mouth is beginning to feel quite sore now. [lose its effect]

on

A: Waiter, why is my apple pie all squashed?
B: Well, you did ask me to **step on it!*** [hurry]
They **lay on** extra trains during the rush hour. [provide]
That music will never **catch on.** [become popular]

"Well, you did ask me to step on it!"

out

I was going to take part in the London Marathon but I **bottled out*** at the last moment. [lost my courage and decided not to do it]
I'm finding my job very unpleasant at the moment but I'm going to try to **stick it out*** until the end of this year. [persevere with it]
Jim always relies on his wife to **sort out** all the arrangements for their holidays. [organise]

up

I was about to leave work when a problem **cropped up.** [occurred]
It's said to be better to share your feelings with someone rather than to **bottle them up***. [keep feelings hidden]
It was raining heavily earlier on, but it's **easing up** a bit now. [becoming less intense]

TIP You may find it helpful to note such phrasal verbs down in your vocabulary book according to the preposition or particle. Try to note down an example sentence to help you remember the phrasal verb.

Exercises

94.1 Complete these sentences by adding a verb from the opposite page in each of the gaps.

1 Before I can go home, I must .... out the papers in my in-tray.
2 My grandfather has the talent of being able to .... off at any time in any place.
3 Jo's been .... away at her revision all morning. Why don't you take her a cup of coffee?
4 The company agreed to .... on some food at the party but workers would have to provide their own drinks.
5 We would have gone for a walk if it hadn't been .... down.
6 I'm sorry, I'm going to be late home again tonight. Something urgent has just .... up.
7 The escaped convict .... away on an oil tanker.
8 I really hate my job and don't think I can .... it out much longer.
9 We were very busy at the weekend but things have .... up a bit now.
10 Every year the management is .... away at jobs. Now there are fewer than 100 employees in the whole company.

94.2 Look at the underlined nouns in each of the sentences below. What do you think they mean? They are all connected with one of the phrasal verbs on the opposite page.

1 Thanks to a <u>tip-off</u>, the police were able to locate the bomb before it exploded.
2 Look at the cat having a <u>doze</u> on the window ledge. It's a wonder it doesn't fall off.
3 Two <u>stowaways</u> were found in the hold of the aircraft just before take-off.
4 I've finished the book now but I found it quite a <u>slog</u>.
5 The team has been badly affected by a <u>crop</u> of injuries.
6 The President is said to be very good at making people feel at <u>ease</u>.

94.3 What is the literal meaning of the basic verb in these phrasal verbs? Does this meaning have any connection with the meaning of the phrasal verb?

1 bottle up	3 step on it	5 crop up	7 stick it out
2 pelt down	4 stow away	6 sort out	8 whittle away

94.4 Does each of the six particles opposite seem to convey any specific idea that might help you to work out the meanings of the phrasal verbs? Note that there is more than one meaning for each of the particles/prepositions.

EXAMPLE **away** conveys the ideas of: at a distance (stow away)
continuous activity (whittle away, slog away)

94.5 New phrasal verbs are constantly being invented in English, particularly ones based on more unusual words. Can you use your knowledge about the meanings of basic verbs and prepositions in English, as well as the context, to work out what these underlined phrasal verbs mean?

1 I'm <u>conferenced out</u> now. I'm really ready to go home.
2 The advertising campaign led to sales <u>rocketing off</u>.
3 We decided to <u>tile up</u> the old fireplace.
4 The children <u>surfed away</u> on the Internet all day long.

95 Phrasal verbs 3

In this unit we look at two other ways of organising phrasal verbs.

A

You may want to group together verbs which have two prepositions or particles. Here are some examples:

Because Joe was often ill as a child, he **missed out on** a lot of schooling. [was not able to receive]
Capital punishment was **done away with** in Britain forty years ago. [abolished]
The sales manager really seems to **have it in for** her new secretary. She criticises her work all the time. [be determined to find fault with]

Why don't you come round for a cup of coffee this evening and we can **catch up with** all the gossip? [get up-to-date with]
I've been meaning to tidy my desk for ages but I just never **get round to** it. [find time for]
Eva has **gone/come down with** flu and won't be able to attend today's meeting. [started to suffer from]
Bill **fell out with** his brother when they were in their twenties and they didn't see each other for fifteen years. [quarrelled with]
When parents are stressed at work, they sometimes **take it out on** their children. [get unfairly cross with]

B

You may also be able to organise some phrasal verbs by topic. Here are some verbs classified according to a couple of topics which produce a lot of phrasal verbs.

Work and business

Our business went through a bad patch last year, but things seem to be **picking up** now. [improving]
Last year the company decided to **branch out** into some new lines. [expand]
We've **been snowed under** with work all month. [had a lot to deal with]
Two hundred workers have been **laid off** at the British Aerospace factory. [made redundant from their jobs]
House prices fell steeply earlier this year but now they seem to have **bottomed out.** [reached the lowest point from which they will not fall any further]

Mood and emotions

He's looking so miserable! What can we do to **cheer him up**? [make him feel happier]
Come to the bar with us – work isn't everything. You need to **chill out**! [informal: relax]
You really must try to stay calm. Don't get so **worked up** about it. [upset]
He's still angry. Wait until he has **simmered down** before talking to him. [become calmer]
The food looked so good, I **got** a bit **carried away** and ordered far too much. [lost control, became excited]
Knowing that I wouldn't tell anyone else, Susanna **opened up** to me a little. [told some secrets]
Being spoken to like that really **took me aback**. [surprised/shocked me]
Anne was **bubbling over with** excitement at the thought of seeing her boyfriend again. [full of]

"I got a bit carried away."

Exercises

95.1 Put the words in the right order to make sentences. To help you the first and last words are already in the correct position.

1 as / away / on / out / was / Juan / missed / the / he / fireworks
2 I've / temperature / and / with / got / think / I / a / be / down / going / may / something
3 I / on / day / but / need / take / out / know / had / no / to / you've / bad / there's / it / a / me
4 most / wish / schools / away / end-of-term / students / that / with / would / do / exams
5 it / time / really / is / painting / got / to / round / the / we / house
6 I / going / fall / to / with / over / other / each / we're / hope / not / who / is / to / out / going / pay
7 one / other / in / for / had / since / me / ever / in / has / work / of / it / I / waiters / started / the / that / restaurant
8 I / think / can / with / don't / I've / catch / break / take / as / I / a / lunch / to / today / some / up / got / work

95.2 Complete these sentences with either a verb or a preposition or particle.

1 Alex was feeling very miserable when he got home but a good meal and his favourite TV programme .... him up.
2 Jade was quite taken .... when she realised that she was the only person at the party who was in fancy dress.
3 Janet always gets terribly .... up over her exams.
4 Mel's decided to leave his job and .... out on his own.
5 It is rumoured that they are planning to .... off more staff next month. I hope I'm not one of them.
6 The children haven't talked to me at all about the accident but they might just .... up to their grandmother.
7 I'm absolutely snowed .... at work. I hope things ease up soon.
8 Sales have been very poor so far this year but there are signs that they may be .... up now.

95.3 Can you reword each of these sentences using one of the phrasal verbs from either A or B?

1 There's no point in trying to talk to your father until he's a bit less angry.
2 Do you think it would be a good idea to abolish selective education?
3 Sam's father died when he was six and so he grew up without a male role model at home.
4 When Mr Brown was made redundant, the family decided to emigrate to Australia.
5 Emily was very moved by the emotional way in which Richard read the poem.
6 Do you consider that oil prices have now fallen as low as they are going to?
7 You take life too seriously. Relax!
8 The newly married couple were full of happiness.

95.4 Look at the phrasal verbs in Unit 94. Which of these could also be included in either the *Work and business* or *Mood and emotions* categories?

95.5 A number of the phrasal verbs in B are based on metaphors. Find four examples and explain what the metaphor is and why it is appropriate.

96 Divided by a common language: American and British English

A Streets and roads

Street has a wider range of meaning in American English.
American speaker: Let's cross the **street** here. There's more traffic further down.
However a British speaker would normally say cross the **road**, especially in a busy city.
Here are some more examples of American English words and expressions not used in British English. The British English expressions are given in square brackets.

Go two blocks down and the car rental office is **kitty-corner** to [informal: diagonally opposite] the **gas station** [petrol station].
You should always use the **crosswalk** to cross the street. [pedestrian crossing / zebra crossing]
There's a **trail** [path] that leads down to the **creek** [stream, small river].
Take a left [turn left] here and you'll come to the **Interstate** [major motorway in the US connecting different states] after about three miles.
After the **intersection**, look for a sign saying 'International Airport'. [road junction]
I hit a shopping **cart** [trolley] in the **parking lot** [car park] when I was **backing up** [reversing].
Look for the **overpass** [flyover, i.e. bridge that carries one road over another] and then take the next exit for downtown Chicago.
Note: in British English road numbers use *the*, in American English no article is used.
British English: Take **the M4** as far as Newbury, then turn off on to **the A34** for Oxford.
American English: Take **I-45** north for about 20 miles, then take **25** west.

B Air travel

A number of expressions to do with air travel are different in British and American English. Here are some announcements you might hear at American and British airports.

American	*British*
Statewide Airlines announces the arrival of Flight 606 from Phoenix. This flight will **deplane momentarily**.	Monarch Airlines announces the arrival of Flight 505 from Lisbon. Passengers will be **disembarking shortly**.
Coach class passengers may now board.	**Economy** class passengers may now board.
Passengers are reminded that **carry-on** baggage is restricted to one item only.	Passengers are reminded that **hand** baggage is restricted to one item only.

C Around the home

This cable is the **ground** (US)/**earth** (UK).
[cable that takes electricity safely into the ground]
We need a **dumpster** (US)/**skip** (UK) to put all this old furniture in. [large metal container for putting rubbish in]
I left the **faucet** (US)/**tap** (UK) running and nearly flooded the kitchen.
I have to cook for five people, so we need a big **stove** (US)/**cooker** (UK). [piece of kitchen equipment to cook food]
I fried the fish in a **skillet** (US)/**frying pan** (UK).

THE FAR SIDE® By GARY LARSON

"Something's wrong here, Harriet. ... This is starting to look less and less like Interstate 95."

Exercises

96.1 **Who do you think is most likely to be speaking, an American or a British person? What would someone who speaks the *other* variety have said instead?**

1 I lost my way at the big intersection just south of the city.
2 Why are there always so many shopping trolleys left in the car park?
3 Cross the road at the pedestrian crossing, then turn left.
4 You can't drive any further; you'll have to back up, the street is very narrow.
5 You'll see the petrol station just after the flyover on the A56.
6 Once you get on to the Interstate, it will only take you two hours to get there.
7 The bookstore is kitty-corner to the Chinese restaurant.
8 There's a creek at the end of the trail. It's about three miles from here.

96.2 **Match the words on the left with their equivalent on the right, and write US for American English and UK for British English in the boxes.**

1 dumpster	☐	skillet	☐
2 ground	☐	skip	☐
3 frying pan	☐	stove	☐
4 cooker	☐	earth	☐

96.3 **Fill the gaps with a British English (UK) word or an American English (US) word.**

1 Do you want to check in that bag or take it on board as .... ? (UK)
2 Zodiac Airlines wishes to announce the arrival of Flight 347 from San Francisco. This flight will .... momentarily. (US)
3 .... class is always the cheapest way of flying. (US)

96.4 **In English, we often respond to something someone says with a single adjective or adverb instead of *yes* or *no*, or in order to express our feelings or reaction.**

EXAMPLE

A: Here's that book I promised you.
B: Oh, **lovely**. Thanks.

A: Could you hold this for me?
B: **Sure**. No problem.

Research shows that in conversation some words used as short responses are much more frequent in one variety of English than the other. The ticks (✓) in this table show in which variety the word is more frequent.

US	word	UK
	lovely	✓
✓	sure	
	fine	✓
	brilliant	✓
✓	cool	
	marvellous	✓
✓	wonderful	

Now cover the table and label these conversations with US (most likely American) or UK (most likely British).

1 A: The plane arrives at 6.30.
B: Brilliant. I'll meet you at the exit.

2 A: I'm coming to town this weekend.
B: Wonderful! Let's eat together Friday.

3 A: Will you help us tomorrow?
B: Sure, no problem!

4 A: I'll pick you up at 8.30.
B: Fine.

5 A: I just got a new bike.
B: Cool!

97 Other Englishes: diversity and variety

English is spoken in a wide range of countries outside of Great Britain and the USA. In this unit we look at some other varieties of English you may encounter.

A Ireland

Irish English has some words and phrases you may see or hear on a visit to Ireland which are different from British English. Many of them come from the Gaelic language of Ireland. Here are some examples.

word	*meaning*
craic /kræk/	fun, enjoyment
guards or **gardai** /gɑːr'diː/	police
boreen /bɔː'riːn/	narrow, quiet country lane
fleadh /flæː/	festival, usually of traditional music
Taoiseach /'tiːʃɒk/	Prime Minister

B Australia

Many people feel that Australian English has introduced a relaxed, informal tone to English vocabulary. Australian slang is sometimes called 'strine'. Here are some examples.

You'll have to forgive him; he's just an ignorant **ocker**. [person who is not well educated and does not behave in a polite way]

There was a young Australian in the shopping centre playing a **didgeridoo**. [/dɪdʒərɪ'duː/ ancient Australian wind instrument which produces long deep notes]

They live on a sheep **station** north of here. [large farm; also used in New Zealand]

'**Struth!** [gosh/wow] Look at that **bloke** [man] over there, **mate** [informal way of addressing a male]!'

Be careful of the **dingos** [kind of wild dog] when you're out in the **bush** [the natural, uncultivated land away from towns]. (*Bush* is also used in this way in African varieties of English.)

Travelling across the **outback** [the wild, uncultivated land, especially the desert] in **Oz** [slang name for Australia] can be dangerous, but there are some **beaut** [/bjuːt/ beautiful] places to see.

C Some other English varieties

variety	*example*	*meaning/comments*
Malaysian	We **shifted** a month ago. Here's my new address.	moved house
Canadian	The **washroom** is on the left.	public toilet
Hong Kong	We have to pay at the **shroff**.	car park payment office
Scottish	They have three **bairns**. /beənz/	children

Exercises

97.1 **Look at these news extracts and decide whether they are likely to have appeared in an Australian newspaper or in an Irish newspaper.**

1

Will the 2002 Fleadh be held here?

The city and environs could be in for a multi-million pound boost next year.

2

OZ SNAPS UP $100m US GEAR

American sports clothing has become a mega-business of the decade

3

BEAUT BANGLES – Diamond fiesta

Drooling at diamonds is probably not a healthy pastime, unless you're a born money bags.

4

He pointed out that all three men had apologised to the Gardai on the day following the incident.

97.2 **Answer these questions.**

1 What is the name for a kind of wild dog found in Australia?
2 Who or what is the Taoiseach?
3 When an Australian talks about the outback, what are they referring to?
4 What is an Irish person referring to when they talk of 'the craic'?
5 Where would you find a boreen?
6 Where would you find a station without trains or buses?
7 What would you do with a didgeridoo?
8 Is an ocker a person or thing? Explain.

97.3 **Match the words on the left with their definitions on the right. Try to guess the answers for those words not on the opposite page.**

1 shroff	Scottish word for 'small'
2 joker	Scottish word for a child
3 wee	Malaysian word for 'university'
4 varsity	Australian word for 'person'
5 bairn	Caribbean word for a godmother
6 washroom	Hong Kong word for a payment office at a car park
7 macommere	Irish word for 'idiot/fool'
8 eejit	South African word for flat, open countryside with few trees
9 veld	Canadian word for a public toilet

FOLLOW UP

If you can, read Chapter 7 on 'World English' of *The Cambridge Encyclopedia of the English Language* by David Crystal, published by Cambridge University Press, where you will find examples of English from different parts of the world.

98 Language and gender

A Gender awareness and vocabulary

A number of vocabulary changes are being introduced as a result of the feminist movement and heightened awareness of the sexist nature of some English vocabulary. David Crystal in *The Cambridge Encyclopedia of the English Language* writes:

Attention has been focused on the replacement of 'male' words with a generic meaning by neutral items – *chairman*, for example, becoming *chair* or *chairperson* (though not without controversy) or *salesman* becoming *sales assistant*. In certain cases, such as job descriptions, use of sexually neutral language has become a legal requirement. There is continuing debate between extremists and moderates as to how far such revisions should go – whether they should affect traditional idioms such as *man in the street*[1] and *Neanderthal Man*[2], or apply to parts of words where the male meaning of man is no longer dominant such as *manhandle*[3] and *woman*. The vocabulary of marital status has also been affected with the introduction of *Ms* as a neutral alternative to *Miss* or *Mrs*.

[1] a typical person (could be replaced by *person in the street*) [2] primitive people who lived in Europe and Asia 2.5 to 3 million years ago [3] handle roughly, using force

Here are some examples of non-sexist variations of vocabulary:

older usage	*current usage*
spokesman	spokesperson
fireman	firefighter
male nurse	nurse
to man	to staff
man-hours	working hours

older usage	*current usage*
air hostess	flight attendant
cleaning lady	cleaner
foreman	supervisor
manpower	human resources
mankind	human race

B Words relating to gender

words	*meaning/comment*	*example*
male, female	used for gender classification in biology	**male** and **female** bees
masculine, feminine	having qualities felt to be typically male or female	**masculine** pride, **feminine** charm
manly, womanly	having positive qualities felt to be typically male or female	**manly** strength, **womanly** grace
virile	manly (usually used in a sexual context)	handsome and **virile** men
effeminate	resembling a woman (used of men, negative)	his **effeminate** walk
mannish	resembling a man (used of women, negative)	her **mannish** haircut
a tomboy	a young girl who behaves and dresses like a boy	She's a real **tomboy**.
a sissy	a boy who behaves like a girl, or a weak and cowardly person (informal, negative)	He's such a **sissy**!
butch	used of men and women, aggressively masculine in looks and behaviour (informal)	**butch** stars of cowboy films

Exercises

98.1 Answer these questions about the text.

1 Why do you think there have been attempts to introduce non-sexist language of the kind described by David Crystal?
2 How would you explain this expression: male words with a generic meaning?
3 Why do you think there might have been controversy about attempts to change the word *chairman*?
4 What do more extreme advocates of making English sexually neutral want to do that is unacceptable to the moderates?
5 Why was *Ms* introduced and why is it useful?

98.2 A modern editor would probably alter these sentences. How would this be done?

1 Three firemen helped put out a fire at a disused warehouse last night.
2 A spokesman for the Department of Education provided us with a statement.
3 Cleaning lady wanted for house in Priory Street.
4 The switchboard is continuously manned even during holiday periods.
5 All our air hostesses are fluent in at least three languages.
6 Miss Jones is in charge of the Manpower Department of the company.
7 Policemen today spend more time in cars than on the beat.
8 Brenda's husband is a male nurse.
9 It took a great many man-hours to clean up the stadium after the concert.
10 This was a great step for mankind.
11 The man in the street has little time for such issues.
12 They manhandled the hostage into the van.

98.3 Circle the best of the underlined words to complete each sentence.

1 That suit makes her look rather <u>mannish/manly</u>.
2 Go on, jump. Don't be such a <u>tomboy/sissy</u>!
3 Younger men are said to be more <u>male/virile</u> than older ones.
4 She always dresses in a very <u>feminine/effeminate</u> way. You never see her in trousers.
5 The <u>masculine/male</u> cat is less aggressive than his sister.

98.4 Answer these questions.

1 Does your language ever use male words generically?
2 If so, have there been attempts to change them to avoid sexual stereotyping?
3 Do you think that using sex-biased words does affect people's attitudes to men and women's roles in society?
4 How do you feel about imposing language changes of the different kinds that David Crystal describes?
5 Do terms of address (i.e. Mr, Mrs, etc.) in your language indicate whether people are married?
6 Do you think it is better if terms of address indicate marital status or not? Why?
7 A grammatical problem in this area is the use of *he/his* to refer to a person of either sex. In the sentence 'A government minister may have to neglect his family.' the minister could be a man or a woman. However the use of 'his' assumes, perhaps wrongly, that it is a man. How could you rewrite this sentence to avoid this problem?

99 Language of age and social class

A

In English, certain expressions will date the speaker or place them in a particular social or age group. People are often judged on the way they speak and listeners may decide that the person is either **posh** (upper class, negative) or **common** (lower class, negative). Here are some disapproving words which are used to comment on a person's class.

expression	*refers to*	*comment*
a pleb	lower-class person	adjectives **plebby** (informal) and **plebeian** (formal)
an oik	lower-class man	implies bad behaviour
riff-raff	lower social class	implies lack of culture
hoi polloi	ordinary people	excludes the rich or the educated
the chattering classes	well-educated middle-class people	implies readiness to express an opinion on any subject
bourgeois	middle class	implies someone who is narrow-minded and materialistic (can also be used more objectively in a historical context)
the upper crust	upper class	people with money and influence
stuck-up / snooty	behaving in a snobbish way to lower-class people	implies someone who thinks that he or she is better than other people
new money	people who have recently become rich	implies spending money in a showy way
a toff	rich upper-class person	usually used humorously

B

People often continue to use the expressions that were popular when they were young. **Cool!** or **Wicked!** are the current terms of approval, whereas in the 1940s it was **Spiffing!** Similarly, the words people choose to use for inventions may also date them because older people may continue to use a name that was the everyday word in their youth but which has since changed. Thus, some older people may refer to a car as a **motor** (**car**), to a radio as a **wireless**, to trousers as **slacks**.

In general, older people, particularly older people from the upper classes, are more likely to use **one** as a pronoun, often where the meaning is really I:
One doesn't always agree with what she has to say.

C

Social class in English affects vocabulary choice in some possibly unexpected ways as certain words are, for no obvious reason, held to be either common or posh, depending on your point of view.

Luncheon, for example, is an upper-class version of lunch. **Toilet** is considered by some people to be a more lower-class way of referring to the lavatory or loo. Addressing parents as Mother or Father rather than Mum or Dad also suggests that the speaker is likely to be upper class. These distinctions are probably less marked than they used to be, but you may come across them in works of fiction where they may be used by writers to indicate the social background of their characters.

Exercises

99.1 **Choose the best word or expression from the box to fit each sentence.**

bourgeois	chattering classes	oik	common
new money	riff-raff	upper crust	stuck-up

1 They're probably called the .... because they like to spend hours sitting at a pine dinner table over their fettucine discussing the latest book or exhibition.
2 Pink Rolls Royces are much more likely to be owned by .... than the old aristocracy.
3 I don't know why they allow such .... in a lovely classy restaurant like this.
4 Although her dad's a duke, she's not at all ....
5 Karl was glad to have escaped the .... attitudes of the small town he had grown up in and to be living in the much more liberal atmosphere of a city.
6 Her parents sent her to a private school mainly because they did not want her to grow up talking in a way that they considered ....
7 The expression .... derives from the fact that the most important people in the medieval dining hall were given the best or top part of a loaf of bread.
8 Maria's parents, Lord and Lady De Vere, are very upset that she wants to marry someone whom they consider to be an ignorant ....

99.2 **What does the language used in the sentences below tell you about the speakers?**

1 The whole family used to gather together and listen to the wireless every Sunday evening.
2 We all still dress for dinner even when no one is expected. One has to do one's best to keep up standards.
3 Old Jack has bought a spiffing new motor.
4 Your new mobile is wicked – I'll text you from uni this afternoon.
5 We wasn't doing nothing, was we, Tracey?

99.3 **The comic novels by the writer P.G. Wodehouse about a 'toff' called Bertie Wooster make extensive use of a now rather dated upper-class dialect of English. What do you think the underlined words, typical of these novels, mean?**

1 Don't be such a <u>chump</u>! Aunt Angela won't bite you!
2 You must help me, old <u>sport</u>. I'm in an awful <u>fix</u>.
3 I'm short of money now but I'm hoping an old uncle, who's <u>rolling in stuff</u>, will <u>kick the beam</u> soon and leave me his fortune.

FOLLOW UP

Read the play *Pygmalion* by Bernard Shaw which is based on the relationship between class and English. In the play, a professor tries to teach a poor lower-class girl to speak English in such a way that she can pass as a duchess. You can access the text of the play at: www.bartleby.com/138

100 Newspaper headline language

A Features of headline language

Here are some typical examples of headlines from **tabloid newspapers** with comments on their use of language. [popular papers with smaller pages than more serious papers]

EXPERT REVEALS NEW MOBILE DANGERS

- Articles, prepositions and auxiliary verbs are often omitted from headlines.
- This use of the present simple instead of the past tense makes the story sound more immediate.
- The use of language is often ambiguous. It is not entirely clear, for example, what *mobile* refers to here. It is actually about the dangers of mobile phone use but it could have referred to dangers that can move in some way. Readers have to look at the story in order to find out.
- Words with dramatic associations such as *danger* are often used.

TV STAR TRAGIC TARGET FOR MYSTERY GUNMAN

This story is about how a well-known television actor was shot by an unknown killer.

- Tabloid newspapers like to use references to royalty or popular figures like film or pop stars or sports personalities in order to attract readers' attention.
- Alliteration such as TV Star Tragic Target is often used to attract the eye in headlines and to make them sound more memorable.
- Newspapers tend to use strong, simple words such as 'gunman' in order to express an idea or image as briefly and as vividly as possible.

B Violent words

Violent and militaristic words are often used in newspaper headlines, especially in tabloid newspapers, in order to make stories seem more dramatic.

EU acts to **crush terror** of the **thugs**
Crackdown on soccer **louts**
Palace **besieged** by journalists
Typhoon **rips** through town

C Playing with words

Many newspaper headlines in English attract readers' attention by playing on words in an entertaining way. For example, a story about the theft of traffic signs erected to help tourists coming to see a solar eclipse in the area was headlined **Dark deeds**. In this collocation *dark* usually carries the meaning of *wicked*, but the headline is cleverly playing with the word *dark* because at the time of an eclipse the sky goes dark.

Another example is the use of the headline **Ruffled feathers** to describe an incident where a wife was angry with her husband, a wildlife expert, for allowing a Russian steppe eagle to sleep in their bedroom. We use the idiom **to smooth someone's ruffled feathers**, meaning to pacify someone after an argument. It is apt to use it here as the story is about a bird (although, of course, it was the woman's feathers which were ruffled).

TIP The English newspaper *The Guardian* is particularly fond of playing with words in its headlines. See if you can find some examples at its website: www.guardian.co.uk

Exercises

100.1 Read these headlines. What do you think the stories might be about?

1 **MOSCOW BLAST TERROR**
2 **PM TO REVEAL SOCCER LOUT PLANS**
3 **TOP MP IN LONE BATTLE**
4 *CRACKDOWN ON PORN*
5 **THUGS BESIEGE TEEN STAR**
6 COPS TARGET LOUTS

100.2 These headlines were written in a pretend tabloid newspaper about Ancient Greece. Match them with the subjects of their stories (a) to (e) below and comment on the features of headline language they contain.

1 **NUDE SCIENTIST IN BATHTUB SENSATION**
2 **KING PHIL'S MACEDONIAN MASH-UP**
3 ***MARATHON MAN IN DROP-DEAD DASH***
4 QUADRUPLE ROYAL MURDER SENSATION
5 **IT'S CURTAINS FOR CORINTH**

a) Mysterious death of four members of the royal family.
b) Philip of Macedonia wins battle against city states of Athens and Thebes.
c) Archimedes' discovery of the laws governing the displacement of water.
d) Burning of city of Corinth to ground by the Romans.
e) Long-distance runner brings news of battle victory to Athens and then dies.

100.3 Match the headline to its story and explain the play on words in each case.

1 ***Bad blood***
2 **Happy days?**
3 **Shell-shocked**
4 **False impressions**
5 **Happy haunting**
6 Hopping mad
7 Flushed
8 Highly embarrassed
9 Round-up

a) A grandfather's breathing problems were solved when doctors found four false teeth at the entrance to his lungs. They had been forced down his windpipe in a car crash eight years ago.
b) A 25-year-old terrapin is being treated for a fractured shell after surviving a 200ft drop.
c) A Shetland teacher has suggested labradors or golden retrievers could be used to control pupils in playgrounds.
d) A ghost society has been told not to scare off a friendly female apparition at a hotel.
e) Adults who have never quite grown up are to be offered school theme nights including uniforms, register, assembly and primary school dinners by a Nottingham hotel.
f) An ex-public loo in Hackney, East London, is to be sold for £76,000.
g) A Whitby curate has attacked the resort's attempts to profit on its connections with Dracula: 'a pale-faced man with a bad sense of fashion, severe dental problems and an eating disorder.'
h) A toad triggered a police alert when it set off a new hi-tech alarm system.
i) Firemen had to scale a 30-foot tree in St Leonard's, East Sussex, to rescue a man who was trying to capture his pet iguana.

Key

Unit ii

ii.1
1 signify
2 written record
3 punishment given by a judge
4 small in amount
5 pretending to have
6 mark above a letter to show how you pronounce it
7 part which you say loudest
8 issues

ii.2
1 famished
2 brilliant
3 worn out
4 gorgeous
5 pouring
6 excruciating
7 appropriate
8 annoying

ii.3
1 to contemplate your future
2 to dismiss a worker
3 to do some gardening
4 to dribble a ball
5 to have a good time
6 to make a mistake
7 to pay a compliment
8 to plead innocence
9 to set an example
10 to shuffle cards
11 to waste an opportunity
12 to wind a rope

ii.4
1 A horseshoe, a mascot and a black cat are lucky in British English (though black cats are unlucky in the US) and the number 13 is unlucky.
2 It is associated with Christmas because it is used as a decoration at that time of year and with kissing because tradition says you can kiss anyone who is standing under the mistletoe.
3 The standard meanings are:
loaf = large piece of bread before it is cut into slices
bread = food made from flour and water
nick = cut slightly
kid = young goat
wicked = evil, morally bad

The informal meanings are:
loaf = head [This is an example of Cockney rhyming slang, which is spoken in some parts of London: Use your loaf (of bread) = Use your head!]
bread = money
nick = prison, steal
kid = child
wicked = wonderful
4 a) language appropriate to a particular situation, e.g. formal, informal, academic, etc.
b) record of the absences of pupils
c) all the notes a musical instrument or a person's voice can produce

Unit iii

iii.1 *Dissimilar* is normally used in the negative; for example:
These yellow flowers are **not dissimilar** to the ones I have in my garden.

iii.2 *For* and *to* are the normal prepositions; for example:
He will be **liable for** the cost of repairs to the car since the accident was his fault. [legally responsible for]

You will be **liable to** a fine of £200 if you send your tax declaration in late. [subject to / obliged to pay]

iii.3 *Aught* is an old-fashioned or regional dialect word meaning 'anything'; e.g. Is there **aught** you want?

iii.4 The two verbs may sometimes mean the same, i.e. 'to make up for not doing something because you did not have enough time'.
I must **catch up on** some sleep this weekend. I've stayed up late studying every night this week.
I'm trying to **catch up with** my work. I've missed two classes because I had a cold.

Catch up with also means 'to discover that someone has done something wrong and punish them'.
He committed a number of small crimes years ago, but the police **never caught up with** him.

Catch up with also means 'to meet someone you have not seen for some time'.
I'm hoping to **catch up with** Freda when I'm in Toronto next week. I have an address for her there. I haven't seen her for about three years.

Unit iv

iv.1
1 real
2 real
3 real/genuine
4 genuine
5 genuine

iv.2
1 c
2 d
3 a
4 b
5 c

iv.3
1 brisk, sharpen
2 toll
3 leisurely
4 perfectly
5 bequeathed
6 rightly
7 visit
8 spoilt

iv.4
1 a powerful car
2 strong tea
3 auburn hair
4 a doleful expression
5 a lengthy meeting

Unit v

A The word that would fill the gaps in all three sentences is **match**.

D
a) an instrument a dentist uses to make holes in your teeth
b) training for marching
c) a pneumatic tool used for making holes in a road

Unit vi

vi.1
a) in the saddle = in charge; idiom taken from horse riding
b) moving the goalposts = changing the rules; idiom from football
c) a half-baked idea = an idea that is not fully thought through; idiom from cookery
d) to tighten our belts = to reduce our spending; idiom from dressing

vi.2 a) All the world's a stage and all the men and women merely players.
The lines suggest that life is like a theatre and that possibly the roles are written in advance, with people being like actors in that they all have different parts to play. (From *As You Like It*)

b) Night's candles are burnt out; and jocund day stands tiptoe on the misty mountain tops.
The lines say that night has finished and day is about to break. 'Night's candles' conjures up an image of the stars because now that dawn has come the stars are no longer visible and so they can be said to have burnt out. Day standing tiptoe suggests that day is poised ready to start a race down the mountain tops. It also implies the quietness of early morning because we tiptoe when we want to be quiet and not wake someone who is sleeping. (From *Romeo and Juliet*)

c) There is a tide in the affairs of men, which, taken at the flood, leads on to fortune.
The lines suggest that our lives have tides like the sea and we must take advantage of lucky opportunities, metaphorical flood tides, in order to be transported to good times. (From *Julius Caesar*)

vi.3 a) This book throws a great deal of fresh light on the history of the period.
This books tells us a great deal that is new about the history .... .
From the concept of intelligence as light.

b) We could save half an hour at least if we went through the wood.
We could gain half an hour .... . From the concept of time as money.

c) Try to keep cool even if he argues with you.
Try to keep calm .... . From the concept of intense feeling as heat.

d) She spent all her life fighting to get her company recognised.
(Two metaphors) She devoted all her life to trying hard to get her company recognised. From the concepts of time as money and business as a military operation.

e) Police tried to control the flow of the fans as they left the concert.
Police tried to control the movement of the fans .... . From the concept of movement of people as water.

Unit vii

vii.1
1 She works in a shop that sells ladies' clothing. (Ladies' garments might be an even more formal equivalent.)
2 I've got some new specs. Do you like them?
3 Did you see that documentary about Wales on telly / on the box last night?
4 Have you met Lily's new bloke? ('Lily's new man' is also possible.)
5 I spent the morning conversing with the Director.
6 Molly was there with her husband. He's a nice man.

vii.2

neutral	*formal*	*informal*
children	offspring	kids
sunglasses		shades
policeman/woman	police officer	cop (*or* bobby)
umbrella		brolly
meal	repast	
make sure	ensure (*or* guarantee)	

vii.3 **In a database totalling ten million words of everyday spoken and written English texts, the words in the list occurred approximately in the ratios given in the second column (for example, *begin* is five times more frequent in written English than in spoken).**

word		*ratio spoken : written*
frequently	W	1 : 11
start	S	2 : 1
begin	W	1 : 5
maybe	S	5 : 1
moreover	W	1 : 60

vii.4
1. pharmacist/chemist
2. girl/young unmarried woman
3. poetry or poem
4. to where / where to

vii.5
1. This computer text could be called written, modern, technical. Terms such as *.pst file*, *shared directory* and *file server* are technical. The style is typically written, especially with the use of passive voice verbs and the word *located*; in non-technical spoken language we would probably just say 'one that is on a file server'.
2. This is typical modern, written academic text. Key written items are *above*, and the citation of other researchers' works. The adjectives *ornery* and *splenetic* (which mean angry/argumentative and bad-tempered/irritable) are very rare outside of academic and literary registers. Other typical academic words are *paradigm* (which means a dominant set of beliefs or methods in an academic field) and the initials *SLA*, which mean *Second Language Acquisition*.
3. This is rather archaic poetry (by the English poet John Donne, 1572–1631). *Thee* is an archaic form of singular *you*; *'tis* is an archaic form of *it is*; *in jest* is rather formal and/or literary and means 'as a joke / not serious'. Other rather formal or literary words are *weariness* and *feigned* (pretended).
4. This is formal spoken language. It is from a speech by US President John F. Kennedy (1917–1963). Key items are the formal *ask not* instead of 'don't ask', *my fellow*, and *the freedom of man* instead of human freedom or freedom for everyone. Formal speeches and lectures are often very close to formal written texts, and this text could possibly also have been a written text (e.g. a political pamphlet or electioneering literature).
5. This is informal, modern conversation. Key items are *mind you* (rare in written language), *telly* instead of television, *cos* instead of *because*, and *yeah* instead of yes. The text is quite fragmented too (*The Rhine. Yeah. The river in Bonn*). Written registers tend to be more integrated (e.g. *The River Rhine in Bonn*).

Unit viii

B **These are the connotations which these words have for most English speakers:**

shark — a dishonest person, someone who persuades other people to pay too much money for something

scar — something ugly which spoils, for example, a landscape

diamond — typical stone in engagement ring; referring to a period of 60 years, e.g. diamond wedding, diamond anniversary; diamonds is one of the red suits in playing cards

D **In English the colours have the following connotations:**

1 blue	miserable
2 green	inexperienced
3 yellow	a coward
4 red	danger
5 white	purity
6 black	evil

Note that these are not the only connotations which these colours have. Blue, green and red, for instance, can also be used to refer to different political parties.

Unit 1

1.1 1 AD 2 i.e. 3 NB 4 e.g.

1.2
1 Alcoholics Anonymous, pronounced as letters
2 pages, pronounced as the word in full
3 miles per hour, usually pronounced as the words in full
4 before Christ, pronounced as letters
5 unidentified flying objects, pronounced either as the words in full, or as an acronym or as letters
6 as soon as possible, pronounced as letters

1.3
1 World Health Organisation
2 United Nations Educational, Scientific and Cultural Organisation
3 International Monetary Fund
4 Order of the British Empire (honour awarded by the monarch for services in any area of life)
5 Greenwich Mean Time (standard time in the UK as measured at the Greenwich Observatory)
6 International Olympic Committee
7 Royal Society for the Prevention of Cruelty to Animals
8 Eastern Standard Time (standard time on the east coast of the USA)

1.4 See you for tea at three, is that all right with you? By the way K's going to be here too.

1.5 *Possible answer:*

3rd girl wanted for s/c f/f flat. Suit n/s prof. C/h. All mod cons / £220 pcm excl.

1.7

1 DUMP	Disposal of Unused Medicines and Pills
2 NOW	National Organisation of Women
3 UNITE	Union of National Income Tax Employees
4 CALL	Computer Assisted Language Learning
5 AAAAA	American Association for the Abolition of Abbreviations and Acronyms

Unit 2

2.1 *Suggested answers:*

1 a 2 b 3 c 4 b 5 a 6 c

2.2
1 The hotel upgraded me to a luxury room (instead of the ordinary one I'd booked).
2 Would you like to stay there overnight or come back the same day?
3 The underlying problem is a very serious one.
4 Cross-cultural misunderstandings are, sadly, very frequent.
5 I think this hotel is overpriced.

6 It's slippery underfoot just here. Be careful.
7 The company experienced an upturn in popularity since it changed its name.
8 I felt that what she said undermined my position.
9 It would be a mistake to underestimate how intelligent Frances is / to underestimate Frances's intelligence.

2.3

1	locate	YES	allocate
2	verse	YES	adverse
3	state	NO	
4	mission	YES	admission
5	pertain	YES	appertain
6	minister	YES	administer
7	drain	NO	

2.4 *Possible answers:*

1 There were several advertisements **promoting** the new range of products.
She was **promoted** to Senior Manager after two years in the job.
2 Mobile phones have **proliferated** in recent years. Now almost everybody has one.
3 I hate people who **procrastinate.** I always try to tackle problems when they arise, and not put them off till tomorrow.
4 Many religious people believe that the only purpose of sexual relations is **procreation.** [having children]

2.5

1 **Ab-** in these words has the idea of something going or being taken away from something.
A king or queen may **abdicate** [give up the throne], a prisoner may **abscond** [run away from prison], and a criminal may **abduct** someone [kidnap them, persuade them to go with them].
2 **A-** here is something like the *-ing* form with verbs. So if something is **ablaze,** it is blazing [burning vigorously]. If a boat is **afloat** it is floating on the water, if it is **adrift** it is drifting out of control.
3 **Extra-** means 'outside of'. Thus **extraterrestrial** means from beyond earth, e.g. from another planet, 'an extraterrestrial being', **extraneous** details are details which are not relevant or outside of the important ones, and **extracurricular** activities are activities outside of the school curriculum, e.g. optional sports during lunchtime, after-school clubs.
4 **Inter-** often means connected or linked one with the other. **Interrelated** refers to a connection between separate things. **Interdepartmental** means 'between different departments'. The **Internet** is a system that connects computers around the world.
5 **Intra-** means within something. **Intravenous** means in the veins. **Intradepartmental** means 'within the department'. **Intranet** is a computer network that operates only within one organisation.

Unit 3

3.1

suffix	*possible examples*
-able	a debatable issue, an uncontrollable child
-conscious	cost-conscious management, money-conscious parents
-free	car-free city centre, sugar-free drinks
-rich	energy-rich drink, information-rich society
-led	French-led fashion, military-led coup
-minded	broad-minded person, sports-minded friends
-proof	bullet-proof car, a fireproof screen
-related	smoking-related illnesses, drugs-related crime
-ridden	flu-ridden office, poverty-ridden society
-worthy	noteworthy pictures, creditworthy person – note that this means someone to whom a bank is prepared to give credit [a financial loan]

3.2 **Here are some of the most likely adjective + noun combinations. You may find others that also work.**

1 additive-free foods, drinks
2 avoidable delay, mistake
3 disposable knives and forks, income
4 guilt-ridden expression, criminal
5 high-minded speech, principles
6 newsworthy story, personality
7 oil-rich economy, country
8 ovenproof glove, dish
9 soundproof room, booth
10 stress-related illness, problems

3.3 *Suggested answers:*

age-conscious, age-related
dust-free, dustproof, dust-related
Byronesque
sugar-free, sugar-rich, sugar-related
workable, work-conscious, work-free, work-rich, work-led, work-minded, work-related

3.4

1 Poisonous mushrooms are easily identifiable.
2 He is so career-minded that he has no time for his family.
3 The new phone boxes are supposed to be vandal-proof.
4 During the Civil War, the country was terror-ridden.
5 The soil on that farm is nutrient-rich.
6 The bank decided that he was not creditworthy.

3.5

1 This depends on who is the current President of the USA. Adjectives relating to past Presidents include Lincolnesque, Kennedyesque, Clintonesque.
2 meat-free
3 class-related
4 vitamin-rich
5 dry-cleanable
6 clothes-conscious
7 government-led

3.6

1 verb
2 adjective
3 adverb
4 adjective
5 verb
6 adjective
7 adverb and adjective
8 verb

Unit 4

4.1
1 a message written and sent from a distance
2 sound carried from a distance
3 something written by yourself about your own life
4 study of sound
5 to go backwards
6 study of writing
7 to make something unstable
8 something written to represent yourself

4.2 *Possible answers:*

telegraph technological bio-technology phonologist telephony retrogressive

4.4
1 She asked the star for his **autograph** on the back of her table napkin.
2 She took a degree in **criminology** at Stockholm University.
3 The novel is largely **autobiographical.**
4 It's **a retrospective exhibition** of the painter's life and work.
5 He believes in **auto-suggestion.**
6 **Teleworking** is becoming increasingly common.
7 Some areas are now deliberately trying to **de-industrialise**.
8 **Cybercrime** is a growing cause for concern.

4.5 *Possible answers:*

1 The firm makes job applicants do a test that analyses their handwriting for what it reveals about their personality.
2 Johnny loves his electronic toy that behaves like a pet.
3 Matt's brilliant at technical things.
4 He's giving a paper at a special event taking place just before a conference in Spain.
5 Is it OK if I write a date on this cheque that is later than today's date?

4.6
1 information + commercial, i.e. a television advert that gives information instead of selling something (e.g. explaining new social welfare regulations)
2 education + entertainment, e.g. a CD-ROM that is intended to teach children by using games
3 cyberspace + library, i.e. a collection of texts often literary or educational that can be accessed via the Internet
4 vegetable + hamburger, i.e. a vegetarian hamburger
5 swimming + marathon, i.e. an event in which people attempt to swim a very long distance (probably done in order to raise money for charity)
6 fun + fantastic, i.e. fantastically good fun (this would be most likely to be seen in an advert trying to attract people to some leisure event or holiday)

Unit 5

5.1 *Possible answers:*

1 source of worry, confusion, inspiration
2 enrich your life, experience, vocabulary
3 classical music, drama, studies
4 linguistic errors, study, puzzle

5.2 1 hammock 2 turban 3 tabby 4 cot

5.3 1 hara-kiri 2 mumps 3 amber 4 tonic 5 roster 6 gimmick

5.4 *Here are some possible answers for speakers of Spanish:*

- food and drink – paella, tapas, rioja
- flora, fauna and landscape features – mosquito, cork, banana
- industrial products and inventions – lasso, fumidor
- clothing and the home – sombrero, mantilla, hammock
- politics and society – junta, guerilla, embargo, mañana, macho
- the arts, sports and leisure activities – flamenco, guitar, toreador

5.5 If possible compare your answers with those of other speakers of your language.

5.6 Notice that these words may not all have originated in English. *Pudding* originates from an old French word, for instance, but it seems to have moved into some other languages from English rather than going directly from French.

Unit 6

6.1
1 interfere
2 stationary [stopped, not moving]
3 compliment
4 avoid
5 sign
6 intervened
7 complemented [added to, made even better]
8 stationery [paper, envelopes, labels, etc.]
9 continually
10 evading [avoiding doing something in an illegal or improper way]
11 signal [a signal usually tells you to react in some way, or that something is happening]
12 continuously

6.2
1 upended
2 outrun [run faster than]
3 outdo
4 upheld
5 outlasted [lasted longer than]
6 ended up
7 outstay [stay longer than you should]
8 run out [are finished/exhausted]

6.3
1 rehearse an end-of-term play
2 revise for an exam
3 change the batteries in the clock
4 alter a garment that's too big
5 pick up a friend at the airport
6 pick flowers in the garden
7 rouse someone who's sleeping
8 arouse someone's suspicions

6.4
1 an outbreak, e.g. There has been an outbreak of violence. [sudden occurrence of]
2 an upset, e.g. I had a stomach upset and couldn't go to work. [sick stomach]
3 an outlook, e.g. He has a very cheerful and positive outlook (on life). [attitude to life and the world]
4 a setup, e.g. His car hadn't been stolen at all. It was all just a setup. [someone had made it look like the car had been stolen]
5 a lookout, e.g. Thieves or robbers often have one person as a lookout, watching for police, etc.
6 a breakout, e.g. There were three breakouts from this prison last year.

Unit 7

7.1 I think I have a good **working relationship** with most of my colleagues. I tried to establish a good **rapport** with them from the very beginning. The person I like most is my **opposite number** in our office in Paris. Generally, when I socialise **with** my colleagues outside of work, we try not to **talk shop**, but it's not easy and sometimes we have a good gossip about people who are not there.

7.2 *Possible answers:*

1 **assembly-line worker** This is a worker who stands at a moving mechanical belt and repeats the same job or process, so it could be called tedious, monotonous, repetitive, mind-numbing [deadens your mind], soul-destroying [destroys your spirit and ambitions and dreams].
2 **shop steward** This is a trade union officer who negotiates with management on behalf of the union members, so it could be called demanding, stressful, hectic, intensive, sensitive, thankless [nobody is ever really grateful to you].
3 **PR officer** A Public Relations Officer gives statements to the press and information to the public in general. This job could be called varied, unpredictable, glamorous [the PR officer might appear on radio and TV], demanding, stressful, never-ending.
4 **bodyguard** This is a job where someone protects a person whose life may be in danger. It is definitely a (potentially) dangerous, stressful, intense, demanding job, for highly-trained people, but it could also be glamorous, exciting and exhilarating.
5 **lifeguard** This is a job where someone saves people who get into difficulties in swimming pools and/or in the sea, and generally watches over their safety, so it could be called rewarding, indispensable, (potentially) dangerous, stressful, demanding, but sometimes monotonous.
6 **trawlerman** This job on a large fishing boat is dangerous, unenviable, essential, stressful, physically demanding, unpredictable.
7 **private eye** A private eye is a private detective, so this job could be called glamorous, exciting, dangerous, fascinating, but for some people it is contemptible [they hate or despise private eyes].
8 **refuse collector** This is a person who collects the rubbish from people's houses, generally a monotonous, unglamorous, unenviable, low-paid, dirty, unpleasant, but essential job.

7.3

1 -to-five job	5 flexi-time	9 self-employed
2 clock in and out	6 a rut	10 end job
3 workload	7 shift work	11 off
4 behind a desk	8 freelance	12 antisocial

7.4 *Possible answers:*

1 a station porter, a labourer [person who does unskilled physical work] on a building site
2 a social worker, an aid worker [person who works for an organisation giving humanitarian aid to people in need]
3 a travelling salesperson, a courier
4 a doctor, a film cameraman
5 a post office worker, a supermarket check-out assistant
6 a journalist, a news reporter
7 a secretary, a clerk

Unit 8

8.1 *Suggested answers:*

1 Do you often look at the job advertisements?
2 I have no sales experience.
3 Selling computers is very lucrative. I made £70,000 last year.
4 We sell quite a diverse range of products.
5 I thought I would apply for the job since I fitted the description.

8.2
1 a very close-knit team
2 a very rewarding job
3 to have (a lot of) drive / to be an achiever
4 a rather dynamic and fast-moving profession
5 a salary increment

8.3
1 A career suggests a progression over time, with promotion and a structure that enables people to move around and up.
2 Unclear situations, which might demand (difficult) decisions.
3 Self-reliance.
4 Resourcefulness.
5 You need a tough mind.
6 The job advertisement is for a youth adventure leader. This is a person who takes young people on challenging outdoor trips and expeditions such as mountain-climbing, canoeing, sailing, etc.

8.4 *Suggested answers:*

1 –
2 +
3 – It means to have far too much work to do.
4 – It means to be given a lower position.
5 – It means to not get the promotion you expected or deserved.
6 – It means to be refused/rejected.
7 + To be short-listed for a job means you are one of perhaps five or six people from all the applicants who are being seriously considered.
8 + To be a high-flyer means to be someone who is rising fast in the job, and will probably be promoted frequently.

8.5
1 I started studying French at university, but I didn't finish my *course* and left after one year. ('Career' is not normally used to refer to university studies; it usually means a job or a profession.)
2 My boss *raised* my salary *by* £2,000 a year. I was delighted. (Don't confuse *rise* (intransitive) with *raise something* (transitive). Verbs of increase and decrease are normally followed by *by + quantity/number*, e.g. The temperature rose by 10 degrees.)
3 I'm *overworked and underpaid*, like everybody! And I'm always stressed *out*. ('Overworked and underpaid' is a binomial expression; normally these cannot be reversed: for example, we say 'a black and white film' in English, never 'a white and black film'.)
4 My holiday *entitlement* is four weeks a year.
5 He got *paternity* leave when his wife had a baby.

8.6 *Possible answers:*

1 You could get a job in a 'dot-com' company (an Internet-based company), where profits can be very high, or else perhaps in the financial sector, or in a highly paid profession such as the law or dentistry.

2 You could try to get a job in a band or orchestra, but it will be tough. Maybe teaching music would be a better option.
3 You could get a job in the computer industry, perhaps setting up systems in companies, or perhaps approach a big international computer company and sell yourself very hard to them.
4 First talk to your superiors, if you have a good rapport with them. If not, look around for another job, but don't give up the one you have (yet).

Unit 9

9.1
1 loss leader
2 capital assets
3 confusion marketing
4 first refusal
5 hard sell
6 inertia selling
7 brand loyalty
8 niche market
9 red tape

9.2 1 under 2 around 3 first 4 cold 5 on 6 bid 7 phone 8 niche

9.3
1 hammer out a deal
2 red tape
3 merging
4 lucrative
5 entrepreneurship
6 swallowed up

9.4 *Possible answers:*
1 cold-calling, hard sell, inertia selling, confusion marketing, red tape, swallowed up
2 buildings, machinery, computers
3 on approval, bidding, first refusal, shop around, brand loyalty
4 loss leader, niche market, telesales, cold-calling, inertia selling, confusion marketing
5 **Red tape** is used to refer to bureaucracy. The metaphor is based on the red ribbon that used to be used to tie up sets of documents and it is appropriate because it relates to documents in large quantities.
Swallowed up is used to refer to a smaller company being taken over by a larger one. It is based on the idea of a larger creature eating a smaller one and is appropriate in that when something is eaten it becomes part of the bigger whole.
Come under the hammer is used to refer to something being sold at auction and it is appropriate in that a hammer is used by the auctioneer when he is announcing that he has taken the final bid. He traditionally uses the words 'going, going, gone' and then hits with his hammer to announce the sale.
Hammer out an agreement is again a metaphor based on hammering. This time the image is one of hammering out a piece of metal to make it flat and acceptable in a way that clearly has associations with getting rid of problems that may stand in the way of an agreement.

Unit 10

10.1
1 Do you have many outstanding accounts?
2 When does your contract expire?
3 Please acknowledge receipt of our payment.
4 It is very important that you meet the deadline.
5 We would like to invite companies to submit tenders for the job.
6 It is company policy to take legal action against customers who default on payment.

10.2 1 project 2 flaw 3 Resources 4 morale 5 lack 6 employee

10.3 1 J.K. Galbraith
2 Mahatma Gandhi
3 Charles, Prince of Wales
4 John D. Rockefeller
5 Theodore Roosevelt

10.4 1 a chief executive
2 a personal gesture
3 a square deal
4 the survival of the fittest
5 an award for achievement
6 to turn your hand to
7 the human factor
8 to amass a fortune
9 to conduct business

10.5 1 chief executive
2 amass a fortune
3 turn his hand to
4 a square deal
5 the human factor
6 to conduct business
7 an award for achievement
8 personal gesture

Unit 11

11.1 1 His PhD **thesis** ...
2 Little Martha did her first **composition** ...
3 We have to hand in a **portfolio** ...
4 The teacher gave us the title of this week's **essay** ...
5 At the end of this course you have to do a 5,000-word **assignment** ...
6 I think I'll do a study of people's personal banking habits for my MSc **dissertation** ...
7 I've chosen to do the **project** ...

11.2 When I'm **cramming** for an exam, I don't see any point in looking up **past papers**, nor is there any point in just learning things **(off) by heart.** I know some people develop very clever **mnemonics** to help them remember the material, but there's no real substitute for **revising** the term's work. It's a good idea to have some sort of **mind-map**, and **rote-learning** is useful, but in a limited way. At the end of the day, you just have to **bury yourself in your books** until you feel you know the subject **inside out.**

11.3 1 b 2 a 3 b 4 c

11.4 1 a first draft
2 a deadline
3 plagiarism
4 submit; assess
5 drop out
6 a paper; in (academic) journals
7 inter-library loan
8 feedback

Unit 12

12.1 1 league tables
2 selective education
3 equality of opportunity
4 perpetuating inequalities

12.2 1 Inequality is **inherent in** the education system.
2 **Elitism** is bad for the country in the long term.
3 **Comprehensive education** is a basic political ideal in many countries.
4 A **two-tier system** of schools **depresses** the opportunities for children from **less well-off** families and favours those from **better-off** families.
5 Some private schools **are well-endowed**, and this means they can have better resources.
6 All parents want their children to **excel** at school.
7 Emphasis on the three Rs is **perceived** by parents to be the key to success.

12.3

1 literacy	4 the three Rs
2 numeracy	5 a mature student
3 curriculum reform	6 one-to-one teaching

12.4 *Answers for Great Britain:*
1 When class sizes become very small, for example in villages in the countryside where people have moved away to towns.
2 Typically, children cannot concentrate, they talk during lessons, they bully one another. Teachers are not allowed to hit children, but they may put them into detention or inform their parents.
3 There may be a teacher who can teach slow learners, or special teachers may come in to help pupils with learning difficulties, but children often have to go to special centres to get help.
4 People of all ages, more and more, are going to universities in Britain, and special courses (called Access Courses) help them to do so. There are also evening classes, usually organised by local councils, which are not very expensive.

12.5 1 PTA: (Parent–Teacher Association) group consisting of teachers and parents who meet regularly
2 School governors: group which oversees all the business of the school
3 Supply teacher: teacher who works in a school when needed (e.g. if someone is sick)
4 Peripatetic teacher: teacher who works in different schools and travels between them

Unit 13

13.1

1 altruistic	selfish
2 diligent	lazy
3 intellectual	low-brow
4 methodical	unsystematic
5 morose	cheerful
6 obliging	unhelpful
7 quick-tempered	placid
8 sensitive	thick-skinned
9 stingy	generous
10 stubborn	flexible

13.4 The speaker has a positive opinion of Pat and Sam, but a negative opinion of Vince and Julie.

13.5 Pat seems very sly and terse. I find Vince thrifty and diligent. Julie is serious and resolute. Sam is unscrupulous and extravagant.

13.6

1 altruism	3 diligence	5 industriousness/industry	7 gallantry	9 moroseness
2 parsimony	4 placidity	6 sagacity	8 terseness	10 unscrupulousness, lack of scruples

13.7 altruistic – unselfish, selfless
parsimonious – mean, tight-fisted
diligent – hard-working
placid – calm, easy-going
industrious – hard-working
sagacious – wise
gallant – polite, chivalrous
terse – abrupt, brusque
morose – miserable, gloomy
unscrupulous – dishonest

Unit 14

14.1
1 ... love at first sight.
2 ... kindred spirits.
3 ... bosom pals.
4 ... head over heels in love.
5 ... hit it off.

14.2
1 eyes
2 well-matched
3 on; on fire
4 infatuated or (much stronger) besotted

14.3

noun	*adjective*
loyalty	loyal
consideration	considerate
passion	passionate
devotion	devoted
fondness	fond
faithfulness/faith*	faithful

noun	*adjective*
respect	respectful
affection	affectionate
romance	romantic
support	supportive
amiability	amiable
trust	trusting/trustworthy*

*Faithfulness is when you are completely loyal to someone; faith is the complete trust or confidence that you have in someone or something.
*If someone is very trusting, they trust you (or other people); if they are trustworthy, you (or other people) can trust them.

14.4 1 to 2 for 3 to 4 of 5 of 6 in

14.5 *Author's answers:*

1 My brother and sister: because they represent for me a link with my childhood and with my parents, who are now dead.
2 A very dear friend of mine: because this friend seems to see the world in exactly the same way as I do and always understands the problems I have.
3 My favourite colleague at work: because he does so many things that I also love to do and he has similar ambitions to me.

Unit 15

15.1
1 disloyal
2 untruthful
3 dishonest
4 unwelcoming
5 discontented
6 cold-hearted (or heartless)

15.2
1 ... we're **business partners.**
2 I've made several **casual acquaintances ...**
3 Were Britain and the USA **allies ...**
4 ... they're **bitter rivals.**

15.3
1 staunch
2 scrupulous
3 deeply
4 complete, unswerving
5 bitter
6 true (or loyal)

15.4
1 Rick and his sister didn't see eye to eye on a lot of things.
2 Her affection for Andrew has turned sour lately. I expect they'll split up.
3 Our relationship broke down because we always misunderstood / never understood each other.

15.5
1 There was a genuine misunderstanding.
2 They come from a broken home.
3 It has had its ups and downs.
4 A serious rift has developed/emerged between the two union leaders.
5 I think it's a family feud.

15.6
1 with 2 of 3 to

15.7
1 To die because of sadness resulting from a love affair which the other person ended, or you have lost the one you love (e.g. because of death), or some other, similar, personal tragedy.
2 To hate someone very much. This is a very informal expression. Formally we might use **to dislike someone intensely.**
3 To take advantage of every opportunity to speak badly of someone and/or to be looking for opportunities to create problems for them.
4 To have a bad relationship with someone.

Unit 16

16.1
1 b
2 c
3 b
4 b
5 c
6 b

16.2
1 hankering
2 covetously
3 rapturously
4 conciliatory
5 implacable
6 placatory; jubilation

16.3
1 Sarah has been walking on air since she got engaged.
2 Beth is full of the joys of spring.
3 Amanda seems to be on top of the world since finishing her thesis.
4 Jill feels enormous pity for children with AIDS.
5 Sam is hankering after a new computer.
6 His parents rejoiced at his good fortune.

16.4 *Possible answers:*

1 Anything that the person is happier not knowing about, e.g. an impending disaster or something unpleasant happening elsewhere.
2 No, appeasement implies being inappropriately conciliatory.
3 Jubilant.
4 Personal answer – you might mention any experience of intense happiness, e.g. when in love.

Unit 17

17.1 *Possible answers:*

1 Tripe, brains, lumpy custard.
2 Having a filling at the dentist, having an oral exam, finding mice that the cat has brought in.
3 A politician who stole a lot of money and then lied in court.
4 I find racism abhorrent.
5 I once felt an instant antipathy to a new colleague – though later we got on quite well!
6 People smoking in public places is my pet aversion.

17.2

1 loathsome	3 abhorrent	5 fickleness
2 repulsive	4 sloppily	6 scornfully

17.3 *These sentences all mean more or less the same as the original:*

1 People who talk with their mouth full revolt me.
2 I have an aversion to people who talk with their mouth full.
3 I find people who talk with their mouth full abhorrent.
4 People who talk with their mouth full fill me with repulsion.

17.4

1 ostentatious/brash	3 obsequious	5 grasping	7 bland
2 fickle	4 sloppy	6 squalid	8 trite

17.5

1 fuddy-duddy	3 nit-picking	5 officious
2 puerile	4 off-hand	6 brash

Unit 18

18.1 'fat' words: stout corpulent portly
'thin' words: scrawny gangling lanky

18.2

1 She looks as if she needs a good meal; **she is so scrawny.**
2 Marian and Frank are very suitable for each other; they're both **lanky** individuals.
3 A rather **portly**, middle-aged man offered to show us the way.
4 A **gangling/gangly** boy carried our bags for us.
5 She's become quite **stout** these days, ever since she stopped playing tennis.
6 A rather **corpulent** gentleman ascended the stairs, red-faced and breathless.

18.3 *Suggested answers:*

1 This person has rather unkempt hair.
2 This person doesn't have a hair out of place.
3 This person has a double chin.
4 This man has a rather/very haggard(-looking) face.

18.4

1 He is biting his nails.
2 He is folding his arms.
3 She is clenching her fists.
4 She is pouting.

5 He is crossing his legs. / He is sitting with his legs crossed.
6 She is shrugging her shoulders.
7 She is scowling.
8 He is picking his nose.

18.5
1 The two meanings are to position one's lips in a sexually attractive way or to position one's lips in a look of annoyance.
2 They probably feel angry or annoyed.
3 A swarthy complexion is a dark complexion, a sallow complexion is rather yellowish and unhealthy-looking.
4 b
5 They might do this if they are puzzled, or perhaps if they are tired, or if their head was itching.
6 Perhaps because they are surprised or shocked.
7 When you were really angry.
8 When they want to show they don't know or understand something, or if they wish to show they just don't care about something.
9 You might tap them on a hard surface such as a table.
10 I often fold my arms when listening to a talk or a lecture, or if I am sitting down when someone takes my photograph. I cross my legs when I'm listening to a talk or lecture, or when sitting and waiting such as at the dentist's or the hairdresser's.

Unit 19

19.1
1 unapproachable (or perhaps reserved)
2 pig-headed
3 They have little self-confidence.
4 an effusive greeting
5 Yes; scrupulous means extremely honest and not wanting to do wrong.
6 Impetuous is more negative.

19.2

adjective	*noun*
excitable	excitability
disdainful	disdain
impetuous	impetuousness or impetuosity
obstinate	obstinacy
modest	modesty

adjective	*noun*
gullible	gullibility
reserved	reserve or reservedness
garrulous	garrulousness or garrulity
conceited	conceit or conceitedness
pig-headed	pig-headedness

19.3
1 impulsive
2 approachable
3 aloof
4 extrovert
5 conscientious
6 obstinate
7 pig-headed
8 conceited
9 self-important
10 garrulous
11 pushy
12 disdainful
13 unscrupulous

19.4 *Suggested answers:*
1 She's a flirt, and doesn't care who knows it.
2 He's always had a tendency to be / tended to be an introvert.
3 Larry is (rather/very) reserved, while his sister is more approachable.
4 I'm an impulsive buyer rather than thinking about what I really need.
5 He was a (very) garrulous man, and taciturn is a word I would never associate with him.

Unit 20

20.1

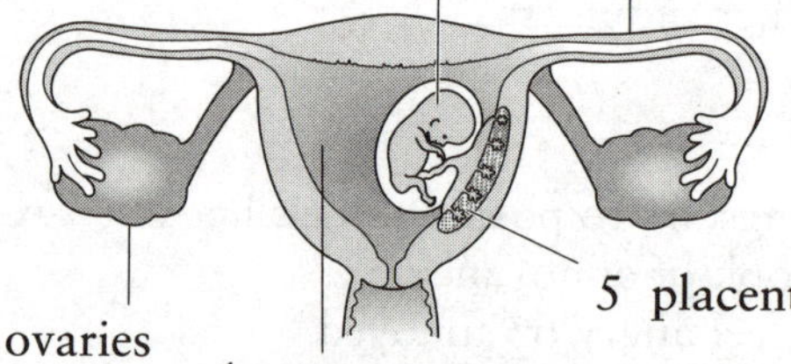

20.2 fertilisation, conception (these could be said to happen at the same time as they both suggest the point where the egg is fertilised and a baby is conceived – though some might say that conception happens a little later, when the fertilised egg implants itself into the wall of the uterus)
pregnancy
labour
delivery

20.3
1 The whole country is in **mourning** after the President's death.
2 I'd like my **ashes** scattered at sea.
3 My **late** grandfather was a shepherd all his life.
4 I'm afraid her elderly godmother has just passed **away**.
5 My car is on its last **legs**.
6 My grandfather **bequeathed** me his gold watch in his will.
7 Mrs Wilson seems to have been at death's **door** for years.
8 Over two thousand people **perished** in the earthquake.
9 It was amazing there **were** no **fatalities** when the bridge collapsed.
10 My uncle left me a **bequest** of five hundred pounds in his will.

20.4
1 Both my sisters are expecting at the moment.
2 Amanda Harrison gave birth to twins last Monday.
3 She has been taking fertility drugs (to help her conceive).
4 All my grandparents lived to a ripe old age.
5 My grandmother is 90 but she still has all her wits about her.
6 Unfortunately the deceased died without leaving a will.
7 John's three nephews each inherited £1,000 from him.

20.5
1 perished
2 fatalities
3 slaughtered
4 deceased
5 passed away
6 bequeathed
7 inherited
8 bequest

Unit 21

21.1
1 therapeutic
2 lucrative
3 relaxing/calming/therapeutic
4 fruitful
5 rewarding
6 time-consuming

21.2 1 a couch potato 2 a doer 3 a culture vulture 4 a dabbler

21.3 *Author's answers:*
1 Playing folk music on the violin.
2 a shopaholic
3 a) a workaholic b) a sportaholic c) a chocaholic (not a chocolataholic)
4 I could be called a 'fiddlaholic' (a lover of the violin – fiddle is an informal word for a violin, especially if you play folk music on it).

21.4
1 time off, leisure time, free time or leisure
2 split fifty/fifty
3 labour-saving
4 mechanisation, automation
5 mass production

21.5
1 My daughter's **into** folk music. She buys a lot of folk CDs.
2 He **locks** himself **away** in his darkroom and does photography for hours on end.
3 She's (**totally**) **hooked on** ice hockey these days. She watches every competition on TV.
4 I have a **full diary** for the rest of the month.
5 What do you **get up to** when you aren't working, Nigel?

Unit 22

22.1
1 She meant that she tends to dress in an untidy, careless way.
2 Jeans, trainers [sports shoes] and sweatshirt [informal top with long sleeves, usually made of thick cotton].
3 *Personal answer*
4 She is about to do her finals [last university exams] and so stop being a student and begin working. In the work environment clothes tend to be more important than they are for a student.
5 They do not want pastel colours, shoulder pads or very short skirts. They also do not want to appear frumpy.
6 She would like it to be smart, young and modern. It should be conventional enough to fit most dress codes but also with some individuality to show a potential employer that she is a person with a degree of special style and originality.
It also must not be too expensive.
7 This will depend, but in many workplaces, the dress code for men is a suit with a shirt and tie. For women it may be a dress or skirt rather than trousers.
8 There are many ways of answering this question, of course, but the article from which the extract was taken went on to recommend a honey-coloured trouser suit in stretch fabric.

22.2
1 kill
2 smart-casual
3 dress down
4 designer (label); high street
5 snazzy
6 baggy

22.3 *Possible answers:*
1 Mini scooters and dresses with uneven hemlines.
2 Platform shoes, sarongs and pashminas.
3 That they must be rather stupid and insecure to need to follow fashion so closely. (Note that this expression is disapproving so it would be unusual to have a positive opinion about people described in this way.)
4 Not very interested at all.
5 Film stars, pop stars, business people who wish to make money from selling new fashions.

22.4
1 I'm no good at speaking off the cuff.
2 Although he's the head of a large company, his wife wears the trousers at home.
3 Have you any idea what all these cloak-and-dagger meetings at work are about?
4 Be careful what you say to Helen – she's hand in glove with the boss.
5 I wouldn't invite them to stay if I were you – they'll take/have the shirt off your back before you know where you are.
6 The new legislation has really put us in a straitjacket.

22.5 1 The literal meaning of frill is a piece of cloth with folds along one side which is sewn onto another piece of material for decoration. The metaphorical meaning of no frills is basic, simple, no extras.
2 The literal meaning of the verb hem is to sew up the bottom edge of e.g. a dress so that it does not develop loose threads. Hemmed in means completely surrounded.
3 A seam is a line of sewing joining two pieces of material so that if, say, a bag is bursting at the seams, it is almost splitting open. The metaphorical meaning of bursting at the seams is very, very full.
4 Literally, to cloak is to cover with a cloak. The metaphorical meaning of cloaked is kept secret.
5 Literally a feather in someone's cap is simply a feather decorating one's cap or hat. The metaphorical meaning of the expression is an achievement to be proud of.

Unit 23

23.1 *Possible answers:*

accommodation	*What kind of person lives there?*	*Would you like to live there? Why/Why not?*
squat	a homeless person or someone with very little money	I wouldn't like it because you never know when you might be evicted.
pied à terre	someone who is wealthy enough to have a small second home which they use occasionally	I'd love to be able to afford a flat in the capital so that I could stay there if I wanted to have a weekend shopping and going to theatres.
council housing	people who do not have enough money to buy a house of their own	It would depend on the area – some council housing is very nice and has a friendly atmosphere. Other areas are rather run-down and depressing.
granny flat	an elderly relative of the people who live in the main house	When I'm old I would like to live close to my family but with at least a degree of independence.
high-rise flat	any type of person might live in one of these, though it would probably be someone in a large city	I prefer to live in a house because it is good to have a garden.
hovel	a very poor person or someone who is not good at looking after themselves	I should hate to live somewhere dirty and in a bad condition.
penthouse	someone with a lot of money	You might have wonderful views from a penthouse flat, but I prefer to live somewhere that has a garden.

23.2 1 Feng Shui 3 minimalism 5 New Age
2 the rat race 4 subsistence farming

23.3 *Author's answers:*

Young, fashionable people are most likely to be attracted to **minimalist** décor. It would be very hard for people with children or people who like collecting souvenirs to live in such a way. I'm afraid it is not suited to my way of life because I have collected too much clutter over the years.

Post-modernism is likely to appeal to people who are quite eclectic in their tastes. It appeals to me because I think it allows you to put together all sorts of different things without having to try to be consistent in your approach.
New Age is likely to attract rather unconventional younger people, especially those who are tired of a more materialist way of life. Some aspects of it interest me, but I enjoy the comforts of a conventional life too much to be tempted by a totally New Age lifestyle.
Subsistence farming is often something that is forced on people by circumstance rather than adopted by choice. However, it is an attractive life for people who like the outdoor life and who enjoy hard physical work. I like the idea of growing all my own food, as you would know that it had not been contaminated by chemicals of different kinds. Also, home-grown food tends to be fresher and to taste better. However, it would be a difficult lifestyle to have and would not be one that I personally would choose.

23.4 1 house 2 home truths 3 write 4 story

23.5
1 We **had the time of our life/lives** on holiday this year.
2 As soon as spring comes I feel as if I'm **getting a new lease of life.**
3 The problems caused by the floods are only **hitting home** now.
4 I imagine that being a servant in the past was **a dog's life.**
5 All over the world McDonald's **is a household name.**

Unit 24

24.1
1 a stag party (if you're a man) and a hen party (if you're a woman) – note than *hen party* is usually, but not exclusively, used about pre-wedding parties for women
2 a wedding reception
3 a housewarming (party)
4 a launch (party)
5 a reception
6 a fancy dress party

24.2 *Suggested answers:*
1 It's always good to see Hugh but somehow he always manages to **stay too long.**
2 You wouldn't believe it but Helen and Mark **are now going out together** (**as boyfriend and girlfriend**)!
3 I don't really approve of the way Erica **actively makes contacts with influential people,** but I'm sure it'll help her to make a success of going freelance.
4 Don't forget your old friends when your film becomes a hit and **you're mixing socially with** the rich and famous.
5 I'm going to a birthday **party** this weekend. Should be fun.
6 We must invite Jane to **our party.** She **adores going to parties!**
7 Mike'll want **to spend an evening going round different pubs** as soon as his exams finish.
8 Let's **spend an evening enjoying the various entertainments available in the town** as the children are with their grandparents tonight.

24.3 The answers to these questions will mainly depend on your own personal circumstances. Note, however, the following points about questions 3, 4 and 7.
3 Note that other networks that may influence progress up the career ladder include family connections and contacts made in clubs or churches.
4 People who want to succeed in a political or business career are likely to need to do some networking.
7 If you use the word 'cliquey' you do not like the atmosphere because you feel that people are in exclusive little groups which you are not able to join.

24.4 1 private/public 5 putting
2 boy/school tie 6 togethers
3 hung 7 shoulders
4 chummy/pally

Unit 25

25.1 1 far-fetched 2 hackneyed 3 overrated 4 understated 5 disjointed

25.2 *Suggested answers:*

1 The musical **was rather/a bit risqué** and was attacked by several politicians and religious figures. (*Risqué* is often used with a modifier such as *rather, very, a bit,* etc.)
2 Her performance was **memorable/unforgettable**, simply marvellous.
3 I can't remember the last time I saw such a **gripping film.**
4 It was a **very/deeply moving** play.
5 It's a **harrowing** film.
6 Some of his films are absolutely **impenetrable.**

25.3 *Most likely answers:*

1 Yes, it would probably be good, since all the critics say it's very good.
2 Yes, usually.
3 Probably not, as it's probably a bad film.
4 The Oscars, or, more correctly, the Academy Awards.
5 No, because then it's difficult for them to get a variety of different parts.
6 False. An *ovation* means applause, and if people stand up to applaud, it means they have enjoyed the performance a great deal.

25.4 1 portrayal
2 miscast
3 cliffhanger
4 keep you on the edge of your seat
5 budding (like the buds of a flower, which will open up and grow)
6 blockbuster (film/movie)
7 cops-and-robbers
8 masterpiece

Unit 26

26.1 1 false 2 true 3 true 4 false 5 true 6 false

26.2 1 detractors 4 fad
2 voted with their feet 5 pull the wool over his wife's eyes
3 dumbing down 6 inured/immune

26.3 *usually positive associations*
dazzling evocative exquisite intriguing peerless
usually negative associations
highbrow lowbrow impenetrable undemanding pedestrian uninspiring clumsy dreary run-of-the-mill
negative or positive associations
transparent challenging tongue-in-cheek earnest sophisticated primitive

26.4 *Possible answers:*

I think soap operas are usually rather lowbrow as they are intended to appeal to a mass audience.
I find some modern sculpture rather impenetrable as I neither know what it is meant to represent nor find it beautiful in any way.
I think operas by the German composer Wagner are very sophisticated in that you need to have had some musical education in order to appreciate them.
I find paintings by the surrealist artist Salvador Dali rather challenging as they contain so many curious and unexpected images.
I recently saw a performance of the ballet *Swan Lake*, which I thought was rather pedestrian because it contained nothing original.
I find paintings by Toulouse-Lautrec very evocative of the Paris of a century or so ago because they make me feel as if I am there myself.
In my opinion the designs on ancient Chinese porcelain are often exquisite as they are so delicate and so carefully executed.
I found a recent work that won a prestigious art prize – an unmade, rather grubby bed – extraordinarily dreary as it made me feel miserable rather than uplifted, as I believe art should.
I believe that Turner's paintings of the sea are peerless as no other painter seems to capture the colour and light of the sea so effectively.
Most articles and books by the writer Sue Townsend are tongue-in-cheek as they do not take anything too seriously.

26.5

1 lowbrow	3 sophisticated	5 exquisite
2 tongue-in-cheek	4 dreary	6 challenging

Unit 27

27.1 1 memoirs 2 manual 3 anthology 4 (academic) journal

27.2 *Suggested rewrites:*

1 I just could not seem to **get into** the story, so I stopped reading it.
2 It's **quite/rather lightweight**.
3 It's **quite/rather heavy going**.
4 Take it to bed with you; it's **good bedtime reading**. All the time I was reading it I just **couldn't put it down**. (*Or*: It was **a** real **page-turner** the whole time I was reading it.)
5 **It's compulsive reading.**

27.3

1 lugubrious	3 chilling	5 enigmatic	7 breathtaking
2 wry	4 evocative	6 poignant	8 macabre

27.5

1 section on 'troubleshooting'	manual
2 concise information about a subject	compendium
3 record of a recent examination or test of a lorry	logbook
4 day-to-day record of life during a war in 1776	journal

27.6 *Possible answers:*

1 Some books will be forgotten soon after we have read them; others will always be great, and will last in people's memories for all time.
2 Some books can be just read in parts, some should be read completely, and some should be read carefully and thought about.

Unit 28

28.1

1 The consumer often thinks that the labels provide information, but manufacturers often use meaningless terms just to make the product appear more attractive.
2 Because people feel happier with the idea that foods are natural rather than synthetic.
3 It refers to *egg*. It is, however, rather ambiguous and manufacturers exploit this.
4 *Organic* means that artificial fertilisers and chemicals have not been used in the food's production.
Wholemeal refers to flour that contains all the natural fibres of the grain with nothing removed through processing.
Vegetarian means without meat, i.e. suitable for eating by vegetarians.
5 Genetically modified. In other words, it refers to food which has had its genes modified in some way in order to make the crop more profitable.
6 DNA stands for deoxyribonucleic acid: the chemical at the centre of living things which controls the structure and purpose of each cell and carries genetic information.
7 *Cereal bars* are a kind of snack made from cereal with fruit or nuts and sugar and moulded into a kind of biscuit.
Fish fingers are slices of filleted fish coated in batter ready for frying. They are called fingers because they (slightly) resemble fingers in their shape.
Vegetable burgers are burgers that are not made of meat but of vegetables (typically lentils or beans).
8 It is a kind of pudding – like solid fruit juice made by adding gelatine to juice. In US English *jelly* means what is called *jam* in British English.
9 There must be less than 5% fat in *low-fat* cheese. In *reduced fat* cheese there would be 25% less fat than in standard cheese.

28.2 **The following should taste nicer:**

1 strawberry flavoured yoghurt: because at least some of the flavour will have come from real strawberries
2 orange juice: because it contains the juice from oranges instead of artificial flavourings
3 raspberry jam: because it has been made using real raspberries
4 free-range chicken: because the chicken was able to move freely on the farm rather than being kept in a small cage (battery farming)

28.3

1 fair hair (opposite: dark)
2 a gentle wind (opposite: a strong wind)
3 a comedy that has no serious content (opposite: a black comedy)
4 someone who wakes easily from sleep (opposite: a heavy sleeper)
5 to put a match to a fire to ignite it (opposite: to extinguish or put out a fire)
6 a small aircraft used for carrying only a few passengers or a small load
7 the joy of my life (opposite: the bane of my life)
8 Have you got a lighter or match (i.e. something to light a cigarette with)?
9 to find the solution by chance
10 Taking into consideration the information which the reports provide ...

28.4

ingredients – foodstuffs needed to make a dish
dilute – make another liquid weaker by mixing it with water
stew – cook slowly for a long time in liquid
grill – cook under or over a hot flame
half-baked – not fully cooked (of bread, biscuits or cakes)
spice up – make tastier by using spices like chilli powder, cinnamon, ginger, etc.

Although **savoury** is used about food (meaning the opposite of sweet in taste), **unsavoury** is only used in this metaphorical sense.
turn sour – lose its pleasant taste
juicy – full of tasty liquid, e.g. like a ripe orange

28.5
1 My mother **grilled** me about where I had been last night.
2 Let's **spice up** the evening by organising some party games.
3 What's been happening while I was on holiday? You must fill me in on all the **juicy** gossip.
4 Don't tell her that her briefcase has been found. Let her **stew** for a bit longer – perhaps she'll be more careful with it in future.
5 It might be a good idea to **dilute** these investments in your portfolio by exchanging some of them for others in a different line of business.
6 They lived together happily for many years, but things **turned sour** when his mother came to live with them.
7 Patience combined with interest in your pupils is a teacher's **recipe for** success / the **recipe for** success for a teacher.
8 Lance's ideas are always **half-baked.**

Unit 29

29.1 *Suggested answers:*
1 No, please. Put your credit card away. **Dinner's on me.**
2 Let me **get this (one)**. You can pay next time.
3 Visitors to the company's head office in London are always **wined and dined** in/at the best restaurants.
4 **Would you like to join us** for lunch tomorrow?
5 When we eat out as a group, **we usually split the bill.**
6 **I'd like you to be my guest** at the theatre tomorrow night.

29.2
1 I'm teetotal.
2 I haven't got a sweet tooth.
3 Do you have any special/particular dietary requirements?
4 Just a small portion for me, please. I don't want to overdo it.
5 She's become very calorie-conscious. / She's counting the calories.
6 Sasha is such a fussy eater. It's difficult to find things she likes.

29.3
1 a savoury dish
2 a sullen/overbearing waiter
3 an informal get-together
4 courteous staff
5 sluggish service
6 impeccable service

29.4
1 take pot luck
2 say when
3 grab a bite to eat
4 nibbles
5 seconds (note plural)
6 an informal get-together

29.5 **Cordially** is a formal word meaning 'in a friendly or welcoming way'.
Black tie normally means a black dinner jacket, white shirt and black bow tie for men, and very formal, long dresses for women.
RSVP means répondez s'il vous plaît, French for 'please reply'.
To toast is to raise your glass and drink with others to wish someone success or happiness.
Aperitifs are alcoholic drinks normally taken before a meal.

Unit 30

30.1
1 towaway
2 tailback
3 pile-ups
4 give-way
5 right of way
6 hit-and-run
7 exhaust emissions
8 breathalyser, drink-driving
9 sound/hoot/toot; horns

30.2 *Suggested answers:*

1 B: Oh, so you skidded?
2 B: Oh, I guess it was a case of road rage.
3 B: Oh, so you didn't have the minimum depth of tyre tread?
4 B: Oh, so it was a head-on collision/crash.
5 B: Oh, really? I didn't know they could give on-the-spot fines.
6 B: Oh, so it's not roadworthy.

30.3 *Suggested answers:*

1 All the traffic in all directions was unable to move.
2 I've spent six hours driving.
3 The police car made me stop at the side of the road.
4 I had a small accident where I hit something or another car, but without serious damage.
5 My car broke down.
6 He's an irritating person who sits in the passenger seat and thinks he can tell the driver how to drive.

Unit 31

31.1 *Suggested answers:*

1 I hate charter flights.
2 It was an Apex ticket.
3 The ticket allowed us a three-night stopover in Singapore.
4 You can get a shared cabin on the ferry. / You can get a four-berth cabin ...
5 We hired a car with unlimited mileage.
6 When you get there, the transfers are included in the cost of the holiday.
7 It was a budget fare, but there were restrictions.

31.2

1 bed and breakfast
2 full board
3 self-catering
4 unlimited mileage
5 exotic island
6 value for money

31.3 *Most likely answers:*

1 self-catering holiday: to be your own boss
2 camping trip: to rough it (i.e. to live in very basic conditions, without any extra comforts), to be out in the wilds (i.e. away from civilisation), to sleep under the stars (i.e. out in the open, without a roof over your head)
3 staying in an inn or a guest house: a cosy atmosphere
4 skiing holiday: an exhilarating experience, perhaps also a real learning experience
5 trekking holiday: to keep on the move, to be out in the wilds, to sleep under the stars
6 cruise: to lounge around (i.e. to sit or lie and relax for long periods), to just drift along (to go along with the pace and rhythm of the ship)
7 sightseeing holiday: to spend a fortune on entrance fees, a real learning experience
8 holiday with car hire: to go as you please, to just drift along (i.e. not drive fast, no particular plan), to keep on the move

31.4 *Suggested answers:*

1 lounged around / drifted along
2 be my own boss

3 roughing it / sleeping under the stars / being out in the wilds
4 an exhilarating experience
5 to spend a fortune on entrance fees
6 a real learning experience
7 a cosy atmosphere

31.5 *Possible answers:*

1 A sightseeing holiday, looking at ancient monuments (Egyptian pyramids in this case). For many people, Egypt is an exotic destination.
2 A beach/seaside holiday, in this case we could also say a 'family holiday'. Activities typically include sunbathing, swimming, lounging around on the beach.
3 This picture shows Sydney Harbour, with its famous bridge and Opera House. Sydney is a great destination for cultural activities, sightseeing, shopping, etc. Cruise ships might also call in there.
4 This looks like a hiking or trekking holiday, since the man is carrying a rucksack and wearing clothes suitable for climbing mountains.
5 Beach holidays or holidays by the sea are good for snorkelling and underwater activities such as scuba-diving (which the picture shows).

Unit 32

32.1

1 boasts
2 sector
3 fauna
4 wander; beaten
5 hordes
6 get; nature
7 seeking; ordinary
8 escape
9 tracts; virgin; wealth
10 promising

32.2 *Possible answers:*

1 The list of times and events for the sea-cruise includes three trips to places on land, and 10 nights travelling by sea.
2 The flights are not guaranteed, but depend on seats being available from the airline.
3 An extra £30 per night is payable for a single room.
4 You can make a booking immediately or be given a price you can think about.
5 You can choose a package that includes a flight and car hire.

32.3

1 unrivalled
2 heartland
3 stunning
4 unbeatable
5 awe-inspiring
6 waterfront
7 unwind
8 recharge

32.4

1 trek, hike, ramble
2 savour
3 discerning
4 in Africa or Australia
5 four by four; it is a vehicle powered by four wheels, instead of the usual two

Unit 33

33.1

1 coniferous forest 2 industrial nation 3 paddy field 4 chemical industry
5 sugar plantation

Note that some other matches could be made although they do not appear in the text. Less strong but also possible is coniferous plantation. Note, however, that paddy cannot collocate with anything else and it is not possible to talk about crop fields.

33.2 *Suggested answers:*

plantation: tea, coffee, rubber
industry: manufacturing, pharmaceutical, textile
forest: deciduous, rain, dense
field: oil, wheat, ripe (ready to harvest)
nation: civilised, independent, sovereign

Note that oil and rubber could also collocate with 'industry'.

33.3
1 ancestors
2 emigrants
3 immigrants/migrants
4 migrants/immigrants
5 descendants

33.4
1 About 80% of the population lives in or around cities along the coast where life is easier than in the remote towns and farms of the outback. (*Australia*)
2 400 years ago it was the centre of the Inca Empire that stretched the length of South America. (*Peru*)
3 Two thirds of the farmland is under water but deliberately so, because the fields are flooded to grow rice. (*Vietnam*)
4 To the east of a long, narrow peninsula more than a hundred islands make up the rest of the country. (*Denmark*)
5 Much of the land is desert, dotted with oases, but parts of the coastline are more fertile. (*Oman*)
6 A line of volcanoes, many still active, dominates the landscape of this small country and forests, once rich with cedar, mahogany and oak, have been cut down for farmland. (*El Salvador*)

Unit 34

34.1 *Possible answers:*

1 Yes, extremely chilly.
2 Mm. Isn't it hot!
3 Yes, terribly humid.
4 Very windy!
5 Yes, it's dreadfully oppressive.
6 Yes, what a deluge/downpour!
7 Yes, it's very humid.
8 Yes, isn't it oppressive/sultry!

34.2
1 coldness
2 coldness, inhospitableness
3 covered with a great amount of something
4 rapid, moving quickly
5 lots of hard things that one can't stop or escape from
6 not bright and cheerful, something hidden
7 lack of clearness
8 loud deep noise

34.3 *Possible answers:*

1 moral, social, economic, current, mild, harsh
2 winds, view, climate, opinion, mood
3 the issue, the horizon, someone's judgement, someone's thinking, someone's vision
4 change, democracy, discontent, fear, recession
5 reception, look, glance, response
6 bullets, gunfire, abuse, missiles, insults

34.4 *Possible answers:*

1 mean	6 solar radiation
2 arid	7 moderate
3 elevation	8 continental
4 latitude	9 seasonality
5 precipitation	

Unit 35

35.1
1 glass ceiling = invisible barrier
2 ivory tower = life away from unpleasant realities
3 brick wall = barrier
4 back door = unofficial way in
5 key feature = most important characteristic

35.2

1 went	3 opens	5 hit	7 shut/closed
2 hold/provide	4 come	6 towers	8 fell

35.3
1 My brother is always **a tower of strength** whenever I have a problem.
2 I would be reluctant to work for a company that does a lot of business **through/by the back door.**
3 The fee for this work will depend on the time it takes but **there is / it has a ceiling** of twenty thousand dollars.
4 The cost of petrol **has gone through the roof** in the last six months.
5 Having children often **cements a marriage.**
6 Vancouver is **the gateway to** Western Canada.
7 The **key** decision we have to take now is where to locate our business.
8 The professor has spent all his life **in an ivory tower** and really finds it very difficult to cope in the real world.

35.4
1 The company has been involved in a legal battle for several years now.
2 The speaker's request for questions was met with total silence.
3 Working on this project together should help to provide the starting point for a good relationship in the future.
4 Her eyes were firmly fixed on mine as she told me she was planning to go abroad.
5 When Jack returned to this country he found his marriage had completely broken down.
6 This government should put things right in its own immediate sphere of influence / close to home before criticising other countries.

Unit 36

36.1
1 nipped in the bud
2 a budding poet
3 grass roots
4 the root of the problem
5 to reap rewards
6 to take root
7 the seeds of discontent

36.2
1 Alec has spent most of his life in London but he is keen to **go** back to his roots when he retires.
2 The business is firmly **rooted** in the west of England.
3 The idea took some time to **take** root but it's very fashionable now.

4 His grandfather sowed the **seeds** of the business's success.
5 The US bookshop chain is opening a number of **branches** in the UK.
6 It's about time she **put** down some roots.
7 The idea for her novel **stems/stemmed** from her interest in mountain climbing.
8 The St James's Drama College turns out a hundred **budding** actors every year.

36.3 *Possible answers:*

1	fade	lose colour and strength
2	shrivel	dry up, lose volume
3	flourish	do very well, look strong and healthy
4	sprout	proliferate, lots of new growth
5	germinate	start to grow successfully
6	weed out	remove what is felt to be negative
7	prune back	cut back (with the aim of improving long-term results)
8	wilt	lose vitality
9	reap	gather the results of what one has worked for
10	wither	cause bad feelings or gradually die

36.4 *Possible answers:*

1 budding romance, film star, footballer
2 flourishing business, trade, nightlife
3 withering look, attack, contempt
4 fading dreams, hopes, looks (= appearance)
5 deeply rooted customs, ideas, values, fears, anxieties

36.5 *Possible answers:*

1 I'd like to shed one or two of my work commitments.
2 When I got an increased salary because I had passed an exam.
3 A couple of new friendships are flourishing.
4 I last felt that I was wilting when the office air conditioning broke down.

36.6
1 Your teacher likes you very much.
2 Something is growing or developing rapidly, just like mushrooms do.
3 They live very luxuriously.
4 Someone who is not very active and prefers to sit at home watching television.
5 The discussions are successful and produce positive results.

Unit 37

37.1 *Suggested rewrites:*

1 There are dozens of different types of **rodent** living in the woods.
2 A whale isn't a fish, it doesn't lay eggs. It's actually a **mammal**.
3 There are some interesting **reptiles** near the river.
4 Everyone thinks these animals are **carnivores**, but in fact they are **herbivores**.
5 The mother bird protects her eggs from **predators**.

37.2 1 docile 2 fierce/savage 3 domesticated 4 tame 5 wild

37.3 1 habitat 2 sanctuary 3 reserve 4 shelter

37.4
1 blood sports
2 the ivory trade
3 poachers
4 They would say that it is cruel to kill animals just to provide people with luxury clothes.

37.5 Stressed syllables are in bold for comparison.

noun	*verb*	*adjective*
carnivore		car**ni**vorous
herbivore		her**bi**vorous
predator	prey (on)	**pre**datory
poacher	poach	

Unit 38

38.1 *Suggested answers:*

1 **Carbon dioxide emissions from** cars and factories is a major problem.
2 These flowers here are **an endangered species**, so it's illegal to pick them.
3 A lot of wild animals have to survive in **shrinking habitats.**
4 Most of Patagonia is a **pristine environment.**
5 We have to look after **the finite resources of the planet.**
6 If **deforestation** continues, there will be no forest left ten years from now.
7 Burning **fossil fuels** causes a lot of pollution.
8 **There will be rising sea levels / Sea levels will rise if global warming** continues.
9 Increasing population **exerts severe pressure on** economic resources.
10 **The ecological balance** is very delicate.

38.2

noun	*verb*	*adjective*	*adverb*
climate		climatic	
demography		demographic	demographically
projection	project	projected	
sustainability	sustain	sustainable	sustainably

38.3 **Prophets of doom** and gloom are always saying that we are heading for an environmental catastrophe, and that unless we adopt a policy of **sustainable** development we will cause irreparable damage to the planet. The worst **case scenario** is of a world choked by overpopulation, the greenhouse **effect** and traffic gridlock. Much of what is claimed is exaggerated, but politicians are influenced by such voices and are always trying to improve their green **credentials** in the eyes of the voters.

38.4 1 amphibians: creatures which live on land and in water, e.g. frogs
2 endangered species

Unit 39

39.1 1 on hold; back to
2 dispatch
3 responsive
4 prompt/quick/swift
5 backlog
6 shoddy/substandard
7 obliging/accommodating
8 helpline

39.2 *Author's answers:*

1 I always have a backlog of e-mails to answer.
2 Yes, a travel agent was very helpful and arranged a complicated journey for me which was not the typical kind people make.

3 Computer companies usually have helplines. I used one when I got my new computer. It was not very successful, as the person on the other end of the line seemed to assume I understood all the computer terminology he was using!
4 Yes, I wanted to change to a non-smoking room in a hotel and the person on the reception desk was not willing to help and would not even check to see if one was available.

39.3 1 e 2 b 3 i 4 f 5 a 6 h 7 d 8 g 9 c

Unit 40

40.1 *Suggested answers:*

1 You'll have to show a **vaccination certificate** for tropical diseases when you enter the country.
2 People entering from war-torn countries often **seek political asylum.**
3 You have to **clear customs** if you arrive on an international flight at San Francisco airport, even if you are flying on within the USA.
4 You have to fill in a **customs declaration (form)** before going through customs control.
5 Some of the people were **economic migrants**, rather than genuine political refugees.
6 *Passenger to airline cabin attendant:* Could you give me **a landing card** before we arrive, please?
7 At the airport the security guards had **sniffer dogs.**
8 You'll need a visa; the **entry restrictions** are very strict.
9 You have to fill in the **port of entry** in this box here.

40.2 *Possible answers for Great Britain:*

1 To see if they are overloaded, to see if their brakes work, to check how many hours the driver has been driving without a rest.
2 If they have failed a breathalyser test and the subsequent blood test.
3 If the person is suspected of involvement in terrorism or drug smuggling. To tap means to listen to phone calls without the people involved knowing.
4 If they are suspicious of someone late at night.
5 If the police suspect the person of involvement in terrorism or drug smuggling, or any serious crime.
6 If someone has escaped from a nearby prison (all traffic is stopped and checked).
7 If they are looking for a person whose description they have. (A photofit picture is a computer-generated image based on someone's description of a person.)
8 If you witnessed a crime or if you are involved in a serious accident.

40.3
1 a plain clothes (police) officer
2 a paramilitary police force
3 the anti-corruption squad
4 a parking ticket
5 the drug squad
6 the security forces

Unit 41

41.2
1 stems from, derives from
2 seeks
3 are anxious to
4 universally
5 range
6 with little in common

41.3 1 implausible 2 credible 3 benefit 4 likely 5 buy 6 salt 7 credence 8 attributed

41.4 1 eradicate 2 converts 3 ingenuous 4 tenets 5 adherents 6 ascribe 7 credence 8 postulate 9 pinch

Unit 42

42.1 *Suggested answers:*

1 For Christians, Christmas **celebrates** the birth of Jesus Christ.
2 The **festivities** included parades, sports and musical gatherings.
3 There was a **celebratory feeling** about the whole weekend.
4 For the country people, the spring festival **symbolises the renewal of / is a symbol of the renewal of / is a symbolic renewal of** the fertility of the land.
5 There was a **ceremonial** atmosphere as the military bands marched round the main square.
6 People tend to be in a **festive** mood when the harvest is successfully completed.
7 You should go and see the lantern festival. It's always **a great/real spectacle.**

42.2 *Suggested answer:*

"Well, it's called the Festival of Flowers, and it's **associated with** the coming of spring, after the **sombre** winter months. It **can be traced back to** a religious tradition of taking flowers to the church to offer them to God. Spring flowers are the main **focus of** the festival, and there's always a **parade of people** dressed in traditional costumes. It's all very **flamboyant** and **raucous,** and it **is very atmospheric.** The flowers **symbolise** new life, and **were believed to guarantee/to be a guarantee of** a good harvest later in the year if they were offered to God. Nowadays most people **are not so superstitious,** but there's still a **pagan** atmosphere about it all ..."

42.3 Mother's Day is a day when people send cards and give gifts to their mother.
Independence Day (e.g. 4th July in the USA) is celebrated in many countries which were formerly colonised by other countries.
May Day is the first of May, and is celebrated in many countries as a commemoration of all workers.
Valentine's Day is 14th February. On this day, people send romantic messages (often anonymously) to someone they are in love with.

Unit 43

43.1

1 Slavic	3 Semitic	5 Austronesian	7 Indo-Arian
2 Celtic	4 Germanic	6 Romance	8 Slavic

43.2

1 P-U-N tilde-O	4 F-A-C-C cedilla-A tilde-O
2 G-A umlaut-R-E-N	5 S-I-E grave (accent)-G-E
3 G-R-A circumflex-C-E	6 C-A-F-E acute (accent)

43.3 *Suggested answers:*

1 The **orthography** of Burmese / Burmese **orthography** is quite difficult for a foreign learner.
2 Japanese uses several different writing systems with hundreds of **characters.**
3 The **lexicon** of a language like English is constantly changing. A lot of new technical words are based on **Graeco-Latin** roots, rather than **Anglo-Saxon** words.
4 Unlike English, some world languages have very few vowel **phonemes** and no **diphthongs.**
5 This ancient and beautiful alphabet uses **pictograms** to express meaning.
6 *Windscreen* is a **compound noun / a noun compound / a nominal compound.**
7 **Modality is** expressed in different forms in different languages.

43.4 *Stressed syllables are in bold.*

noun	*adjective*	*change in stress?*
or**thog**raphy	ortho**graph**ic	yes
lexicon	**lex**ical	no
mo**dal**ity	**mo**dal	yes

Unit 44

44.1 *Possible answers (about Russia):*

1 It can be argued that Boris Godunov **usurped** the throne of Russia.
2 The so-called False Dmitry I was a **pretender to the** Russian **throne** in the early seventeenth century.
3 Peter the Great **succeeded to the throne** in 1682 when he was only 10 and Sofia Miloslavsky acted as his **regent** for seven years.
4 Catherine the Great **succeeded** her husband, Peter III, **to the throne.**
5 She **acceded to the throne** in 1762 after overthrowing, and probably organising the murder of, her husband, Peter III.
6 The Romanov tsars enjoyed **absolute power** in Russia.

44.2 1 chariot 2 jester 3 armour 4 cart 5 galleon 6 highwayman

44.3 1 b 2 b 3 b 4 a 5 b 6 b 7 a 8 a

Unit 45

45.1
1 *False* **Human** poverty takes health factors into account as well as money.
2 *True* This is implied by the figures rather than stated directly in the text.
3 *False* 15 people **have a combined wealth** that is worth more than the GDP of sub-Saharan Africa.
4 *False* The US gives **less than** 0.7% of its GNP to overseas aid.
5 *False* The proportion of GNP given as overseas aid is **decreasing.**
6 *True*
7 *False* Just **less than** a quarter of overseas aid actually goes to the poorest countries.

45.2 1 National; Domestic 2 malnutrition 3 servicing 4 relative; absolute 5 alleviation 6 sanitation

45.3
1 poverty line
2 life expectancy
3 overseas aid
4 minimum standard
5 debt servicing
6 infant malnutrition
7 trade deal
8 income poverty

The above are the collocations used in the text in A and are the strongest collocations. However some other collocations are also possible, for example: lifeline (one word), overseas deal, minimum aid.

45.4 1 destitute 2 mouth 3 tight 4 deprived 5 breadline

Unit 46

46.1
1 False (Hidden pressures are more influential.)
2 True
3 True
4 True
5 False (Most lobbying is concealed from the public.)
6 True
7 False (The individual can try to get support from his or her own MP.)

46.2 *Possible answers:*
1 Members of Parliament, constituents, directors, ministers, civil servants, lobbyists, Chancellor
2 centralised, close-knit, well-funded, scattered, fragmented, powerful, public, non-commercial, effective
3 win, change, lobby, counter, appeal

46.3
1 commerce – commercial, non-commercial
2 mass-produced – producers
3 constituency – constituents
4 petitioner – petitions
5 consumption – consumers
6 pressurise – pressures
7 legislate – legislation
8 representative – represent

46.4
1 representative
2 petitioner
3 mass-produced
4 legislate
5 constituency
6 pressurise
7 consumption
8 commerce

46.5 *Possible answers:*

Text A:
to influence = to affect (to influence public opinion, to influence a child)
assiduously = showing hard work or attention to detail (to study assiduously, to avoid something assiduously)
a climax = most important or exciting point (to reach a climax, the climax of the play)
to press for = to argue in favour of (to press for reform, to press for change)

Text B:
close-knit = tightly connected (a close-knit community, a close-knit fraternity)
backstairs = hidden from the public (backstairs pressures, backstairs influences)
relentlessly = without stopping (to campaign relentlessly for something, prices rise relentlessly)
intimidate = to frighten or threaten someone (to be intimidated into doing something, to intimidate a younger child)
encircle = to surround (to encircle a town, to encircle the enemy camp)

46.6
1 counter
2 lobby
3 appeal
4 minister
5 civil
6 counter

Unit 47

47.1
1 impeached
2 lodge
3 overturned
4 sets
5 award/grant
6 bend
7 are infringing / infringed
8 perverting
9 annulled
10 quashed

47.2
1 trespass
2 embezzlement
3 joyriding
4 perjury

47.3 1 a civil court
2 an indictable offence
3 The signatories have to do what they have agreed to do.
4 discretionary

47.4 abrogation contravention impeachment infringement perversion indictment discretion statute

47.5 1 indictment 2 discretion 3 infringement 4 statute 5 perversion

Unit 48

48.1
1 They had stopped thinking of it as something heroic and glorious and began thinking of it as something terrifying.
2 He thought his invention had such a potential to destroy that it would end up making wars illegal because they would be so terribly destructive. He wanted to reward people who help to further the cause of peace.
3 It mentions the invention of dynamite, aerial warfare and nuclear weapons and their use as a deterrent.
4 Warfare now uses increasingly terrifying methods of destruction. These wipe out ordinary people and places as well as soldiers and army bases. This means that people inevitably have a less romantic view of war than used to be the case when they had more control over their own level of risk.
5 People who believe that their own national, ethnic or political cause is worth killing for.

48.2

	verb	*noun*	*adjective*
1	deter	deterrent	deterrent
2		warfare, war	warring, warlike
3	outlaw	outlaw	outlawed
4	empower, power	power	powerful
5		nucleus	nuclear
6	revolt	revulsion, revolt	revolting
7	annihilate	annihilation	annihilated
8	cause	cause	causal

48.3 *Possible answers:*
1 an area of life; an area in the north
2 military operations; surgical operations
3 a modern society; an English language society at school
4 for the good of the cause; the cause of the accident
5 the outbreak of war; an outbreak of measles
6 a last resort; a holiday resort
7 an act of war; an act in a play; to put on an act [pretend]
8 a means to an end; a means of transport

48.4 *Possible answers:*
Roman armies waged wars all round Europe and the Mediterranean.
In the First World War hostilities ceased in November 1918.
The castle was besieged by an enemy army.
William the Conqueror won the Battle of Hastings in part because he managed to successfully ambush parts of Harold's army.
Traditionally armies in the First World War called a truce for Christmas Day.
Both sides agreed on a ceasefire during the peace negotiations.
The Scots were routed at the Battle of Flodden in 1513.
The UN sends peacekeeping troops to areas of serious conflict in the world.
An international observer in an area of conflict has to remain impartial.
Napoleon's campaign in Russia failed because he did not take the winter climate there sufficiently into account.
Police and ambulances were called when an incendiary device went off at a busy train station.
Germ warfare has been illegally used on a number of occasions.

48.5 1 explode 2 ambush 3 siege 4 truce 5 bomb

Unit 49

49.1
1 sustainable
2 following (*pursuing* is also possible), reduce (*alleviate* is also possible)
3 encouraging (*positive* is also possible)
4 deep (*abject* is also possible)
5 recovered
6 achieve
7 lasting (*long-term* is also possible)
8 access

49.2
1 Over a period of five years, the country **incurred** huge debts which it could not **repay**.
2 **Debtor countries** are completely at the mercy of the rich nations.
3 **The burden of debt** is so great in some countries that their economies are collapsing.
4 Richer countries could do a lot to **ease/alleviate** the debt of poor countries, and indeed, in some cases, could **cancel** (or **write off**) the debt altogether.

49.3
1 trade war
2 (a) to impose (b) to lift
3 restrictive practices
4 monetary union
5 development grants
6 a war-torn economy
7 ailing

Unit 50

50.1
1 a charge card
2 credit card fraud
3 put/stick it on my (credit) card
4 make it out to
5 bounced
6 broke/skint
7 strapped for cash
8 bit tight

50.2
1 premium
2 loan shark
3 mortgage /ˈmɔːɡɪdʒ/
4 excess
5 health cover
6 pension plan

50.3
1 handshake
2 rolling
3 lump
4 life
5 portfolio
6 ends meet

50.4 *Author's answers:*

1 I have a credit card, a charge card and a store card.
2 02/04 (end of February, 2004)
3 I have a store card for a big department store in my hometown. A lot of people would probably like to own a store card for a big store like Harrods in London.
4 Around 20% at the moment.

Unit 51

51.1
1 classified ads or adverts/advertisements
2 an agony aunt
3 the obituaries / obituary column
4 a leader / a leading article / an editorial
5 a supplement
6 a feature

51.2

1 manual	3 brochures	5 leaflet	7 prospectus
2 flyers/leaflets	4 pamphlets	6 booklet	

51.3 *Books:*

spine (the vertical edge of the book which usually has the title on it)
jacket (the cover)
foreword (a piece of text before the main text of the book begins)
edition

Magazines:

subscription (a payment that buys you a certain number of issues in advance, e.g. for one year)
issue (publication printed for a particular day/week/month)
binder (a file or special jacket to collect and bind a set of issues together)
quarterly (a magazine issued every three months)

51.4 1 b 2 c 3 a

51.5
1 c
2 d
3 a
4 e If something **gives you the lowdown on something** (informal), it gives all the most important information.
5 f
6 b **Small print** refers to the details, rules and restrictions that often accompany legal documents such as guarantees, contracts, insurance policies, etc., which are often written in very small letters.

Unit 52

52.1
1 attachment: file sent at the same time as an e-mail message
2 cookie: program sent to your computer from the Internet, used to follow your activities
3 spam: unwanted web pages (e.g. advertisements) sent to you via the Internet
4 chat room: Internet site where people with common interests can e-mail each other online
5 ISP: company that gives you access to the Internet and offers news pages, shopping, etc.

52.2

	word	*opposite*	*exists*	*doesn't exist*
1	delete	undelete	✓	
2	download	upload	✓	
3	update	downdate		✓
4	inbox	outbox	✓	
5	online	offline	✓	
6	install	uninstall	✓	

52.3 1 upload, online 2 inbox 3 install 4 undelete 5 offline

52.4 *Suggested answers:*
1 E-signatures are a way of identifying yourself on the Internet with a unique code or name, which you could use, for example, to agree to pay for goods.
2 E-learning means taking courses over the Internet instead of going to a school or college to do your studies.
3 E-enabled here means that all the study materials can be accessed and worked with through the Internet.
4 E-books are books which you buy from the Internet or on CD-ROM, and which you then read on your computer or on your hand-held PDA (personal digital assistant).
5 The dotcom economy refers to Internet companies, whose web addresses typically end in '.com', for example, a company that sells bicycles over the Internet might call itself *newbikes.com*, which would be read aloud as 'new bikes dot com'.

Unit 53

53.1 1 lap 2 crowd 3 rock 4 art 5 with 6 to 7 put/leave 8 galore

53.2 1 B 2 C 3 E 4 C 5 D 6 A, F 7 E, F 8 B

53.3
1 a logo
2 a banner
3 sports sponsorship
4 a billboard
5 a sandwich board
6 a carrier bag
7 classified ads
8 sky-writing

53.4 The language used in the advert makes use of lots of words which have attractive associations (soft, smooth, natural, life-giving, freshness, glow, etc.); it suggests the product contains beneficial ingredients; it suggests that it can make you look younger and better; it uses alliteration (radiance renewed, soft and smooth, compliments on your complexion).

53.5 *Possible answer:*

> **Pamper yourself!**
>
> ❄ Try our tantalisingly tempting new range of lipsticks
> ❄ Unsurpassed value
> ❄ Scientifically proven to last longer and to retain their gloss
> ❄ You'll outshine the other girls!

Unit 54

54.1

1 air your views
2 issue a statement
3 muck-raking
4 press conference
5 pressure groups
6 silly season
7 sound bite
8 tap sources

54.2 1 rag 2 copy 3 deadline 4 went 5 hot 6 cuttings

54.3

1 No, because rag is too informal a word for this context and also it implies that you think the newspaper is not of good quality.
2 You have a low opinion of them.
3 Deadlines.
4 *Vogue.*
5 'Exclusive' and 'scoop'.
6 The story breaks and the story hits the headlines.
7 Libel and defamation of character: these both involve saying things that lower a person's reputation. Defamation is broader than libel in that it covers slander as well as libel. Slander is spoken defamation of character and libel is written defamation of character.
8 She might keep articles about her, such as copies of reviews of her films or of interviews with her.

54.4

1 Every newspaper inevitably puts its own spin on events.
2 I have to find some articles from some back copies of *The Times*.
3 Read all about the royal divorce! Hot off the press!
4 The floods took up more column inches in the papers than any other story this week.
5 Politicians are always ready and willing to air their views to/in the press.
6 The story about the scandal surrounding her uncle hit the headlines on her wedding day.
7 Any newspaper does all it can to prevent being sued for defamation of character.
8 Muck-raking is a characteristic activity of the gutter press.

Unit 55

55.1

1 **chol**era (stress on first syllable)	dia**be**tes bron**chi**tis **chol**era
2 sore **throat** (stress on second word)	**heart** attack sore **throat** **lung** cancer
3 **ty**phoid (stress on first syllable)	hepa**ti**tis **ty**phoid tubercu**lo**sis
4 di**sease** (stress on last syllable)	**ill**ness di**sease** **sick**ness
5 con**sul**tant (stress on middle syllable)	con**sul**tant **doc**tor **sur**geon
6 trans**fu**sion (stress on middle syllable)	**hos**pital **am**bulance trans**fu**sion
7 T**B** (stress on last syllable)	**heart** disease **sur**gery T**B**

55.2 *positive meanings:*
be over the worst
be on the mend
be back on one's feet again
get over

negative meanings:
be poorly
feel a bit under the weather
come down with

Whether you consider *fight off* to be positive or negative depends on whether you feel that 'fighting something off' is always used in a negative situation, or whether you are succeeding in 'fighting off' your cold/flu/headache, etc., in which case you might see it as positive.

1 'Hello, Frank, good to see you **back on your feet again.**'
2 'Jo, I won't be in today, I've **come down with** a cold.'
3 'Oh, I'm OK. I'm **over the worst** now. I still feel bad, but I should be out within a week or so.' (*Over the worst* suggests getting better, but that you are still quite ill. *On the mend* [see 7 below] suggests the person is getting back to normal health.)
4 'Don't worry, darling. Everyone has a cold now and then. You'll **get over** it.'
5 'Don't worry. It's nothing serious. I'm just feeling **a bit under the weather**, that's all.'
6 'I'm trying to **fight off** the flu, but nothing seems to help. I don't think I'll be in work tomorrow.'
7 Hilary was quite ill last week, but she's **on the mend** now and should be back at work next week. (*Or:* 'she's **back on her feet again** now'.)

55.3
1 Her mother died **of/from** skin cancer.
2 Is there a prescription **charge** in your country? (*Price* is the fixed cost of goods; it is not normally used for services such as prescribing medicines.)
3 In Britain, national **insurance** is a separate tax from income tax. (The mixed collocation here is with *social security*, which is the financial support paid to people who are unemployed, or who have no means of support.)
4 Correct
5 Are there insurance **schemes** for private healthcare in your country? (A *scheme* means a plan or contract you can enter into with an insurance company.)
6 Correct
7 She suffers **from** a severe allergy and can't be in a smoky room.

Unit 56

56.1
1 She was feeling **under** the weather and a bit **feverish** so she took the day off.
2 I felt really **off colour** yesterday and my head was **throbbing**, so I took a tablet.
3 I felt a bit **out of sorts** and seemed to have more **aches and pains** than usual.
4 My arms are **aching** after carrying that heavy suitcase of yours.

56.2
1 feverish
2 a nauseous feeling
3 dizzy
4 bunged up
5 a stiff neck
6 trembling

56.3
1 allergic to
2 dosage
3 vaccinations
4 medication
5 prescription
6 symptoms
7 sick note

56.4 1 herbal medicine 2 aromatherapy 3 acupuncture 4 homeopathy 5 chiropractic

56.5 1 d 2 c 3 a 4 b

Unit 57

57.1

verb	noun	adjective
become pregnant, make someone pregnant, impregnate	pregnancy	pregnant
breastfeed	breastfeeding	breast-fed
sensitise	sensitivity	sensitive
clot	clot	clotted
drug	drug	drugged
dehydrate	dehydration	dehydrated
ulcerate	ulcer	ulcerous, ulcerated
affect	effect	effective

57.2

1 Excitement **reached fever pitch** as the day of the final match dawned.
2 Unfortunately, a number of our investments are **ailing** at the moment.
3 There has been a **rash of** car thefts in our part of town.
4 Unfortunately, she **still carries the scars of / is still scarred by** her divorce.
5 Ralph's jealousy is **symptomatic of** a person with general low self-esteem.
6 What do you think the **prognosis** is for the peace talks? (Note that the verb has to change to the singular here.)

57.3

1 paralysed
2 ailing
3 fatal
4 rash
5 contagious
6 fever
7 disease
8 prognosis

Unit 58

58.1 *Possible answers:*

1 Heart attacks and strokes may be caused by too much cholesterol.
2 You want to prevent plaque on teeth because it contains bacteria which can cause decay.
3 They are all cholesterol-rich foods.
4 Fruit, vegetables and wholemeal breads, for example, contain a lot of fibre.
5 It speeds up the digestion process and helps the body to get rid of waste.

58.2

1 high levels of cholesterol, high blood pressure, diabetes
2 three miles
3 It varies according to your weight. Heavier people burn more calories.
4 depression
5 It produces a hormone, serotonin, which is believed to improve people's mood.

58.3

1 clog
2 tolerance
3 raise
4 enhancer
5 swift
6 lose

58.4

scoring an own goal, moving the goalposts, level playing field: football
in the running, neck and neck: horse racing
skate around: skating
sail through: sailing

58.5 1 Sarah sailed through her exams.
2 I wish he'd stop skating around the point.
3 I've been told that I'm in the running for the job of supervisor.
4 Although he meant it as a compliment, Rick scored an own goal when he told Helen she looked as if she had put on some weight.
5 It's hardly a level playing field when 18-year-olds take the same exam as 15-year-olds.
6 It's hard to know what to do when the goalposts are constantly being moved.

58.6 *Possible answers:*
1 The teacher hated to have any interruptions when she was presenting new material to her class.
2 The king banished his rival from the country.
3 Louise works much more efficiently than any of our previous secretaries.
4 At the front of a railway engine is a buffer for protection if it hits anything.
5 The painting showed a harbour full of picturesque sailing vessels.
6 He is not known for his tolerance – indeed he is the most intolerant person I know.
7 People's resistance to new ideas usually increases with age.
8 Some churches spend a lot of time and money attempting to convert people to their faith.
9 Don't burn this newspaper – I want to cut out some articles from it.
10 The village was built in a depression in the hills.

58.7 *Possible answers:*
1 Eating too much cholesterol can lead to blocked arteries and kidney disease.
2 If necessary, increase your intake of fruit and vegetables to make sure that you eat plenty of fibre.
3 Run on a regular basis as it is a particularly efficient form of cardiovascular exercise.
4 All-round exercise can enhance your mood as well as improve your physical fitness.
5 Eat plenty of fibre so that you help your body to excrete what it does not need.

Unit 59

59.1 *Suggested answers:*
1 service industries, manufacturing industries
2 high-technology/high-tech industries, low-technology/low-tech industries
3 State ownership (*or* Nationalisation), privatisation
4 Heavy industry, light industry

59.2 1 a sweetener
2 a public-private partnership
3 subsidies
4 inward investment
5 a lame duck (industry)
6 red tape
7 a sweatshop economy
8 to switch production, to relocate

59.3 1 Industrial piracy [illegal production of goods using another company's brand name]
2 industrial espionage [stealing or destroying a rival company's plans or secrets]
3 Copyright infringement [publishing or copying a book or work of art without the author's permission]
4 Money laundering [passing money illegally earned through the normal banking system without being caught]
5 black market [secret, illegal trade]

Unit 60

60.1 1 PDA 2 laptop or notebook 3 handheld or palmtop 4 desktop

60.2 1 thumbnail [small pictures you can make bigger before downloading them]
2 computer nerd [a rather negative term for a person obsessed with computers and who devotes most of their time to them at the expense of a normal social life]
3 techie
4 analogue
5 screensaver [image that appears on your computer screen if you do not use the computer for a certain period of time]
6 footprint
7 icon [small symbol representing the program]
8 trackpad

60.3 1 satellite communications
2 ergonomics
3 biotechnology
4 digital technology
5 artificial intelligence

Unit 61

61.1 1 gridlocked traffic
2 genetic modification
3 human genome
4 virtual reality
5 global village

61.2 1 genetically modified food, or GM food
2 a smart card
3 virtual reality
4 a clone
5 extraterrestrial beings
6 genetic engineering
7 gene therapy
8 a designer baby

61.3 1 The doomsday scenario for human society is that we will destroy ourselves with nuclear weapons.
2 Interplanetary travel may become normal in the coming centuries.
3 E-commerce will become more and more normal.
4 The team of scientists is doing research into the human genome.

61.4 1 genetic modification
2 the nuclear family
3 cloning
4 gene therapy
5 globalisation, or the global village, or the global economy
6 interactive TV

61.5 All of the ideas are in fact true (as reported in newspapers and news magazines), except for number 3.

Unit 62

62.1
1 poky: suitable here in this informal context
2 roomy: often used for cars
3 compact: in fact, a whole class of small cameras is referred to as 'compact cameras' by manufacturers and advertisers
4 cramped: suitable in this slightly more formal context (compare 1)
5 spacious
6 extensive

62.2

Kingsmead House, Letchwood.

The property is **spacious**, with a **compact** garden, and is situated only ten minutes away from the **bustling** town centre. There are **extensive** leisure facilities nearby.

Shops, banks, restaurants and other services are located in the pleasantly designed neighbourhood. Viewing by appointment. Offers in the region of £220,000.

Ref 023DW446

Rambling usually suggests a rather chaotic collection of rooms, and a *labyrinth* suggests they are confusingly laid out.
Cramped and *poky* suggest that somewhere is too small to be comfortable.
Congested and *crowded* are negative. *Bustling* suggests that somewhere is busy, interesting and full of life.
Excessive means too many, and no one wants *expensive* facilities.

62.3 *Suggested rewrites:*
1 The kitchen is so small you can't/couldn't swing a cat in it. (*Or*: The kitchen is so small there isn't enough room to swing a cat in it.)
2 I suffer from claustrophobia.
3 I got/was hemmed in in the office car park the other day.
4 Holidays in Australia are great if you love wide open spaces.
5 I hate the London Underground during rush hour. Everyone is packed/crammed in like sardines in the trains.
6 I dropped a glass and tiny pieces were scattered all over the floor.
7 The buildings in the holiday complex are (quite/rather) spread out.
8 The train was very full but I just managed to squeeze in before the doors closed.

62.4
1 Hundreds of people spent years incarcerated in the cells of this dark, damp castle.
2 I quickly stuffed a few clothes and a couple of books in a rucksack and set off at once. (*stuffed* is a good word here because it also suggests putting things in quickly and without much care)
3 She suffers from agoraphobia.
4 We'll all have to try and squeeze into my little car; Larry hasn't got his with him today.
5 I always get claustrophobia when I'm in a lift.
6 I don't think we should try and cram everything into one suitcase. Let's take two. (*squeeze* and *stuff* would also be possible here)

Unit 63

63.1
1 They've been living in the same house since the year dot.
2 We got to the airport just in the nick of time. (*Or*: We just got to the airport in the nick of time.)
3 John gave it to Sarah for keeps. (*Or*: Sarah gave it to John for keeps.)
4 Together we can get it done in less than no time.
5 He's never been further than the nearest town in all his born days.
6 We got to the hospital in the nick of time.

63.2
1 a lingering scent
2 a transient (feeling of) joy
3 persistent criticism
4 an incipient headache
5 pristine sheets
6 the inexorable ageing process
7 a fleeting grin
8 a protracted investigation

63.3
1 lingering kiss
2 fleeting appearance
3 incipient wrinkles
4 inexorable advance of time
5 persistent smell
6 pristine beach
7 protracted peace negotiations
8 transient population

63.4
river current is strong carried away ocean-tide swim
(You could also include the words never-resting, rolling, rushing on, which also suggest a torrent of water.)

63.5
Marcus Aurelius: Everything passes.
Thomas Carlyle: We all quickly become insignificant as time passes.
Janet Frame: The concept of tenses is an artificial one.
Hector Berlioz: Age brings wisdom but unfortunately we do not live long enough to be able to make use of that wisdom.

In general the quotations are more powerful because the images they create through their use of metaphor are memorable and convey the ideas much more effectively than a factual statement can.

63.6
1 Jo's worked in the same office for donkey's years.
2 We'll be ready to leave in less than no time.
3 Most of the members of the band may be in their fifties but they're certainly not over the hill.
4 You can argue with him till the cows come home, but he'll never see sense.
5 My grandmother's lived all her born days in the same house. (*Or*: My grandmother's lived in the same house since she was born.)
6 Kit promised he'd get here in a flash and he kept his word.

63.7
Author's answers:
1 There are some advantages but I personally think that greater variety is more interesting.
2 I'd happily eat chocolate eclairs till the cows come home.
3 I personally prefer to travel and see more of the world.
4 Have my hair cut!
5 I am more likely to do things I enjoy at a rate of knots and things I am reluctant to do at a snail's pace.

Unit 64

64.1
1 trudged If you strut, you can't have your shoulders hunched. You are also unlikely to be weary.
2 tiptoed If you trudge you are tired and weary and your steps are heavy, so you might well wake someone who is sleeping lightly. A bedroom is also a very small place for someone to trudge across.
3 hobble Ambling is an easy, comfortable kind of walking and so is not appropriate for when someone is wearing tight shoes.
4 limped Stamping is something which you usually do when you are angry and there is no obvious connection between having an accident and stamping.
5 staggered or lurched Striding cannot be unsteady.
6 trample Daisies are too small to be stumbled on.
7 chased Tramped suggests moving slowly and so the dog would then be unlikely to catch the postman. Tramped also suggests too heavy a movement to be appropriate for a little dog as opposed to a big, heavy dog.
8 lurching or staggering It would be extremely difficult to tiptoe if the sea is rough and the ship is moving violently.

64.2 *Possible answers:*
1 It was not at all successful or enjoyable – the verb limped makes that clear.
2 No, it was clearly in difficulties for a few years before it failed totally.
3 People didn't expect her to do as well as she did.
4 No, the government gave the impression of being out of control.
5 She is probably calm, easy-going and relaxed.
6 They destroy or spoil them, for example, by laughing at them.
7 He or she might send them letters reminding them to pay, or they might phone them.

64.3
flowed: moved smoothly, without ceasing
spilled: fell out, in an uncontrolled fashion, starting suddenly and moving in all directions
streamed: a lot of people moving at a fairly constant pace from one direction
pouring: coming all the time, in large numbers, possibly from all directions
trickle: a few people, here and there
meandered: not going in a straight line, no definite purpose
flooding: coming in large numbers, spreading in all directions

64.4 *Possible answers:*
The River Amazon flows into the South Atlantic.
Try not to spill your orange juice on the new white tablecloth.
Tears were streaming down her face.
Janet poured us all a nice cup of tea.
I must fix a new washer on the tap – I can't stand the constant trickle of water.
The river meandered through the valley.
The river often floods at this time of year.

64.5 *Possible answers:*
1 Rudi took his first steps towards becoming a doctor today when he **attended his first lectures at medical school.**
2 **The invention of the printing press** was a very significant step for humankind.
3 Yesterday the British government took the unprecedented step of **recommending the abolition of the monarchy.**

4 It was a big step for me to **decide to hand in my notice.**
5 I think you took a backward step when you **decided to move to the country.**
6 The business took a critical step today when it **floated its shares on the stock market.**

64.6

verb	*type of movement*	*reason for type of movement*
file	lots of people moving in a straight line, one after the other	to control large numbers of people
saunter	relaxed, confident	pleasure
sidle	approaching someone in a slightly sneaky way	intending to do something dishonest or unpleasant in some way
glide	smooth, as if not moving one's feet	to make effortless movement or to make movement seem effortless
mill around	lots of people all moving in different directions	to meet or to talk to different people

64.7
1 Graceful dancers glide.
2 Guests at a cocktail party mill around or mill about.
3 Schoolchildren going into class file into the classroom.
4 Someone who is irritatingly anxious to make you like them might sidle up to you.
5 Tourists exploring in a relaxed way might saunter round a city.

Unit 65

65.1

positive associations	*negative associations*
gentlemanly	offhand
ladylike	prissy
	starchy
	strait-laced

65.2
1 code of etiquette
2 elders and betters
3 give up your seat
4 mind your Ps and Qs
5 oil the wheels
6 social graces
7 stand on ceremony
8 the done thing

65.3
1 She might do this because she wants Rob to find her attractive. Perhaps she wants to go out with him.
2 No, he was probably feeling nervous.
3 She didn't like them.
4 He probably flinched because his arm hurt. Perhaps he had recently broken it.
5 It must have been rather surprising or shocking in some way. They were probably swearing.
6 Tanya, because a smirk is not a pleasant smile.
7 No, he was probably not pleased. A titter is rather a weak laugh and more from embarrassment than amusement.

65.4

1 snorted	3 squirm	5 flinch
2 twitch	4 eyelashes	6 sniff

65.5 1 They are all ways of laughing.
2 They are all ways of using the face to indicate displeasure or anger.
3 They are all ways of looking at someone or something.
4 They are all ways of crying.

Unit 66

66.1 *Most likely answers:*

1 noiselessly
2 quiet
3 silent
4 soundlessly (we might normally expect some sound from its wings)
5 silent

66.2 *Possible answers:*

1 Suddenly, a shot rang out. Somebody was firing at the birds on the lake.
2 The door creaked. It was very old, made of oak and difficult to open.
3 The music was pounding through the walls. It was as if the musicians were playing in our bedroom.
4 The chicken sizzled in the frying pan. The sound and the smell made me even more hungry.
5 The rusty door hinges are squeaking. I think they need some oil.
6 She tooted her horn. I looked out of the window and saw her car parked outside.
7 I could hear the waves crashing. It was wonderful to be so near the sea.
8 We heard police sirens wailing. There must have been an accident, or perhaps a robbery.

66.3 1 deafening 2 eerie 3 piercing 4 grating 5 high-pitched

66.4 1 It was so quiet you could have **heard a pin drop**.
2 I've had some noisy, hectic days with all those kids, now I'm looking forward to some **peace and quiet**.
3 Turn that music down! I can't **hear myself think**!
4 I don't even notice that Jack is in the flat sometimes. He's **as quiet as a mouse**.

Unit 67

67.1 1 cumbersome (or unwieldy)
2 ponderous
3 weighty
4 lumbering
5 burdensome
6 cumbersome (or unwieldly)

67.2 *Suggested answers:*

1 lumbering	dinosaur vehicle goods train	3 weighty	encyclopedia topic issue
2 cumbersome	fax machine procedure suitcase	4 ponderous	tone of voice sermon narrative

67.3
1 I weighed **out** a kilo of the flour and then added water to it.
2 He's very irritating. When you're trying to have a rational discussion, he always has to weigh **in** with his own selfish point of view.
3 I owe Gerry £150; it's been weighing **on** my mind for weeks. I must pay him.
4 We were weighed **down** with huge suitcases and bags, and the airport was terribly crowded; it was a nightmare.
5 I have to weigh **up** the various options before I decide which job to accept.

67.4
1 To thin out the customer's hair.
2 thicken: The fog has thickened.
3 It will probably congeal and be difficult to wash out.
4 It means you must add water. You have to dilute it / water it down before using it.
5 You could use a sieve to sift flour to make it less lumpy.
6 No, because insults do not penetrate their consciousness.
7 It is impermeable.
8 The story or argument is so dense you cannot begin to understand it.
9 It lacks complexity and seriousness.
10 thin out: The traffic is thinning out.

Unit 68

68.1
1 jet black, ginger, mousy, chestnut
2 ginger (cat), chestnut (horse), jet black
3 crimson
4 scarlet, crimson, turquoise, shocking pink
5 navy and beige
6 scarlet
7 auburn (this colour is more attractive than 'mousy')
8 pitch black

68.2
1 I think he's going to be sick.
2 Yes, ever since his wife left him.
3 Yes, he can't stand the presenter.
4 Yes, it's not at all clear what we should do.
5 I wonder what they've got against him?
6 No, they make me feel sick.
7 Yes, but they need qualifications.
8 Yes, they want to do their bit for the environment.

68.3 *Possible answers:*

There are some great black and white films on TV on Sunday afternoons. (Note: not white and black.)
He gave me such a black look that I stopped talking immediately.
At last I have received the cheque I was waiting for and our account is in the black again.

It was only a white lie when I told her I loved her new hairdo.
I'd love to go white-water rafting though I know it's quite dangerous.
That shop sells mainly white goods – fridges, cookers and the like.

I wouldn't pay any attention to what they're suggesting – it's only a red herring.
I hate it when my bank account is in the red – they charge so much interest.
Don't talk to him about the present government – it's like a red rag to a bull.

Come and sit next to the fire – you look quite blue with cold.
We were driving along when, out of the blue, another car turned out of a side street and stopped just in front of us.
I'm not very keen on blue cheese.
He likes to imply that he's blue-blooded but really most of his ancestors were farm labourers.

You can't park there – there are double yellow lines.
If you want to find a plumber, look in the Yellow Pages.

Her garden is wonderful – she has green fingers.
It's almost impossible to get permission to build houses in the green belt.
The government has recently published a green paper on the Health Service.

68.4
1 ruby, emerald, jade, amber, sapphire, turquoise, coral
2 magnolia, violet, forget-me-not, cornflower, poppy
3 strawberry, burgundy, lime
4 magnolia, violet, coral
5 *pink/red* – strawberry, ruby, burgundy, poppy, coral
blue – forget-me-not, cornflower, sapphire, turquoise (turquoise could also be classified as green)
green – emerald, lime, jade
other – amber (orangy yellow), violet (light purple), magnolia (creamy white)
6 emerald, turquoise
7 forget-me-not, cornflower
8 a) burgundy b) magnolia c) amber

Unit 69

69.1
1 in a hurry 3 dawdling 5 rocket 7 career 9 to be creeping up
2 speed up 4 a traffic jam 6 totter 8 person who races 10 fast

69.2
1 not pleased
2 not pleased
3 not pleased
4 pleased
5 not pleased
6 not pleased

69.3 1 c 2 b 3 d 4 c 5 b 6 d 7 d 8 b

69.4 They are all one-syllable words. This is appropriate because they sound faster than a longer word and they are all used to convey an idea of speed.

Unit 70

70.1
1 generated (*Produced* is also quite acceptable here, with little difference in meaning, except perhaps that it focuses more on the result, while *generated* focuses more on the process of getting the result.)
2 produce (*Produce* is the most frequent collocation for *list*, but in more formal, technical contexts, *generate* can also be used.)
3 caused (*Brought about* is also possible here.)

4 sparked off / precipitated (*Caused*, *produced* and *provoked* would all also be possible here, but *spark off* and *precipitate* are ideal for things which explode suddenly and violently.)
5 resulted (No other possibilities: *result* collocates with *in*.)
6 given (*Brought* or *provided me with* could also be used with the same meaning here.)
7 provoked (*Caused, produced* and *generated* are also possible, but *provoke* is ideal for negative responses and emotions.)
8 precipitate (*Cause* or *bring about* are also possible here, but would be less dramatic.)

70.2 *Possible answers:*

1 No one knows what **incited** him to commit such a violent crime. (Often used when someone or something makes someone do something wrong.)
2 Your letter has **prompted** me to respond immediately and to offer my apologies. (Used to indicate how something gave someone a reason to act.)
3 The news **induced** a feeling of terror in everybody. (Usually connected with states and emotions, often, but not always, negative ones, e.g. *tiredness, despair.*)
4 Poverty **breeds** crime and misery. (Often used with words denoting social problems, e.g. *discontent, lawlessness.*)

70.3 *Possible answers:*

1 Owing to / As a result of / As a consequence of the crash on the motorway, all traffic is being severely delayed.
2 We got there in time, thanks to your advice. (*Thanks to* is usually for good results, but can be used ironically/sarcastically for bad things.)
3 My computer crashed, as a result of which I lost all the data. (*Or* more formally: ...crashed, as a consequence of which ... . *Owing to which* is not normally used, and sounds very awkward.)
4 As a consequence of / As a result of one bad decision after another, he's lost all his money.
5 The flight was cancelled due to / owing to bad weather.

70.4 *Possible answers:*

2 The higher taxes have sparked off riots in three cities.
3 Icy roads have caused a number of serious accidents this week.
4 Thanks to a brave bank assistant, two robbers were in jail last night.
5 My old car has caused me / given me endless problems and involved me in a lot of expense.
6 This software can generate stunning images and graphics.
7 Jealousy caused the breakup of his marriage.

Unit 71

71.1 Distinct is followed by **from**. All the others are followed by **to**.

1 dissimilar to
2 tantamount to
3 corresponds to
4 akin to
5 distinct from

71.2
1 between; and
2 with
3 from
4 with

71.3 1 disparate 2 diverse 3 dissimilar 4 distinct 5 divergent 6 discrete

71.4
1 distinct
2 dissimilar
3 discrete
4 divergent
5 disparate
6 diverse

Unit 72

72.1 1 dilemma 2 glitches 3 hardship 4 ordeal 5 snag 6 impediment 7 pitfalls 8 stumbling block

72.2
1 obstructive
2 stiff
3 traumatic
4 abstruse
5 wayward
6 insufferable
7 convoluted (or abstruse)
8 gruelling (or arduous or tough)

72.3 1 into 2 guts 3 death 4 hassle 5 drag/pain 6 fix/spot/hole 7 with 8 sticky/tricky 9 hook 10 woods

Unit 73

73.1
1 Are you going clubbing tonight? You must be joking! I'm much too old.
2 I've just handed in my notice. What, may I ask, was the point of that?
3 The car won't start. Shall I have a look at it?
4 You might find buried treasure. I should be so lucky!
5 I'm afraid I've broken a cup. Don't worry. Accidents will happen.
6 Jane and Joe have just had twins. They must be very happy.
7 Someone's at the door. It'll be the Patels.
8 I only just managed to escape. You must have been terrified.

73.2
1 It is obligatory to put on a life jacket.
2 The odds are (that) Harry'll take over his father's job.
3 If I were in your shoes, I'd apologise to him at once.
4 You have no option but to do what the police officer says.
5 They're bound to settle down eventually.

73.3 *Possible answers:*
1 If I were you, I'd have a haircut before the interview!
2 I hope you'll take this in the spirit in which it is intended, but that skirt is a bit too short for an interview.
3 Let me give you one tip/hint/suggestion: don't forget to make eye contact with the interviewers.
4 It would be sensible to allow plenty of time to get there.
5 It would be wise to make a list of questions you want to ask.

73.4 *Possible answers:*
1 It is essential to arrive at school on time every day.
2 It is compulsory to pay a deposit before you can borrow tapes from the library.
3 Wearing uniform is optional.
4 It is obligatory to wear soft-soled shoes in the sports hall.

73.5

1 anxiety
2 determination
3 yearning
4 resolutions
5 desirous
6 eagerness
7 longing
8 wishful

Unit 74

74.1

1 sighting
2 rodents
3 quadrupled
4 quotient
5 expenditure
6 per
7 sustain
8 factor

74.2 *Suggested answers:*

1 There seems to be a discrepancy between the two reports of the accident.
2 The value of the shares has increased four-fold.
3 Job satisfaction seems to be in inverse proportion to educational achievement.
4 The water levels didn't fluctuate as much as we'd expected last year.
5 I don't need to know all the individual figures – just give me the aggregate.
6 His moods are erratic – one minute he's happy, the next he's depressed.

74.3

1 b
2 a
3 a
4 at least $1,000
5 55
6 the weather forecast or competing companies' advertising campaigns

74.4

verb	*noun*	*adjective*
deviate	deviation	deviant
	discrepancy	discrepant
flaw	flaw	flawed
invert	inversion	inverse
	inconsistency	inconsistent
err	error	erratic

Unit 75

75.1

1 vetoed
2 condone/countenance
3 acquiesced
4 outlaw/ban
5 authorised/endorsed
6 barred/banned
7 accede
8 clamp

75.2

1 give someone carte blanche: carte blanche is French for 'white card'
2 to give the green light: when traffic lights turn green, traffic is allowed to move
3 countenance
4 to give the go-ahead

75.3

1 c An **embargo** means an official prohibition on something. If the prohibition is cancelled, the embargo is **lifted**.
2 a A **franchise** is permission to operate some sort of service or commercial activity, usually for a set period of time.
3 d **Zero-tolerance** means that not even the smallest crime or misbehaviour will be allowed.
4 b **Sanctions** are restrictions on some activity.

Unit 76

76.1 *Possible answers:*

1 Informal. A formal version: *I take great exception to your rudeness!*
2 Formal. An informal version: *You've got to do something about your unfair rules.*
3 Informal. A formal version: *The state of your desk is most unsatisfactory!*
4 Formal. An informal version: *I've just about had enough of the awful station facilities!*
5 Informal. A formal version: *I really must object to your going out in that dress!*
6 Formal. An informal version: *I'm fed up with this behaviour!*

76.2

1 about	3 to	5 done	7 do
2 take/took	4 with	6 wouldn't	8 well

76.3 *Possible answers:*

1 Honestly! I'm fed up with their loud music so late at night!
2 I wish you wouldn't play your music quite so loud after midnight.
3 Most people take considerable exception to being forced to listen to other neighbours' music when they are ready themselves to go to sleep.
4 I'm not at all satisfied about the changes to our working hours.
5 I've just about had enough of working longer hours.
6 I wish to complain in the strongest terms about the changes in our working hours.

76.4 *Possible answers:*

1 We must open the window at once.
2 Jack's work is very careless.
3 Simon is often late for work.
4 You're not suited to this job.
5 This room really needs decorating.
6 The TV must be turned down.

76.5 *Possible answers:*

1 While appearance should not, of course, be a teacher's highest priority, I think that some of you have got into the habit of coming to school dressed in a way that is perhaps a bit too informal to give the right message to our pupils.
2 The portions tend to be a bit too small.
3 The train company would be well advised to lay on a few more trains.
4 You'd really benefit from taking a bit more exercise, darling.

Unit 77

77.1 *Suggested answers:*

1 perfect	4 cast-iron/perfect
2 lame/flimsy/weak	5 sincere/heartfelt
3 flimsy	

77.2

1 excuses	3 forgive, forgive
2 repent	4 apologise, apologies

77.3

1 The President granted him a **reprieve** just an hour before he was due to be executed.
2 He was **acquitted** of murder in 1984, but two years later was convicted of armed robbery in the same courtroom.
3 She showed a complete lack of **remorse/repentance** for her evil deeds and just laughed when the judge sentenced her.

4 The Public Inquiry **exonerated** him from all blame for the accident at the factory.
5 Most Christians believe that if you **repent** your bad deeds just before you die, God will forgive you.
6 Ten years after his death, John Wilson was given a **posthumous** pardon by the government when another man confessed to the crime he had been hanged for.

77.4 *Suggested answers:*

1 The two armies **declared/announced/agreed a truce** during the religious holiday.
2 Both governments **agreed/assented** to the terms of **the peace treaty** and it was signed on 15th August, 1954.
3 The long-standing **accord** between the government and the unions is in danger of **collapsing**.
4 The generals **signed the armistice** at midday on 25th February, 1968.

Unit 78

78.1

1 fish	4 to	7 widely/highly
2 singing	5 take, as	8 damning
3 paying	6 shower/heap	

78.2

1 The performers were given a standing ovation.
2 In the speech the new manager paid tribute to his predecessor.
3 They're always extolling the virtues of living in the country.
4 Matt's design earned him the highest plaudits from the judges.
5 The teacher gave Becky a pat on the back for her drawings.
6 The new young Czech player was the toast of the tennis world.

78.3 *Suggested answers:*

1 He's always flattering the boss. (neutral)
He's always licking the boss's boots. (informal)
He's always making up to the boss. (informal)
He's always crawling to the boss. (informal)

2 I wish she wasn't so slimy. (informal)
I wish she wasn't such a crawler. (informal)
I wish she wasn't so servile. (formal)
I wish she wasn't so obsequious. (formal)

78.4

verb	*noun*	*adjective*
compliment	compliment	complimentary
praise	praise	praiseworthy
congratulate	congratulations	congratulatory
laud		laudable, laudatory
flatter	flattery, flatterer	flattering
crawl	crawler	crawling
smarm		smarmy

78.5

1 complimentary (= free)
2 flatterer
3 congratulatory
4 laudable/praiseworthy (Both are possible – laudable is a little more formal.)
5 congratulations

6 Flattery
7 laud/praise (Both are possible – laud is a little more formal.)

Unit 79

79.1 1 b
2 b *Swore*, possibly because of its close associations with taboo language, sounds much less formal than *vowed*.
3 a
4 b Because *New Year's resolutions* is the standard phrase and such resolutions are perhaps best known for being quickly broken, *vow* sounds much more formal.

79.2

1 promised	3 best	5 kept
2 oath	4 flutter	6 life

79.3 *Suggested answers:*
1 Your best bet would be to see a doctor.
2 My mother swears by these herbal teas.
3 John's been rather lazy with his homework but he has promised to turn over a new leaf next year.
4 I could have sworn I locked the door when I went out.
5 The new production of the play promises to be most unusual.
6 I'd put money on the Democratic Party winning the next election.
7 Do you ever have a flutter on the horses?
8 Her mother disliked the film because it contained so many swear words / so much swearing.

79.4 2 Swift is making the point that many people don't take promises seriously. His point is effective because of the comparison of a solemn thing like a promise with such an everyday thing as a piecrust, which is of course intended to be broken. It has to be for the pie to be eaten.
3 Most people probably do agree that making someone promise not to do something may often serve to put the idea of doing it actually into their head!

Unit 80

80.1

1 used	5 rose-tinted
2 schooldays	6 became
3 have	7 must
4 touch/contact	8 stands

80.2 1 I'm disappointed in my results.
2 I rue the day I agreed to go into business with him.
3 I feel a certain remorse for what I said to her.
4 I regret not apologising for what I said.
5 I mourn my lost youth.
6 It's disappointing that we didn't make a go of it.

80.3 *Suggested answers:*

1 getting married	6 shouldn't have spoken
2 films	7 what happened
3 good old	8 forget how (beautiful)
4 didn't invite	9 sorry
5 I'd known then what	10 pity/shame you/I have

80.4 *Author's answers:*

1 I used to do a lot of sport when I was a child.
2 I regret not taking an opportunity to visit Thailand.
3 I'll never forget climbing a mountain and seeing other mountain peaks above the clouds.
4 I keep in touch with several friends I knew at primary school.
5 I know what happened to some but not all of them.
6 What stands out in my mind is how I didn't have anything to worry about then.
7 I feel remorse for some of my actions in the past.
8 I have found a lot of popular films rather disappointing.
9 They often lament lost love, lost youth and the passing of time.

80.5 *Suggested answers:*

1 I regret not buying her a birthday present.
2 I'm disappointed that you won't play the piano for us.
3 I wish he wasn't/weren't so unreliable.
4 I lament the passing/demise of trams in our town.
5 I mourn our lost youth / the passing of time.

Unit 81

81.1

verb	*preposition*
approve	of
conform	to
tally	with
coincide	with
concur	with
compromise	on
be in accord	with

1 conforms
2 tallies/coincides
3 concur(red)
4 tally/concur
5 approve
6 accord
7 compromise

81.2 1 c 2 e 3 a 4 d 5 b

81.3 *Suggested answers:*

1 The President has **made a/the concession** that the opposition party should be allowed a place on the committee.
2 I think one should always **exercise/use** as much **discretion** as possible when it is a question of people's private lives.
3 The landowners **reached a settlement in** their dispute with the authorities over the route of the road.
4 The negotiating team were able to **reach a compromise** and put an end to the long strike.

Unit 82

82.1 1 overlap; complements 2 deduce 3 advocates 4 inferred

82.2 1 authoritative 2 empirical 3 ambiguous 4 coherent 5 comprehensive

82.3 1 b
2 They are square numbers and the next two numbers are 49 (7 squared) and 64 (8 squared).
3 James's mark was either the highest or the lowest in the class.

4 c
5 No, she's selecting her subjects in a random fashion.

82.4
1 We believe the information **resides** in archives that must not be opened until 2050.
2 He **conceived** his theory while still a young man.
3 Each of the signs in the phonetic alphabet **denotes** a sound rather than a letter.
4 This study **contradicted** what was previously held to be true and so **triggered** a great deal of discussion amongst specialists in the field.
5 Details of the experiment **are appended** to the report for those who wish to see how we arrived at our data.

82.5

The study was initially **conceived** in order to validate a new method of enquiry **whereby** genetic information could be **utilised** to predict disease. Our work **contradicts** the findings of Hill (2001); indeed it would appear to **demonstrate** the **converse** of what he claimed. We **perceive** our work as presenting a **somewhat** different view of the genetic factors which **trigger** disease. **Notwithstanding**, our work does not **negate** Hill's as his studies served the **crucial** purpose of devising symbols to **denote** certain tendencies, **thereby** facilitating further research. We hope that Hill will **likewise** find our work to be valid and that when international researchers **convene** next April, they will concur that much of value **resides** in both our and Hill's studies. Our results are **appended**.

Unit 83

83.1
1 The response from the public **underscores** the importance of having a full investigation of the facts.
2 This view of the world was originally **expounded** by the Ancient Greek philosophers.
3 It is not easy to **account for** the fall in population of these birds.
4 Economists have **posited** a link between exchange rates and a general lack of confidence in the European Union.
5 I should like to **reiterate** here that the issue is not one that can be easily resolved.
6 The recent events **epitomise** the dilemma faced by politicians the world over.

83.2 *Suggested answers:*

1 70% of the landmass is comprised of mountain ranges. / Mountain ranges comprise 70% of the landmass.
2 The book embraces a wide variety of subjects. (Note that *embrace* is usually used in the active voice.)
3 I think these three sections can all be subsumed under one heading.
4 Poems are not easily amenable to being categorised. / Poems are not easily categorised.

83.3

verb	*noun*
categorise	category
preface	preface
allude to	allusion
cite	citation
reiterate	reiteration
epitomise	epitome /ɪˈpɪtəmɪ/

83.4
1 return
2 brings
3 touches
4 address
5 beyond the scope of
6 ascending
7 forced to conclude
8 deal with

Unit 84

84.1
1 Let me just **jot down** your e-mail address, or I'll forget it.
2 I'll just **scribble** a note for Jim to tell him where we've gone.
3 I spent the whole lesson just **doodling** in the margin of my exercise book, I was so bored.
4 She's been writing **up** her PhD thesis for the last three months, that's why no one has seen her.
5 I'll send you a **draft** of the letter so you can suggest any changes before we send it.

84.2
1 bold
2 upper case
3 italics
4 new font size
5 new typeface
6 lower case
7 block capitals
8 chain (brackets)
9 square (brackets)
10 diamond (brackets)

84.3
2 subtitle
3 chapter heading
4 sub-heading
5 bullet
6 asterisk

84.4 1 typescript 2 format 3 manuscripts 4 paste

Unit 85

85.1
1 make such a big thing = make such a fuss
2 has got a thing about = really likes / is obsessed with
3 The thing is = The problem is
4 things = the situation; get away for a holiday = go on holiday
5 things = subjects/items; get through = deal with
6 get on with = have a good relationship with; For one thing = Firstly; like different things = have different tastes; For another (thing) = In addition / Secondly
7 get = understand; I didn't get a thing = I didn't understand anything
8 get everything sorted out = solve all our problems; got it together = organised things

85.2
1 corkscrew
2 Leonardo DiCaprio
3 protractor
4 pliers
5 colander
6 Leonard Nimoy

85.3
2 Look, isn't that whosit? The actor who was in *Titanic*.
3 I can't find the thingumajig for measuring angles.
4 Have you got a thingy for pulling out nails?
5 Where's the whatsit for draining potatoes?
6 The book is about Leonard whatsisname – the guy who was in that sci-fi series.

85.4 *Possible answers:*

1 We don't need to rush as we have plenty of time.
2 I've invited her out a great many times, but she always makes some excuse.
3 He hasn't done any useful work here since he was first employed by us.
4 I have a large number of papers which I would like to dispose of.
5 Pat invited a great many people to her party at the weekend.
6 Sue possesses a great deal of energy – I don't know where it all comes from!

85.5 1 company 2 included 3 offence 4 mind 5 possible

Unit 86

86.1
1 to bicker
2 without a murmur
3 to lisp (*or* to speak with a lisp, have a lisp)
4 shout, yell, scream (*also* roar, shriek)
5 *roar* is a deeper sound, like a lion; *shriek* is a very high-pitched sound
6 to gossip, to slag (someone) off
7 to wind (someone) up

86.2
1 stuttered/stammered
2 tongue-tied
3 mumbling/muttering
4 yell/shout
5 murmured
6 gossip
7 slurring
8 lisp

86.3
1 whining not whineing; whing(e)ing not winging
2 winding me *up*
3 butter me up, not banter me up
4 nagging, not nigging

86.4

	[1] S		[2] S			
[3] C	H	A	T	T	E	R
	O		A			
[4] M	U	R	M	U	[5] R	
	T		M		O	
			E		A	
			R		R	

Unit 87

87.1 *Suggested answers:*

1 The company will invest in excess of £10.3 million in new technology over the next five years.
2 It will cost you in the region of / around / about £7,000 to have the whole house redecorated.

3 (informal) It could take seven hours, give or take an hour, to drive to Aberdeen, depending on the traffic. (*or* It could take seven hours or so ...)
(formal) It could take approximately seven hours to drive to Aberdeen, depending on the traffic.

4 Quite a few students failed the exam. I was rather surprised and disappointed.

87.2

1 Her hair's a sort of reddish colour, and I'd say she's, well, forty, forty-fiveish.
Sort of is used here with an adjective, but it can be used with almost any type of word. The *-ish* suffix is used here with a descriptive adjective and a number denoting age, but it is also often used with clock times (e.g. We arrived around half-past sevenish). *Well* is often used to make things less direct.

2 The garden was a bit on the big side, but it was very pretty.
The expression *a bit on the ... side* is used with adjectives to denote a quality that is not what we want or hope for (e.g. The living room was a bit on the dark side, but we bought some new lamps and it was OK).

3 There was a kind of elasticky thing that held the two parts together, and I've lost it.
Kind of and *sort of* can both be used with adjectives and with almost any other word class. Putting the *-y* suffix on a noun or adjective to make it indirect or less precise occurs in informal conversation (e.g. It was a browny colour. It has a kind of acidy taste).

4 They're good shoes. They're comfortable on long walks and that.
And that just means 'and similar things'. It is very informal. Here it is used with a noun, but people often use it with verbs too (e.g. They were singing and that at the party last night).

5 I've been to the doctor's and had treatments and suchlike and I'm sure it helps in one way or another.
And suchlike normally follows a plural noun, but could also be used with an uncountable one (e.g. It'll be useful for your work and suchlike).

87.3

1 oodles/lashings 2 dash 3 lashings 4 smattering 5 dollop

87.4

Possible answers:

1 worrying/strange/odd
2 nuisance/pain/problem
3 embarrassing
4 sandwich/snack
5 relax/watch TV/have a sleep
6 souvenirs/pots/jewellery/pictures
7 sightseeing

87.5

1 a thing for measuring spaces, distances, objects or people
2 stuff for cleaning shoes
3 a thing for removing corks from bottles
4 a thing for knocking nails into wood or other materials
5 stuff you don't finish eating at a meal which you can eat later
6 stuff you spread on your body to protect you from the sun

Unit 88

88.1

I always try (1) to make the most of any opportunity to make new friends, such as a party or a social event. But it's not always easy (2) to break the ice, and when you don't know someone, it's so easy (3) to put your foot in it by saying something insensitive or something which unexpectedly (4) rubs someone up the wrong way. But if you (5) keep an eye on what you say, (6) play it by ear and just try to act naturally, it can (7) make all the difference and you may find you (8) stand a good chance of making a new acquaintance or even a good friend.

1 get the maximum benefit from a situation
2 create a relaxed social atmosphere
3 say or do something socially embarrassing
4 irritates someone
5 be watchful/careful about something
6 don't plan in advance, just see how things go
7 have a very positive effect
8 there is a strong possibility

88.2 1 at 2 under 3 from 4 in 5 on 6 in 7 out

88.3 *Suggested answers:*

1 I hate being (kept) in the dark about things at work.
2 The terrorists killed all the hostages in cold blood.
3 The mountains and ski slopes are on our doorstep; we're so lucky.
4 Out of the blue she received a letter from her long-lost brother.
5 I often find Jane and I are at cross purposes.
6 It looks as if they'll have to start from scratch (again).
7 Keith's been looking under the weather recently, hasn't he?.

88.4 1 nitty-gritty 2 saving grace 3 make-believe 4 long-winded 5 half-hearted

Unit 89

89.1
1 clockwork
2 dream
3 up
4 to plan
5 into place
6 and running

89.2 *Suggested answers:*

1 It's a mystery to me how she can eat so much food and yet stay so slim.
2 The traffic in the city centre is a real nightmare on Saturdays.
3 What a pain! We have to be at the airport at 5.30 a.m.
4 It's the calm before the storm.
5 It was just a storm in a teacup.
6 She asked me a question that completely threw me.
7 This is like a bad dream.
8 Oh no! That's the last thing I wanted to hear!
9 I'm sorry; our wires must have got crossed.
10 I'm sorry; you've lost me there.

89.3
1 to brush something under the carpet
2 at the eleventh hour
3 I can't see the wood for the trees

89.4
1 a (complete/total) shambles
2 a close call/thing
3 as clear as mud
4 muddy the waters

Unit 90

90.1 pleased: 1, 3, 8
displeased: 2, 4, 5, 6, 7

90.2
1 It's no fun spending time with Jez and Sal as they only have **eyes** for each other.
2 Try to solve these problems by using your **grey** matter.
3 Most parents weren't born **yesterday** – they have a good idea of what their kids get up to.
4 Maggie could talk the **hind** legs off a donkey.
5 Mary's on cloud **nine** now she's at university. (*or* Mary's in seventh heaven now she's at university.)
6 They are head over **heels** in love.
7 I haven't the **foggiest** idea what we should do about this letter.
8 Gilly has a soft **spot** for Jim – she's always talking about him.
9 Ruth and Paul **raved about** the play.

90.3

1 dreams	10 clue
2 to	11 heels
3 fire	12 back
4 soft	13 nose
5 mine	14 all
6 element	15 nothing
7 what	16 dumps
8 planks	17 seventh
9 top	

90.4

1 B	4 A
2 A	5 C
3 C	6 B

90.5
1 Amanda **thinks the world of her father.**
2 When I met my penfriend, we immediately **hit it off.**
3 I wanted to keep the present a secret but my little boy **let the cat out of the bag.**
4 Why have the children **been looking as miserable as sin** all evening?
5 If you come round this evening **I'll put you in the picture.**
6 **I've been walking on air** ever since I heard your good news!

Unit 91

91.1 *Possible answers:*
1 You might be pleased to be called 'very much your own person' or 'a dark horse' (as it makes you sound mysterious).
2 You would almost certainly not want to be called 'a soft touch' or 'your own worst enemy'.

91.2
1 went ballistic / blew a fuse / hit the roof/ceiling
2 are full of beans
3 was at a (complete) loss for words
4 (all) at sea
5 was dead on my feet
6 driving me round the bend / driving me crazy / driving me nuts
7 wanted to curl up and die
8 put a brave face on it
9 turns my stomach
10 at the end of my tether

91.3 1 rub 2 loggerheads 3 snake 4 benefit

91.4
1 Aunt Vicky is a soft touch.
2 Mike is a dark horse.
3 Maria's a snake in the grass.
4 He or she is full of beans.
5 She was at a (complete) loss for words.
6 I was all at sea.
7 Helena's in a world of her own.

91.5
1 a rope attached to an animal, keeping it within a fixed piece of land
If you are at the end of your tether, you have gone as far as the rope allows you to go. Obviously this is likely to cause frustration and annoyance.
2 to go into a small ball
If you curl up you look smaller, which is how we wish we looked when we have done something we feel is embarrassing or stupid.
3 a small safety part in an electrical device which causes it to stop working if the electricity is too powerful
The idiom suggests a strong reaction caused by a surge of anger rather than electricity.
4 a valuable stone
Diamonds are very hard and they need to be cut to give them their full beauty – a rough diamond can similarly be a person whose strong qualities are hidden behind a rough exterior.
5 used to refer to a weapon that is shot through the air
The idiom suggests a violent, aggressive reaction like that of a powerful weapon against its enemy.

Unit 92

92.1
1 the blue
2 my own business
3 it in my bones
4 our thumbs
5 as a by-your-leave

92.2
1 to cut a long story short
2 you live and learn
3 it's a small world
4 I lived to tell the tale
5 it just goes to show that ...
6 it was just one of those things

92.3
1 as luck would have it
2 famous last words
3 in next to no time
4 all's well that ends well
5 to crown it all
6 would you believe it

92.4 1 b 2 e 3 a 4 f 5 c 6 d

Unit 93

93.1 *Possible answers:*
1 The police asked people to stand back from the injured man.

2 When he was at school, John always used to stand up for his younger brothers in the playground.
3 Michael Porter has decided to stand down from his post as Minister of Defence because of the scandal.
4 I always knew that Laura would stand by me, come what may.
5 The Socialist Workers' Party stands for the rights of the working classes.
6 On my first day as a teacher I had to stand in for a gym teacher who had broken his leg.
7 I would never dream of standing anyone up.
8 Masha is considering standing for the local council in next year's elections.

93.2 The letters AA can **stand for** either Automobile Association or Alcoholics Anonymous. [be short for]
I won't **stand for** such behaviour in my house. [tolerate]

93.3

1 out	4 up	7 up	10 up
2 through	5 apart	8 up	11 off
3 on	6 over	9 down	12 on

93.4 1 Please keep off the grass.
2 Sam is going to the dentist to have a tooth pulled out this afternoon.
3 This is such a lovely photo. I'd like to have it blown up and framed for my wall.
4 Rod's going to apply for the job, but the fact that he has so little experience will tell against him.
5 Her idea for a new business is brilliant. I just hope she can pull it off.
6 Do you think that Ken might be keeping something from us?

93.5 *Possible answers:*

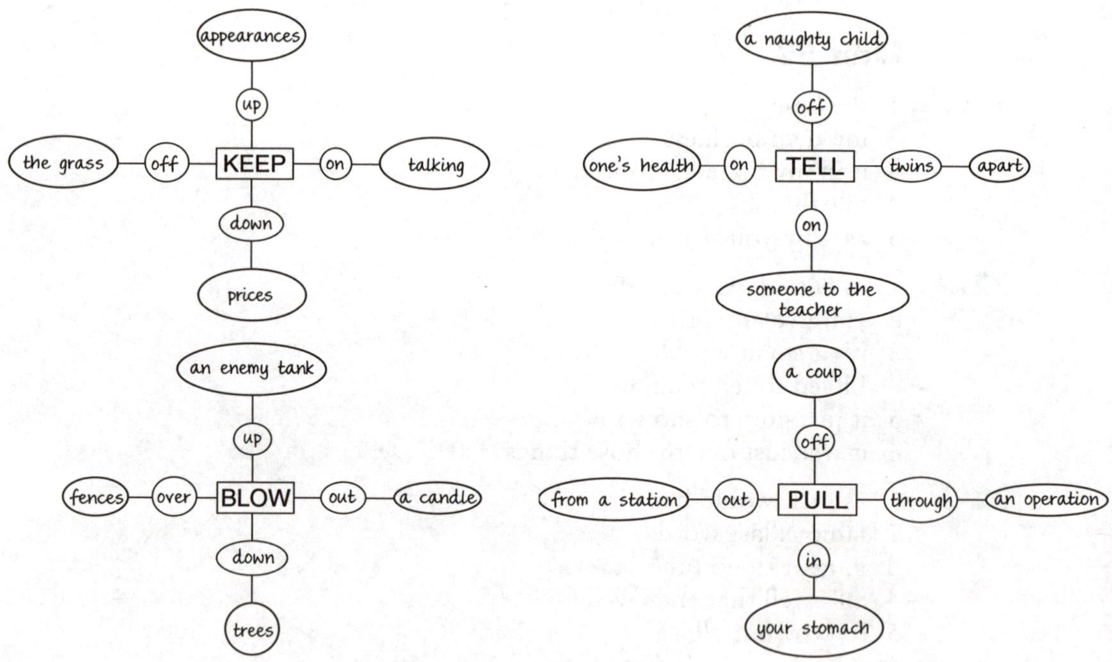

93.6 *Suggested answers:*

1 Ron waited an hour for Alice, then he realised she had decided not to come and, furious, went home.
2 You should always support your friends when they are in trouble.
3 You should also defend your principles, even if it makes you unpopular.
4 The house is a little way from the road, so you wouldn't notice it as you drive past.

5 There are three candidates for election in this constituency.
6 The party that I support is in favour of equality and improved social services.
7 I often had to substitute for other teachers who were absent.
8 After ten years as Mayor, Damian Taylor decided it was time to stop putting his name forward for election.

Note that when you change sentences like this, the new sentences do not always have exactly the same meaning or connotation as the original sentence.

Unit 94

94.1

1	sort	6	cropped
2	doze	7	stowed
3	slogging	8	stick
4	lay	9	eased
5	pelting	10	whittling

94.2

1 information provided by a secret informer
2 a sleep
3 people trying to travel illegally by finding a hiding place on some means of transport
4 hard work
5 a number of instances appearing suddenly and at more or less the same time
6 comfort (at ease = comfortable, relaxed)

94.3

1 *to bottle:* to enclose in a bottle. This clearly connects with the idea of bottling up feelings.
2 *to pelt:* to throw something repeatedly in order to attack. This has a clear connection with heavy rainfall.
3 *to step:* to stand. The image in *step on it* is from stepping on the accelerator to make a car go faster and so there is a connection between the basic verb and the phrasal verb.
4 *to stow:* to put something away carefully, neatly and out of sight. It is particularly used about packing things on some means of transport where space is often at a premium.
5 *to crop:* to provide a good crop. This unusual verb is related to the more common noun *crop*. So there is a connection between something growing and something appearing.
6 *to sort:* to organise or classify. The particle *out* really adds very little to the basic meaning of the verb.
7 *to stick:* to fix with glue. So the connection is one of remaining fixed in one place.
8 *to whittle:* to cut or scrape thin slices off wood, typically with a penknife. The connection is thus one of removing slowly but steadily.

Note that sometimes the literal meaning of the basic verb helps you to understand the meaning of the phrasal verb but sometimes the connection is not close enough to give much of a clue to the phrasal verb's meaning.

94.4

1 *down* may have the meaning of:
downward movement (pelt down)
decreasing (dumb down, play down)
2 *off* may have the meaning of:
movement away (doze off, pull it off)
3 *on* may have the meaning of:
touching (step on it)
adding (lay on, catch on)
4 *out* may have the idea of:
completing something (sort out, stick it out)
excluding (bottle out)
5 *up* may have the idea of:
an improvement (ease up)
an upward movement (crop up)

As you encounter new phrasal verbs, see if the prepositions or particles seem to fit these meanings. Some of them will, but some won't. Appreciating the meanings of the particles or prepositions will sometimes help, but not always.

94.5
1 conferenced out: have had enough of conferences
2 rocketed off: rose at great speed
3 tile up: cover with tiles
4 surfed away: occupied themselves on the Internet continuously

Unit 95

95.1
1 As Juan was away he missed out on the fireworks.
2 I've got a temperature and think I may be going down with something.
3 I know you've had a bad day but there's no need to take it out on me.
4 Most students wish that schools would do away with end-of-term exams.
5 It really is time we got round to painting the house.
6 I hope we're not going to fall out with each other over who is going to pay.
7 One of the other waiters has had it in for me ever since I started work in that restaurant.
8 I don't think I can take a lunch break today as I've got to catch up with some work.

95.2

1 cheered	5 lay
2 aback	6 open
3 worked	7 under
4 branch	8 picking

95.3
1 There's no point in trying to talk to your father until he's simmered down.
2 Do you think it would be a good idea to do away with selective education?
3 Sam's father died when he was six and so he missed out on having a male role model at home.
4 When Mr Brown was laid off, the family decided to emigrate to Australia.
5 Emily was carried away by the emotional way in which Richard read the poem.
6 Do you consider that oil prices have now bottomed out?
7 You take life too seriously. Chill out!
8 The newly married couple were bubbling over with happiness.

95.4
The most obvious verbs to include in *Work and business* are:
slog away   ease up

The most obvious verbs to include in *Mood and emotions* are:
bottle out   stick something out   bottle something up

95.5
To branch out is based on the metaphor of a tree. It is appropriate because it suggests that the business is growing and spreading out as a tree does.
To be snowed under is based on the metaphor of being covered by snow. It is appropriate because it suggests being buried by work in a way that makes it difficult to escape from it.
To chill out, simmer down and *bubble over* are all based on the temperature of liquid and they are appropriate because they compare being *cool* to being relaxed, being *heated* to being angry (simmer down) and *bubbling over* to excitement. *Bubble over* may also have associations with a glass of champagne or some other fizzy drink bubbling over the edge of the glass. This kind of literal effervescence is also comparable to an excited mood.

Unit 96

96.1
1 American. British version: I lost my way at the big **junction** just south of the city.
2 British. American version: Why are there always so many shopping **carts** left in the **parking lot**?
3 British. American version: Cross the **street** at the **crosswalk**, then **take a left**.
4 American. British version: You can't drive any further; you'll have to **reverse**, the **road** is very narrow.

5 British. American version: You'll see the **gas station** just after the **overpass** on **I-34** (or Highway 26, or some other typical American road designation).
6 American. British version: Once you get on to the **motorway**, it will only take you two hours to get there.
7 American. British version: The book**shop** is **diagonally opposite** the Chinese restaurant.
8 American. British version: There's a **stream** at the end of the **(foot)path**. It's about three miles from here.

96.2

1 dumpster US = skip UK
2 ground US = earth UK
3 frying pan UK = skillet US
4 cooker UK = stove US

96.3 1 hand baggage 2 deplane 3 coach

96.4 1 UK 2 US 3 US 4 UK 5 US

Unit 97

97.1

1 Irish
2 Australian
3 Australian
4 Irish

97.2

1 a dingo
2 the Prime Minister of Ireland
3 the wild land, especially the central deserts of Australia
4 fun / social enjoyment
5 in Ireland
6 in Australia or New Zealand
7 blow into it
8 a person; someone who is not very polite

97.3

1 Hong Kong word for payment office at a car park
2 Australian word for 'person'
3 Scottish word for 'small'
4 Malaysian word for 'university'
5 Scottish word for a child
6 Canadian word for a public toilet
7 Caribbean word for a godmother
8 Irish word for 'idiot/fool'
9 South African word for flat, open countryside with few trees

Unit 98

98.1

1 To try to make the language less stereotyped with regard to gender and also perhaps to try to alter sexist attitudes in this way.
2 The expression means words that have male connotations but are referring to people in general.
3 There might have been controversy perhaps because some people felt it was an unnecessary change or that it was impossible to try to impose language change artificially.
4 They want to get rid of 'male' words in traditional idioms like *man in the street* by using such phrases as the *person in the street* or the *average person* instead. They even want to get rid of *man* in words like *manhandle* and *woman* where the male idea has really been lost.

5 It was introduced as a title which does not focus on whether a woman is married or not. It is useful if you do not know what a woman's marital status is or if a woman does not want people to know her marital status.

98.2
1 Three **firefighters** helped put out a fire at a disused warehouse last night.
2 A **spokesperson** for the Department of Education provided us with a statement.
3 **Cleaner** wanted for house in Priory Street.
4 The switchboard is continuously **staffed** even during holiday periods.
5 All our **flight attendants** are fluent in at least three languages.
6 Ms Jones is in charge of the **Human Resources** Department of the company.
7 **Police officers** today spend more time in cars than on the beat.
8 Brenda's husband is **a nurse**.
9 It took a great many **working** hours to clean up the stadium after the concert.
10 This was a great step for the **human race**.
11 The average person has little time for such issues.
12 They pushed the hostage into the van.

98.3 1 mannish 2 sissy 3 virile 4 feminine 5 male

98.4
1–6 personal answers
7 The sentence can be altered by either using *he* or *she*: A government minister may have to neglect his or her family.
Or by making it plural: Government ministers may have to neglect their families.
It is also becoming increasingly common and acceptable for *their* to be used as a generic pronoun with a singular referent, e.g. A government minister may have to neglect their family. Note that some people consider this to be incorrect.
Note that some writers use the pronoun *s/he* instead of *he* or *she*.

Unit 99

99.1
1 chattering classes
2 new money
3 riff-raff
4 stuck-up
5 bourgeois
6 common
7 upper crust
8 oik

99.2
1 The speaker is probably an older person reminiscing – this is suggested by the use of the word *wireless*.
2 The speaker is upper class and older – the meaning of the sentence suggests this as does the use of *one* as a pronoun meaning *we*.
3 The speaker is probably quite old because of the use of *spiffing* and *motor*.
4 This is probably a young person talking to a contemporary – young people tend to abbreviate – *mobile* for *mobile phone*, *uni* for *university*.
5 The speaker is probably working class – the use of 'incorrect' grammar like *we was / we ain't done nothing* is a feature of some working class speech.

99.3
1 idiot
2 friend; difficult situation
3 very rich; die **To be rolling in money** is still used to mean 'very rich' but 'stuff' is a dated piece of slang. **To kick the bucket** is a similar idiom meaning to die which is still in use.

Unit 100

100.1 *Suggested answers:*

1 A bomb explosion in Moscow terrorises the population there.
2 The Prime Minister is going to announce plans for dealing with football hooligans.
3 A high-ranking Member of Parliament is fighting for or trying to achieve something on his own.
4 A strong campaign against pornography has been launched.
5 Violent men surround a teenage star.
6 The police decide to focus on dealing with violently behaved and offensive young men.

100.2
1c use of nudity; use of dramatic words like 'sensation' to attract attention
2b use of familiar name for King (shows either lack of respect or friendly familiarity); colloquial and dramatic expression 'mash-up' for battle
3e alliteration of Marathon Man and Drop-dead Dash; dramatic words and image
4a royalty and scandal – favourite topics for tabloids
5d colloquial expression 'It's curtains for …' [It's the end for ...]; alliteration of curtains and Corinth

100.3
1g Dracula was a vampire known for drinking blood. **Bad blood** is also an expression used to mean bad feelings between people. There will probably be bad blood between the vicar of Whitby and the people who are making a profit from the Dracula connections of the town.
2e School days are often referred to as the 'happiest days of one's life'.
3b **Shell-shocked** means traumatised or in a state of great shock. It is referring to how soldiers in the trenches in World War I felt after they had been subjected to shells or bombs for a long time. Terrapins and tortoises have shells and they would certainly be shocked (in the medical sense) by falling from such a height.
4a Dentists make impressions of teeth and **false impressions** is a common collocation used to mean incorrect impressions created by a person.
5d This is meant to recall the phrase 'happy hunting'. Haunting, however, is what a ghost does. An apparition is a kind of ghost.
6h **Hopping mad** is a collocation meaning extremely cross. It is appropriate here as toads and frogs hop along the ground. Hopping mad is also no doubt how the police felt when they discovered they had been called out by a toad.
7f A loo is a toilet and toilets flush (= water passes through them). **Flushed** also means to have a pink colour in one's skin because one is happy. It collocates strongly with the phrase 'flushed with success', as the people who have sold the toilet for such a large sum of money are likely to be.
8i **Highly embarrassed** is a collocation meaning extremely embarrassed. It is doubly appropriate here as the man is so high up the tree that he has to be rescued by the fire brigade – certainly an embarrassing situation.
9c Sheepdogs **round up** sheep. Labradors and golden retrievers are kinds of dogs and it is suggested that they should round up the children.

Phonemic symbols

Vowel sounds

Symbol	Examples		
/iː/	sleep	me	
/i/	happy	recipe	
/ɪ/	pin	dinner	
/ʊ/	foot	could	pull
/uː/	do	shoe	through
/e/	red	head	said
/ə/	arrive	father	colour
/ɜː/	turn	bird	work
/ɔː/	sort	thought	walk
/æ/	cat	black	
/ʌ/	sun	enough	wonder
/ɒ/	got	watch	sock
/ɑː/	part	heart	laugh
/eɪ/	name	late	aim
/aɪ/	my	idea	time
/ɔɪ/	boy	noise	
/eə/	pair	where	bear
/ɪə/	hear	beer	
/əʊ/	go	home	show
/aʊ/	out	cow	
/ʊə/	pure		

Consonant sounds

Symbol	Examples		
/p/	put		
/b/	book		
/t/	take		
/d/	dog		
/k/	car	kick	
/g/	go	guarantee	
/tʃ/	catch	church	
/dʒ/	age	lounge	
/f/	for	cough	
/v/	love	vehicle	
/θ/	thick	path	
/ð/	this	mother	
/s/	since	rice	
/z/	zoo	houses	
/ʃ/	shop	sugar	machine
/ʒ/	pleasure	usual	vision
/h/	hear	hotel	
/m/	make		
/n/	name	now	
/ŋ/	bring		
/l/	look	while	
/r/	road		
/j/	young		
/w/	wear		

Index

*The numbers in the index are **Unit** numbers not page numbers.*

Acknowledgements

We would like to thank several individuals and also the students and staff at various institutions in different parts of the world who provided us with invaluable feedback on the initial manuscript: Olga Afanasyeva, Moscow, Russia; Faramarz Amiri, University of Wolverhampton; Andrew Arleo, Saint Nazaire, France; L Baranochnikova, Russia; Tomasz Bilau, Gdansk, Poland; Judith d'All, Angers, France; Celso Frade, Brazil; Reiko Furuya, Japan; Monika Galbarczyk, Warsaw, Poland; Ana Llinares Garcia, Madrid, Spain; Olga Gasparova, Moscow, Russia; Virginia Gavathas, Athens, Greece; Carolyne Ardron, Milan, Italy; Ludmila Gorodetskaya, Moscow, Russia; Eryl Griffiths, Cambridge, UK; Ewa Gumul, Sosnowiec, Poland; Sarah Hamilton, London, UK; Kathy Keohane, Stockport, UK; Cath King, London, UK; Marina Kulinich, Samara, Russia; Gillian Lazar, London, UK; Marilyn Lewis, Auckland, New Zealand; Elena Marinina, Moscow, Russia; Geraldine Mark, Cheltenham, UK; Ewa Modrzejewska, Gdansk, Poland; Anne O'Keefe, Limerick, Ireland; Paul Pauwels, Antwerpen, Belgium; Chen Pei Tsen, Tainan, Taiwan; Guy Perring, Tokyo, Japan; David Perry, Valencia, Spain; Chaz Pugliese, Paris, France; Tony Robinson, Cambridge, UK; Shiomi Sasanuma, Tokyo, Japan; Diane Slaouti, University of Manchester, UK; Ruth Wajnryb, Sydney, Australia.

Particular thanks are due to our editors at Cambridge University Press, Nóirín Burke and Martine Walsh, who have contributed far beyond the call of duty to this book at all the stages of its development. We are extremely grateful to them for their generous help and support and we are well aware that this book would have been very different and much poorer had it not been for them. We are also very grateful to Jane Cordell, who contributed to the project in its initial stages, and to Alyson Maskell for the experience which she brought to the final editing. Last but not least, we would both like to thank our domestic partners for their patience and their assistance in many ways throughout the process of writing *English Vocabulary in Use: advanced.*

Michael McCarthy & Felicity O'Dell

Cambridge, January 2002

The authors and publishers would like to thank the following for permission to reproduce copyright material in *English Vocabulary in Use: advanced.* While every effort has been made, it has not been possible to identify the sources of all the material used and in such cases the publishers would welcome information from copyright owners.

pp.28 and *214* extracts from *The Cambridge Encyclopedia of the English Language* by David Crystal (Cambridge University Press, 1995); *p.33 Making time to meet* from USA TODAY Snapshots, Copyright 2000, USA TODAY. Reprinted with permission; *p.34* advert © The Observer 1998; *p.36* from The Times online (2000); *p.38* from *DOGBERT'S Top Secret Management Handbook.* Copyright © 1996 United Feature Syndicate, Inc.; *p.49* The Far Side® by Gary Larson © 1980 FarWorks, Inc. All Rights Reserved. Used with permission; *p.48* extract by William Davis from *High Life*, Headway Publishing (1998); *p.58* (top) extract by Cherry Norton first published in The Independent 11 September 1999; *p.58* (middle) extract by Keith Waterhouse from *Night and Day Magazine* 1999; *p.61* extract by Elaine Glusac, from *American Way* (2000); *p.62* by Julian Robson © Telegraph Group Limited; *p.70 Art* © Adrian Searle (2000) from The Guardian ©; *p.74* article by Christine Michael, from *Top Santé* (1999); *p.82* extract from article by Images, Words, Ltd. in The Observer © 2000; *p.84* adapted from *The Dorling Kindersley Geography of the World* (Dorling Kindersley 1996) copyright 1996 Dorling Kindersley Ltd; *p.95 Number of threatened species in USA* from USA TODAY Snapshots, Copyright 2000, USA TODAY. Reprinted with permission; *p.102* (top right) extract from *Culture Shock! Taiwan* by Chris & Lang-Li Bates © 1995 Times Media Pte Ltd. Published by Times Books International, an imprint of Times Media Pte Ltd; *p.102* (top left) extract reprinted by kind permission of the Tourism Bureau R.O.C., Taiwan; *p.108* extract from *New Internationalist* (www.newint.org) © 1999; *p.110* from *The Essential Anatomy of Britain: Democracy in Crisis*, copyright ©1993 by Anthony Sampson, reprinted by permission of Harcourt Inc.; *p.114* from *No More War Heroes* by Dorothy Thompson in *New Internationalist* (www.newint.org) © 1999; *p.116* © Crown copyright 1999; *p.132* adapted from a Patient Information Leaflet from the Wallis Laboratory Ltd.; *p.134* (middle) by Ursula Kenny in The Observer © (1999); *p.134* (top) by Jane Clarke, author and nutritionist, published in The Observer © (1999); *p.166* from *Facts from Planet Gauge* by Morgan, HarperCollins Publishers Ltd; *p.210* The Far Side® by Gary Larson. © 1981 FarWorks, Inc. All Rights Reserved. Used with permission; *p.218* two headlines taken from The Guardian © 1999, reproduced with permission; *p.219* headlines reproduced from *Greek Gazette* by permission of Usborne Publishing, 83-85 Saffron Hill, London, EC1N 8RT. Copyright Usborne Publishing Ltd © 1997.

The publisher has used its best endeavours to ensure that the URLs for external websites referred to in this book are correct and active at the time of going to press. However, the publisher has no responsibility for the websites and can make no guarantee that a site will remain live or that the content is or will remain appropriate.

Illustrations by:
O.D.I. *pp.29, 78, 88, 130, 131* and *138*
Sam Thompson *pp.32, 54, 55* and *200*
Kathy Baxendale *pp.44, 81* and *107*
Phil Burrows *pp.62, 78, 124, 125, 141, 164, 170, 178, 189, 196, 202, 206* and *208*

Cover design by John Dunne
Designed and typeset by Oxford Designers & Illustrators